SECOND EDITION

ETHICAL ISSUES IN BUSINESS

A Philosophical Approach

Edited by

Thomas Donaldson

Patricia H. Werhane

Loyola University of Chicago

Prentice-Hall, Inc., *Englewood Cliffs, New Jersey 07632*

Library of Congress Cataloging in Publication Data
Main entry under title:

Ethical issues in business.

Includes bibliographical references.
1. Business ethics—Addresses, essays, lectures.
2. Industry—Social aspects—Addresses, essays, lectures.
I. Donaldson, Thomas, 1945– . II. Werhane, Patricia Hogue.
HF5387.E8 1983 174'.4 82-13255
ISBN 0-13-290148-X

Editorial/production supervision and interior design by Patricia V. Amoroso
Cover design by Wanda Lubelska
Manufacturing buyer: Harry P. Baisley

Printed in the United States of America

10 9 8 7 6 5 4 3 2

ISBN 0-13-290148-X

PRENTICE-HALL INTERNATIONAL, INC., *London*
PRENTICE-HALL OF AUSTRALIA PTY. LIMITED, *Sydney*
PRENTICE-HALL OF CANADA INC., *Toronto*
PRENTICE-HALL OF INDIA PRIVATE LIMITED, *New Delhi*
PRENTICE-HALL OF JAPAN, INC., *Tokyo*
PRENTICE-HALL OF SOUTHEAST ASIA PTE. LTD., *Singapore*
WHITEHALL BOOKS LIMITED, *Wellington, New Zealand*

CONTENTS

PREFACE

When the first edition of this book appeared, the field of business ethics was in its infancy. Most teachers adopted a personally designed collection of materials to a subject matter that remained undefined. Today, as the second edition appears, the field has matured considerably. A variety of textbooks have appeared and tens of thousands of courses are taught each year in the United States and in other countries. For those who wish to do advanced research, professional journals and monographs are now available.

Because of the excellent reception to this book's first edition, we have decided to retain the original format that combines case studies of decision-making dilemmas in business with theoretical articles about specific issues. Yet, thanks to the many new case studies and articles that have appeared in the last four years, we have been able to improve and update the material while, we hope, retaining the best of the earlier edition.

This book stresses the importance of analyzing business issues from the standpoint of theoretical philosophy. When philosophy has been coupled with other disciplines the result has invariably been the enrichment of both philosophy and the discipline involved. The ideas and methods of philosophy have yielded especially fruitful consequences when applied to fields such as law, science, medicine, and now to business. The union of philosophy and business is a natural one. Ethics has always served as one of the major elements in the philosopher's repertoire, and morality has always been one of the major issues in the world of business. Today, ethical issues are becoming even more important in the evaluation of business practices and organizational structures. It is thus a natural course of events for the ethical aspects of business and philosophy to be synthesized in a way which sheds light on both fields.

This anthology contains both modern and traditional philosophical material which relates to business problems. It also incorporates one of the most significant innovations in business education—the case study method. This method, which invites students to consider theoretical issues in the context of actual cases, is practiced in most major business schools. The role of the instructor in such studies is largely neutral; he or she guides and encourages the students without hindering the student's personal reflection. Even a casual reading of this book will reveal the significant debt it owes to those who contributed to its many case studies.

We are deeply obliged to Loyola University of Chicago for its continuing encouragement and support of our projects in business ethics, and the Mellon Foundation for its generous grant with which we initiated work on this anthology. A number of individuals have also been of invaluable assistance. Among them are Professors Richard De George, Al Gini, Kenneth Goodpaster, Michael Hoffman, Stephen Massey, David Ozar, Thomas McMahon, C. S. V., and Manuel Valesquez—all of whom offered intellectual and editorial assistance. We wish to thank also the secretaries and typists, Cynthia Rudolph and Tella Roberts, who contributed enormously to this project. Finally, a special word of thanks goes to Raymond O'Connell and Pattie Amoroso for their helpful editorial assistance.

THOMAS DONALDSON

PATRICIA H. WERHANE

GENERAL INTRODUCTION

There is one and only one social responsibility of business . . . to increase its profits. . . .

Milton Friedman

Business executives and the companies they serve have a personal and vested interest in the resolution of ethical and social responsibility dilemmas.

Steven Brenner and Earl Molander

It has often been suggested—though perhaps in jest—that the idea of business ethics constitutes a contradiction in terms. "Business is business," it has been said, "and ethics is not business." Yet each day we hear of the controversies about discrimination in hiring, consumer rights, deceptive advertising, bribery and payoffs, and pollution problems of such magnitude that we cannot remain unaffected.

Ethical problems in business are as old as business itself. Just as we are acutely aware of the problems surrounding the Pinto case or the sale of infant formula in developing countries, earlier generations were aware of other ethical issues confronting business. Names such as the "Teapot Dome scandal" or the "Mississippi bubble" are not familiar today, but they were once as well known as "Ford Pinto" and "Nestle" are now. The issues about which there has been public concern include trusts and monopolies, child labor, working hours and conditions, meat packing standards, the distribution of salaries, and the liability of producers for dangerous products. Not only complaints but attempts at reform have a long and interesting history. The Code of Hammurabi, written nearly two thousand years before Christ, records the fact that Mesopotamian rulers attempted to legislate honest prices from local merchants by instituting wage and price controls.

To explain the special relationship between business and ethics, it is necessary to see how focusing merely on problems of business efficiency and profit-making may overlook important moral issues. For example, when the manufacture of a certain product can be linked eventually to human disease or a decrease in the quality of human life, then the issues surrounding it are no longer simply traditional "business" issues. No amount of expertise in marketing, accounting, or management can deal adequately with such problems, and yet they are clearly connected to the activities of the business world. Nor can situations like these be reduced simply to legal problems, understandable only to the lawyer. When Ralph Nader claimed in the late 1960s that General Motors was producing automobiles which, despite their many consumer advantages, were contributing to thousands of highway deaths each year, he was not arguing that GM's practices were against the law—because at that time they were not illegal at all. Rather, Nader was arguing that General Motors had special obligations to its consumers, which were not simply of a traditional business nature, and that the company was not living up to them. Those obligations were *ethical* or *moral* ones.

It appears, then, that confronting questions like those implied by the Nader case—as "Does business have an obligation to its consumers (or to others) which extends beyond its obligation to make a profit and satisfy its investors?"—means confronting ethical and moral issues. The words "ethical" and "moral" in this book are not simply used as they might be by a modern newspaper, e.g., "That movie is thoroughly immoral" (meaning, "That movie is pornographic"). Instead, they are used as philosophers have traditionally used them, as words which arise from the study of what is good or right. Although there is dispute even among philosophers over how to define the subject matter of ethics, most would agree that it includes the study of what people ought to pursue, i.e., what the *good* is for people, or alternatively, the determination of which actions are the *right* actions for people to perform. Such general definitions may leave one with the feeling that studying ethics must be a hopelessly vague task; yet interestingly, ethical philosophers have succeeded in presenting a great many detailed ethical theses and in conducting a number of successful investigations into specific ethical topics.

The word "ethics," then, refers generally to the study of whatever is right and good for humans. The study of *business* ethics seeks to understand business practices, institutions, and actions in light of some concept of human value. Traditional business ends, e.g., profit making, growth, or technical advance are certainly relevant to the subject of business ethics insofar as they could be related to the achievement of some human good. In other words, business ethics looks at corporate profits not for their own sake but with respect to the achievement of some basic human good, perhaps increased investor satisfaction, higher levels of employment, or increased capacity to improve working conditions.

Because business ethics involves relating business activities to some concept of human good, it is a study which has as one of its aspects the *evaluation* of business practices. Indeed, most of the fundamental criticisms and commendations of contemporary business practices are cast in terms of how modern business either contributes or fails to contribute to the general human good. For example, when modern corporations are criticized for their failure to respond to environmental needs by limiting the amount of pollutants they discharge, they are being evaluated on ethical grounds—the charge is that they are neglecting the public good. Alternatively, when businesses are praised for achieving high levels of efficiency and satisfying consumer needs, it is implied that efficiency and consumer satisfaction contribute directly to the sum total of human good. Even traditional conservative economic theory justifies economic practices in the light of their contribution to human good: The classical economist, Adam Smith, for example, justifies the pursuit of self-interest in business by referring to the public benefits which such action secures.

Another aspect of the evaluative dimension in business ethics—or any ethical study—is seen in the contrast between evaluation and simple description. There is a special difference between answering a moral question and answering a question in the areas of, say, marketing and economics. In the latter, it is often sufficient to establish the immediate facts which pertain to the subject. For example, if one hopes to determine the best advertising strategy for the introduction of a new product, then one would only need to determine that a certain advertising strategy will have, as a matter of fact, the desired effect, i.e., that it *will* sell the product. It is usually possible in such cases to utilize indicators which more or less establish whether or not a given strategy will be effective: consumer polls, trends in sales, etc. These indicators are then used as factual information upon which one's strategy is based.

However, answering an ethical question may demand very different methods. Determining the immediate and specific facts may only be the first step in a long process which, in the end, may take one far beyond immediate facts. For example, if one wants to determine whether discriminatory hiring practices by corporations *ought* to be corrected by instituting affirmative action programs that favor women and minorities, there may be no question at all about the immediate facts. Two people could thoroughly agree that discrimination of a certain type has taken place and that blacks and women need equal job opportunities to reach relevant levels of social equality. Yet, after agreeing on all these facts the two people may still disagree—and disagree vehemently—over whether affirmative action programs *ought* to be imposed in the wake of past discriminatory practices. Thus, solving an ethical problem will require making *evaluative* judgments about issues which seem far removed from the facts at hand.

Even though business ethics focuses primarily on evaluative issues, its scope is surprisingly large. Insofar as it is concerned with relating business practices to some concept of human good, almost any business issue which relates to human value may become part of its subject matter. Thus the scope of business ethics includes such issues as

1. advertising practices, e.g., false or misleading advertising;
2. product safety;
3. monopolistic price schemes and their effects on the consumer;

4. pursuit of profits;
5. treatment of workers, including salaries, working conditions, worker participation, access to pension plans and benefits, etc.;
6. effects of pollution, both economic and environmental;
7. payments of "sensitive" sums of money to foreign governments, foreign agents, or local politicians;
8. proper roles of shareholders, management, government, and the public in determining corporate policy;
9. discriminatory hiring policies, conditions, and policies of advancement;
10. limits of private ownership.

The analysis of such issues requires a systematic investigation of both general ethical theory and specific business practices. To accomplish this goal, the editors of this anthology have selected a series of writings which includes not only theoretical and philosophical material relevant to business practices but actual case descriptions of ethical problems found in the business world. The philosophical material often has gained wide support in traditional ethical philosophy, and the cases include ones that have had a dramatic impact upon our society. This book has not attempted to provide a list of ethical codes of conduct. Such codes have often proven unsuccessful in achieving their presumed purpose; and more important, their existence can imply something false about the field of business ethics: that the work needed to understand ethical issues can be made unnecessary, and that serious issues can be resolved by simply writing and studying lists of ethical rules.

The advantage of investigating ethical problems from a philosophical point of view should be apparent. One cannot successfully examine a case involving payments made by U.S. corporations to foreign governments until one has considered the more general issue of whether different ethical attitudes (as might exist in the United States and in foreign countries) affect the morality of such actions. This question has traditionally been treated by philosophers under the heading of "ethical relativism," and studying the contributions of philosophers can be of great help.

INTRODUCTION TO ETHICAL REASONING

What is the basis for making ethical decisions? Should Joan challenge Fred the next time he cracks a chauvinist joke? Should John refrain from lying on his job application despite his temptation to do so? What, if anything, should make Hillary decide that eating meat is corrupting whereas vegetarianism is uplifting? It is obvious that the kind of evidence required for an ethical decision is different from that needed to make a nonethical one; but what is the nature of the difference? These questions give rise to a search for a *method* of ethical justification and decision making, a method that will specify the conditions which any good ethical decision should meet.

To see how such questions arise concretely, consider the following case.[1]

> Some years ago, a large German chemical firm, BASF, decided to follow the lead of many other European firms and build a factory in the United States. BASF needed land, lots of it (1,800 acres), an inexpensive labor pool, almost 5 million gallons of fresh water every day, a surrounding area free of import taxes, and a nearby railroad and ocean port. Obviously, only a handful of locations could meet all these requirements. The spot the company finally picked seemed perfect, an area near the coast of South Carolina called Beaufort County. It purchased 1,800 acres.
>
> South Carolina and Beaufort County were pleased with BASF's decision. The surrounding area, from which the company would pick its workers, was economically depressed and per capita income stood well below the national average. Jobs of any kind were desperately needed. Even the Governor of South Carolina and his staff were eager for BASF to build in South Carolina, and although BASF had not yet finalized its exact production plans, the State Pollution Central Authority saw no problems with meeting the State pollution laws. BASF itself said that although it would dump chemical byproducts into the local Colleton River, it planned not to lower the river's quality.
>
> But trouble started immediately. To see why, one needs to know that Beaufort County is the home of the internationally famous resort area called "Hilton Head." Hilton Head attracts thousands of vacationers every year—most of them with plenty of money—and its developers worried that the scenic splen-

> dor of the area might be marred by the air and water pollution. Especially concerned about water pollution, resort developers charged that the proposed chemical plant would pollute the Colleton River. They argued that BASF plants in Germany had polluted the Rhine and, in Belgium, the Schelde River. Further, they noted that on BASF's list of proposed expenditures, pollution control was allocated only one million dollars.
>
> The citizens of Beaufort County, in contrast to the Hilton Head Developers, welcomed BASF. They presented the company with a petition bearing over 7,000 signatures endorsing the new plant. As one local businessman commented, "I would say 80 percent of the people in Beaufort County are in favor of BASF. Those who aren't rich." (William D. McDonald, "Youth Corps Looking for Jobs," *The State,* February 23, 1970.)

The manager of BASF's U.S. operations was clearly confronted by an economic and moral dilemma. He knew that preventing massive pollution was virtually impossible and, in any case, outrageously expensive. The eagerness of South Carolina officials for new industry suggested that pollution standards might be "relaxed" for BASF. If it decided to go ahead and build, was the company to push for the minimum pollution control it could get away with under the law? Such a policy might maximize corporate profits and the financial interests of the shareholders, while at the same time it would lower the aesthetic quality of the environment. It might make jobs available to Beaufort County while ignoring the resort industry and the enjoyment of vacationers. Moreover, the long-term effects of dumping chemicals was hard to predict, but past experience did not give the manager a feeling of optimism. Pollution seemed not to be only a business issue, but a *moral* one. But how should the manager sort out, and eventually decide upon, such a moral issue?

To solve his moral problem, BASF's manager might try a variety of strategies. He might, for example, begin by assuming that he has three basic options: (1) Build with minimal pollution control; (2) Build with maximal pollution control; (3) Do not build.

Then, he might reason:

> The consequences of option (1) will be: significant but tolerable water pollution, hostility from the Hilton Head Developers, high short-term corporate profits, and satisfied shareholders.
>
> The consequences of option (2) will be: unnoticeable pollution, no complaints from the Hilton Head Developers, high pollution control costs, low profits, unsatisfied stockholders.
>
> The consequences of (3) will be: approval from the Hilton Head Developers, low short-term profits (while a search for a new location is underway), strong disapproval from the local townspeople.
>
> My job from a *moral* perspective is to weigh these consequences and consider which of the alternatives constitutes a maximization of good. Who will benefit from each decision? How many people will be adversely affected and in what ways?

Or the manager might reason:

> Both BASF Corporation and I are confronted with a variety of *duties, rights,* and *obligations.* First there is the company's obligation to its stockholders, and my duty as manager is to protect the economic interests and rights of our stockholders. Next there are the rights of those Beaufort residents and visitors in the area to clean air and water. Finally there are the rights of other property owners in the area, including the Hilton Head Developers, not to be harmed unreasonably by other industries. There is an implied obligation to future generations to protect the river. And finally, there are broader considerations: Is this an act I would want others to do? What kind of moral example will I be setting?
>
> My job from a *moral* perspective is to balance and assess these duties, rights, and obligations—and determine which have priority.

Finally, the manager might reason:

> I cannot confront a moral problem from either the abstract perspective of "consequences," or of "duties, rights, and obligations." Instead, I must utilize a concrete concept of *human nature* to guide my deliberations. Acts that aid persons to develop their potential human nature are morally good: ones that do the opposite are bad.
>
> I believe that the crucial potentialities of human nature include such things as: health, knowledge, moral maturity, meaningful employment, political freedom, and self-respect.
>
> My job from a *moral* perspective is to assess the situation in terms of its harmony or disharmony with these basic concepts of human potential.

Notice how different each of these approaches is! The first focuses on the concept of *consequences;* the second on *duties, rights, and obligations;* and the third on *human nature.* Of course the three methods may overlap; for example, applying the concept of "human nature" in the third approach may necessitate referring to concepts drawn from the first and second, such as "consequences" and "rights," and vice versa. Even so, the approaches reflect three classical types of ethical theory in the history of philosophy. Each has been championed by a well-known traditional philosopher, and most ethical theories can be catagorized under one of the three headings. The first may be called "consequentialism," the second, "deontology," and the third, "human nature ethics."

CONSEQUENTIALISM

As its name implies, a consequentialist theory of ethical reasoning concentrates on the consequences of human actions, and all actions are evaluated in terms of the extent to which they achieve desirable results. Such theories are also frequently labeled "teleological," a term derived from the Greek word "telos," which refers to an end or purpose. According to consequentialist theories, the concepts of right, wrong, and duty are subordinated to the concept of the end or purpose of an action.

There are at least two types of consequentialist theory. The first—advocated by only a few consequentialists—is a version of what philosophers call "ethical egoism." It construes right action as action whose consequences, considered among all the alternatives, maximizes *my* good, that is, which benefits *me* the most or harms *me* the least. (Ethical egoism is discussed in more detail in Part I, section 2, of this book.) The second type—advocated by most consequentialists—denies that right action concerns only *me,* rather right action must maximize *overall* good; that is, it must maximize good (or minimize bad) from the standpoint of the entire human community. The best accepted label for this type of consequentialism is "utilitarianism." This term was coined by the eighteenth-century philosopher Jeremy Bentham, although its best known proponent was the nineteenth-century English philosopher, John Stuart Mill. As Bentham formulated it, the principle of utility states that an action is right if it produces the greatest balance of pleasure or happiness over pain or unhappiness. The Principle of Utility thus evaluates the rightness or wrongness of actions by measuring this balance of happiness and unhappiness in light of alternative actions. Mill supported a similar principle using what he called the "proof" of the principle of utility, namely, the recognition that the only proof for something's being desirable is that someone actually desires it. Since everybody desires pleasure or happiness it follows, according to Mill, that happiness is the most desirable thing. The purpose of moral action is to achieve greatest overall happiness, and actions are evaluated in terms of the extent to which they contribute to this end. The most desirable state of affairs, the greatest good and the goal of morality, said Mill, is the "greatest happiness for the greatest number."

While later utilitarians accept the general framework of Mill's argument, not all utilitarians are hedonists, that is, not all utilitarians equate "the good" with pleasure or happiness. Some utilitarians have argued that in maximizing the "good," one must be concerned not only with maximizing pleasure, but with maximizing other things such as knowledge, moral maturity, and friendship. Although it could be claimed that such goods *also* bring pleasure and happiness to their possessor, it is arguable whether their goodness is ultimately *reducible* to whatever pleasure they bring. These philosophers are sometimes called "pluralistic" utilitarians. Still other philosophers have adapted utilitarianism to modern methods of economic theory by championing what is known as "preference utilitarianism." Instead of referring to the maximization of specific goods, such as pleasure or knowledge, preference utilitarians understand the ultimate foundation of goodness to be the set of preferences people actually possess. One person prefers oysters to strawberries, another prefers rock music to Mozart. Each person has a *set* of preferences, and so long as the set is internally consistent it makes no sense to label one set morally superior to another. Preference utilitarianism thus interprets right action as that which is "optimal" among alternatives in terms of everyone's preferences. Disputes, however, rage among preference utilitarians and their critics over how to specify the meaning of "optimal."

Bentham and Mill thought that utilitarianism was a revolutionary theory both because it reflected accurately human motivation and because it had clear application to the political and social problems of their day. If one could measure the benefit or harm of any action, rule or law, they believed, one could sort out good and bad social and political legislation as well as good and bad individual actions.

But how, specifically, *does* one apply the traditional principle of utility? To begin with, one's race, religion, intelligence, or condition of birth is acknowledged to be irrelevant in calculating one's ultimate worth. Each person counts for "one," and no more than "one." Second, in evaluating happiness one must take into account not only present generations but ones in the future. In calculating the effects of, say, pollution, one must measure the possible effects pollution might have on health, genetics, and the supply of natural resources for future generations. Third, pleasure or happiness is measured *en toto* so that the thesis does not reduce to the idea that "one ought to do what makes the most persons happy." Utilitarianism does not reduce to a dictatorship of majority interests. One person's considerable unhappiness might outweigh the minor pleasures of many other persons added together. Utilitarians also consider the long-term consequences for single individuals. For instance, it might be pleasurable to drink a full bottle of wine every evening, but the long-term drawbacks of such a habit might well outweigh its temporary pleasures.

Finally, according to many utilitarians (such as Mill), some pleasures are *qualitatively* better than others. Intellectual pleasure, for example, is said to be higher than physical pleasure. "Better to be Socrates unsatisfied," writes Mill, "than a pig satisfied." The reasons that drove Mill to formulate this qualitative distinction among pleasures are worth noting. Since Mill believed that the optimal situation was one of "greatest happiness for the greatest number," then what was he to say about a world of people living at the zenith of merely *physical* happiness? If science could invent a wonder drug, like the "soma" in Aldous Huxley's *Brave New World,* that provided a permanent state of drugged happiness (without even a hangover), would the consequence be a perfect world? Mill believed not, and to remedy this difficulty in his theory, he introduced *qualitative levels* of happiness: e.g., he said that the happiness of understanding Plato is "higher" than that of drinking three martinis. But how was Mill to say *which* pleasures were higher? Here he retreated to an ingenious proposal: when deciding which of two pleasures is higher, one should poll the group of persons who are experienced, that is, who know *both* pleasures. Their decision will indicate which is the higher pleasure. Ah, but might the majority decision not be wrong? Here Mill provides no clear answer.

Modern day utilitarians divide themselves roughly into two groups, *act utilitarians* and *rule utilitarians.* An *act* utilitarian believes that the Principle of Utility should be applied to individual acts. Thus one measures the consequences of each *individual action* according to whether it maximizes good. For example, suppose a certain community were offered the opportunity to receive a great deal of wealth in the form of a gift. The only stipulation was that the community force some of its citizens with ugly, deteriorated houses, to repair and beautify them. Next, suppose the community held an election to decide whether to accept the gift. Now an act utilitarian would analyze the problem of whether to vote for or against the proposal from the standpoint of the *individual voter.* Would an individual's vote to accept the gift be more likely to maximize the community's overall good than would a vote to the contrary?

A *rule* utilitarian, on the other hand, believes that instead of considering the results of specific actions, one must weigh the consequences of adopting a *general rule* exemplified by that action. According to the rule utilitarian, one should act according to a general rule which, if adopted, would maximize good. For example, in the hypothetical case of the community deciding whether to accept a gift, a rule utilitarian might adopt the rule, "Never vote in a way which lowers the self-respect of a given class of citizens." She might accept this rule because of the general unhappiness that would ensue if society systematically treated some persons as second-class citizens. Here the focus is on the general rule and not on the individual act.

Critics raise objections to utilitarianism. Perhaps the most serious is that it is unable to account for justice. Because the utilitarian concentrates on the consequences of an action for a majority, the employment of the Principle of Utility can be argued to allow injustice for a small minority. For example, if overall goodness were maximized in the long run by making slaves of 2 percent of the population, utilitarianism seemingly is forced to condone slavery. But clearly this is unjust. Utilitarianism's obvious response is that such slavery will not, as a matter of empirical fact, maximize goodness. Rule utilitarians, as we have seen, can argue that society should embrace the rule, "never enslave others," because following such a principle, in the long run, will maximize goodness. Even so, the battle continues between utilitarians and their critics. Can utilitarianism account for the widely held moral conviction that injustice to a minority is wrong *regardless* of the consequences? The answer is hotly contested.

Another criticism concerns the determination of the good to be maximized. Any consequentialist has the problem of identifying and ranking whatever is to be maximized. For a utilitarian such as Mill, as we have seen, the problem involves distinguishing between higher and lower pleasures. But for "pluralistic" utilitarians a similar problem exists: What is the basis for selecting, for example, friendship and happiness as goods to be maximized and not, say, aesthetic sensitivity? And even granted that this problem can be solved, there is the further problem of arbitrating trade-offs between goods such as happiness and friendship when they *conflict.* When one is forced to choose between enhancing happiness and enhancing friendship, which gets priority? And under what conditions?

An interesting fact about consequentialist reasoning is that most of us employ it to some degree in ordinary decisions. We weigh the consequences of alternatives in choosing colleges, in deciding on a career, in hiring and promoting others, and in many other judgments. We frequently weigh good consequences over bad ones and predict the long- and short-term effects of our choices. We often even cite consequentialist style principles: for example, "No one should choose a college where he or she will be unhappy." Or, "No one should pollute the environment when his or her action harms others."

However, for a variety of reasons including the objections to utilitarianism mentioned earlier, some philosophers refuse to acknowledge consequentialism as an adequate theory of ethics. They argue that the proper focus for ethical judgments should not be consequences, but moral *precepts,* that is, the rules, norms, and principles we use to guide our actions. Such philosophers are known as "deontologists," and the next section will examine their views.

DEONTOLOGY

The term "deontological" comes from the Greek word for duty, and what is crucial according to the deontologist are the rules and principles that guide actions. We shall discuss here two approaches to deontological ethical reasoning that have profoundly influenced ethics. The first is that of the eighteenth-century philosopher Immanuel Kant and his followers. This approach focuses on duty and universal rules to determine right actions. The second—actually a subspecies of deontological reasoning—is known as the "social contract" approach. It focuses not on individual decision-making, but on the general social principles that rational persons in certain ideal situations would agree upon and adopt.

Kantian Deontology

Kant believed that ethical reasoning should concern activities that are rationally motivated and should utilize precepts that apply universally to all human actions. To this end he opens his treatise on ethics by declaring,

> It is impossible to conceive anything at all in the world, . . . which can be taken as good without qualification except a *good* will.[2]

This statement sums up much of what Kant wants to say about ethics —and is worth unraveling. What Kant means is that the only thing which can be good or worthwhile without any provisos or stipulations is an action of the will freely motivated for the right reasons. Other goods such as wealth, beauty, and intelligence are certainly valuable, but they are not good *without qualification* because they have the potential to create both good and bad effects. Wealth, beauty, and intelligence can be bad when they are used for purely selfish ends. Even human happiness—which Mill held as the highest good—can, according to Kant, create complacency, disinterest, and excessive self-assurance under certain conditions.

According to Kant, reason is the faculty that can aid in the discovery of correct moral principles; thus it is *reason,* not *inclination,* that should guide the will. When reason guides the will, Kant calls the resulting actions ones done from "duty." Kant's use of the term "duty," turns out to be less formidable than it first appears. Kant is simply saying that a purely good and free act of the will is one done not merely because you have an *inclination* to do it, but because you have the right reasons for doing it. For example, suppose you discover a wallet belonging to a stranger. Kant would say that despite one's inclination to keep the money (which the stranger may not even need), one should return it. This is an act you know is right despite your inclinations. Kant also believes you should return the wallet even when you believe the *consequences* of not returning it are better. Here his views are at sharp odds with consequentialism. Suppose the stranger is known for her stinginess, and that you plan to donate the money to a childrens' hospital. No matter. For Kant, you must return the wallet. Thus the moral worth lies in the act itself and not in either your happiness or the consequences brought about by the act. Acts are good because they are done for the sake of what is right and not because of the consequences they might produce.

But how do I know what my duty is? While it may be clear that one should return a wallet, there are other circumstances where one's duty is less evident. Suppose you are in a six-person lifeboat at sea with five others and a seventh person swims up? What is one's duty here? And how does one even know that what one *thinks* is right *is* right? To settle such problems Kant claims that duty is more than doing merely what you "feel" is right. Duty is acting with *respect for other rational beings.* It almost goes without saying, then, that "acting from duty" is not to be interpreted as action done in obedience to local, state, or national laws, since these can be good or bad. Rather "duty" is linked to the idea of universal principles that should govern all our actions.

But is there any principle that can govern *all* human beings? Kant believes the answer is yes, and he calls the highest such principle the "Categorical Imperative." He formulates the Categorical Imperative in three ways (although we shall only consider two formulations here). The first formulation, roughly translated, is:

> One ought only to act such that the principle of one's act could become a universal law of human action in a world in which one would hope to live.

For example, one would want to live in a world where people followed the principle, "return property that belongs to others." Therefore one should return the stranger's wallet. We do not, however, want to live in a world where everyone lies. Therefore one should not adopt the principle "lie whenever it seems helpful."

The second formulation of the categorical imperative is:

> One ought to treat others as having intrinsic value in themselves, and *not* merely as means to achieve one's ends.

In other words, one should respect every person as a rational and free being. Hitler treated one group of persons as nonpersons in order to achieve his own ends, and thus acted contrary to the categorical imperative.

Another instance of treating persons as means would occur if a teacher looked up the grade records of new students to determine how to assign grades in her own class. She would be treating students as if they had no control over their destinies. Such actions are immoral according to Kant because they fail to respect the inherent dignity of rational beings.

Ethical reasoning for Kant implies adopting principles of action and evaluating one's actions in terms of those principles. Even Kant grants that the evaluation is sometimes difficult. For example, there is the problem of striking the proper level of generality in choosing a principle. A principle which read, "If one is named John Doe and attends Big State University and has two sisters, then he should borrow fifty dollars without intending to repay it," is far too specific. On the other hand the principle "you should always pay your debts," might be too general since it would require that a starving man repay the only money he possesses to buy a loaf of bread. Because of the problem of striking the proper degree of generality, many modern deontologists have reformulated Kant's basic question to read: "Could I wish that everyone in the world would follow this principle *under relevantly similar conditions?*"

As with utilitarianism, critics challenge deontological reasoning. Some assert that fanatics such as Hitler could at least *believe* that the rule "Persecute Jews whenever possible," is one that the world should live by. Similarly a thief might universalize the principle, "Steal whenever you have a good opportunity." Moreover a strict interpretation of dentological ethical reasoning is said to allow no exceptions to a universal principle. Such strict adherence to universal principles might encourage moral rigidity and might fail to reflect the diversity of responses required by complex moral situations. Finally, critics argue that in a given case two principles may conflict without there being a clear way to decide which principle or rule should take precedence. Jean-Paul Sartre tells of his dilemma during World War II when he was forced to choose between staying to comfort his ill and aging mother, and fighting for the freedom of France. Two principles seemed valid: "Give aid to your father and mother," and "Contribute to the cause of freedom." But with conflicting principles, how is one to choose? Nevertheless, deontological ethical reasoning represents a well-respected and fundamentally distinctive mode of ethical reasoning, one which, like consequentialism, appears in the deliberations of ordinary persons as well as philosophers. We have all heard actions condemned by the comment, "what would it be like if everyone did that?"

The Contractarian Alternative

Kant assumes that the Categorical Imperative is something all rational individuals can discover and agree upon. A different version of deontology is offered by many philosophers who focus less on the actions of individuals, and more on the principles that govern society at large. These include two philosophers whose writings appear in our book: the seventeenth-century political philosopher John Locke and the twentieth-century American philosopher John Rawls. They and others try to establish universal principles of a just society through what might be called "social contract thought experiments." They ask us to imagine what it would be like to live in a situation where there are no laws, no social conventions and no political state. In this so-called "state of nature" we imagine that rational persons gather to formulate principles or rules to govern political and social communities. Such rules would resemble principles derived through the categorical imperative in that they are presumably principles to which every rational person would agree and which would hold universally.

Locke and Rawls differ in their approach for establishing rules or principles of justice, and the difference illustrates two distinct forms of contractarian reasoning. Locke argues from what is called a "natural rights" position, while Rawls argues from what is called a "reasonable person" position. Locke claims that every person is born with, and possesses, certain basic rights that are "natural." These rights are inherent to a person's nature, and they are possessed by every one equally. Like other inherent traits they cannot be taken away. They are, in the words of the Declaration of Independence, "inalienable." When rational persons meet to formulate principles to govern the formation of social and political communities they construct a social contract that is the basis for an agreement between themselves and their government, and whose rules protect natural rights. Rights, then, become deontological precepts by which one forms and evaluates rules, constitutions, governments, and socio-economic systems. While many philosophers disagree with Locke's view that each of us has inherent or *natural* rights, many do utilize a theory of human rights as the basis for justifying and evaluating political institutions. More will be said about rights in Part IV of this volume.

Rawls adopts a different perspective. He does not begin from a natural rights position. Rather he asks which principles of justice would rational persons formulate if they were behind a "veil of ignorance," i.e., if each person knew nothing about who he or she was. That is, one would not know whether one were old or young, male or female, rich or poor, highly motivated or lazy, or anything about one's personal status in society. Unable to predict which principles, if picked, will favor them personally, Rawls argues, persons will be forced to choose principles that are fair to all.

Rawls and Locke are not in perfect agreement about which principles would be adopted in such hypothetical situations, and more will be said about their views later in the book. For now it is important to remember that the social contract approach maintains a deontological character. It is used to formulate principles of justice which apply universally. Some philosophers note, however, that from an original position in a "state of nature" or behind a "veil of ignorance," rational persons, logically speaking, *could* adopt consequentialist principles as rules for a just society. Thus, while the social contract approach is deontological in style, the principles it generates are not necessarily ones which are incompatible with consequentialism. In business the contractual approach is exemplified in the idea of the "social contract" between business and society discussed by Thomas Donaldson in Part II of this book.

In the moral evaluations of business, all deontologists, contractarians included, would ask questions such as:

(a) Are the rules fair to everyone?
(b) Do they hold universally even with the passage of time?
(c) Is every person treated with equal respect?

What may be missing from a deontological approach to ethical reasoning is a satisfactory means of coping with valid exceptions to general rules. Under what circumstances, if any, are exceptions allowed? Deontologists believe that they can answer this qustion, but their solutions vary. Suffice it to say that deontologists, just as utilitarians, have not convinced everyone.

HUMAN NATURE ETHICS

According to some contemporary philosophers, the preceding two modes of ethical reasoning exhaust all possible modes: that is to say, all theories can be classified as either "teleological" or "deontological." Whether this is true cannot be settled here, but it will be helpful to introduce briefly what some philosophers consider to be a third category, namely the "human nature" approach.

A "human nature" approach assumes that all humans have inherent capacities that constitute the ultimate basis for all ethical claims. Actions are evaluated in terms of whether they promote or hinder, coincide with, or conflict with, these capacities. One of the most famous proponents of this theory was the Greek philosopher, Aristotle. In Aristotle's opinion, human beings have inherent *potentialities* and thus human development turns out to be the struggle for self-actualization, or in other words, the perfection of inherent human nature. Consider the acorn. It has the natural potential to become a sturdy oak tree. Its natural drive is not to become an elm or a cedar, or even a stunted oak, but to become the most robust oak tree possible. Diseased or stunted oak trees are simply deficient; they are instances of things in nature whose potential has not been fully developed. Similarly persons, according to Aristotle, are born with inherent potentialities. Persons, like acorns, naturally are oriented to actualize their potentialities, and for them this means more than merely developing their *physical* potential. It also means developing their mental, moral, and social potential. Thus human beings on this view are seen as basically good; evil is understood as a deficiency that occurs when one is unable to fulfill one's natural capacities.

Here it is important to understand that the concept of human nature need not be an individualistic one. According to Aristotle, persons are "social" by nature, and cannot be understood apart from the larger community in which they participate. "Man," Aristotle writes, is a "social animal." For Aristotle, then, fulfilling one's natural constitution implies developing wisdom, generosity, and self-restraint, all of which help to make one a good member of the community.

The criterion for judging the goodness of any action is whether or not the action is compatible with one's inherent human capacities. Actions which enhance human capacities are good; those that deter them are bad unless they are the best among generally negative alternatives. For example, eating nothing but starches is unhealthy, but it is clearly preferable to starving.

This theory puts great emphasis on the nature of persons, and obviously how one understands that "nature" will be the key to determining both what counts as a right action and how one defines the proper end of human action in general. Aristotle argued that intelligence and wisdom are uniquely human potentialities and consequently that intellectual virtue is the highest virtue. The life of contemplation, he believed, is the best sort of life, in part because it represents the highest fulfillment of human nature. Moral virtue, also crucial in Aristotle's theory, involves the rational control of one's desires. In action where a choice is possible, one exercises moral virtue by restraining harmful desires and cultivating beneficial ones. The development of virtue requires the cultivation of good habits, and this in turn leads Aristotle to emphasize the importance of good upbringing and education.

One problem said to affect human nature theories is that they have difficulty justifying the supposition that human beings *do* have specific inherent capacities and that these capacities are the same for all humans. Further, critics claim that it is difficult to warrant the assumption that humans are basically good. Perhaps the famous psychoanalyst Sigmund Freud is correct in his assertion that at bottom we are all naturally aggressive and selfish. Third, critics complain that it is difficult to employ this theory in ethical reasoning, since it appears to lack clear-cut rules and principles for use in moral decision making. Obviously, any well-argued human nature ethic will take pains to spell out the aspects of human nature which, when actualized, constitute the ultimate ground for moral judgments.

CONCLUSION

The three approaches to ethical reasoning we have discussed, consequentialism, deontology, and human nature ethics, all present theories of ethical reasoning distinguished in terms of their basic methodological elements. Each represents a type or "model" of moral reasoning that is applicable to practical decisions in concrete situations. Consider, for example, the case study with which we began our discussion, involving BASF and its proposed new plant. As it happened, BASF chose option (3) and decided to build elsewhere. In making his decision, did the BASF manager actually use any or all of the methods described above? Although we cannot know the answer to this question, it is clear—as we saw earlier—that each of the methods was at least applicable to his problem. Indeed, the three methods of moral reasoning are sufficiently broad that each is applicable to the full range of problems confronting human moral experience. The question of which method, if any, is superior to the others must be left for another time. The intention of this essay is not to substitute for a thorough study of traditional ethical theories—something for which there is no substitute—but to introduce the reader to basic modes of ethical reasoning that will help to analyze the ethical problems in business that arise in the remainder of the book.

P. H. W.
T. D.

NOTES

1. See "BASF Corporation vs. The Hilton Head Island Developers," in *Business and Society,* Robert D. Hay, et.al., eds. (Cincinnati: South-Western Publishing Co, 1976), pp. 100–12.
2. Immanuel Kant, *Groundwork of the Metaphysic of Morals,* trans. H. J. Paton (New York: Harper & Row, 1948; rpt. 1956), p. 61.

PART I

General Issues in Ethics

> At a time when the reputation of business in general is low . . . at such a time one would expect corporate executives to be especially sensitive even to appearances of conflict of interest. . . . Yet this seems not, on the whole, to be the case. . . .
>
> *Irving Kristol*

If you were operating a branch of a U.S. company in a foreign country, would you follow the necessary foreign procedures for filing taxes even if (1) these conflicted with procedures in the United States, or (2) they clearly involved what you considered unethical practices?

If you were an employee of a large corporation producing equipment for the aircraft industry, would you protest the manufacture of defective products even if it meant the loss of your job?

Suppose you, as an employee of an advertising agency, felt that one of the advertisements for which you were responsible presented false or misleading information about a product. Would you request a change in the advertisement?

Each of these questions is drawn from an actual business situation, and such incidents occur more frequently than one might expect. Understanding their ethical implications requires not only an awareness of the concrete situation, but also the ability to subsume business problems under categories of more general ethical concern. The philosophical material in Part I involves three traditional ethical issues: ethical relativism, truth telling, and ethical egoism. Stated as questions, these issues are:

1. *Ethical relativism:* are values simply relative to the people who espouse them, or is it possible to identify universal values which apply to all?
2. *Ethical egoism:* Is it morally acceptable for one to act always in one's own self-interest?

3. *Truth telling:* What obligations exist, if any, for individuals and organizations to communicate honestly?

ETHICAL RELATIVISM

The questions of self-interest and honesty are difficult issues in practice because they must be faced every day. The issue of the relativity of value judgments is less obviously commonplace. It asks whether some moral principles apply universally or whether, instead, all values and ethical judgments are relative to particular cultural contexts. This question is particularly acute in contemporary business, because most major corporations today are what are called "transnational" or "multinational" corporations who conduct business in many countries. How should business operate in foreign countries? Should it adopt the practices of the host country even when those practices conflict with an American way of doing business or are morally questionable? For example, should one lie, bribe, or submit to extortion in a foreign country if that activity is common business practice in that culture?

According to the view of ethical relativism one cannot say that bribery is wrong if it is an acceptable practice in that value system; for according to the ethical relativist there are no universal standards by which one can judge the moral principles of different cultures.

Ethical relativism frequently uses evidence provided by another, but closely related, point of view known as *cultural* relativism. The latter argues that the way in which people reason about morality varies in different cultures because of different customs, religious traditions, and methods of education. Using this argument the *ethical* relativist goes ahead to claim that there are no ultimate, universal ethical principles and that all value judgments are relative to particular cultural contexts. Richard Brandt, in his article "Ethical Relativism," which is included in this section, suggests that for at least some ethical disagreements between cultures there is no single correct view—thus offering some support to the ethical relativists' position.

An obvious way to challenge ethical relativism is to argue that there are some values which are universal—that is, which apply without exception. For example, one might argue that skinning live babies for sport is not acceptable anywhere, despite anyone's belief. W. T. Stace, in his article "Ethical Relativity and Ethical Absolutism," defends just such a point of view. He recognizes that there are practical difficulties in specifying particular ethical principles which apply universally, but these difficulties do not imply that ethical relativism is correct. In an intricate set of arguments Stace tries to show that a thoroughgoing position of ethical relativism results in the conclusion that one cannot make *any* value judgments whatsoever.

The case study, "The Lockheed Aircraft Corporation," raises specifically the question of which ethical principles or value system, if any, a multinational corporation should adopt, when doing business in a foreign country. Lockheed, trying to gain business favors, made "sensitive payments" to Japanese government officials; but the former president of Lockheed defended these payments, even though they would have been considered both illegal and unethical if made in this country. He defended them as consistent with (1) practices of other multinational corporations, and (2) accepted cultural practice in other countries. Hence, if Lockheed refused to bribe, he concluded, it would lose in the race with its competitors. Arguments such as (1) and (2) involve ethical relativism insofar as right and wrong are assumed to depend on the particular corporate or cultural context being considered. Other U.S. companies involved in foreign bribes have offered a third justification, that (3) American corporations provide needed technology and economic services to foreign countries, thus raising the standards for citizens in these countries. The means through which one makes these goods and services available, e.g., sensitive payments, are thus justified by long-range economic results.

If Stace's arguments are correct, they might be used to show that justifications such as (1) and (2) for sensitive payments abroad are questionable and that other justifications such as (3) are inconsistent with (1) and (2). For when some corporations defend their activities by referring to the economic advantages for the foreign countries in which they operate, are they not assuming that economic growth is a universal value and should be espoused by every country?

The conduct of multinational corporations has been under severe scrutiny in recent years. As a result of bribery incidents such as Lockheed's, the U.S. Congress passed in 1977 the Foreign Corrupt Practices Act (FCPA). The FCPA is an attempt to legislate standards of conduct for multinational corporations by making it a crime to offer or to acquiesce to sensitive payments to officials of foreign governments. The Act implies that what *we* in this country think is morally right should be exported in our dealings with *other* countries. This act would be criticized by an ethical relativist since, according to him, value differences between cultures preclude the justification of such exportation.

The FCPA raises the issue of whether one can justify sensitive payments, e.g., bribery and extortion, in any context. Michael Hooker and Mark Pastin consider this question in their article, "Ethics and the Foreign Corrupt Practices Act." They argue that the moral rule prohibiting bribery is a *prima facie* rule that can be overridden to prevent a greater harm, the greater harm in this instance being the loss of American business and the accompanying loss of jobs by American multinational corporations which cannot compete in the international market. In responding to this article Kenneth Alpern suggests that one cannot justify overriding a moral rule such as that prohibiting bribery except in dire circumstances, a situation which hardly describes the state of American business. Abolishing the FCPA, according to Alpern, is tantamount to endorsing a policy of bribery.

THE PROBLEM OF EGOISM

Ethical egoism is a theory about the justification of human conduct. The ethical egoist holds that all actions should be motivated by a desire to achieve one's own self-interest—and nothing else. In short, he or she insists that we should consider what benefits us, and then act to maximize our own gratification. The ethical egoist defends the view of self-interested motivation as a *normative* theory of ethics, that is, as one about what people *should* do.

Yet any discussion of ethical egoism would be incomplete without some understanding of a closely related theory known as *psychological egoism.* Ethical egoism is, as its name implies, an ethical theory, whereas psychological egoism is a factual theory about how people are motivated. The latter says human beings are motivated exclusively by self-interest. It argues, simply, that we are all constituted in such a way that we are motivated exclusively by our own desires and self-interests. Therefore, all actions are directed toward the satisfaction of merely personal ends, and even actions which appear to be disinterested in fact are motivated by one's long-term self-gain.

It is possible to defend ethical egoism without defending psychological egoism. One could deny that people *do* always act in a self-interested manner, thus granting that purely benevolent actions are possible, but still assert that people *ought* to act always in their self-interest. Perhaps such an ethical egoist views all forms of benevolent behavior as forms of human weakness; or perhaps he believes that there are simply no reasons to show that a person should not act in his own self-interest.

The seventeenth-century philosopher, Thomas Hobbes, may be understood primarily as a psychological egoist. In the selections from Hobbes' *Leviathan* included in this section, he argues that persons in their original natural state are passionate and selfish. They are motivated by three interests: self-preservation, achieving power over other men, and self-gain. Hobbes argues, however, that in addition to being passionate and self-interested, men are also rational, and he makes the reasonable assumption that obtaining even selfish ends is impossible in a state where all people are allowed to pursue their own selfish ends unhampered. Therefore, he concludes, people form political societies, called "commonwealths," in order to control the unlimited pursuit of self-interest. A properly constructed commonwealth, however, should reflect the truth of psychological egoism by insuring the orderly development of the self-interests of all members of the society.

It may be true, as Hobbes suggests, that persons by nature are motivated only by self-interest. But it does not follow immediately from this that one *should* be motivated to act only and always in one's own self-interest. One cannot automatically assume because something *is* the case, that it *ought* to be the case. Interestingly, some have charged defenders of ethical egoism with inconsistency: if one should always act in one's own self-interest, then in order to maximize that self-interest, it seems one should lie and defend, not egoism but benevolence.

In sharp contrast to the egoism of Hobbes, Joseph Butler argues in excerpts from his *Fifteen Sermons* that people are motivated not only by self-interest but by an interest in society, or benevolence. A bishop of the Anglican Church in eighteenth-century England, Butler wanted to expose the logical flaws which he believed existed in all doctrines of egoism. He claims that both egoism and benevolence participate in human motivation and moreover, that the actions of all people are *evaluated* in terms of the benevolence of those acts, and not on how much self-gain is achieved. The heart of the ethical issue raised in this section, then, rests with the dispute between Hobbes and Butler. Is Hobbes right to conclude that people are naturally selfish and that we should structure our institutions to reflect this fact? Or is Butler right in his claims that people can and should be motivated by benevolence, and if so, what implications arise for the design of social institutions?

The ethical egoist focuses his or her attention on the motivating principles of human conduct and not on the consequences of his or her actions for the well-being of other people. Even so, an ethical egoist may argue that self-interested actions often result in benefits for others. Indeed, it seems likely that the eighteenth-century philosopher and economist Adam Smith (whose views we shall examine in Part II) believed that self-interested actions frequently benefit others—at least when the actions are economically motivated. Such an argument does not follow necessarily from an ethical egoist's position, because an ethical egoist is concerned primarily with justifying self-interested activity by itself rather than in relation to possible benefits. But many people discuss ethical egoism, just as Smith does, in the light of its possible contribution to the general welfare.

The case study, "The Aircraft Brake Scandal," presented in this section illustrates one aspect of the issue of egoism in business. A large U.S. Corporation, B. F. Goodrich, became involved in serious ethical problems over the testing procedures it used in the fulfillment of a government contract for jet aircraft brakes. The case has been labeled a scandal because the pressures upon corporate employees, including those of job security and advancement in this incident, were strong enough to result in the falsifying of engineering specifications so that Goodrich could market dangerous and defective aircraft brakes. The dilemma of one employee, Vandivier, who finally blew the whistle on Goodrich, is a revealing illustration of some of the conflicts which can occur between self-interest and one's sense of a moral obligation to tell the truth, conflicts which in this case entailed serious societal consequences.

TRUTH TELLING

The issue of ethical egoism constitutes a fundamental locus for discussion of *motivation,* self-interested or otherwise, in business. Truth telling represents a fundamental point of departure for discussions about *communication* in business and can be used to investigate a wide variety of issues, including honesty in advertising, the accuracy of consumer information, and the responsibilities a business has to communicate honestly with its employees and stockholders.

A philosopher who is well known for his vigorous defense of truth-telling is the eighteenth-century German philosopher, Immanuel Kant. In this section, selections from his *Lectures on Ethics* are presented in which Kant claims that truth telling is an essential feature of right action. He equates honesty both with frankness and reserve, and he supports the principle of never telling a lie on three grounds. First, the principle of truth telling is one which each of us would like everyone else to follow. In other words, it is a principle which Kant calls "universalizable," meaning that each of us would like to see it universally followed by all human beings. Second, truth telling is a necessary element for society because all societies depend upon mutual bonds of honesty and truthfulness to enforce their unity and orderly continuation. Finally, lying destroys the major source of human development, i.e., knowledge, since it thwarts the discovery of new truths.

In contrast to Kant, Albert Carr, in a lively article, "Is Business Bluffing Ethical?", suggests that truth telling depends on the context in which the activity takes place. For example in advertising, although few advertisers actually lie about their products, many advertisements "puff" their products or make unfair comparisons between their product and the competition. This is all right, according to Carr, because everyone understands the "game" of advertising and no one is really fooled by the puffery. However, advertisers as well as philosophers are worried about the impact of the "game" of advertising on the public. Is bluffing or puffery justified when some persons affected by them do not understand the "game" and are deceived or misled?

If Carr's game analogy is questionable in advertising, the reader might want to consider its application to other aspects of business. Does the analogy ever justify making an exception to Kant's dictum that one should never lie? For example, the case study, "Italian Tax Mores," presents a situation in which truth telling (as well as relativism) is a major issue. The case concerns an American executive working at a branch of a U.S. company in Italy who finds that typical Italian practices encourage actions that he believes constitute both bribery and lying. Is it morally acceptable to misrepresent the company's income tax figures *if* it appears that most other companies in Italy do the same thing? Should the executive "play the game" and adopt the practices of the Italian tax system when the practices involve outright lying? Or can the manager justify providing the truth to the Italian tax authorities even when this might threaten the well-being of his bank?

ETHICAL RELATIVISM

Case Study—Lockheed Aircraft Corporation

CARL KOTCHIAN

My initiation into the chill realities of extortion, Japanese style, began in 1972. In August of that year I flew to Tokyo to work for the sale to a Japanese airline of Lockheed's wide-bodied TriStar passenger plane.

Soon after landing I found myself deep in conversation with Toshiharu Okubo, an official of Marubeni, the trading company that was serving as Lockheed's representative and go-between in the already ongoing TriStar negotiations.

Beaming, Okubo reviewed Marubeni's efforts on behalf of TriStar, then gave me the good news that "tomorrow at seven-thirty A.M., we are seeing Prime Minister Tanaka" about the matter. I was quite impressed with and encouraged by the "power of Marubeni"—power that made it possible to make an appointment with the prime minister only 24 hours after I had asked Marubeni to set up such a meeting. Then came an unexpected development: when we began to discuss in detail how to bring about the sale of TriStar, Okubo suddenly suggested that I make a "pledge" to pay money for a major favor like this. Though the proposal did not appall and outrage me, I was nonetheless quite astonished that the question of money had been brought up so abruptly—especially since in broaching the idea Okubo mentioned the name of the prime minister's secretary, Toshio Enomoto.

"How much money do we have to pledge?" I asked.

"The going rate when asking for a major favor is usually five hundred million yen [roughly $1.7 million]. It can be smaller. . . ."

I was now faced with the problem of whether to make a payment to Japan's highest government office. If I refused, declining Marubeni's advice, and should our sale fail, I was certain that the full responsibility would be placed squarely upon me by Marubeni's officials, who could say to me, "We told you so. You did not listen to us."

Sensing my hesitation, Okubo reiterated, "If you wish to be successful in selling the aircraft, you would do well to pledge five hundred million yen."

A. Carl Kotchian, "The Payoff: Lockheed's 70-day Mission to Tokyo," *Saturday Review*, July 9, 1977, pp. 7–12.

During this exchange, Okubo never mentioned for whom the money was intended. But we both knew that our whole conversation had been about the meeting between Prime Minister Tanaka and Chairman Hiyama of Marubeni, scheduled for early in the morning of the next day. Stalling for time and hoping to discover for whom the money was intended, I asked, "How do you deliver that money?"

"We do not have to worry about it," Okubo assured me, "because Mr. Ito [Hiroshi Ito, another executive of Marubeni] is very close to Mr. Enomoto, the prime minister's secretary."

This exchange left me with no doubt that the money was going to the office of Japan's prime minister. Then, in response to my further questions, Okubo concretely spelled out the details of the arrangement—the amount, 500 million yen; the way it had to be put together, in Japanese yen, cash; the fact that it had to be ready when we were given the signal; and the way the delivery of the money was to be accomplished, through the prime minister's secretary. This, then, was how I got involved in the now much publicized secret payments to Japanese government officials.

And "involved" is the word, for later that day I had a meeting near Tokyo's Sony Building with Yoshio Kodama, Lockheed's confidential consultant in Japan. So Byzantine were the TriStar maneuverings that Marubeni, our "above ground" agents and consultants, had no idea that Kodama was on Lockheed's payroll! In keeping with the air of mystery surrounding these dealings, Kodama always insisted on meeting me in the evening, because, I gather, he did not want employees in the other offices to see a highly conspicuous, six-foot-tall *gaijin*—a Japanese word for "foreigner"—going in and out of his office.

During the meeting, I asked about the chances of Lockheed's enlisting the support of Kenji Osano, an intimate of Prime Minister Tanaka whom some people had urged on me as an adviser, since he was "the most influential person in Japan." On this point, Kodama told me without hesitation, "In order to include Mr. Osano, we need an extra five hundred million yen." Frankly, I was quite surprised that he had come up with this figure so readily, as though it had already been decided on well in advance.

So my education in Japanese business practices was proceeding apace: it was the second time that day that I had been asked for "five hundred million yen." I felt that this particular figure must be used quite often in Japan!

In fact, as I thought about it back in my room at the Hotel Okura, I had now had *three* requests for around 500 million yen—520 million yen for Kodama on our contract with him, a second 500 million yen requested by Okubo to make a "payment pledge," and finally the third 500 million yen requested by Kodama for the inclusion of Osano in our campaign. I could not help thinking about these payments while I was having a room service dinner with my wife, Lucy. I was in fact thinking of calling Okubo to stop the 500 million yen that I had promised to pledge; but if I did that, I thought, I would have to tell him about the 500 million yen requested by Kodama. I decided at the last minute not to do that.

But why, you may wonder, did Lockheed put up at all with these under-the-counter demands? Why not just throw up our hands and try to sell our planes in some other country?

The truth is that—for the moment, at least—Lockheed had nowhere else to go *but* Japan. Although our planes were, and still are, first-rank products, fully competitive with if not superior to any other planes in the world, we had just come off a run of bad luck in the European market. To our chagrin and dismay, we had lost out on contract after airline contract—especially with Italy's Alitalia, Germany's Lufthansa, and Belgium's Sabena airlines.

Further, we were having difficulties with U.S. Defense Department contracts for the "Cheyenne" helicopter and the giant C5A Galaxie transport plane.

This bleak situation all but dictated a strong push for sales in the biggest untapped market left—Japan. This push, if successful, might well bring in revenues upwards of $400 million. Such a cash inflow would go a long way toward helping to restore Lockheed's fiscal health, and it would, of course, save the jobs of thousands of the firm's employees.

Against this background, I could hardly afford simply to fly away in disgust at the mere mention of these payments—payments which were in any case not forbidden under U.S. law. Realistically, the best I could hope for was to bend a bit in the face of these demands, while keeping our payments to a minimum percentage of any sale that went through.

While I was working in the Lockheed office at about 10:00 A.M. the next day, August 23, I received a telephone call from Okubo. He asked me to come to his office.

When I got there an hour or so later, I found him in a very jovial mood. He told me, "I accompanied Mr. Hiyama, Marubeni's chairman, to Prime Minister Tanaka's residence this morning."

According to Okubo, the two men had seen Prime Minister Tanaka briefly, and then Okubo left while Hiyama stayed to talk with the prime minister. He did not tell me what the three of them talked about or what Hiyama talked about with the prime minister. But then Okubo confided:

"That pledge has been made, too."

I do not know specifically how the pledge was made to the office of the prime minister, since these transactions seemed to be such a uniquely Japanese method. All I know is that I was given no paper saying, for instance, "If Lockheed is successful, we will pay 500 million yen," and the like. First of all, it was not clear whether the pledge was made to the prime minister himself or to his secretary. But I did not ask Okubo about this point, nor did I have any intention of doing so. I knew from the beginning that this money was going to the office of the prime minister and there was no need for me to have to pin down exactly to whom it was going or how the money was going to be delivered.

For the next few months, as summer passed over into fall, I stayed on in Tokyo, trying with little success to force-feed the situation, while delays, diversions, and frustrations piled up.

Then, to make things worse, late in October I was knocked flat by the pain and fever of a severe "bug" infection. Doctors, antibiotics, and bed rest seemed to do me no good: all I could do was lie there in my hotel suite, aching and perspiring and thinking darkly about jumping out the window. I suspect that it was only my wife's comforting presence that kept me from doing something drastic.

On October 29, when I was at my lowest ebb physically and mentally, our telephone started ringing. I picked up the receiver thinking, Who can it be at this time on a Sunday night? It was Okubo. Judging from the way his voice sounded, he seemed to be telephoning from a faraway place. After we exchanged pleasantries, he pointed out that the final decision by All Nippon Airlines (ANA)—the largest Japanese domestic carrier—would be made very shortly and said:

"If you do three things, Mr. Kotchian, you will definitely succeed in selling the TriStar."

I was struck with the importance of what Okubo was trying to say to me, and I straightened out the receiver in my hand and asked him, like a pupil asking questions of a teacher, "What are these three things that I have to do?" There was a tension in Okubo's voice, and for my part I listened to him with the phone pressed hard against my ear.

His first few stipulations were relatively minor, having to do with the maintenance of any planes Lockheed might sell to All Nippon Airlines. I readily agreed to them. And then came the "hook." According to Okubo, I had to get together as soon as possible $400,000—that is, 120 million Japanese yen—cash. "If possible, the first thing tomorrow morning, it has to be ready," Okubo urged me. As I'm sure he knew, it would have been impossible to have such a large sum of money ready on such short notice. I began asking questions; above all, What is the money for?

"To give three hundred thousand dollars [90 million yen] to Mr. Wakasa, president of All Nippon Airlines," Okubo blandly explained, "and also to make payments to six politicians."

As Okubo mentioned the six politicians by name, I wrote the names down on a hotel memo pad.

"If we give three hundred thousand dollars to Mr. Wakasa and to each of the six politicians, won't that make two million one hundred thousand dollars—six hundred thirty million yen?" I asked.

Suffering from a high fever and pain, I really became sick at the thought of such a preposterous sum. Okubo had, I reflected, already asked me for 500 million yen in August and I had agreed to make the pledge. Now he's asking more money for payments to politicians. What is he trying to do to me? Okubo hurriedly objected to my 630-million-yen figure: "No, not such a large sum."

"Is it, then, three hundred thousand dollars altogether, including the payments to the politicians?"

"No, that is not correct either. What I'm trying to say is. . . ."

In the end, it came down to this: the amount of money that had to be delivered to Mr. Wakasa, the president of ANA, was $300,000 altogether. This amount was calculated on the basis of $50,000 for each of the six airplanes ANA planned to purchase initially. In addition to this $300,000 for ANA, Okubo mentioned that an additional $100,000 should be prepared in Japanese yen—cash—and that this money should go to the following six politicians:

> Tomisaburo Hashimoto, secretary-general of the Liberal Democratic party.
>
> Susumu Nikaido, chief cabinet secretary.
>
> Hideyo Sasaki, minister of transportation.
>
> Kazuomi Fukunaga, chairman of the liberal Democratic party's special committee on aviation.
>
> Takayuki Sato, former parliamentary vice-minister of transportation.
>
> Mutsuki Kato, present parliamentary vice-minister of transportation.

Of the six politicians, I had not heard of Kazuomi Fukunaga and Mutsuki Kato. Of the remaining four, I had never met or talked with even one (and have never met them since, either); but I had heard of them and had seen their names in the newspapers. The hotel's telephone memo paper, on which I jotted down their names in romanized Japanese, was the so-called "memo" that had the names of the high Japanese government officials; it is this memo that became a great subject of curiosity when the Lockheed incident was disclosed in the United States.

As for the breakdown of this money for the politicians, Okubo expressed the intention of distributing the money as follows: 7 million yen each to Hashimoto and Nikaido, and 4 million yen each to Sasaki, Fukunaga, Sato, and Kato.

"If you do this first thing tomorrow morning," said Okubo, full of confidence, "we can formally get ANA's order tomorrow without fail." I had a feeling that these figures and the names must have been carefully thought about by someone. The problem, however, was that it was already past midnight and it was going to be very difficult to prepare such a large sum of money so quickly.

"By what time do we have to prepare this amount?" I asked.

"I would like you to have the whole sum of money ready by ten A.M. tomorrow," responded Okubo.

"That is impossible. I could not have it ready so quickly."

"The thirty million yen [for the politicians] is highly important. Couldn't you have that much ready at least?"

"Well, I'll try to do my best," I responded, adding, "and I will have the remaining ninety million yen ready at the earliest possible date. I will let you know on this remaining amount tomorrow morning."

If some third party had heard this conversation, he could ask why I responded to this request for secret payments. However, I must admit that it was extremely persuasive and attractive at that time to have someone come up to me and confidently tell me, "If you do this, you will surely get ANA's order in twenty-four hours." What businessman who is dealing with commercial and trade matters could decline a request for certain amounts of money when that money would enable him to get the contract? For someone like myself, who had been struggling against plots and severe competition for over two months, it was almost impossible to dismiss this opportunity.

At about 10:00 A.M. the next day, a Lockheed representative in Tokyo called to tell me that—pursuant to my instructions—he had delivered the 30 million yen to Okubo. (As for the remaining 90 million yen, I believe it was delivered on November 6, after I left Japan.)

Later that day, a group of us who had been working on the TriStar sale met in the lobby of the Kasumigaseki Building; Mr. Matsui of Marubeni got into the elevator with us, and together we went up to the head office of All Nippon Airlines. When we were ushered into one of the conference rooms in the main office, the top management of ANA had already assembled. I was told, "Congratulations, Mr. Kotchian, you have won the contract."

Feverish and light-headed though I was from my illness, I nonetheless felt very happy when I heard this and had a warm feeling inside me. I came back to the hotel at about seven o'clock and waited a little bit longer until it was Monday morning, California time. Then I called up our main office in Burbank and informed Mr. Haughton, our chairman, of the good news. He was delighted and told me that on my return they were going to have a big celebration party for all of us who had worked on the sale.

Now, finally, I began to feel a sense of victory after the most intense sales campaign of my life. It was a victory of pain after 70 straight days of battle in which I had literally run around the great city of Tokyo without getting a chance to know it at all. At about seven o'clock on the evening of October 31, our suite was filled with happy Lockheed men and women who had worked many weeks for this occasion. Everybody's face looked so happy and bright; champagne was opened, one bottle after another. I even poured champagne over the head of Peter Mingrone, a Lockheed executive who had helped enormously in the sales campaign.

After returning to the States, I began to take care of the areas of my responsibility other than Japan. Having completed the official signing of the contract document, I thought that the sales campaign of the TriStar in Japan had been completed.

I believe it was around June 25, 1973, although I do not specifically remember the date, that I received an unexpected telephone communication from Okubo, who said, "Now is the time for you to honor that pledge."

For one second, I wondered what he was talking about, but then I realized that by the word *pledge,* he was talking about the pledge of 500 million yen that we made to the office of Prime Minister Tanaka the previous August. The word *pledge* had been used frequently at that time in Okubo's office when we were talking about the subject. Nevertheless, there had been a ten-month lapse since August. It had been almost half a year since Lockheed and ANA officially signed the formal contract in January. I wondered why he was bringing this up now, when the sales campaign of the TriStar to ANA had long ago been completed.

"I am very surprised, Mr. Okubo, because it all happened six or eight months ago; and we haven't heard anything about it. Frankly, as our campaign has been completed, I don't have that kind of budget now," I told him.

"Yes, but that is the pledge that you agreed upon and accepted," Okubo insisted.

"But you have not communicated with us for such a long time on this matter. The whole deal was completed six months ago," I repeated.

I expressed strong opposition to doing this kind of thing this late. Therefore I asked him: "Are you sure it's necessary, Mr. Okubo?"

Okubo said, "Let me check into it. If it's really necessary, I'll get back to you."

This is how our telephone conversation ended on that day. Three days later, Okubo called me again and said: "This is very serious, Mr. Kotchian, and you must carry out that pledge."

Okubo *sounded* very serious and worried. He said that he had talked to Mr. Hiyama, the chairman of the board of Marubeni, on this matter, and that Mr. Hiyama asked him to tell me that if Lockheed did not stand by its pledge, we would never be able to sell anything in Japan again. Worse still, Okubo said, if the pledge was not honored, "Mr. Hiyama will have to leave Japan."

It was quite shocking for me to hear that the chairman of Marubeni would have to leave Japan. I interpreted this as meaning that Hiyama would be forced into exile.

"You have convinced me, Mr. Okubo, that the matter is indeed serious," I told him, promising that I would get in touch with him early the next week.

After hanging up the telephone, I went home and thought about the matter overnight. I decided on the basis of what Okubo had told me that we could not possibly risk any retaliation against Lockheed or against Marubeni. If we did not make the payment on this matter, Hiyama would be forced into exile, Lockheed might not be able to sell anything in Japan again, and our relations with Marubeni might be completely disrupted. Consequently, the more I thought about it, the more I was convinced that there was no alternative but to make the payment. In the end, after talking it over with other Lockheed officials, I called Okubo and told him we would honor the pledge.

Throughout these three international telephone calls on this matter, Okubo never once mentioned the name of the person for whom the money was intended, or the amount; and neither did I. Perhaps we were both mindful of the fact that the conversation was going through the telephone exchange and we did not want to be overheard by anybody; but more than anything else, we were both aware that this 500 million yen was going to the office of the prime minister. I never asked why the payment was necessary at this particular stage, after so many months had passed. All I know is that the designated amount was paid—spread over the remainder of 1973 to early 1974. I did not know then that it was made in four shipments or when it was paid specifically.

When I visited Japan in October 1973, on my way back from Iran, to arrange the date for the delivery of the first plane, All Nippon Airlines had already decided to make a firm order for the additional eight TriStars on which they had an option. After this second contract was concluded, Okubo again demanded $400,000 from us, calculated on the basis of $50,000 per plane for eight planes, to be delivered to Mr. Wakasa, the president of ANA, as a secret payment.

When Okubo called me by international telephone from Tokyo and demanded this amount, I responded rather harshly, saying, "Wasn't it a one-time expenditure at that time only?"

"No," Okubo said emphatically. "I'm sure I told you these payments were necessary for all of the planes—all of the twenty-one planes."

I had no intention of paying this kind of money until the actual order was made and the initial down payment for the next eight planes was made to Lockheed, and I told this to Okubo. Here again, I could have declined. However, if I had declined and they had said, "Well, we will not order any more planes from Lockheed," what would we do?

The most I could say to this additional demand for money was: "When the initial down payment is received, we will pay what we have to."

The down payment started coming in, and by August of the next year, 1974, down payment for the first four of the eight planes had been received by Lockheed. I thought that if I paid the $400,000 requested by Okubo at that stage I would expedite the down payment for the remaining four planes. So it was around this time that I finally approved the payment of $400,000 to ANA and instructed our representative to arrange such a delivery per instructions from Okubo. I don't know how this money was paid, where, and in what manner—or what kind of receipts were used.

As for the purpose of the $700,000 (calculated on the basis of $50,000 per plane for the 14 planes), Okubo never explained to me, nor did I ask any questions about it. It could be inferred, however, from the way that Okubo spoke that the money was to be used at the discretion of the top management of ANA, although none of the ANA people ever talked about this in our meetings.

Such were some of the payments for the sale of the TriStar in Japan, viewed from my perspective. Above all, there are three things I would like to stress about the whole sequence I have described.

The *first* is that the Lockheed payments in Japan, totaling about $12 million, were worthwhile from Lockheed's standpoint, since they amounted to less than 3 percent of the expected sum of about $430 million that we would receive from ANA for 21 TriStars. Further, as I've noted, such disbursements *did not violate American laws.* I should also like to stress that my decision to make such payments stemmed from my judgment that the TriStar payments to ANA would provide Lockheed workers with jobs and thus redound to the benefit of their dependents, their communities, and stockholders of the corporation.

Secondly, I should like to emphasize that the payments to the so-called "high Japanese government officials" were all requested by Okubo and were *not brought up from my side.* When he told me "five hundred million yen is necessary for such sales," from a purely ethical and moral standpoint I would have declined such a request. However, in that case, I would *most certainly* have sacrificed commercial success.

Finally, I want to make it clear that I never discussed money matters with Japanese politicians, government officials, or airline officials.

It would be simple if selling were merely a matter of presenting a product on its merits. Lockheed conducted its business in Japan much as other aircraft companies, its competitors, had done over the years. All have found it helpful to have nationals advise them, in Japan as in many other countries. Much has been made in press accounts in both Japan and the United States of secret agents and secret channels for sales efforts. Of course these consultations with advisers were secret: competitors do not tell each other their strategy or even their sales targets.

And if Lockheed had not remained competitive by the rules of the game as then played, we would not have sold the TriStar and would not have provided work for tens of thousands of our employees or contributed to the future of the corporation. Nor would ANA have had the services of this excellent airplane.

From my experience in international sales, I knew that if we wanted our product to have a chance to win on its own merits, we had to follow the functioning system. If we wanted our product to have a chance, we understood that we would have to pay, or pledge to pay, substantial sums of money in addition to the contractual sales commissions. We never *sought* to make these extra payments. We would have preferred not to have the additional expenses for the sale. But, always, they were recommended by those whose experience and judgment we trusted and whose recommendations we therefore followed.

Every investigation campaign requires an "example," a "scapegoat," and Lockheed is that today in the current international climate of reform. The requirement to assess responsibility in Japan has brought the embarrassment of public accusation to some persons associated with the company. To others it has brought the humiliation of arrest and imprisonment. We, too, have suffered. We are anguished that some of our friends and their families have had to bear this agony. We hope it will not have been without benefit.

Ethical Relativity and Ethical Absolutism

WALTER STACE

Any ethical position which denies that there is a single moral standard which is equally applicable to all men at all times may fairly be called a species of ethical relativity. There is not, the relativist asserts, merely one moral law, one code, one standard. There are many moral laws, codes, standards. What morality ordains in one place or age may be quite different from what morality ordains in another place or age. The moral code of Chinamen is

From W. T. Stace, *The Concept of Morals* (New York: The Macmillan Co., 1937); renewed 1965 by Walter T. Stace; reprinted by permission of The Macmillan Co.

quite different from that of Europeans, that of African savages quite different from both. Any morality, therefore, is relative to the age, the place, and the circumstances in which it is found. It is in no sense absolute.

This does not mean merely—as one might at first sight be inclined to suppose—that the very same kind of action which is *thought* right in one country and period may be *thought* wrong in another. This would be a mere platitude, the truth of which everyone would have to admit. Even the absolutist would admit this—would even wish to emphasize it—since he is well aware that different peoples have different sets of moral ideas, and his whole point is that some of these sets of ideas are false. What the relativist means to assert is, not this platitude, but that the very same kind of action which is right in one country and period may *be* wrong in another. And this, far from being a platitude is a very startling assertion.

It is very important to grasp thoroughly the difference between the two ideas. . . . We fail to see that the word "standard" is used in two different senses. It is perfectly true that, in one sense, there are many variable moral standards. We speak of judging a man by the standard of his time. And this implies that different times have different standards. And this, of course, is quite true. But when the word "standard" is used in this sense it means simply the set of moral ideas current during the period in question. It means what people *think* right, whether as a matter of fact it is right or not. On the other hand when the absolutist asserts that there exists a single universal moral "standard," he is not using the word in this sense at all. He means by "standard" what *is* right as distinct from what people merely think right. His point is that although what people think right varies in different countries and periods, yet what actually is right is everywhere and always the same. And it follows that when the ethical relativist disputes the position of the absolutist and denies that any universal moral standard exists he too means by "standard" what actually is right. . . .

To sum up, the ethical relativist consistently denies, it would seem, whatever the ethical absolutist asserts. For the absolutist there is a single universal moral standard. For the relativist there is no such standard. There are only local, ephemeral, and variable standards. For the absolutist there are two senses of the word "standard." Standards in the sense of sets of current moral ideas are relative and changeable. But the standard in the sense of what is actually morally right is absolute and unchanging. For the relativist no such distinction can be made. There is only one meaning of the word standard, namely, that which refers to local and variable sets of moral ideas.

Finally—though this is merely saying the same thing in another way—the absolutist makes a distinction between what actually is right and what is thought right. The relativist rejects this distinction and identifies what is moral with what is thought moral by certain human beings or groups of human beings. . . .

I shall now proceed to consider, first, the main arguments which can be urged in favour of ethical relativity; and secondly, the arguments which can be urged against it. . . .

There are, I think, [two] main arguments in favour of ethical relativity.

The first is that which relies upon the actual varieties of moral "standards" found in the world. . . .

The investigations of anthropologists have shown that there exist side by side in the world a bewildering variety of moral codes. On this topic endless volumes have been written, masses of evidence piled up. Anthropologists have ransacked the Melanesian Islands, the jungles of New Guinea, the steppes of Siberia, the deserts of Australia, the forests of central Africa, and have brought back with them countless examples of weird, extravagant, and fantastic "moral" customs with which to confound us. We learn that all kinds of horrible practices are, in this, that, or the other place, regarded as essential to virtue. We find that there is nothing, or next to nothing, which has always and everywhere been regarded as morally good by all men. Where then is our universal morality? Can we, in face of all this evidence, deny that it is nothing but an empty dream?

This argument, taken by itself, is a very weak one. It relies upon a single set of facts—the variable moral customs of the world. But this variability of moral ideas is admitted by both parties to the dispute, and is capable of ready explanation upon the hypothesis of either party. The relativist says that the facts are to be explained by the non-existence of any absolute moral standard. The absolutist says that they are to be explained by human ignorance of what the absolute moral standard is. And he can truly point out that men have differed widely in their opinions about all manner of topics including the subject-matters of the physical sciences—just as much as they differ about morals. And if the various different opinions which men have held about the shape of the earth do not prove that it has no one real shape, neither do the various opinions which they have held about morality prove that there is no one true morality.

Thus the facts can be explained equally plausibly on either hypothesis. There is nothing in the facts themselves which compels us to prefer the relativistic hypothesis to that of the absolutist. And therefore the argument fails to prove the relativist conclusion. If that conclusion is to be established, it must be by means of other considerations. . . .

The [second] argument in favour of ethical relativity is a very strong one. . . . It consists in alleging that no one has ever been able to discover upon what foundation an absolute morality could rest, or from what source a universally binding moral code could derive its authority.

If, for example, it is an absolute and unalterable moral rule that all men ought to be unselfish, from whence does this *command* issue? For a command it certainly is, phrase it how you please. There is no difference in meaning between the sentence "You ought to be unselfish" and the sentence "Be unselfish." Now a command implies a commander. An obligation implies some authority which obliges. Who is this commander, what this authority? Thus the vastly difficult question is raised of *the basis of moral obligation.* Now the argument of the relativist would be that it is impossible to find any basis for a universally binding moral law; but that it is quite easy to discover a basis for morality if moral codes are admitted to be variable, ephemeral, and relative to time, place, and circumstance.

No such easy solution of the problem of the basis of moral obligation is open to the absolutist. He believes in moral commands, obedience to which is obligatory on all men, whether they know it or not, whatever they feel, and whatever their customs may be. Such uniform obligation cannot be founded upon feelings, because feelings are—or are said to be—variable. And there is no set of customs which is more than local in its operation. The will of God as the source of a universal law is no longer a feasible suggestion. . . . Where then is the absolutist to turn for an answer to the question? And if he cannot find one, he will have to admit the claims of the ethical relativist; or at least he will have to give up his own claims. . . .

This argument is undoubtedly very strong. It is absolutely essential to solve the problem of the basis of moral obligation if we are to believe in any kind of moral standards other than those provided by mere custom or by irrational emotions. It is idle to talk about a universal morality unless we can point to the source of its authority—or at least to do so is to indulge in a faith which is without rational ground. To cherish a blind faith in morality may be, for the average man whose business is primarily to live aright and not to theorize, sufficient. Perhaps it is his wisest course. But it will not do for the philosopher. His function, or at least one of his functions, is precisely to discover the rational grounds of our everyday beliefs—if they have any. Philosophically and intellectually, then, we cannot accept belief in a universally binding morality unless we can discover upon what foundation its obligatory character rests.

But in spite of the strength of the argument thus posed in favour of ethical relativity, it is not impregnable. For it leaves open one loop-hole. It is always possible that some theory, not yet examined, may provide a basis for a universal moral obligation. The argument rests upon the negative proposition that *there is no theory which can provide a basis for a universal morality.* But it is notoriously difficult to prove a negative. How can you prove that there are no green swans? All you can show is that none have been found so far. And then it is always possible that one will be found tomorrow. So it is here. The relativist shows that no theory of the basis of moral obligation has yet been discovered which could validate a universal morality. Perhaps. But it is just conceivable that one might be discovered in the course of this book.

It is time that we turn our attention from the case in favour of ethical relativity to the case against it. Now the case against it consists, to a very large extent, in urging that, if taken seriously and pressed to its logical conclusion, ethical relativity can only end in destroying the conception of morality altogether, in undermining its practical efficacy, in rendering meaningless many almost universally accepted truths about human affairs, in robbing human beings of any incentive to strive for a better world, in taking the life-blood out of every ideal and every aspiration which has ever ennobled the life of man. . . .

First of all, then, ethical relativity, in asserting that the moral standards of particular social groups are the only standards which exist, renders meaningless all propositions which attempt to compare these standards with one another in respect of their moral worth. And this is a very serious matter indeed. We are accustomed to think that the moral ideas of one nation or social group may be "higher" or "lower" than those of another. We believe, for example, that Christian ethical ideals are nobler than those of the savage races of central Africa. Probably most of us would think that the Chinese moral standards are higher than those of the inhabitants of New Guinea. In short we habitually compare one civilization with another and judge the sets of ethical ideas to be found in them to be some better, some worse. The fact that such judgments are very difficult to make with any justice, and that they are frequently made on very superficial and prejudiced grounds, has no bearing on the question now at issue. The question is whether such judgments have any *meaning.* We habitually assume that they have.

But on the basis of ethical relativity they can have none whatever. For the relativist must hold that there is no *common* standard which can be applied to the various civilizations judged. Any such comparison of moral standards implies the existence of some superior standard which is applicable to both. And the existence of any such standard is precisely what the relativist denies. According to him the Christian standard is applicable only to Christians, the Chinese standard only to Chinese, the New Guinea standard only to the inhabitants of New Guinea.

What is true of comparisons between the moral standards of different races will also be true of comparisons between those of different ages. It is not unusual to ask such questions as whether the standard of our own day is superior to that which existed among our ancestors five hundred years ago. And when we remember that our ancestors employed slaves, practiced barbaric physical tortures, and burnt people alive, we may be inclined to think that it is. At any rate we assume that the question is one which has meaning and is capable of rational discussion. But if the ethical relativist is right, whatever we assert on this subject must be totally meaningless. For here again there is no common standard which could form the basis of any such judgments.

There is indeed one way in which the ethical relativist can give some sort of meaning to judgments of higher or lower as applied to the moral ideas of different races or ages. What he will have to say is that we assume *our* standards to be the best simply because they are ours. And we judge other standards by our own. If we say that Chinese moral codes are better than those of African cannibals, what we *mean* by this is that they are better *according to our standards.* We mean, that is to say, that Chinese standards are *more like our own* than African standards are. "Better" accordingly *means* "more like us." "Worse" means "less like us." It thus becomes clear that jugments of better and worse in such cases do not express anything that is really true at all. They merely give expression to our perfectly groundless satisfaction with our own ideas. In short, they give expression to nothing but our egotism and self-conceit. Our moral ideals are not really better than those of the savage. We are simply deluded by our egotism into thinking they are. The African savage has just as good a right to think his morality the best as we have to think ours the best. His opinion is just as well grounded as ours, or rather both opinions are equally groundless. . . .

Thus the ethical relativist must treat all judgments comparing different moralities as either entirely meaningless; or, if this course appears too drastic, he has the alternative of declaring that they have for their meaning-content nothing except the vanity and egotism of those who pass them. . . .

I come now to a second point. Up to the present I have allowed it to be taken tacitly for granted that, though judgments comparing different races and ages in respect of the worth of their moral codes are impossible for the ethical relativist, yet judgments of comparison between individuals living within the same social group would be quite possible. For individuals living within the same social group would presumably be subject to the same moral code, that of their group, and this would therefore constitute, as between these individuals, a common standard by which they could both be measured. We have not here, as we had in the other case, the difficulty of the absence of any common standard of comparison. It should therefore be possible for the ethical relativist to say quite meaningfully that President Lincoln was a better man than some criminal or moral imbecile of his own time and country, or that Jesus was a better man than Judas Iscariot.

But is even this minimum of moral judgment really possible on relativist grounds? It seems to me that it is not. For when once the whole of humanity is abandoned as the area covered by a single moral standard, what smaller areas are to be adopted as the loci of different standards? Where are we to draw the lines of demarcation? We can split up humanity, perhaps—though the procedure will be very arbitrary—into races, races into nations, nations into tribes, tribes into families, families into individuals. Where are we going to draw the *moral* boundaries? Does the *locus* of a particular moral standard reside in a race, a nation, a tribe, a family, or an individual? Perhaps the blessed phrase "social group" will be dragged in to save the situation. Each such group, we shall be told, has its own moral code which is, for it, right. But what *is* a "group"? Can anyone define it or give its boundaries? . . .

. . . Does the American nation constitute a "group" having a single moral standard? Or does the standard of what I ought to do change continuously as I cross the continent in a railway train? Do different States of the Union have different moral codes? Perhaps every town and village has its own peculiar standard. This may at first sight seem reasonable enough. "In Rome do as Rome does" may seem as good a rule in morals as it is in etiquette. But can we stop there? Within the village are numerous cliques each having its own set of ideas. Why should not each of these claim to be bound only by its own special and peculiar moral standards? And if it comes to that, why should not the gangsters of Chicago claim to constitute a group having its own morality, so that its murders and debaucheries must be viewed as "right" by the only standard which can legitimately be applied to it? And if it be answered that the nation will not tolerate this, that may be so. But this is to put the foundation of right simply in the superior force of the majority. In that case whoever is stronger will be right, however monstrous his ideas and actions. And if we cannot deny to any set of people the right to have its own morality, is it not clear that, in the end, we cannot even deny this right to the individual? Every individual man and woman can put up, on this view, an irrefutable claim to be judged by no standard except his or her own.

If these arguments are valid, the ethical relativist cannot really maintain that there is anywhere to be found a moral standard binding upon anybody against his will. And he cannot maintain that, even within the social group, there is a common standard as between individuals. And if that is so, then even judgments to the effect that one man is morally better than another become meaningless. All moral valuation thus vanishes. There is nothing to prevent each man from being a rule unto himself. The result will be moral chaos and the collapse of all effective standards.

Perhaps, in regard to the difficulty of defining the social group, the relativist may make the following suggestion. If we admit, he may say, that it is impossible or very difficult to define a group territorially or nationally or geographically, it is still possible to define it logically. We will simply define an ethical group as any set of persons (whether they live together in one place or are scattered about in many places over the earth) who recognizes one and the same moral standard. As a matter of fact such groups will as a rule be found occupying each something like a single locality. The people in one country, or at least in one village, tend to think much alike. But theoretically at least the members of an ethical group so defined might be scattered all over the face of the globe. However that may be, it will now be possible to make meaningful statements to the effect that one individual is morally better or worse than another, so long as we keep within the ethical group so defined. For the individuals of the ethical group will have as their common standard the ethical belief or beliefs the acknowledgement of which constitutes the defining characteristic of the group. By this common standard they can be judged and compared with one another. Therefore it is not true that ethical relativity necessarily makes all such judgments of moral comparison between individuals meaningless.

I admit the logic of this. Theoretically judgments of comparison can be given meaning in this way. Nevertheless there are fatal objections to the suggestion. . . .

. . . Even if we assume that the difficulty about defining moral groups has been surmounted, a further difficulty presents itself. Suppose that we have now definitely decided what are the exact boundaries of the social group within which a moral standard is to be operative. And we will assume —as is invaribly done by relativists themselves—that this group is to be some actually existing social community such as a tribe or nation. How are we to know, even then, what actually *is* the moral standard within that group? How is anyone to know? How is even a member of the group to know? For there are certain to be within the group—at least this will be true among advanced peoples—wide differences of opinion as to what is right, what wrong. Whose opinion, then, is to be taken as representing *the* moral standard of the group? Either we must take the opinion of the majority within the group, or the opinion of some minority. If we rely upon the ideas of the majority, the results will be disastrous. Wherever there is found among a people a small band of select spirits, or perhaps one man, working for the establishment of higher and nobler ideals than those commonly accepted by the group, we shall be compelled to hold that, for that people at that time, the majority are right, and that the reformers are wrong and are preaching what is immoral. . . .

The ethical relativists are great empiricists. *What* is the actual moral standard of any group can only be discovered, they tell us, by an examination on the ground of the moral opinions and customs of that group. But will they tell us how they propose to decide, when they get to the ground, which of the many moral opinions they are sure to find there is *the* right one in that group? To some extent they will be able to do this for the Melanesian Islanders—from whom apparently all lessons in the nature of morality are in future to be taken. But it is certain that they cannot do it for advanced peoples whose members have learnt to think for themselves and to entertain among themselves a wide variety of opinions. They cannot do it unless they accept the calamitous view that the ethical opinion of the majority is always right. We are left therefore once more with the conclusion that, even within a particular social group, anybody's moral opinion is as good as anybody else's, and that every man is entitled to be judged by his own standards.

Finally, not only is ethical relativity disastrous in its consequences for moral theory. It cannot be doubted that it must tend to be equally disastrous in its impact upon practical conduct. If men come really to believe that one moral standard is as good as another, they will conclude that their own moral standard has nothing special to recommend it. They might as well then slip down to some lower and easier standard. It is true that, for a time, it may be possible to hold one view in theory and to act practically upon another. But ideas, even philosophical ideas, are not so ineffectual that they can remain for ever idle in the upper chambers of the intellect. In the end they seep down to the level of practice. They get themselves acted on.

These, then, are the main arguments which the anti-relativist will urge against ethical relativity. And perhaps finally he will attempt a diagnosis of the social, intellectual, and psychological conditions of our time to which the emergence of ethical relativism is to be attributed.

Ethical Relativism

RICHARD BRANDT

ARE THERE ULTIMATE DISAGREEMENTS ABOUT ETHICAL PRINCIPLES?

No one seriously doubts that there are differences of ethical principle. . . .However, there is a question about these differences, and its answer is controversial. In order to mark this question, let us use the phrase "*ultimate* difference of ethical principle," . . .

What is meant by an "ultimate" difference of principle? Consider first an example of conflicting evaluations of a particular action. Suppose Smith gives his father an overdose of sleeping pills, resulting in death. Suppose

From Richard Brandt, *Ethical Theory* (Englewood Cliffs, N.J.: Prentice-Hall, Inc., 1959); reprinted by permission of the publisher.

further that Jones hears of this event, but thinks no worse of Smith for this reason, because he knows that Smith's father was dying from cancer and in a very painful condition, and he believes Smith's act was done as an act of mercy. We might say he thinks Smith's act was right, because it was of the kind ABC. Suppose, now, that Brown also learns of Smith's act, but, unlike Jones, he thinks its was wrong. Brown knows that Smith's father was wealthy and that Smith was penniless, and he believes Smith's act was done to expedite the transfer of his father's property to him. Brown, then thinks Smith's act was wrong, since he assumes that it was of the kind ADE. Brown and Jones, then, differ in their appraisal of the act, but possibly they do not differ at all in their ethical principles, but only in their factual beliefs about the properties of the act. It may well be that Brown and Jones both agree that all acts of the kind ABC are right, and that all acts of the kind ADE are wrong. In this case, we do not wish to say there was any *ultimate* disagreement between them.

Let us now turn to disagreements about ethical principles. . . . the Romans decidedly did not think it right to put one's parents to death. In some of the Eskimo groups, however, this is thought proper. One observer has told of an Eskimo who was getting ready to move camp, and was concerned about what to do with his blind and aged father, who was a burden to the family. One day the old man expressed a desire to go seal-hunting again, something he had not done for many years. His son readily assented to this suggestion, and the old man was dressed warmly and given his weapons. He was then led out to the seal grounds and was walked into a hole in the ice, into which he disappeared.[1] The Romans, we may expect, would have been shocked at this deed. The Eskimos think it right, in general, to drown a parent who is old and a burden; the Romans, we guess, think this is wrong. The Romans, we may say, think that all acts of the kind ABC are wrong; the Eskimos deny this.

But may it not be that the Eskimos and the Romans in some sense have different acts in mind? Suppose that Eskimos, through their experience with the hardships of living, think of parricide as being normally the merciful cutting short of a miserable, worthless, painful old age. And suppose the Romans think of parricide as being normally the getting rid of a burden, or a getting one's hands on the parent's money—an ungrateful, selfishly motivated aggression against one whose care and sacrifices years ago have made the child's life a rich experience. The Eskimos are more-or-less unconsciously taking for granted that putting a parent to death is euthanasia under extreme circumstances; the Romans are more-or-less unconsciously taking for granted that putting a parent to death is murder for gain. In this case, although the Romans and the Eskimos may use the very same words to describe a certain sort of act—and then may express conflicting ethical appraisals of it—actually in some sense they have in mind quite different things. The Eskimos, perhaps, are accepting something of the kind ABCD; the Romans are condemning something of the kind ABFG. In this situation, we do not want to say there is necessarily any ultimate disagreement of principle between them. . . .

It is not easy to answer the question whether there is ultimate disagreement on ethical principles between different groups. Most of the comparative material assembled . . . is of little value for this purpose, for in large part what it tells us is simply whether various peoples approve or condemn lying, suicide, industry, cleanliness, adultery, homosexuality, cannibalism, and so on. But this is not enough. We need, for our purpose, to know how various peoples *conceive* of these things. Do they eat human flesh because they like its taste, and do they kill slaves merely for the sake of a feast? Or do they eat flesh because they think this is necessary for tribal fertility, or because they think they will then participate in the manliness of the person eaten? Perhaps those who condemn cannibalism would not do so if they thought that eating the flesh of an enemy is necessary for the survival of the group. If we are to estimate whether there is ultimate disagreement of ethical principle, we must have information about this, about the beliefs, more or less conscious, of various peoples, about what they do. However, the comparative surveys seldom give us this.

In view of the total evidence, then, is it more plausible to say that there is ultimate disagreement of ethical principle, or not? Or don't we really have good grounds for making a judgment on this crucial issue?

. . . The writer inclines to think there is ultimate ethical disagreement, and that it is well established. Maybe it is not very important, or very pervasive; but there is some. Let us look at the matter of causing suffering to animals. It is notorious that many peoples seem quite indifferent to the suffering of animals. We are informed that very often, in Latin America, a chicken is *plucked alive*, with the thought it will be more succulent on the table. The reader is invited to ask himself whether he would consider it justified to pluck a chicken alive, for this purpose. Or again, take the "game" played by Indians of the Southwest (but learned from the Spaniards, apparently), called the "chicken pull." In this "game," a chicken is buried in the sand, up to its neck. The contestants ride by on horseback, trying to grab the chicken by the neck and yank it from the sand. When someone succeeds in this, the idea is then for the other contestants to take away from him as much of the chicken as they can. The "winner" is the one who ends up with the most chicken. The reader is invited to ask himself whether he approves of this sport. The writer had the decided impression that the Hopi disapproval of causing pain to animals is much milder than he would suppose typical in suburban Philadelphia—certainly much milder than he would feel himself. For instance, children often catch birds and make "pets" of them. A string is tied to their legs, and they are then "played" with. The birds seldom survive this "play" for long: their legs are broken, their wings pulled off, and so on. One informant put it: "Sometimes they get tired and die. Nobody objects to this." Another informant said: "My boy sometimes brings in birds, but there is nothing to feed them, and they die."[2] Would the reader approve of this, or permit his children to do this sort of thing?

Of course, these people might believe that animals are unconscious automata, or that they are destined to be rewarded many times in the afterlife if they suffer martyrdom on this earth. Then we should feel that our ethical principles were, after all, in agreement with those of these individuals. But they believe no such thing. The writer took all means he could think of to discover some such belief in the Hopi subconscious, but he found none. So probably—we must admit the case is not definitively closed—there is at least one ultimate difference of ethical principle. How many more there are, or how important, we do not say at present.

It is obvious that if there is *ultimate* disagreement of ethical opinion between two persons or groups, there is also disagreement in *basic* principles—if we mean by "basic ethical principle"... the principles we should have to take as a person's ethical premises, if we represented his ethical views as a deductive system. We have so defined "ultimate disagreement" that a difference in the ethical theorems of two persons or groups does not count as being "ultimate" if it can be explained as a consequence of identical ethical premises but different factual assumptions of the two parties. Since ultimate ethical disagreements, then, cannot be a consequence of the factual assumptions of the parties, it must be a consequence of their ethical premises. Hence, there is also disagreement in "basic" principles. Our conclusion from our total evidence, then, is that different persons or groups sometimes have, in fact, conflicting basic ethical principles....

ARE CONFLICTING ETHICAL OPINIONS EQUALLY VALID?

A Greek philosopher who lived in the fifth century B.C., named Protagoras, seems to have believed two things: first, that moral principles cannot be shown to be valid for everybody; and second, that people ought to follow the conventions of their own group.[3] Something like this combination of propositions probably had been thought of before his time. Primitive people are well aware that different social groups have different standards, and at least sometimes doubt whether one set of standards can really be shown to be superior to others. Moreover, probably in many groups it has been thought that a person who conforms conscientiously to the standards of his own group deserves respect.

Views roughly similar to those of Protagoras may be classified as forms of *ethical relativism.* The term "ethical relativism," however, is used in different senses, and one should be wary when one comes across it. Sometimes one is said to be a relativist if he thinks that an action that is wrong in one place might not be in another, so that one is declared a relativist if he thinks it wrong for a group of Eskimos to strip a man of his clothing twenty miles from home on January 1, but not wrong for a tribe at the equator. If "relativism" is used in this sense, then practically everyone is a relativist, for practically everyone believes that particular circumstances make a difference to the morality of an act—that, for instance, it is right to lie in some circumstances but wrong in others. Again, one is sometimes said to be a relativist if he asserts a pair of causal propositions: that different social groups sometimes have different values (ethical opinions) as a result of historical developments; and that an individual's values are near-replicas of the tradition of his group, however strongly he may feel that they are "his own" or that they are "valid" and can be supported by convincing reasons. We shall not use "ethical relativism" for either of these views, but reserve it for a theory at least fairly close to that of Protagoras. . . .

It is clarifying to substitute, in place of our initial statement of Protagoras' view, the following, as a brief formulation of the relativist thesis in ethics: "*There are conflicting ethical opinions that are equally valid*." But this formulation requires discussion in order to be clear.

The first thing to notice—although the fact will not be obvious until we have explained the phrase "equally valid"—is that the statement is *about* ethical opinions or statements, but is not an ethical statement itself. It is not like saying, "Nothing is right or wrong!" or "Some things are both right and wrong!" It is a metaethical theory.

Next, the statement is cautious. It does not say that no ethical opinions are valid for everybody. It says only that some ethical opinions are not more valid than some other ethical opinions that conflict with them.

Third, our relativist thesis is not merely the claim that different individuals sometimes in fact have conflicting ethical opinions. It does assert this, but it goes further. It holds that the conflicting ethical opinions are *equally valid.*

. . .Now, the ethical relativist is not merely making the uninteresting claim, when he says two conflicting ethical statements are equally valid, that the two statements are equally plausible in the light of the facts known at present. He is saying something much more radical, about what would happen if one were testing these statements by the best possible ethical methodology, and in the light of a complete system of factual or nonethical knowledge. In other words, he is saying that the application of a "rational" method in ethics would support, equally, two conflicting ethical statements even if there were available a complete system of factual knowledge—or else that there is no "rational" method in ethics comparable to an ideal inductive method for empirical science. . . .

We can now explain exactly what it means to say that two conflicting ethical statements are "equally valid." What it means to say this, is that *either* there is *no* unique rational or justified method in ethics, *or* that the use of the unique rational method in ethics, in the presence of an ideally complete system of factual knowledge, would still not enable us to make a distinction between the ethical statements being considered.

The ethical relativist asserts that there are at least *some* instances of conflicting ethical opinions that are equally valid in this sense. . . .

The facts of anthropology are also relevant to our question, and in the following way. In the first place . . . studies of cultural change in primitive societies suggest that facts like personal conflicts and maladjustments, the attitudes of one's close relatives (for example, whether favorably oriented toward White civilization), and personal success in achieving status in one's group or outside one's groups (for example, with White men) play an important role in the development of the values of adults. This finding is some support for our reading of the observational evidence of psychology. In the second place, there is the fact that various groups have different values. The mere fact that different ethical standards exist in different societies, of course, by itself proves nothing relevant to our present problem.

Nevertheless, something important is proved if the facts bear testimony that different standards can prevail even if different groups have the *same beliefs* about the relevant event or act, and if there is no reason to suppose that the group standards reflect group differences in respect of other "qualifications." (We must remember that attitudes common to a group cannot usually be discounted as being a result of personal interest or of an abnormal frame of mind.) The fact of variation of group standards, in these circumstances, would tend to show that attitudes are a function of such variables, that attitudes could differ even if our "ideal qualifications" were all met.

Is there such variation of group standards? We have seen that there is one area of ethical opinion where there is diversity in appraisal and at the same time possible identity of belief about the action—that about the treatment of animals. On the whole, primitive groups show little feeling that it is wrong to cause pain to animals, whereas the columns of *The New York Times* are testimony to the fact that many persons in the U.S.A. take a vigorous interest in what goes on in slaughterhouses. . . . Nevertheless, we cannot be sure that attitudes of the groups here in question really do fulfill our "qualifications" equally well. Primitive peoples rarely make pets of the animals they maltreat. There is at least some question whether they have a vivid imagination of what the suffering of an animal is like, comparable to that of the authors of letters to the *Times*. The writer has assured himself by personal investigation that there is no definite discrepancy between the Hopi *beliefs*, about the effects of maltreating animals, and those of what seems a representative sample of educated White Americans. Degrees of *vividness* of belief, however, do not lend themselves to objective investigation, and it is not clear how we may definitely answer questions about them, either way. Perhaps the sanest conclusion is just to say that, as far as can be decided objectively, groups do sometimes make divergent appraisals when they have identical beliefs about the objects, but that the difficulties of investigation justify a healthy degree of skepticism about the conclusiveness of the inquiry.

The fact that objective inquiry is difficult naturally works both ways. It prevents us from asserting confidently that, where there are differences of appraisal, there is still identity of factual belief. But equally it prevents us from denying confidently that there is identity of belief, where appraisals differ.

The anthropological evidence, taken by itself, then, does not give a *conclusive* answer to our question. At the present time, the anthropologist does not have two social groups of which he can say definitely: "These groups have exactly the same beliefs about action *A*, on all points that could be seriously viewed as ethically relevant. But their views—attitudes—about the morality of the acts are vastly different." Whether, everything considered, the relativist reading of the facts is not the more balanced judgment, is another question. The writer is inclined to think it is the better judgment.

If we agree that the ethical standards of groups are not a function solely of their beliefs (or the vividness of these), it is reasonable to suppose that "ideally qualified" attitudes may well conflict with respect to the very same act or event. . . .

NOTES

1. G. de Poncins, *Kabloona* (New York: Reynal & Hitchcock, 1941).
2. See the writer's *Hopi Ethics* [(Chicago: University of Chicago Press, 1954)], pp. 213–15, 245–46, 373; and Wayne Dennis, *The Hopi Child* (New York: Appleton-Century-Crofts, Inc., 1940).
3. For Protagoras' views, see Plato, *Theaetetus*, pp. 166ff.; and F. J. Copleston, *A History of Philosophy*, I (London: Burns Oates & Washbourne Ltd., 1956), pp. 87–90.

Ethics and the Foreign Corrupt Practices Act

MARK PASTIN AND MICHAEL HOOKER

Not long ago it was feared that as a fallout of Watergate, government officials would be hamstrung by artificially inflated moral standards. Recent events, however, suggest that the scapegoat of post-Watergate morality may have become American business rather than government officials.

One aspect of the recent attention paid to corporate morality is the controversy surrounding payments made by American corporations to foreign officials for the purpose of securing business abroad. Like any law or system of laws, the Foreign Corrupt Practices Act (FCPA), designed to control or eliminate such payments, should be grounded in morality, and should therefore be judged from an ethical perspective. Unfortunately, neither the law nor the question of its repeal has been adequately addressed from that perspective.

On December 20, 1977 President Carter signed into law S.305, the Foreign Corrupt Practices Act (FCPA), which makes it a crime for American corporations to offer or provide payments to officials of foreign governments for the purpose of obtaining or retaining business. The FCPA also establishes record keeping requirements for publicly held corporations to make it difficult to conceal political payments proscribed by the Act. Violators of the FCPA, both corporations and managers, face severe penalties. A company may be fined up to $1 million, while its officers who directly participated in violations of the Act or had reason to know of such violations, face up to five years in prison and/or $10,000 in fines. The Act also prohibits corporations from indemnifying fines imposed on their directors, officers, employees, or agents. The Act does not prohibit "grease" payments to foreign government employees whose duties are primarily ministerial or

Mark Pastin and Michael Hooker, "Ethics and the Foreign Corrupt Practices Act," *Business Horizons*, December, 1980, pp. 43–47, reprinted with permission.

clerical, since such payments are sometimes required to persuade the recipients to perform their normal duties.

At the time of this writing, the precise consequences of the FCPA for American business are unclear, mainly because of confusion surrounding the government's enforcement intentions. Vigorous objections have been raised against the Act by corporate attorneys and recently by a few government officials. Among the latter is Frank A. Weil, former Assistant Secretary of Commerce, who has stated, "The questionable payments problem may turn out to be one of the most serious impediments to doing business in the rest of the world."[1]

The potentially severe economic impact of the FCPA was highlighted by the fall 1978 report of the Export Disincentives Task Force, which was created by the White House to recommend ways of improving our balance of trade. The Task Force identified the FCPA as contributing significantly to economic and political losses in the United States. Economic losses come from constricting the ability of American corporations to do business abroad, and political losses come from the creation of a holier-than-thou image.

The Task Force made three recommendations in regard to the FCPA:

- The Justice Department should issue guidelines on its enforcement policies and establish procedures by which corporations could get advance government reaction to anticipated payments to foreign officials.
- The FCPA should be amended to remove enforcement from the SEC, which now shares enforcement responsibility with the Department of Justice.
- The administration should periodically report to Congress and the public on export losses caused by the FCPA.

In response to the Task Force's report, the Justice Department, over SEC objections, drew up guidelines to enable corporations to check any proposed action possibly in violation of the FCPA. In response to such an inquiry, the Justice Department would inform the corporation of its enforcement intentions. The purpose of such an arrangement is in part to circumvent the intent of the law. As of this writing, the SEC appears to have been sucessful in blocking publication of the guidelines, although Justice recently reaffirmed its intention to publish guidelines. Being more responsive to political winds, Justice may be less inclined than the SEC to rigidly enforce the Act.

Particular concern has been expressed about the way in which bookkeeping requirements of the Act will be enforced by the SEC. The act requires that company records will "accurately and fairly reflect the transactions and dispositions of the assets of the issuer." What is at question is the interpretation the SEC will give to the requirement and the degree of accuracy and detail it will demand. The SEC's post-Watergate behavior suggests that it will be rigid in requiring the disclosure of all information that bears on financial relationships between the company and any foreign or domestic public official. This level of accountability in record keeping, to which auditors and corporate attorneys have strongly objected, goes far beyond previous SEC requirements that records display only facts material to the financial position of the company.

Since the potential consequences of the FCPA for American businesses and business managers are very serious, it is important that the Act have a rationale capable of bearing close scrutiny. In looking at the foundation of the FCPA, it should be noted that its passage followed in the wake of intense newspaper coverage of the financial dealings of corporations. Such media attention was engendered by the dramatic disclosure of corporate slush funds during the Watergate hearings and by a voluntary disclosure program established shortly thereafter by the SEC. As a result of the SEC program, more than 400 corporations, including 117 of the Fortune 500, admitted to making more than $300 million in foreign political payments in less than ten years.

Throughout the period of media coverage leading up to passage of the FCPA, and especially during the hearings on the Act, there was in all public discussions of the issue a tone of righteous moral indignation at the idea of American companies making foreign political payments. Such payments were ubiquitously termed "bribes," although many of these could more accurately be called extortions, while others were more akin to brokers' fees or sales commissions.

American business can be faulted for its reluctance during this period to bring to public attention the fact that in a very large number of countries, payments to foreign officials are virtually required for doing business. Part of that reluctance, no doubt, comes from the awkwardly difficult position of attempting to excuse bribery or something closely resembling it. There is a popular abhorrence in this country of bribery directed at domestic government officials, and that abhorrence transfers itself to payments directed toward foreign officials as well.

Since its passage, the FCPA has been subjected to considerable critical analysis, and many practical arguments have been advanced in favor of its repeal.[2] However, there is always lurking in back of such analyses the uneasy feeling that no matter how strongly considerations of practicality and economics may count against this law, the fact remains that the law protects morality in forbidding bribery. For example, Gerald McLaughlin, professor of law at Fordham, has shown persuasively that where the legal system of a foreign country affords inadequate protection against the arbitrary exercise of power to the disadvantage of American corporations, payments to foreign officials may be required to provide a compensating mechanism against the use of such arbitrary power. McLaughlin observes, however, that "this does not mean that taking advantage of the compensating mechanism would necessarily make the payment moral."[3]

The FCPA, and questions regarding its enforcement or repeal, will not be addressed adequately until an effort has been made to come to terms with the Act's foundation in morality. While it may be very difficult, or even impossible, to legislate morality (that is, to change the moral character and sentiments of people by passing laws that regulate their behavior), the existing laws undoubtedly still reflect the moral beliefs we hold. Passage of the FCPA in Congress was eased by the simple connection most Congressmen made between bribery, seen as morally repugnant, and the Act, which is designed to prevent bribery.

Given the importance of the FCPA to American business and labor, it is imperative that attention be given to the question of whether there is adequate moral justification for the law. The question we will address is not whether each payment prohibited by the FCPA is moral or immoral, but rather whether the FCPA, given all its consequences and ramifications, is itself moral. It is well known that morally sound laws and institutions may tolerate some immoral acts. The First Amendment's guarantee of freedom of speech allows individuals to utter racial slurs. And immoral laws and institutions may have some beneficial consequences, for example, segregationist legislation bringing deep-seated racism into the national limelight. But our concern is with the overall morality of the FCPA.

The ethical tradition has two distinct ways of assessing social institutions, including laws: *End-Point Assessment* and *Rule Assessment.* Since there is no consensus as to which approach is correct, we will apply both types of assessment to the FCPA.

The End-Point approach assesses a law in terms of its contribution to general social well-being. The ethical theory underlying End-Point Assessment is utilitarianism. According to utilitarianism, a law is morally sound if and only if the law promotes the well-being of those affected by the law to the greatest extent practically achievable. To satisfy the utilitarian principle, a law must promote the well-being of those affected by it at least as well as any alternative law that we might propose, and better than no law at all. A conclusive End-Point Assessment of a law requires specification of what constitutes the welfare of those affected by the law, which the liberal tradition generally sidesteps by identifying an individual's welfare with what he takes to be in his interests.

Considerations raised earlier in the paper suggest that the FCPA does not pass the End-Point test. The argument is not the too facile one that we could propose a better law. (Amendments to the FCPA are now being considered.[4]) The argument is that it may be better to have *no* such law than to have the FCPA. The main domestic consequences of the FCPA seem to include an adverse effect on the balance of payments, a loss of business and jobs, and another opportunity for the SEC and the Justice Department to compete. These negative effects must be weighed against possible gains in the conduct of American business within the United States. From the perspective of foreign countries in which American firms do business, the main consequence of the FCPA seems to be that certain officials now accept bribes and influence fron non-American businesses. It is hard to see that who pays the bribes makes much difference to these nations.

Rule Assessment of the morality of laws is often favored by those who find that End-Point Assessment is too lax in supporting their moral codes. According to the Rule Assessment approach: A law is morally sound if and only if the law accords with a code embodying correct ethical rules. This approach has no content until the rules are stated, and different rules will lead to different ethical assessments. Fortunately, what we have to say about Rule Assessment of the FCPA does not depend on the details of a particular ethical code.

Those who regard the FCPA as a worthwhile expression of morality, despite the adverse effects on American business and labor, clearly subscribe to a rule stating that it is unethical to bribe. Even if it is conceded that the payments proscribed by the FCPA warrant classifications as bribes, citing a rule prohibiting bribery does not suffice to justify the FCPA.

Most of the rules in an ethical code are not *categorical* rules; they are *prima facie* rules. A categorical rule does not allow exceptions, whereas a prima facie rule does. The ethical rule that a person ought to keep promises is an example of a prima facie rule. If I promise to loan you a book on nuclear energy and later find out that you are a terrorist building a private atomic bomb, I am ethically obligated not to keep my promise. The rule that one ought to keep promises is "overridden" by the rule that one ought to prevent harm to others.

A rule prohibiting bribery is a prima facie rule. There are cases in which morality requires that a bribe be paid. If the only way to get essential medical care for a dying child is to bribe a doctor, morality requires one to bribe the doctor. So adopting an ethical code which includes a rule prohibiting the payment of bribes does not guarantee that a Rule Assessment of the FCPA will be favorable to it.

The fact that the FCPA imposes a cost on American business and labor weighs against the prima facie obligation not to bribe. If we suppose that American corporations have obligations, tantamount to promises, to promote the job security of their employees and the investments of shareholders, these obligations will also weigh against the obligation not to bribe. Again, if government legislative and enforcement bodies have an obligation to secure the welfare of American business and workers, the FCPA may force them to violate their public obligations.

The FCPA's moral status appears even more dubious if we note that many of the payments prohibited by the Act are neither bribes nor share features that make bribes morally reprehensible. Bribes are generally held to be malefic if they persuade one to act against his good judgment, and consequently purchase an inferior product. But the payments at issue in the FCPA are usually extorted *from the seller.* Further it is arguable that not paying the bribe is more likely to lead to purchase of an inferior product than paying the bribe. Finally, bribes paid to foreign officials may not involve deception when they accord with recognized local practices.

In conclusion, neither End-Point nor Rule Assessment uncovers a sound moral basis for the FCPA. It is shocking to find that a law prohibiting bribery has no clear moral basis, and may even be an immoral law. However, this is precisely what examination of the FCPA from a moral perspective reveals. This is symptomatic of the fact that moral conceptions which were appropriate to a simpler world are not adequate to the complex world in which contemporary business functions. Failure to appreciate this point often leads to righteous condemnation of business, when it should lead to careful reflection on one's own moral preconceptions.

ADDENDUM TO "ETHICS AND THE FOREIGN CORRUPT PRACTICES ACT," AUGUST 1981.

There has been an increasing outcry against the FCPA since this article originally appeared. The Reagan administration has called for weakening of the law, especially the burdensome accounting provisions. While we view such weakening of the law as commendable, on the ground that it decreases the cost of the law to business and the American public, the key issue has not been joined. That issue is whether the payments proscribed by the law, heavy-handedly or otherwise, are in fact unethical. There is no doubt that many executives and government officials hold the view that these payments are not unethical. But it is unacceptable to publicly argue that bribes to foreign officials are ethical. Thus it will take considerable audacity to argue for total repeal of the FCPA. Only an increasing appreciation of the barriers to international trade attributable to the law, and of the ethical pointlessness of the law, can be effective.

MARK PASTIN

NOTES

1. *National Journal,* June 3, 1978: 880
2. David C. Gustman, "The Foreign Corrupt Practices Act of 1977," *The Journal of International Law and Economics,* Vol. 13, 1979: 367–401, and Walter S. Surrey, "The Foreign Corrupt Practices Act: Let the Punishment Fit the Crime," *Harvard International Law Journal,* Spring 1979: 203–303.
3. Gerald T. McLaughlin, "The Criminalization of Questionable Foreign Payments by Corporations," *Fordham Law Review,* Vol. 46: 1095.
4. "Foreign Bribery Law Amendments Drafted," *American Bar Association Journal,* February 1980: 135.

Moral Dimensions of the Foreign Corrupt Practices Act: Comments on Pastin and Hooker

KENNETH D. ALPERN

Michael Hooker and Mark Pastin[1] claim that the Foreign Corrupt Practices Act (FCPA) is not supported by either utilitarian or deontological ("rule-based") moral considerations. I will argue that deontological moral considerations do in fact support the FCPA and that much utilitarian criticism of it is not conceptually well-founded.[2]

Hooker and Pastin offer two argument sketches intended to show that the Act does not receive support from deontological considerations. Spelling out the first gives roughly this:

1. The FCPA is essentially a prohibition of bribery. (Allowed for the sake of argument.)
2. Bribery is morally wrong in the sense that there is a *prima facie* moral obligation not to engage in bribery.
3. Corporations have (*prima facie*) moral obligations to protect the investments of their shareholders and the jobs of their employees. The federal government may also have a *prima facie* moral obligation to secure the welfare of American business and workers.
4. There are situations governed by the FCPA in which the *prima facie* moral obligations of corporations and government override the *prima facie* moral obligation not to bribe.[3]
5. Situations in which the FCPA requires actions that are thus contrary to morality are numerous or of great moral moment.
6. Therefore, the FCPA does not have the support of morality from a deontological perspective.

There is much to agree with in this argument. Its pattern of reasoning is good—the premises do license the conclusion. It is certainly the case that any moral rule prohibiting bribery cannot be absolute. And it is surely true that corporations have some sort of obligation to pursue profit. It could even be allowed that situations are conceivable in which the prohibition of bribery is overridden by other moral obligations of corporations. Nonetheless, the conclusion of the argument is still false.

Much of the argument's appeal derives from its apparent discovery of a second moral principle, the principle that promises should be kept. In situations covered by the FCPA, the principle of promise-keeping is supposed to weigh against and outweigh the moral principle prohibiting bribery, though Hooker and Pastin do not go far enough into the argument to

Kenneth D. Alpern, "Moral Dimensions of the Foreign Corrupt Practices Act: Comments on Hooker and Pastin." Reprinted with permission of the author.

indicate which sorts of considerations are supposed to tip the scales in favor of promise-keeping.

Against this position I will argue that the supposed conflict is only apparent and that the introduction of the rule of promise-keeping at this place in the argument is misleading and largely irrelevant. Furthermore, I will argue that the moral considerations which do properly stand in the place thought to be held by the obligation to keep promises are insufficient on conceptual grounds to justify bribery. In order to make my case, it is necessary to look more closely at the way obligations to keep promises enter the picture.

Hooker and Pastin mention three specific obligations deriving from the principle of promise-keeping: (1) an obligation of corporations to promote the investments of their shareholders; (2) an obligation of corporations to protect the security of their employees' jobs; and (3) an obligation which the federal government may possibly be under to protect the welfare of American business and workers. I will focus on the first obligation, which I take to be most important, and comment only briefly on the other two obligations.

The obligation of corporations to their investors seems to come about in this way: corporations are *agents* for their investors. In effect a corporation says: "If you allow us the use of your capital, we promise to return to work to increase the value of your investment."[4] Having made the promise to act as agents, corporations are morally obligated, by virtue of the moral rule that promises be kept, to promote the financial interests of their principals.

What difference does this promise make to the morality of international corporate bribery? The answer is: none. The promise merely *transfers* the responsibility for looking after the investors' interests. It does nothing to affect the type or weight of claim that can be made in behalf of those interests against other moral considerations. In the situations with which we are concerned, who the guardian is and how that guardianship comes about makes no difference outside the relationship between the agent and the principal. If this were not the case, then one could indefinitely increase the moral righteousness of one's causes merely by enlisting a series of agents each promising the other to pursue one's ends.[5]

Talk of the solemn promises or sacred trusts of corporations, while it may refer to actual obligations, is irrelevant to the issue of the weight of investor interests against moral rules. There is no conflict here between a moral principle requiring that promises be kept and a moral principle prohibiting bribery. What stands in opposition to the moral rule prohibiting bribery is not a moral principle at all, but is, at best, merely the *self-interest* of the investors.

Now it must be recognized that unadorned self-interest may carry moral weight. However, it is quite unlikely that this weight will often be great enough to render international corporate bribery moral. For, first of all, within the deontological perspective (which we are being asked to take), moral rules are just the sort of things that override claims of self-interest. As long as we view morality from this perspective, there is strong *a priori* reason to hold that the rule prohibiting bribery controls. Second, though the rule prohibiting bribery may have exceptions—e.g. Hooker and Pastin's case of bribing a doctor as the only means by which to secure essential medical treatment for a dying child—the relevant exceptions appear to exhibit two characteristic features: (1) the personal interest at issue is not a mere desire, but a dire need, and (2) the rule is broken on a special occasion, not as a continuing general policy.[6] In contrast, when we are asked to reject the FCPA, we are asked to endorse a *policy* of bribery, and this for the promotion of interests that are not literally matters of life and death. Finally, to the objection that the moral claim of corporate investors' interests is considerable and thus outweighs the bribery rule, it should be pointed out that not all interests are of equal moral weight. Classical utilitarianism is mistaken in holding that equal additions to the sum total happiness or well-being are morally indifferent. For example, an increase in happiness which satisfies a need is of greater moral moment than the same increment added to the total happiness by way of providing someone with adventitious pleasure. It is morally better to raise a person from poverty to security than to add an equal amount to the total happiness in effecting a person's rise from ease to opulence. So, when it comes to comparing personal interests against moral rules, interests based on mere desires, and not needs, have comparatively little moral weight. This point applies to the FCPA in two ways. First, although American investors include pension plans, philanthropic organizations, and people of modest income, "the average American investor" is nonetheless quite comfortable by world standards and return on investment is not a matter of survival. Secondly, even if return on investment were a matter of survival, corporations can and in fact do derive substantial profits from activities not calling for bribery; most American corporations have dealt successfully in international trade without resorting to payments made unlawful by the FCPA.

One misunderstanding of the preceding argument must be forestalled. At issue is not the comparative need of American investors and the need of citizens of the country in which the bribery takes place. Rather, the point is that because American investors are, on the whole, not in dire need, the moral weight of their financial interests is small compared to the moral weight of moral *principles.*

It remains to say something, necessarily very brief, about the obligation of corporations to their employees and the obligation of the federal government to American business and workers. First, corporations are not morally obligated to secure profits "by whatever means it takes" in order to fulfill their responsibilities to their employees. There are restrictions, such as those imposed by law. If a corporation fails to meet its obligations due to the costs and effects of adhering to the law, then, other things being equal, the employees can have no *moral* complaint against the corporation.

In addition to restrictions imposed on profit-seeking activities through the law, I submit that there are also moral restrictions. For example, corporations are not morally culpable for reduced profits incurred by a failure to be ruthless, even when ruthlessness is within the limits set by the law. Employees (and other interested parties) cannot complain on *moral* grounds that they have suffered because the corporation failed to cheat, lie, deceive, bribe, or pay extortion.

The situation with respect to the moral obligations of the federal government is similar to that of corporations. Roughly, a government can have no *moral* (contrasted with legal or political) obligation to promote the welfare of its citizens by means which are themselves immoral. Bribery, we have been allowing, is immoral. So the government cannot be morally obligated to promote the welfare of American businesses or workers by allowing bribery.

In their second argument against the FCPA, Hooker and Pastin marshal three distinct considerations behind the idea that "many of the payments prohibited by the Act are neither bribes nor share features that make bribes morally reprehensible": (1) payments often are not bribes, but rather are *extorted* from corporations;[7] (2) failure to make payments may lead to the purchase of what are in fact *inferior* products; and (3) such payments may be in accordance with local practices and so lack the deceptiveness of bribery.

Against these considerations it may be pointed out that a payment needn't be bribery to be morally objectionable. Caving in to extortion demands contributes to corruption and fosters its expansion in the country in which payments are made; it leads to unfair competition if the payments are concealed, and even more immediately to the disintegration of free bargaining and a return to a Hobbsian state of nature—in which anything goes—if they are not. These morally objectionable results will generally outweigh harm resulting from the purchase of inferior products. Engaging in such practices *openly* hardly does much to excuse them.

Some business people may feel that international corporate competition *is* in fact a Hobbsian state of nature. However, this is surely hyperbole: murder is still fairly rare in negotiating contracts; not everyone in the business community behaves like the Mafia. But even if they did, that would not make it *moral* to do so. It is also worth pointing out that the state of nature is not a condition that we *want* to be in—few of us *want* to deal with a government like Amin's Uganda or live in a world in which that was the norm.

Hooker and Pastin's third point, that it would be wrong for us to try to impose our standards in countries in which bribery and extortion are commonly practiced, raises important conceptual issues about intercultural social, legal, and moral standards which are too complex to be treated adequately here. However, I can offer a few comments which I think considerably reduce the problems about how one ought to act. First, it is absolutely essential to distinguish between practices that are engaged in, recognized, even tolerated, and those that are condoned and held to be moral. To say simply that in many countries bribery is the norm disguises the fact that what is regularly done may not be what is held to be proper or moral even in the countries where that is the practice. A rough indicator of international moral judgment is the illegality of bribery in every part of the world.[8] Second, requiring American corporations to adhere to "our" moral standards with respect to bribery and extortion is hardly to *impose* our standards on the rest of the world: for a Muslim to refrain from eating pork in England is not for him to impose Muslim standards on the British. Finally, there is some reason for us to refrain from a practice that *we* judge to be wrong and harmful to others even if we do not receive agreement: that settlers in the upper Amazon hunt native Indians for sport does not give us good reason to conform to that practice when in their company. Obviously, more needs to be said on these issues, but I hope that it has been made clear that a passing reference to moral relativism establishes nothing and that there are a number of lines of defense which can be taken against more serious relativistic criticism.

In closing, I want to add a few short remarks. First, in asserting that the FCPA is supported by moral considerations, I am not claiming that the Act defines the morally best behavior in every single case. All laws can be improved; an imperfect law can still be moral and just. Second, it should be noted that if Hooker and Pastin were correct, their arguments would go a long way toward justifying bribery and extortion *within* the United States by both foreign and domestic companies—unless we are to believe that a return to the state of nature is morally acceptable in one place (someone else's country) but not in another. Finally, I think that I have shown that the FCPA is supported by considerations of morality. This should count heavily in favor of retaining the law. However, I do not claim to have necessarily provided *motivation* for supporting this law or adhering to its stipulations. Morality may require sacrifice, in this case at least sacrifice of financial gain. For those who care more for financial gain and for the ruthlessness through which it can be obtained than for the moral values of justice and integrity, I cannot claim to have provided motivation.

NOTES

1. See this volume, pp. 46–51.
2. The arguments sketched in this paper are more fully defended in my forthcoming "International Corporate Bribery." The present paper is a considerably shortened version of a paper read at the Conference on Business and Professional Ethics, in Chicago, May, 1981.
3. That is, in some cases, considered individually and other things being equal, corporations *morally ought to bribe* and the government *morally ought not to punish* corporations for bribing. Thus, as the law now stands, some actions are legally required that are contrary to morality.
4. This promise must be understood as a promise to endeavor to a reasonable extent to increase investment value, not to maximize it at all costs.
5. The general moral principle here is, very roughly, that a promise to pursue the interests of another cannot increase the moral weight of those interests against moral considerations external to the relationship of promiser and promisee.
6. For continuing treatment of the child or in situations in which there is continuing and widespread corruption among doctors, it would be necessary to endorse bribery as a policy. However, then one's obligation would not be merely to engage in bribery, but rather to engage in bribery while doing what one can to rectify the situation. Regardless of the precise way this is to be worked out, a simple endorsement of bribery is not what is justified in such cases.

7. In practice it may be difficult to distinguish between bribery and extortion on the one hand, and goodwill gestures (e.g., gifts) and facilitating payments (so-called "grease") on the other. However, the conceptual issue of the wrongness of extortion does not turn on how the practical problem is solved.
8. Judson J. Wambold, "Prohibiting Foreign Bribes: Criminal Sanctions for Corporate Payments Abroad" (*Cornell International Law Journal* 10 (1977), pp. 235–237). Wambold also found that though bribery is generally illegal, corporate contributions to political parties are acceptable in many countries. This complicates the moral evaluation of the FCPA. The next two points in my text suggest directions in which to go to defend the Act in this connection.

EGOISM

Case Study—The Aircraft Brake Scandal

KERMIT VANDIVIER

The B. F. Goodrich Company is what business magazines like to refer to as "a major American corporation." It has operations in a dozen states and as many foreign countries; and of these far-flung facilities, the Goodrich plant at Troy, Ohio, is not the most imposing. It is a small, one-story building, once used to manufacture airplanes. Set in the grassy flatlands of west-central Ohio, it employs only about six hundred people. Nevertheless, it is one of the three largest manufacturers of aircraft wheels and brakes, a leader in a most profitable industry. Goodrich wheels and brakes support such well-known planes as the F111, the C5A, the Boeing 727, the XB70, and many others.

Contracts for aircraft wheels and brakes often run into millions of dollars, and ordinarily a contract with a total value of less than $70,000, though welcome, would not create any special stir of joy in the hearts of Goodrich sales personnel. But purchase order P-237138—issued on June 18, 1967, by the LTV Aerospace Corporation, ordering 202 brake assemblies for a new Air Force plane at a total price of $69,417—was received by Goodrich with considerable glee. And there was good reason. Some ten years previously, Goodrich had built a brake for LTV that was, to say the least, considerably less than a rousing success. The brake had not lived up to Goodrich's promises, and after experiencing considerable difficulty, LTV had written off Goodrich as a source of brakes. Since that time, Goodrich salesmen had been unable to sell so much as a shot of brake fluid to LTV. So in 1967, when LTV requested bids on wheels and brakes for the new A7D light attack aircraft it proposed to build for the Air Force, Goodrich submitted a bid that was absurdly low, so low that LTV could not, in all prudence, turn it down.

Goodrich had, in industry parlance, "bought into the business." The company did not expect to make a profit on the initial deal; it was prepared, if necessary, to lose money. But aircraft brakes are not something that can be ordered off the shelf. They are designed for a particular aircraft, and once an aircraft manufacturer buys a brake, he is forced to purchase all replacement parts from the brake manufacturer. The $70,000 that Goodrich would get for making the brake would be a drop in the bucket when compared with the cost of the linings and other parts the Air Force would have to buy from Goodrich during the lifetime of the aircraft.

There was another factor, besides the low bid, that had undoubtedly influenced LTV. All aircraft brakes made today are of the disk type, and the bid submitted by Goodrich called for a relatively small brake, one containing four disks and weighing only 106 pounds. The weight of any aircraft is extremely important: the lighter a part is, the heavier the plane's payload can be.

The brake was designed by one of Goodrich's most capable engineers, John Warren. A tall, lanky, blond graduate of Purdue, Warren had come from the Chrysler Corporation seven years before and had become adept at aircraft brake design. The happy-go-lucky manner he usually maintained belied a temper that exploded whenever anyone ventured to offer criticism of his work, no matter how small. On these occasions, Warren would turn red in the face, often throwing or slamming something and then stalking from the scene. As his coworkers learned the consequences of criticizing him, they did so less and less readily, and when he submitted his preliminary design for the A7D brake, it was accepted without question.

Warren was named project engineer for the A7D, and he, in turn, assigned the task of producing the final production design to a newcomer to the Goodrich engineering stable, Searle Lawson. Just turned twenty-six, Lawson had been out of the Northrop Institute of Technology only one year when he came to Goodrich in January 1967. He had been assigned to various "paper projects" to break him in, and after several months spent reviewing statistics and old brake designs, he was beginning to fret at the lack of challenge. When told he was being assigned to his first "real" project, he was elated and immediately plunged into his work.

The major portion of the design had already been completed by Warren, and major subassemblies for the brake had already been ordered from Goodrich suppliers. Naturally, however, before Goodrich could start making the brakes on a production basis, much testing would have to be done. Lawson would have to determine the best materials to use for the linings and discover what minor adjustments in the design would have to be made.

Then, after the preliminary testing and after the brake was judged ready for production, one whole brake assembly would undergo a series of grueling, simulated braking stops and other severe trials called qualification tests. These tests are required by the military, which gives very detailed specifications on how they are to be conducted, the criteria for failure, and so on. They are performed in the Goodrich plant's test laboratory, where huge machines called dynamometers can simulate the weight and speed of almost any aircraft.

Searle Lawson was well aware that much work had to be done before the A7D brake could go into production, and he knew that LTV had set the last two weeks in June 1968 as the starting dates for flight tests. So he decided to begin testing immediately. Goodrich's suppliers had not yet delivered the brake housing and other parts, but the brake disks had arrived, and using the housing from a brake similar in size and weight to the A7D brake, Lawson built a prototype. The prototype was installed in a test wheel and placed on one of the big dynamometers in the plant's test laboratory. Lawson began a series of tests, "landing" the wheel and brake at the A7D's landing speed and braking it to a stop. The main purpose of these preliminary tests was to learn what temperatures would develop within the brake during the simulated stops and to evaluate lining materials tentatively selected for use.

During a normal aircraft landing the temperatures inside the brake may reach 1,000 degrees, and occasionally a bit higher. During Lawson's first simulated landings, the temperature of his prototype brake reached 1,500 degrees. The brake glowed a bright cherry-red and threw off incandescent particles of metal and lining material as the temperature reached its peak. After a few such stops, the brake was dismantled and the linings were found to be almost completely disintegrated. Lawson chalked this first failure up to chance, and ordering new lining materials, tried again.

The second attempt was a repeat of the first. The brake became extremely hot, causing the lining materials to crumble into dust.

After the third such failure, Lawson, inexperienced though he was, knew that the fault lay not in defective parts or unsuitable lining material but in the basic design of the brake itself. Ignoring Warren's original computations, Lawson made his own, and it didn't take him long to discover where the trouble lay—the brake was too small. There simply was not enough surface area on the disks to stop the aircraft without generating the excessive heat that caused the linings to fail.

The answer to the problem was obvious, but far from simple—the four-disk brake would have to be scrapped, and a new design, using five disks, would have to be developed. The implications were not lost on Lawson. Such a step would require junking the four-disk-brake subassemblies, many of which had now begun to arrive from the various suppliers. It would also mean several weeks of preliminary design and testing and many more weeks of waiting while the suppliers made and delivered the new subassemblies.

Yet, several weeks had already gone by since LTV's order had arrived, and the date for delivery of the first production brakes for flight testing was only a few months away.

Although John Warren had more or less turned the A7D over to Lawson, he knew of the difficulties Lawson had been experiencing. He had assured the younger engineer that the problem revolved around getting the right kind of lining material. Once that was found, he said, the difficulties would end.

Despite the evidence of the abortive tests and Lawson's careful computations, Warren rejected the suggestion that the four-disk brake was too light for the job. He knew that his superior had already told LTV, in rather glowing terms, that the preliminary tests on the A7D brake were very successful. Indeed, Warren's superiors weren't aware at this time of the troubles on the brake. It would have been difficult for Warren to admit not only that he had made a serious error in his calculations and original design but that his mistakes had been caught by a green kid, barely out of college.

Warren's reaction to a five-disk brake was not unexpected by Lawson, and, seeing that the four-disk brake was not to be abandoned so easily, he took his calculations and dismal test results one step up the corporate ladder.

At Goodrich, the man who supervises the engineers working on projects slated for production is called, predictably, the projects manager. The job was held by a short, chubby, bald man named Robert Sink. Some fifteen years before, Sink had begun working at Goodrich as a lowly draftsman. Slowly, he worked his way up. Despite his geniality, Sink was neither respected nor liked by the majority of the engineers, and his appointment as their supervisor did not improve their feelings toward him. He possessed only a high-school diploma, and it quite naturally rankled those who had gone through years of college to be commanded by a man whom they considered their intellectual inferior. But, though Sink had no college training, he had something even more useful: a fine working knowledge of company politics.

Puffing on a Meerschaum pipe, Sink listened gravely as young Lawson confided his fears about the four-disk brake. Then he examined Lawson's calculations and the results of the abortive tests. Despite the fact that he was not a qualified engineer, in the strictest sense of the word, it must certainly have been obvious to Sink that Lawson's calculations were correct and that a four-disk brake would never work on the A7D.

But other things of equal importance were also obvious. First, to concede that Lawson's calculations were correct would also mean conceding that Warren's calculations were incorrect. As projects manager, not only was he responsible for Warren's activities, but in admitting that Warren had erred he would also have to admit that he had erred in trusting Warren's judgment. It also meant that, as projects manager, it would be he who would have to explain the whole messy situation to the Goodrich hierarchy, not only at Troy but possibly on the corporate level at Goodrich's Akron offices. And having taken Warren's judgment of the four-disk brake at face value, he had assured LTV, not once but several times, that about all there was left to do on the brake was pack it in a crate and ship it out the door.

There's really no problem at all, he told Lawson. After all, Warren was an experienced engineer, and if he said the brake would work, it would work. Just keep on testing and probably, maybe even on the very next try, it'll work out just fine.

Lawson was far from convinced, but without the support of his superiors there was little he could do except keep on testing. By now, housings for the four-disk brake had begun to arrive at the plant, and Lawson was able to build a production model of the brake and begin the formal qualification tests demanded by the military.

The first qualification attempts went exactly as the tests on the prototype had. Terrific heat developed within the brakes, and after a few short, simulated stops the linings crumbled. A new type of lining material was ordered and once again an attempt to qualify the brake was made. Again, failure.

Experts were called in from lining manufacturers, and new lining "mixes" were tried, always with the same result. Failure.

It was now the last week in March 1968, and flight tests were scheduled to begin in seventy days. Twelve separate attempts had been made to qualify the brake, and all had failed. It was no longer possible for anyone to ignore the glaring truth that the brake was a dismal failure and that nothing short of a major design change could ever make it work.

On April 4, the thirteenth attempt at qualification was begun. This time no attempt was made to conduct the tests by the methods and techniques spelled out in the military specifications. Regardless of how it had to be done, the brake was to be "nursed" through the required fifty simulated stops.

Fans were set up to provide special cooling. Instead of maintaining pressure on the brake until the test wheel had come to a complete stop, the pressure was reduced when the wheel had decelerated to around 15 mph, allowing it to "coast" to a stop. After each stop, the brake was disassembled and carefully cleaned, and after some of the stops, internal brake parts were machined in order to remove warp and other disfigurations caused by the high heat.

By these and other methods, all clearly contrary to the techniques established by the military specifications, the brake was coaxed through the fifty stops. But even using these methods, the brake could not meet all the requirements. On one stop the wheel rolled for a distance of 16,000 feet, or over three miles, before the brake could bring it to a stop. The normal distance required for such a stop was around 3,500 feet.

On April 11, the day the thirteenth test was completed, I became personally involved in the A7D situation.

I had worked in the Goodrich test laboratory for five years, starting first as an instrumentation engineer, then later becoming a data analyst and technical writer. As part of my duties, I analyzed the reams and reams of instrumentation data that came from the many testing machines in the lab, then transcribed all of it to a more usable form for the engineering department. When a new-type brake had successfully completed the required qualification tests, I would issue a formal qualification report.

Qualification reports are an accumulation of all the data and test logs compiled during the qualification tests and are documentary proof that a brake has met all the requirements established by the military specifications and is therefore presumed safe for flight testing. Before actual flight tests are conducted on a brake, qualification reports have to be delivered to the customer and to various government officials.

On April 11, I was looking over the data from the latest A7D test, and I noticed that many irregularities in testing had been noted on the test logs.

Technically, of course, there was nothing wrong with conducting tests in any manner desired, so long as the test was for research purposes only. But qualification test methods are clearly delineated by the military, and I knew that this test had been a formal qualification attempt. One particular notation on the test logs caught my eye. For some of the stops, the instrument that recorded the brake pressure had been deliberately miscalibrated so that, while the brake pressure used during the stops was recorded as 1,000 psi (pounds per square inch)—the maximum pressure that would be available on the A7D aircraft—the pressure had actually been 1,100 psi.

I showed the test logs to the test lab supervisor, Ralph Gretzinger, who said he had learned from the technician who had miscalibrated the instrument that he had been asked to do so by Lawson. Lawson, said Gretzinger, readily admitted asking for the miscalibration, saying he had been told to do so by Sink.

I asked Gretzinger why anyone would want to miscalibrate the data-recording instruments.

"Why? I'll tell you why," he snorted. "That brake is a failure. It's way too small for the job, and they're not ever going to get it to work. They're getting desperate, and instead of scrapping the damned thing and starting over, they figure they can horse around down here in the lab and qualify it that way."

An expert engineer, Gretzinger had been responsible for several innovations in brake design. It was he who had invented the unique brake system used on the famous XB70. "If you want to find out what's going on," said Gretzinger, "ask Lawson; he'll tell you."

Curious, I did ask Lawson the next time he came into the lab. He seemed eager to discuss the A7D and gave me the history of his months of frustrating efforts to get Warren and Sink to change the brake design. "I just can't believe this is really happening," said Lawson, shaking his head slowly. "This isn't engineering, at least not what I thought it would be. Back in school, I thought that when you were an engineer, you tried to do your best, no matter what it cost. But this is something else."

He sat across the desk from me, his chin propped in his hand. "Just wait," he warned. "You'll get a chance to see what I'm talking about. You're going to get in the act too, because I've already had the word that we're going to make one more attempt to qualify the brake, and that's it. Win or lose, we're going to issue a qualification report!"

I reminded him that a qualification report could be issued only after a brake had successfully met all military requirements, and therefore, unless the next qualification attempt was a success, no report would be issued.

"You'll find out," retorted Lawson. "I was already told that regardless of what the brake does on test, it's going to be qualified." He said he had been told in those exact words at a conference with Sink and Russell Van Horn.

This was the first indication that Sink had brought his boss, Van Horn, into the mess. Although Van Horn, as manager of the design engineering section, was responsible for the entire department, he was not necessarily familiar with all phases of every project, and it was not uncommon for those under him to exercise the what-he-doesn't-know-won't-hurt-him philosophy. If he was aware of the full extent of the A7D situation, it meant that Sink had decided not only to call for help but to look toward that moment when blame must be borne and, if possible, shared.

Also, if Van Horn had said, "regardless of what the brake does on test, it's going to be qualified," then it could only mean that, if necessary, a false qualification report would be issued. I discussed this possibility with Gretzinger, and he assured me that under no circumstances would such a report ever be issued.

"If they want a qualification report, we'll write them one, but we'll tell it just like it is," he declared emphatically. "No false data or false reports are going to come out of this lab."

On May 2, 1968, the fourteenth and final attempt to qualify the brake was begun. Although the same improper methods used to nurse the brake through the previous tests were employed, it soon became obvious that this too would end in failure.

When the tests were about half completed, Lawson asked if I would start preparing the various engineering curves and graphic displays that were normally incorporated in a qualification report. I flatly refused to have anything to do with the matter and immediately told Gretzinger what I had been asked to do. He was furious and repeated his previous declaration that under no circumstances would any false data or other matter be issued from the lab.

"I'm going to get this settled right now, once and for all," he declared. "I'm going to see Line [Russell Line, manager of the Goodrich Technical Services Section, of which the test lab was a part] and find out just how far this thing is going to go!" He stormed out of the room.

In about an hour, he returned and called me to his desk. He sat silently for a few moments, then muttered, half to himself, "I wonder what the hell they'd do if I just quit?" I didn't answer and I didn't ask him what he meant. I knew. He had been beaten down. He had reached the point when the decision had to be made. Defy them now while there was still time—or knuckle under, sell out.

"You know," he went on uncertainly, looking down at his desk, "I've been an engineer for a long time, and I've always believed that ethics and integrity were every bit as important as theorems and formulas, and never once has anything happened to change my beliefs. Now this . . . Hell I've got two sons I've got to put through school and I just . . ." His voice trailed off.

He sat for a few more minutes, then, looking over the top of his glasses, said hoarsely, "Well, it looks like we're licked. The way it stands now, we're to go ahead and prepare the data and other things for the graphic presentation in the report, and when we're finished, someone upstairs will actually write the report.

"After all," he continued, "we're just drawing some curves, and what happens to them after they leave here—well, we're not responsible for that."

I wasn't at all satisfied with the situation and decided that I too would discuss the matter with Russell Line, the senior executive in our section.

Tall, powerfully built, his teeth flashing white, his face tanned to a coffee-brown by a daily stint with a sunlamp, Line looked and acted every inch the executive. He had been transferred from the Akron offices some two years previously, and he commanded great respect and had come to be well liked by those of us who worked under him.

He listened sympathetically while I explained how I felt about the A7D situation, and when I had finished, he asked me what I wanted him to do about it. I said that as employees of the Goodrich Company we had a responsibility to protect the company and its reputation if at all possible. I said I was certain that officers on the corporate level would never knowingly allow such tactics as had been employed on the A7D.

"I agree with you," he remarked, "but I still want to know what you want me to do about it."

I suggested that in all probability the chief engineer at the Troy plant, H. C. "Bud" Sunderman, was unaware of the A7D problem and that he, Line, could tell him what was going on.

Line laughed, good-humoredly. "Sure, I could, but I'm not going to. Bud probably already knows about this thing anyway, and if he doesn't, I'm sure not going to be the one to tell him."

"But why?"

"Because it's none of my business, and it's none of yours. I learned a long time ago not to worry about things over which I had no control. I have no control over this."

I wasn't satisfied with this answer, and I asked him if his conscience wouldn't bother him if, say, during flight tests on the brake, something should happen resulting in death or injury to the test pilot.

"Look," he said, becoming somewhat exasperated, "I just told you I have no control over this. Why should my conscience bother me?"

His voice took on a quiet, soothing tone as he continued. "You're just getting all upset over this thing for nothing. I just do as I'm told, and I'd advise you to do the same."

I made no attempt to rationalize what I had been asked to do. It made no difference who would falsify which part of the report or whether the actual falsification would be by misleading numbers or misleading words. Whether by acts of commission or omission, all of us who contributed to the fraud would be guilty. The only question left for me to decide was whether or not I would become a party to the fraud.

Before coming to Goodrich in 1963, I had held a variety of jobs, each a little more pleasant, a little more rewarding than the last. At forty-two, with seven children, I had decided that the Goodrich Company would probably be my "home" for the rest of my working life. The job paid well, it was pleasant and challenging, and the future looked reasonably bright. My wife and I had bought a home and we were ready to settle down into a comfortable, middle-age, middle-class rut. If I refused to take part in the A7D fraud, I would have either to resign or be fired. The report would be written by someone anyway, but I would have the satisfaction of knowing I had had no part in the matter. But bills aren't paid with personal satisfaction, nor house payments with ethical principles. I made my decision. The next morning, I telephoned Lawson and told him I was ready to begin on the qualification report.

I had written dozens of qualification reports, and I knew what a "good" one looked like. Resorting to the actual test data only on occasion, Lawson and I proceeded to prepare page after page of elaborate, detailed engineering curves, charts, and test logs, which purported to show what had happened during the formal qualification tests. Where temperatures were too high, we deliberately chopped them down a few hundred degrees, and where they were too low, we raised them to a value that would appear reasonable to the LTV and military engineers. Brake pressure, torque values, distances, times—everything of consequence was tailored to fit.

Occasionally, we would find that some test either hadn't been performed at all or had been conducted improperly. On those occasions, we "conducted" the test—successfully, of course—on paper.

For nearly a month we worked on the graphic presentation that would be a part of the report. Meanwhile, the final qualification attempt had been completed, and the brake, not unexpectedly, had failed again.

We finished our work on the graphic portion of the report around the first of June. Altogether, we had prepared nearly two hundred pages of data, containing dozens of deliberate falsifications and misrepresentations. I delivered the data to Gretzinger, who said he had been instructed to deliver it personally to the chief engineer, Bud Sunderman, who in turn would assign someone in the engineering department to complete the written portion of the report. He gathered the bundle of data and left the office. Within minutes, he was back with the data, his face white with anger.

"That damned Sink's beat me to it," he said furiously. "He's already talked to Bud about this, and now Sunderman says no one in the engineering department has time to write the report. He wants us to do it, and I told him we couldn't."

The words had barely left his mouth when Russell Line burst in the door. "What the hell's all the fuss about this damned report?" he demanded.

Patiently, Gretzinger explained. "There's no fuss. Sunderman just told me that we'd have to write the report down here, and I said we couldn't. Russ," he went on, "I've told you before that we weren't going to write the report. I made my position clear on that a long time ago."

Line shut him up with a wave of his hand and, turning to me, bellowed "I'm getting sick and tired of hearing about this damned report. Now, write the goddamn thing and shut up about it!" He slammed out of the office.

Gretzinger and I just sat for a few seconds looking at each other. Then he spoke.

"Well, I guess he's made it pretty clear, hasn't he? We can either write the thing or quit. You know, what we should have done was quit a long time ago. Now, it's too late."

Somehow I wasn't at all surprised at this turn of events, and it didn't really make that much difference. As far as I was concerned, we were all up to our necks in the thing anyway, and writing the narrative portion of the report couldn't make me more guilty than I already felt myself to be.

Within two days, I had completed the narrative, or written portion, of the report. As a final sop to my own self-respect, in the conclusion of the report I wrote, "The B. F. Goodrich P/N 2–1162–3 brake assembly does not meet the intent or the requirements of the applicable specification documents and therefore is not qualified."

This was a meaningless gesture, since I knew that this would certainly be changed when the report went through the final typing process. Sure enough, when the report was published, the negative conclusion had been made positive.

One final and significant incident occurred just before publication.

Qualification reports always bear the signature of the person who has prepared them. I refused to sign the report, as did Lawson. Warren was later asked to sign the report. He replied that he would "when I receive a signed statement from Bob Sink ordering me to sign it."

The engineering secretary who was delegated the responsibility of "dogging" the report through publication told me later that after I, Lawson, and Warren had all refused to sign the report, she had asked Sink if he would sign. He replied, "On something of this nature, I don't think a signature is really needed."

On June 5, 1968, the report was officially published and copies were delivered by hand to the Air Force and LTV. Within a week flight tests were begun at Edwards Air Force Base in California. Searle Lawson was sent to California as Goodrich's representative. Within approximately two weeks, he returned because some rather unusual incidents during the tests had caused them to be canceled.

His face was grim as he related stories of several near crashes during landings—caused by brake troubles. He told me about one incident in which, upon landing, one brake was literally welded together by the intense heat developed during the test stop. The wheel locked, and the plane skidded for nearly 1,500 feet before coming to a halt. The plane was jacked up and the wheel removed. The fused parts within the brake had to be pried apart.

That evening I left work early and went to see my attorney. After I told him the story, he advised that, while I was probably not actually guilty of fraud, I was certainly part of a conspiracy to defraud. He advised me to go to the Federal Bureau of Investigation and offered to arrange an appointment. The following week he took me to the Dayton office of the FBI and after I had been warned that I would not be immune from prosecution, I disclosed the A7D matter to one of the agents. The agent told me to say nothing about the episode to anyone and to report any further incidents to him. He said he would forward the story to his superiors in Washington.

A few days later, Lawson returned from a conference with LTV in Dallas and said that the Air Force, which had previously approved the qualification report, had suddenly rescinded that approval and was demanding to see some of the raw test data. I gathered that the FBI had passed the word.

Omitting any reference to the FBI, I told Lawson I had been to an attorney and that we were probably guilty of conspiracy.

"Can you get me an appointment with your attorney?" he asked. Within a week, he had been to the FBI and told them of his part in the mess. He too was advised to say nothing but to keep on the job reporting any new development.

Naturally, with the rescinding of Air Force approval and the demand to see raw test data, Goodrich officials were in a panic. A conference was called for July 27, a Saturday morning affair at which Lawson, Sink, Warren, and I were present. We met in a tiny conference room in the deserted engineering department. Lawson and I, by now openly hostile to Warren and Sink, ranged ourselves on one side of the conference table while Warren sat on the other side. Sink, chairing the meeting, paced slowly in front of a blackboard, puffing furiously on a pipe.

The meeting was called, Sink began, "to see where we stand on the A7D." What we were going to do, he said, was to "level" with LTV and tell them the "whole truth" about the A7D. "After all, " he said, "they're in this thing with us, and they have the right to know how matters stand."

"In other words," I asked, "we're going to tell them the truth?"

"That's right," he replied. "We're going to level with them and let them handle the ball from there."

"There's one thing I don't quite understand," I interjected. "Isn't it going to be pretty hard for us to admit to them that we've lied?"

"Now, wait a minute," he said angrily. "Let's don't go off half-cocked on this thing. It's not a matter of lying. We've just interpreted the information the way we felt it should be."

"I don't know what you call it," I replied, "but to me it's lying, and it's going to be damned hard to confess to them that we've been lying all along."

He became very agitated at this and repeated, "We're not lying," adding, "I don't like this sort of talk."

I dropped the matter at this point, and he began discussing the various discrepancies in the report.

We broke for lunch, and afterward, I came back to the plant to find Sink sitting alone at his desk, waiting to resume the meeting. He called me over and said he wanted to apologize for his outburst that morning. "This thing has kind of gotten me down," he confessed, "and I think you've got the wrong picture. I don't think you really understand everything about this."

Perhaps so, I conceded, but it seemed to me that if we had already told LTV one thing and then had to tell them another, changing our story completely, we would have to admit we were lying.

"No," he explained patiently, "we're not really lying. All we were doing was interpreting the figures the way we knew they should be. We were just exercising engineering license."

During the afternoon session, we marked some forty-three discrepant points in the report; forty-three points that LTV would surely spot as occasions where we had exercised "engineering license."

After Sink listed those points on the blackboard, we discussed each one individually. As each point came up, Sink would explain that it was probably "too minor to bother about," or that perhaps it "wouldn't be wise to open that can of worms," or that maybe this was a point that "LTV just wouldn't understand." When the meeting was over, it had been decided that only three points were "worth mentioning."

Similar conferences were held during August and September, and the summer was punctuated with frequent treks between Dallas and Troy and demands by the Air Force to see the raw test data. Tempers were short, and matters seemed to grow worse.

Finally, early in October 1968, Lawson submitted his resignation, to take effect on October 25. On October 18, I submitted my own resignation, to take effect on November 1. In my resignation, addressed to Russell Line, I cited the A7D report and stated: "As you are aware, this report contains numerous deliberate and willful misrepresentations which, according to legal counsel, constitute fraud and expose both myself and others to criminal charges of conspiracy to defraud . . . The events of the past seven months have created an atmosphere of deceit and distrust in which it is impossible to work . . ."

On October 25, I received a sharp summons to the office of Bud Sunderman. Tall and graying, impeccably dressed at all times, he was capable of producing a dazzling smile or a hearty chuckle or immobilizing his face into marble hardness, as the occasion required.

I faced the marble hardness when I reached his office. He motioned me to a chair. "I have your resignation here," he snapped, "and I must say you have made some rather shocking, I might even say irresponsible, charges. This is very serious."

Before I could reply, he was demanding an explanation. "I want to know exactly what the fraud is in connection with the A7D and how you can dare accuse this company of such a thing!"

I started to tell some of the things that had happened during the testing, but he shut me off saying, "There's nothing wrong with anything we've done here. You aren't aware of all the things that have been going on behind the scenes. If you had known the true situation, you would never have made these charges." He said that in view of my apparent "disloyalty" he had decided to accept my resignation "right now," and said it would be better for all concerned if I left the plant immediately. As I got up to leave he asked me if I intended to "carry this thing further."

I answered simply, "Yes," to which he replied, "Suit yourself." Within twenty minutes, I had cleaned out my desk and left. Forty-eight hours later, the B. F. Goodrich Company recalled the qualification report and the four-disk brake, announcing that it would replace the brake with a new, improved, five-disk brake at no cost to LTV.

Ten months later, on August 13, 1969, I was the chief government witness at a hearing conducted before Senator William Proxmire's Economy in Government Subcommittee. I related the A7D story to the committee, and my testimony was supported by Searle Lawson, who followed me to the witness stand. Air Force officers also testified, as well as a four-man team from the General Accounting Office, which had conducted an investigation of the A7D brake at the request of Senator Proxmire. Both Air Force and GAO investigators declared that the brake was dangerous and had not been tested properly.

Testifying for Goodrich was R. G. Jeter, vice-president and general counsel of the company, from the Akron headquarters. Representing the Troy plant was Robert Sink. These two denied any wrongdoing on the part of the Goodrich Company, despite expert testimony to the contrary by Air Force and GAO officials. Sink was quick to deny any connection with the writing of the report or directing of any falsifications, claiming to have been on the West Coast at the time. John Warren was the man who had supervised its writing, said Sink.

As for me, I was dismissed as a high-school graduate with no technical training, while Sink testified that Lawson was a young, inexperienced engineer. "We tried to give him guidance," Sink testified, "but he preferred to have his own convictions."

About changing the data to figures in the report, Sink said: "When you take data from several different sources, you have to rationalize among those data what is the true story. This is part of your engineering know-how." He admitted that changes had been made in the data, "but only to make them more consistent with the overall picture of the data that is available."

Jeter pooh-poohed the suggestion that anything improper occurred, saying: "We have thirty-odd engineers at this plant . . . and I say to you that it is incredible that these men would stand idly by and see reports changed or falsified . . . I mean you just do not have to do that working for anybody . . . Just nobody does that."

The four-hour hearing adjourned with no real conclusion reached by the subcommittee. But the following day the Department of Defense made sweeping changes in its inspection, testing, and reporting procedures. A spokesman for the DOD said the changes were a result of the Goodrich episode.

The A7D is now in service, sporting a Goodrich-made five-disk brake, a brake that works very well, I'm told. Business at the Goodrich plant is good. Lawson is now an engineer for LTV and has been assigned to the A7D project, possibly explaining why the A7D's new brakes work so well. And I am now a newspaper reporter.

At this writing, those remaining at Goodrich—including Warren—are still secure in the same positions, all except Russell Line and Robert Sink.

Line has been rewarded with a promotion to production superintendent, a large step upward on the corporate ladder. As for Sink, he moved up into Line's old job.

Self-Interest

THOMAS HOBBES

OR THE MATTER, FORM, AND POWER OF A COMMONWEALTH, ECCLESIASTICAL AND CIVIL THE FIRST PART, OF MAN

Chapter VI
Of the Interior Beginnings of Voluntary Motions; Commonly Called the Passions

. . .That which men desire, they are also said to LOVE, and to HATE those things for which they have aversion. So that desire and love are the same thing; save that by desire, we always signify the absence of the object; by love, most commonly the presence of the same. So also by aversion, we signify the absence; and by hate, the presence of the object.

Of appetites and aversions, some are born with men; as appetite of food, appetite of excretion, and exoneration, which may also and more properly be called aversions, from somewhat they feel in their bodies; and some other appetites, not many. The rest, which are appetites of particular things, proceed from experience, and trial of their effects upon themselves or other men. For of things we know not at all, or believe not to be, we can have no further desire than to taste and try. But aversion we have for things, not only which we know have hurt us, but also that we do not know whether they will hurt us, or not.

. . .Whatsoever is the object of any man's appetite or desire, that is it which he for his part calleth *good:* and the object of his hate and aversion, *evil;* and of his contempt, *vile* and *inconsiderable.* For these words of good, evil, and contemptible, are ever used with relation to the person that useth them: there being nothing simple and absolutely so; nor any common rule of good and evil, to be taken from the nature of the objects themselves; but from the person of the man, where there is no Commonwealth; or, in a Commonwealth, from the person that representeth it; or from an arbitrator or judge, whom men disagreeing shall by consent set up, and make his sentence the rule thereof.

. . . Of pleasure or delights, some arise from the sense of an object present; and those may be called *pleasures of sense;* the word *sensual,* as it is used by those only that condemn them, having no place till there be laws. Of this kind are all onerations and exonerations of the body; as also all that is pleasant, in the *sight, hearing, smell, taste,* or *touch.* Others arise from the expectation, that proceeds from foresight of the end, or consequence of things; whether those things in the sense please or displease. And these are

From the *Leviathan* (1651; rpt. London: Oxford University Press, 1967), Part I, Chaps. VI and XIII, Part II, Chap. XVII.

pleasures of the mind of him that draweth those consequences, and are generally called JOY. In the like manner, displeasures are some in the sense, and called PAIN; others in the expectation of consequences, and are called GRIEF. . . .

Chapter XIII
Of the Natural Condition of Mankind as Concerning Their Felicity and Misery

Nature hath made men so equal, in the faculties of the body, and mind; as that though there be found one man sometimes manifestly stronger in body, or of quicker mind than another, yet when all is reckoned together, the difference between man and man, is not so considerable, as that one man can thereupon claim to himself any benefit to which another may not pretend, as well as he. For as to the strength of body, the weakest has strength enough to kill the strongest, either by secret machination, or by confederacy with others, that are in the same danger with himself.

And as to the faculties of the mind, setting aside the arts grounded upon words, and especially that skill of proceeding upon general and infallible rules, called science; which very few have, and but in few things; as being not a native faculty born with us; nor attained, as prudence, while we look after somewhat else, I find yet a greater equality amongst men than that of strength. For prudence, is but experience; which equal time, equally bestows on all men, in those things they equally apply themselves unto. That which may perhaps make such equality incredible, is but a vain conceit of one's own wisdom, which almost all men think they have in a greater degree than the vulgar; that is, than all men but themselves, and a few others, whom by fame, or for concurring with themselves, they approve. For such is the nature of men, that howsoever they may acknowledge many others to be more witty, or more eloquent, or more learned; yet they will hardly believe there be many so wise as themselves; for they see their own wit at hand, and other men's at a distance. But this proveth rather that men are in that point equal, than unequal. For there is not ordinarily a greater sign of the equal distribution of anything, than that every man is contented with his share.

From this equality of ability, ariseth equality of hope in the attaining of our ends. And therefore if any two men desire the same thing, which nevertheless they cannot both enjoy, they become enemies; and in the way to their end, which is principally their own conservation, and sometimes their delectation only, endeavor to destroy or subdue one another. And from hence it comes to pass, that where an invader hath no more to fear, than another man's single power; if one plant, sow, build, or possess a convenient seat, others may probably be expected to come prepared with forces united, to dispossess, and deprive him, not only of the fruit of his labour, but also of his life or liberty. And the invader again is in the like danger of another.

And from this diffidence of one another, there is no way for any man to secure himself, so reasonable as anticipation; that is, by force, or wiles, to master the persons of all men he can, so long, till he see no other power great enough to endanger him: and this is no more than his own conservation requireth, and is generally allowed. Also because there be some, that taking pleasure in contemplating their own power in the acts of conquest, which they pursue farther than their security requires; if others, that otherwise would be glad to be at ease within modest bounds, should not by invasion increase their power, they would not be able, long time, by standing only on their defence, to subsist. And by consequence, such augmentation of dominion over men being necessary to a man's conservation, it ought to be allowed him.

Again, men have no pleasure, but on the contrary a great deal of grief, in keeping company, where there is no power able to overawe them all. For every man looketh that his companion should value him, at the same rate he sets upon himself: and upon all signs of contempt, or undervaluing, naturally endeavours as far as he dares (which amongst them that have no common power to keep them in quiet, is far enough to make them destroy each other), to extort a greater value from his contemners, by damage; and from others, by the example.

So that in the nature of man, we find three principal causes of quarrel. First, competition; secondly, diffidence; thirdly, glory.

The first maketh men invade for gain; the second, for safety; and the third, for reputation. The first use violence, to make themselves masters of other men's persons, wives, children, and cattle; the second, to defend them; the third, for trifles, as a word, a smile, a different opinion, and any sign of undervalue, either direct in their persons, or by reflection in their kindred, their friends, their nation, their profession, or their name.

Hereby it is manifest, that during the time men live without a common power to keep them all in awe, they are in that condition which is called WAR; and such a war, as is of every man, against every man. For WAR, consisteth not in battle only, or the act of fighting; but in a tract of time, wherein the will to contend by battle is sufficiently known: and therefore the notion of *time,* is to be considered in the nature of war, as it is in the nature of weather. For as the nature of foul weather, lieth not in a shower or two of rain, but in an inclination thereto of many days together; so the nature of war, consisteth not in actual fighting, but in the known disposition thereto, during all the time there is no assurance to the contrary. All other time is PEACE.

Whatsoever therefore is consequent to a time of war, where every man is enemy to every man, the same is consequent to the time wherein men live without other security, than what their own strength, and their own invention shall furnish them withal. In such condition, there is no place for industry, because the fruit thereof is uncertain, and consequently no culture of the earth; no navigation, nor use of the commodities that may be imported by sea; no commodious building; no instruments of moving, and removing, such things as require much force; no knowledge of the face of the earth; no account of time; no arts; no letters; no society; and, which is worst of all, continual fear, and danger of violent death; and the life of man, solitary, poor, nasty, brutish, and short. . . .

THE SECOND PART, OF COMMONWEALTH

Chapter XVII
Of the Causes, Generations and Definition of a Commonwealth

The final cause, end, or design of men who naturally love liberty and dominion over others, in the introduction of that restraint upon themselves in which we see them live in commonwealths, is the foresight of their own preservation, and of a more contented life thereby; that is to say, of getting themselves out from that miserable condition of war, which is necessarily consequent . . . to the natural passions of men, when there is no visible power to keep them in awe, and tie them by fear of punishment to the performance of their covenants and observation of those laws of nature set down [previously].

. . . The only way to erect such a common power, as may be able to defend them from the invasion of foreigners and the injuries of one another, and thereby to secure them in such sort as that, by their own industry, and by the fruits of the earth, they may nourish themselves and live contentedly; is, to confer all their power and strength upon one man, or upon one assembly of men, that may reduce all their wills, by plurality of voices, unto one will: which is as much as to say, to appoint one man, or assembly of men, to bear their person; and everyone to own and acknowledge himself to be author of whatsoever he that so beareth their person, shall act or cause to be acted in those things which concern the common peace and safety; and therein to submit their wills, everyone to his will, and their judgments, to his judgment. This is more than consent, or concord; it is a real unity of them all, in one and the same person, made by covenant of every man with every man, in such manner as if every man should say to every man, *"I authorize and give up my right of governing myself to this man, or to this assembly of men, on this condition, that thou give up thy right to him, and authorize all his actions in like manner."* This done, the multitude so united in one person, is called a *commonwealth,* in Latin *civitas.* This is the generation of that great LEVIATHAN, or rather, to speak more reverently, of that *mortal god,* to which we owe under the *immortal God,* our peace and defense. For by this authority, given him by every particular man in the commonwealth, he hath the use of so much power and strength conferred on him, that by terror thereof he is enabled to perform the wills of them all, to peace at home and mutual aid against their enemies abroad. And in him consisteth the essence of the commonwealth; which to define it, is *one person, of whose acts a great multitude, by mutual covenants one with another, have made themselves every one the author, to the end he may use the strength and means of them all, as he shall think expedient, for their peace and common defense.*

And he that carrieth this person, is called *sovereign,* and said to have sovereign power; and everyone besides, his *subject.*

The attaining to this sovereign power is by two ways. One, by natural force; as when a man maketh his children to submit themselves and their children to his government, as being able to destroy them if they refuse; or by war subdueth his enemies to his will, giving them their lives on that condition. The other, is when men agree amongst themselves to submit to some man, or assembly of men, voluntarily, on confidence to be protected by him against all others. This latter may be called a political commonwealth, or commonwealth by *institution;* and the former, a commonwealth by *acquisition*. . . .

Benevolence and Self-Interest

JOSEPH BUTLER

SERMON I
UPON THE SOCIAL NATURE OF MAN

The comparison will be between the nature of man as respecting self, and tending to private good, his own preservation and happiness; and the nature of man as having respect to society, and tending to promote public good, the happiness of that society. These ends do indeed perfectly coincide; and to aim at public and private good are so far from being inconsistent, that they mutually promote each other: yet in the following discourse they must be considered as entirely distinct; otherwise the nature of man as tending to one, or as tending to the other cannot be compared. There can no comparison be made, without considering the things compared as distinct and different.

From this review and comparison of the nature of man as respecting self, and as respecting society, it will plainly appear, that *there are as real and the same kind of indications in human nature, that we were made for society and to do good to our fellow-creatures, as that we were intended to take care of our own life and health and private good: and that the same objections lie against one of these assertions, as against the other.* For,

First, There is a natural principle of *benevolence*[1] in man; which is in some degree to *society,* what *self-love* is to the *individual.* And if there be in mankind any disposition to friendship; if there be any such thing as compassion, for compassion is momentary love; if there be any such thing as the paternal or filial affections; if there be any affection in human nature, the object and end of which is the good of another, this is itself benevolence, or the love of another. Be it ever so short, be it in ever so low a degree, or ever so unhappily confined; it proves the assertion, and points out what we were designed for, as really as though it were in a higher degree and more

From *Fifteen Sermons Preached at Rolls Chapel* (1726; rpt. London: Thomas Tegg & Son, 1835), selections from Sermons I and XI.

extensive. I must, however, remind you that though benevolence and self-love are different; though the former tends most directly to public good, and the latter to private: yet they are so perfectly coincident that the greatest satisfactions to ourselves depend upon our having benevolence in a due degree, and that self-love is one chief security of our right behaviour towards society. It may be added, that their mutual coinciding, so that we can scarce promote one without the other, is equally proof that we were made for both.

Secondly, This will further appear, from observing that the *several passions* and *affections,* which are distinct, both from benevolence and self-love, do in general contribute and lead us to *public* good as really as to *private.* It might be thought too minute and particular, and would carry us too great a length, to distinguish between and compare together the several passions or appetites distinct from benevolence, whose primary use and intention is the security and good of society; and the passions distinct from self-love, whose primary intention and design is the security and good of the individual.[2] It is enough to the present argument, that desire of esteem from others, contempt and esteem of them, love of society as distinct from affection to the good of it, indignation against successful vice, that these are public affections or passions; have an immediate respect to others, naturally lead us to regulate our behavior in such a manner as will be of service to our fellow-creatures. If any or all of these may be considered likewise as private affections, as tending to private good; this does not hinder them from being public affections too, or destroy the good influence of them upon society, and their tendency to public good. It may be added, that as persons without any conviction from reason of the desirableness of life, would yet of course preserve it merely from the appetite of hunger; so by acting merely from regard (suppose) to reputation, without any consideration of the good of others, men often contribute to public good. In both these instances they are plainly instruments in the hands of another, in the hands of Providence, to carry on ends, the preservation of the individual and good of society, which they themselves have not in their view or intention. The sum is, men have various appetites, passions, and particular affections, quite distinct both from self-love and from benevolence: all of these have a tendency to promote both public and private good, and may be considered as respecting others and ourselves equally and in common: but some of them seem most immediately to respect others, or tend to public good; others of them most immediately to respect self, or tend to private good: as the former are not benevolence, so the latter are not self-love: neither sort are instances of our love either to ourselves or others; . . .

Thirdly, There is a principle of reflection in men, by which they distinguish between, approve, and disapprove their own actions. We are plainly constituted such sort of creatures as to reflect upon our own nature. The mind can take a view of what passes within itself, its propensions, aversions, passions, affections, as respecting such objects, and in such degrees; and of the several actions consequent thereupon. In this survey it approves of one, disapproves of another, and towards a third is affected in neither of these ways, but is quite indifferent. This principle in man, by which he approves or disapproves his heart, temper, and actions, is conscience; for this is the strict sense of the word, though sometimes it is used so as to take in more. And that this faculty tends to restrain men from doing mischief to each other, and leads them to do good, is too manifest to need being insisted upon. Thus a parent has the affection of love to his children: this leads him to take care of, to educate, to make due provision for them: the natural affection leads to this; but the reflection that it is his proper business, what belongs to him, that it is right and commendable so to do, this added to the affection becomes a much more settled principle, and carries him on through more labour and difficulties for the sake of his children, than he would undergo from that affection alone, if he thought it, and the course of action it led to, either indifferent or criminal. This indeed is impossible, to do that which is good and not to approve of it; for which reason they are frequently not considered as distinct, though they really are; for men often approve of the actions of others, which they will not imitate, and likewise do that which they approve not. It cannot possibly be denied that there is this principle of reflection or conscience in human nature. Suppose a man to relieve an innocent person in great distress; suppose the same man afterwards, in the fury of anger, to do the greatest mischief to a person who had given no just cause of offence; to aggravate the injury, add the circumstances of former friendship, and obligation from the injured person; let the man who is supposed to have done these two different actions, coolly reflect upon them afterwards, without regard to their consequences to himself: to assert that any common man would be affected in the same way towards these different actions, that he would make no distinction between them, but approve or disapprove them equally, is too glaring a falsity to need being confuted. There is therefore this principle of reflection or conscience in mankind. It is needless to compare the respect it has to private good, with the respect it has to public; since it plainly tends as much to the latter as to the former, and is commonly thought to tend chiefly to the latter. This faculty is now mentioned merely as another part of the inward frame of man, pointing out to us in some degree what we are intended for, and as what will naturally and of course have some influence. The particular place assigned to it by nature, what authority it has, and how great influence it ought to have, shall be hereafter considered.

From this comparison of benevolence and self-love, of our public and private affections, of the courses of life they lead to, and of the principle of reflection or conscience as respecting each of them, it is as manifest, that *we were made for society, and to promote the happiness of it, as that we were intended to take care of our own life, and health, and private good. . . .*

The sum of the whole is plainly this. The nature of man considered in his single capacity, and with respect only to the present world, is adapted and leads him to attain the greatest happiness he can for himself in the present world. The nature of man considered in his public or social capacity leads him to a right behaviour in society, to that course of life which we call virtue. Men follow or obey their nature in both these capacities and respects to a certain degree but not entirely: their actions do not come up to the whole of what their nature leads them to in either of these capacities or respects: and they often violate their nature in both, *i.e.* as they neglect the duties they owe to their fellow-creatures, to which their nature leads them; and are injurious, to which their nature is abhorrent; so there is a manifest negligence in men of their real happiness or interest in the present world, when that interest is inconsistent with a present gratification; for the sake of which they negligently, nay, even knowingly, are the authors and instruments of their own misery and ruin. Thus they are as often unjust to themselves as to others, and for the most part are equally so to both by the same actions. . . .

SERMON XI
UPON THE LOVE OF OUR NEIGHBOUR

Every man hath a general desire of his own happiness; and likewise a variety of particular affections, passions, and appetites, to particular external objects. The former proceeds from, or is, self-love, and seems inseparable from all sensible creatures, who can reflect upon themselves and their own interest or happiness, so as to have that interest an object to their minds: what is to be said of the latter is, that they proceed from, or together make up, that particular nature, according to which man is made. The object the former pursues is somewhat internal, our own happiness, enjoyment, satisfaction; whether we have or have not a distinct particular perception what it is, or wherein it consists: the objects of the latter are this or that particular external thing, which the affections tend towards, and of which it hath always a particular idea or perception. The principle we call self-love never seeks anything external for the sake of the thing, but only as a means of happiness or good: particular affections rest in the external things themselves. One belongs to man as a reasonable creature reflecting upon his own interest or happiness; the other, though quite distinct from reason, are as much a part of human nature.

That all particular appetites and passions are towards *external things themselves,* distinct from the *pleasure arising from them,* is manifested from hence, that there could not be this pleasure, were it not for that prior suitableness between the object and the passion: there could be no enjoyment or delight for one thing more than another, from eating food more than from swallowing a stone, if there were not an affection or appetite to one thing more than another.

Every particular affection, even the love of our neighbour, is as really our own affection, as self-love; and the pleasure arising from its gratification is as much my own pleasure, as the pleasure self-love would have from knowing I myself should be happy some time hence, would be my own pleasure. And if, because every particular affection is a man's own, and the pleasure arising from its gratification his own pleasure, or pleasure to himself, such particular affection must be called self-love. According to this way of speaking, no creature whatever can possibly act merely from self-love; and every action and every affection whatever is to be resolved up into this one principle. But then this is not the language of mankind: or, if it were, we should want words to express the difference between the principle of an action, proceeding from cool consideration that it will be to my own advantage; and an action, suppose of revenge, or of friendship by which a man runs upon certain ruin, to do evil or good to another. It is manifest the principles of these actions are totally different, and so want different words to be distinguished by: all that they agree in is, that they both proceed from, and are done to gratify an inclination in a man's self. But the principle or inclination in one case is self-love; in the other, hatred, or love of another. There is then a distinction between the cool principle of self-love, or general desire of our own happiness, as one part of our nature, and one principle of action; and the particular affections towards particular external objects, as another principle of action. How much soever, therefore, is to be allowed to self-love, yet it cannot be allowed to be the whole of our inward constitution; because, you see, there are other parts or principles which come into it.

Further, private happiness or good is all which self-love can make us desire or be concerned about. In having this consists its gratification; it is an affection to ourselves—a regard to our own interest, happiness, and private good: and in the proportion a man hath this, he is interested, or a lover of himself. Let this be kept in mind, because there is commonly, as I shall presently have occasion to observe, another sense put upon these words. On the other hand, particular affections tend towards particular external things; these are their objects; having these is their end; in this consists their gratification: no matter whether it be, or be not, upon the whole, our interest or happiness. An action, done from the former of these principles, is called an interested action. An action, proceeding from any of the latter, has its denomination of passionate, ambitious, friendly, revengeful, or any other, from the particular appetite or affection from which it proceeds. Thus self-love, as one part of human nature, and the several particular principles as the other part, are themselves, their objects, and ends, stated and shown.

From hence it will be easy to see how far, and in what ways, each of these can contribute and be subservient to the private good of the individual. Happiness does not consist in self-love. The desire of happiness is no more the thing itself, than the desire of riches is the possession or enjoyment of them. People may love themselves with the most entire and unbounded affection, and yet be extremely miserable. Neither can self-love any way help them out, but by setting them on work to get rid of the causes of their misery, to gain or make use of those objects which are by nature adapted to afford satisfaction. Happiness or satisfaction consists only in enjoyment of those objects which are by nature suited to our several particular appetites, passions, and affections. So that if self-love wholly engrosses us, and leaves no room for any other principle, there can be absolutely no such thing at all as happiness or enjoyment of any kind whatever; since happiness consists in the gratification of particular passions, which supposes the having of them. Self-love then does not constitute *this* or *that* to be our interest or good; but our interest or good being constituted by nature and supposed self-love, only puts us upon obtaining and securing it. Therefore, if it be possible that self-love may prevail and exert itself in a degree or manner which is not subservient to this end, then it will not follow that our interest will be promoted in proportion to the degree in which that principle engrosses us, and prevails over others. Nay, further, the private and contracted affection, when it is not subservient to this end, private good, may, for anything that appears, have a direct contrary tendency and effect. And if we will consider the matter, we shall see that it often really has. Disengagement is absolutely necessary to enjoyment; and a person may have so steady and fixed an eye upon his own interest, whatever he places it in, as may hinder him from attending to many gratifications within his reach, which others have their minds free and open to. Overfondness for a child is not generally thought to be for its advantage; and, if there be any guess to be from appearances, surely that character we call *selfish* is not the most promising for happiness. Such a temper may plainly be, and exert itself in a degree and manner which may give unnecessary and useless solicitude and anxiety, in a degree and manner which may prevent obtaining the means and materials of enjoyment, as well as the making use of them. Immoderate self-love does very ill consult its own interest; and how much soever a paradox it may appear, it is certainly true, that, even from self-love, we should endeavour to get over all inordinate regard to, and consideration of, ourselves. Every one of our passions and affections hath its natural stint and bound, which may easily be exceeded; whereas our enjoyments can possibly be but in a determinate measure and degree. Therefore such excess of the affection, since it cannot procure any enjoyment, must in all cases be useless, but is generally attended with inconveniences, and often is down-right pain and misery. This holds as much with regard to self-love as to all other affections. The natural degree of it, so far as it sets us on work to gain and make use of the materials of satisfaction, may be to our real advantage; but beyond or beside this, it is in several respects an inconvenience and disadvantage. Thus it appears that private interest is so far from being likely to be promoted in proportion to the degree in which self-love engrosses us, and prevails over all other principles, that *the contracted affection may be so prevalent as to disappoint itself and even contradict its own end, private good*. . . .

Self-love and interestedness was stated to consist in or be an affection to ourselves, a regard to our own private good: it is, therefore, distinct from benevolence, which is an affection to the good of our fellow-creatures. But that benevolence is distinct from, that is, not the same thing with self-love, is no reason for its being looked upon with any peculiar suspicion, because every principle whatever, by means of which self-love is gratified, is distinct from it. And all things, which are distinct from each other, are equally so. A man has an affection or aversion to another: that one of these tends to, and is gratified by doing good, that the other tends to, and is gratified by doing harm, does not in the least alter the respect which either one or the other of these inward feelings has to self-love.

. . . Thus the principles, from which men rush upon certain ruin for the destruction of an enemy, and for the preservation of a friend, have the same respect to the private affection, are equally interested, or equally disinterested: and it is of no avail, whether they are said to be one or the other.

Therefore, to those who are shocked to hear virtue spoken of as disinterested, it may be allowed, that it is indeed absurd to speak thus of it; unless hatred, several particular instances of vice, and all the common affections and aversions in mankind, are acknowledged to be disinterested too. . . . Is desire of, and delight in the happiness of another any more a diminution of self-love, than desire of and delight in the esteem of another? They are both equally desire of and delight in somewhat external to ourselves: either both or neither are so. The object of self-love is expressed in the term self: and every appetite of sense, and every particular affection of the heart, are equally interested or disinterested, because the objects of them all are equally self or somewhat else. . . .

Thus it appears, that there is no peculiar contrariety between self-love and benevolence; no greater competition between these, than between any other particular affections and self-love. . . .

The short of the matter is no more than this. Happiness consists in the gratification of certain affections, appetites, passions, with objects which are by nature adapted to them. Self-love may indeed set us on work to gratify these: but happiness or enjoyment has no immediate connexion with self-love, but arises from such gratification alone. Love of our neighbour is one of those affections. This, considered as a virtuous principle, is gratified by a consciousness of endeavouring to promote the good of others: but considered as a natural affection, its gratification consists in the actual accomplishment of this endeavour. Now, indulgence or gratification of this affection, whether in that consciousness, or this accomplishment, has the same respect to interest, as indulgence of any other affection; they equally proceed from, or do not proceed from, self-love; they equally include or exclude, this principle. Thus it appears, that "benevolence and the pursuit of public good have at least as great respect to self-love and the pursuit of private good, as any other particular passions, and their respective pursuits."

. . .There is indeed frequently an inconsistency, or interfering between self-love or private interest, and the several particular appetites, passions, affections, or the pursuits they lead to. But this competition or interfering is merely accidental, and happens much oftener between pride, revenge, sensual gratifications, and private interest, than between private interest and benevolence. For nothing is more common than to see men give themselves up to a passion or an affection to their known prejudice and ruin, and in direct contradiction to manifest and real interest, and the loudest calls of self-love: whereas the seeming competitions and interfering between benevolence and private interest, relate much more to the materials or means of enjoyment, than to enjoyment itself.

NOTES

1. Suppose a man of learning to be writing a grave book upon human nature, and to show in several parts of it that he had an insight into the subject he was considering; amongst other things, the following one would require to be accounted for: the appearance of benevolence or good-will in men towards each

other in the instances of natural relation, and in others. (Hobbes, *On Human Nature,* c. ix. § 17.) Cautious of being deceived with outward show, he retires within himself, to see exactly what that is in the mind of man from whence this appearance proceeds; and, upon deep reflection, asserts the principle in the mind to be only the love of power, and delight in the exercise of it. Would not everybody think here was a mistake of one word for another? That the philosopher was contemplating and accounting for some other human actions, some other behaviour of man to man? And could any one be thoroughly satisfied, that what is commonly called benevolence or good-will was really the affection meant, but only by being made to understand that this learned person had a general hypothesis, to which the appearance of good-will could no otherwise be reconciled? That what has this appearance, is often nothing but ambition; that delight in superiority often (suppose always) mixes itself with benevolence, only makes it more specious to call it ambition than hunger, of the two: but in reality that passion does no more account for the whole appearance of good-will than this appetite does. Is there not often the appearance of one man's wishing that good to another, which he knows himself unable to procure him; and rejoicing in it, though bestowed by a third person? And can love of power any way possibly come in to account for this desire or delight? Is there not often the appearance of men's distinguishing between two or more persons, preferring one before another, to do good to, in cases where love of power cannot in the least account for the distinction and preference? For this principle can no otherwise distinguish between objects, than as it is a greater instance and exertion of power to do good to one rather than to another. Again, suppose good-will in the mind of man to be nothing but delight in the exercise of power; men might indeed be restrained by distant and accidental considerations; but these restraints being removed, they would have a disposition to, and delight in mischief, as an exercise and proof of power: And this disposition and delight would arise from, or be the same principle in the mind, as a disposition to, and delight in charity. Thus cruelty, as distinct from envy and resentment, would be exactly the same in the mind of man as good-will: That one tends to the happiness, the other to the misery of our fellow creatures, is, it seems, merely an accidental circumstance, which the mind has not the least regard to. These are the absurdities which even men of capacity run into, when they have occasion to belie their nature, and will perversely disclaim that image of God which was originally stamped upon it; the traces of which, however faint, are plainly discernible upon the mind of man.

If any person can in earnest doubt whether there be such a thing as good-will in one man towards another (for the question is not concerning either the degree or extensiveness of it, but concerning the affection itself), let it be observed, that *whether man be thus or otherwise constituted, what is the inward frame in this particular,* is a mere question of fact or natural history, not provable immediately by reason. It is therefore to be judged of and determined in the same way other facts or matters of natural history are: By appealing to the external senses, or inward perceptions, respectively, as the matter under consideration is cognizable by one or the other: By arguing from acknowledged facts and actions; for a great number of actions of the same kind in different circumstances, and respecting different objects, will prove, to certainty, what principles they do not, and, to the greatest probability, what principles they do proceed from: And, lastly, by the testimony of mankind. Now, that there is some degree of benevolence amongst men, may be as strongly and plainly proved in all these ways as it could possibly be proved, supposing there was this affection in our nature. And should any one think fit to assert, that resentment in the mind of man was absolutely nothing but reasonable concern for our own safety, the falsity of this, and what is the real nature of that passion, could be shown in no other ways than those in which it may be shown, that there is such a thing, in *some degree,* as *real* good-will in man towards man. It is sufficient that the seeds of it be implanted in our nature by God. There is, it is owned, much left for us to do upon our own heart and temper; to cultivate, to improve, to call it forth, to exercise it in a steady uniform manner. This is our work: this is Virtue and Religion.

2. If any desire to see this distinction and comparison made in a particular instance, the appetite and passion now mentioned may serve for one. Hunger is to be considered as a private appetite; because the end for which it was given us is the preservation of the individual. Desire of esteem is a public passion; because the end for which it was given us is to regulate our behaviour towards society. The respect which this has to private good is as remote as the respect that it has to public good; and the appetite is no more self-love, than the passion is benevolence. The object and end of the former is merely food; the object and end of the latter is merely esteem: but the latter can no more be gratified, without contributing to the good of society, than the former can be gratified, without contributing to the preservation of the individual.

TRUTH TELLING

Case Study—Italian Tax Mores

ARTHUR KELLY

The Italian federal corporate tax system has an official, legal tax structure and tax rates just as the U.S. system does. However, all similarity between the two systems ends there.

The Italian tax authorities assume that no Italian corporation would ever submit a tax return which shows its true profits but rather would submit a return which understates actual profits by anywhere between 30 percent and 70 percent; their assumption is essentially correct. Therefore, about six months after the annual deadline for filing corporate tax returns, the tax authorities issue to each corporation an "invitation to discuss" its tax return. The purpose of this notice is to arrange a personal meeting between them and representatives of the corporation. At this meeting, the Italian revenue service states the amount of corporate income tax which it believes is due. Its position is developed from both prior years' taxes actually paid and the current year's return; the amount which the tax authorities claim is due is generally several times that shown on the corporation's return for the current year. In short, the corporation's tax return and the revenue service's stated position are the opening offers for the several rounds of bargaining which will follow.

The Italian corporation is typically represented in such negotiations by its *commercialista,* a function which exists in Italian society for the primary purpose of negotiating corporate (and individual) tax payments with the Italian tax authorities; thus, the management of an Italian corporation seldom, if ever, has to meet directly with the Italian revenue service and probably has a minimum awareness of the details of the negotiation other than the final settlement.

Both the final settlement and the negotiation are extremely important to the corporation, the tax authorities, and the *commercialista.* Since the tax

This case—prepared by Arthur L. Kelly (president and chief operating officer of LaSalle Steel Company; formerly vice-president—International of A. T. Kearney, Inc.)—was presented at Loyola University of Chicago at a Mellon Foundation symposium entitled "Foundations of Corporate Responsibility to Society," April 1977. Printed with the permission of Arthur L. Kelly.

authorities assume that a corporation *always* earned more money this year than last year and *never* has a loss, the amount of the final settlement, i.e., corporate taxes which will actually be paid, becomes, for all practical purposes, the floor for the start of next year's negotiations. The final settlement also represents the amount of revenue the Italian government will collect in taxes to help finance the cost of running the country. However, since large amounts of money are involved and two individuals having vested personal interests are conducting the negotiations, the amount of *bustarella*—typically a substantial cash payment "requested" by the Italian revenue agent from the *commercialista*—usually determines whether the final settlement is closer to the corporation's original tax return or to the fiscal authority's original negotiating position.

Whatever *bustarella* is paid during the negotiation is usually included by the *commercialista* in his lump-sum fee "for services rendered" to his corporate client. If the final settlement is favorable to the corporation, and it is the *commercialista's* job to see that it is, then the corporation is not likely to complain about the amount of its *commercialista's* fee, nor will it ever know how much of that fee was represented by *bustarella* and how much remained for the *commercialista* as payment for his negotiating services. In any case, the tax authorities will recognize the full amount of the fee as a tax deductible expense on the corporation's tax return for the following year.

About ten years ago, a leading American bank opened a banking subsidiary in a major Italian city. At the end of its first year of operation, the bank was advised by its local lawyers and tax accountants, both from branches of U.S. companies, to file its tax return "Italian-style," i.e., to understate its actual profits by a significant amount. The American general manager of the bank, who was on his first overseas assignment, refused to do so both because he considered it dishonest and because it was inconsistent with the practices of his parent company in the United States.

About six months after filing its "American-style" tax return, the bank received an "invitation to discuss" notice from the Italian tax authorities. The bank's general manager consulted with his lawyers and tax accountants who suggested he hire a *commercialista.* He rejected this advice and instead wrote a letter to the Italian revenue service not only stating that his firm's corporate return was correct as filed but also requesting that they inform him of any specific items about which they had questions. His letter was never answered.

About sixty days after receiving the initial "invitation to discuss" notice, the bank received a formal tax assessment notice calling for a tax of approximately three times that shown on the bank's corporate tax return; the tax authorities simply assumed the bank's original return had been based on generally accepted Italian practices, and they reacted accordingly. The bank's general manager again consulted with his lawyers and tax accountants who again suggested he hire a *commercialista* who knew how to handle these matters. Upon learning that the *commercialista* would probably have to pay *bustarella* to his revenue service counterpart in order to reach a settlement, the general manager again chose to ignore his advisors. Instead, he responded by sending the Italian revenue service a check for the full amount of taxes due according to the bank's American-style tax return even though the due date for the payment was almost six months hence; he made no reference to the amount of corporate taxes shown on the formal tax assessment notice.

Ninety days after paying its taxes, the bank received a third notice from the fiscal authorities. This one contained the statement, "We have reviewed your corporate tax return for 19__ and have determined that [the lira equivalent of] $6,000,000 of interest paid on deposits is not an allowable expense for federal tax purposes. Accordingly, the total tax due for 19____ is lira ____." Since interest paid on deposits is any bank's largest single expense item, the new tax assessment was for an amount many times larger than that shown in the initial tax assessment notice and almost fifteen times larger than the taxes which the bank had actually paid.

The bank's general manager was understandably very upset. He immediately arranged an appointment to meet personally with the manager of the Italian revenue service's local office. Shortly after the start of their meeting, the conversation went something like this:

General Manager: "You can't really be serious about disallowing interest paid on deposits as a tax deductible expense."

Italian Revenue Service: "Perhaps. However, we thought it would get your attention. Now that you're here, shall we begin our negotiations?"[1]

Questions

1. Would you, as the general manager of the Italian subsidiary of an American corporation, "when in Rome" do as other Italian corporations do or adhere strictly to U.S. tax reporting practices?
2. Would you, as chief executive officer of a publicly traded corporation (subject to Securities Exchange Commission rules, regulations, and scrutiny), advise the general manager of your Italian subsidiary to follow common Italian tax reporting practices or to adhere to U.S. standards?

NOTE

1. For readers interested in what happened subsequently, the bank was forced to pay the taxes shown on the initial tax assessment, and the American manager was recalled to the United States and replaced.

Ethical Duties Towards Others: "Truthfulness"

IMMANUEL KANT

The exchange of our sentiments is the principal factor in social intercourse, and truth must be the guiding principle herein. Without truth social intercourse and conversation become valueless. We can only know what a man thinks if he tells us his thoughts, and when he undertakes to express them he must really do so, or else there can be no society of men. Fellowship is only the second condition of society, and a liar destroys fellowship. Lying makes it impossible to derive any benefit from conversation. Liars are, therefore, held in general contempt. Man is inclined to be reserved and to pretend. . . . Man is reserved in order to conceal faults and shortcomings which he has; he pretends in order to make others attribute to him merits and virtues which he has not. Our proclivity to reserve and concealment is due to the will of Providence that the defects of which we are full should not be too obvious. Many of our propensities and peculiarities are objectionable to others, and if they became patent we should be foolish and hateful in their eyes. Moreover, the parading of these objectionable characteristics would so familiarize men with them that they would themselves acquire them. Therefore we arrange our conduct either to conceal our faults or to appear other than we are. We possess the art of simulation. In consequence, our inner weakness and error is revealed to the eyes of men only as an appearance of well-being, while we ourselves develop the habit of dispositions which are conducive to good conduct. No man in his true senses, therefore, is candid. Were man candid, were the request of Momus[1] to be complied with that Jupiter should place a mirror in each man's heart so that his disposition might be visible to all, man would have to be better constituted and to possess good principles. If all men were good there would be no need for any of us to be reserved; but since they are not, we have to keep the shutters closed. Every house keeps its dustbin in a place of its own. We do not press our friends to come into our water-closet, although they know that we have one just like themselves. Familiarity in such things is the ruin of good taste. In the same way we make no exhibition of our defects, but try to conceal them. We try to conceal our mistrust by affecting a courteous demeanour and so accustom ourselves to courtesy that at last it becomes a reality and we set a good example by it. If that were not so, if there were none who were better than we, we should become neglectful. Accordingly, the endeavour to appear good ultimately makes us really good. If all men were good, they could be candid, but as things are they cannot be. To be reserved is to be restrained in expressing one's mind. We can, of course, keep absolute silence. This is the readiest and most absolute method of

From *Lectures on Ethics,* trans. Louis Infield (London: Methuen, 1930; rpt. New York: Harper & Row, 1963), pp. 224–35. Reprinted by permission of the publishers.

reserve, but it is unsociable, and a silent man is not only unwanted in social circles but is also suspected; every one thinks him deep and disparaging, for if when asked for his opinion he remains silent people think that he must be taking the worst view or he would not be averse from expressing it. Silence, in fact, is always a treacherous ally, and therefore it is not even prudent to be completely reserved. Yet there is such a thing as prudent reserve, which requires not silence but careful deliberation; a man who is wisely reserved weighs his words carefully and speaks his mind about everything excepting only those things in regard to which he deems it wise to be reserved.

We must distinguish between reserve and secretiveness, which is something entirely different. There are matters about which one has no desire to speak and in regard to which reserve is easy. We are, for instance, not naturally tempted to speak about and to betray our own misdemeanours. Everyone finds it easy to keep a reserve about some of his private affairs, but there are things about which it requires an effort to be silent. Secrets have a way of coming out, and strength is required to prevent ourselves betraying them. Secrets are always matters deposited with us by other people and they ought not to be placed at the disposal of third parties. But man has a great liking for conversation, and the telling of secrets adds much to the interest of conversation; a secret told is like a present given; how then are we to keep secrets? Men who are not very talkative as a rule keep secrets well, but good conversationalists, who are at the same time clever, keep them better. The former might be induced to betray something, but the latter's gift of repartee invariably enables them to invent on the spur of the moment something non-committal.

The person who is as silent as a mute goes to one extreme; the person who is loquacious goes to the opposite. Both tendencies are weaknesses. Men are liable to the first, women to the second. Someone has said that women are talkative because the training of infants is their special charge, and their talkativeness soon teaches a child to speak, because they can chatter to it all day long. If men had the care of the child, they would take much longer to learn to talk. However that may be, we dislike anyone who will not speak: he annoys us; his silence betrays his pride. On the other hand, loquaciousness in men is contemptible and contrary to the strength of the male. All this by the way; we shall now pass to more weighty matters.

If I announce my intention to tell what is in my mind, ought I knowingly to tell everything, or can I keep anything back? If I indicate that I mean to speak my mind, and instead of doing so make a false declaration, what I say is an untruth, a *falsiloquium.* But there can be *falsiloquium* even when people have no right to assume that we are expressing our thoughts. It is possible to deceive without making any statement whatever. I can make believe, make a demonstration from which others will draw the conclusion I want, though they have no right to expect that my action will express my real mind. In that case I have not lied to them, because I had not undertaken to express my mind. I may, for instance, wish people to think that I am off on a journey, and so I pack my luggage; people draw the conclusion I want them to draw; but others have no right to demand a declaration of my will from me.

. . . Again, I may make a false statement, (*falsiloquium*) when my purpose is to hide from another what is in my mind and when the latter can assume that such is my purpose, his own purpose being to make a wrong use of the truth. Thus, for instance, if my enemy takes me by the throat and asks where I keep my money, I need not tell him the truth, because he will abuse it; and my untruth is not a lie (*mendacium*) because the thief knows full well that I will not, if I can help it, tell him the truth and that he has no right to demand it of me. But let us assume that I really say to the fellow, who is fully aware that he has no right to demand it, because he is a swindler, that I will tell him the truth, and I do not, am I then a liar? He has deceived me and I deceive him in return; to him, as an individual, I have done no injustice and he cannot complain; but I am none the less a liar in that my conduct is an infringement of the rights of humanity. It follows that a *falsiloquium* can be a *mendacium*—a lie—especially when it contravenes the right of an individual. Although I do a man no injustice by lying to him when he has lied to me, yet I act against the right of mankind, since I set myself in opposition to the condition and means through which any human society is possible. If one country breaks the peace this does not justify the other in doing likewise in revenge, for if it did no peace would ever be secure. Even though a statement does not contravene any particular human right it is nevertheless a lie if it is contrary to the general right of mankind. If a man spreads false news, though he does no wrong to anyone in particular, he offends against mankind, because if such a practice were universal man's desire for knowledge would be frustrated. For, apart from speculation, there are only two ways in which I can increase my fund of knowledge, by experience or by what others tell me. My own experience must necessarily be limited, and if what others told me was false, I could not satisfy my craving for knowledge.

. . . Not every untruth is a lie; it is a lie only if I have expressly given the other to understand that I am willing to acquaint him with my thought. Every lie is objectionable and contemptible in that we purposely let people think that we are telling them our thoughts and do not do so. We have broken our pact and violated the right of mankind. But if we were to be at all times punctiliously truthful we might often become victims of the wickedness of others who were ready to abuse our truthfulness. If all men were well-intentioned it would not only be a duty not to lie, but no one would do so because there would be no point in it. But as men are malicious, it cannot be denied that to be punctiliously truthful is often dangerous. This has given rise to the conception of a white lie, the lie enforced upon us by necessity—a difficult point for moral philosophers. For if necessity is urged as an excuse it might be urged to justify stealing, cheating and killing, and the whole basis of morality goes by the board. Then, again, what is a case of necessity? Everyone will interpret it in his own way. And, as there is then no definite standard to judge by, the application of moral rules becomes uncertain. Consider, for example, the following case. A man who knows that I have money asks me: "Have you any money on you?" If I fail to reply, he will conclude that I have; if I reply in the affirmative he will take it from me; if I reply in the negative, I tell a lie. What am I to do? If force is used to extort a confession from me, if any confession is improperly used against me, and if I cannot save myself by maintaining silence, then my lie is a weapon of defence. The misuse of a declaration extorted by force justifies me in defending myself. For whether it is my money or a confession that is extorted makes no difference. The forcing of a statement from me under conditions which convince me that improper use would be made of it is the only case in which I can be justified in telling a white lie. But if a lie does no harm to anyone and no one's interests are affected by it, is it a lie? Certainly. I undertake to express my mind, and if I do not really do so, though my statement may not be to the prejudice of the particular individual to whom it is made, it is none the less *in praejudicium humanitatis.* Then, again, there are lies which cheat. To cheat is to make a lying promise, while a breach of faith is a true promise which is not kept. A lying promise is an insult to the person to whom it is made, and even if this is not always so, yet there is always something mean about it. If, for instance, I promise to send some one a bottle of wine, and afterwards make a joke of it, I really swindle him. It is true that he has no right to demand the present of me, but in Idea it is already a part of his own property.

. . . If a man tries to extort the truth from us and we cannot tell it [to] him and at the same time do not wish to lie, we are justified in resorting to equivocation in order to reduce him to silence and put a stop to his questionings. If he is wise, he will leave it at that. But if we let it be understood that we are expressing our sentiments and we proceed to equivocate we are in a different case; for our listeners might then draw wrong conclusions from our statements and we should have deceived them. . . . But a lie is a lie, and is in itself intrinsically base whether it be told with good or bad intent. For formally a lie is always evil; though if it is evil materially as well, it is a much meaner thing. There are no lies which may not be the source of evil. A liar is a coward; he is a man who has recourse to lying because he is unable to help himself and gain his ends by any other means. But a stout-hearted man will love truth and will not recognize a *casus necessitatis.* All expedients which take us off our guard are thoroughly mean. Such are lying, assassination, and poisoning. To attack a man on the highway is less vile than to attempt to poison him. In the former case he can at least defend himself, but, as he must eat, he is defenceless against the poisoner. A flatterer is not always a liar; he is merely lacking in self-esteem; he has no scruple in reducing his own worth and raising that of another in order to gain something by it. But there exists a form of flattery which springs from kindness of heart. Some kind souls flatter people whom they hold in high esteem. There are thus two kinds of flattery, kindly and treacherous; the first is weak, while the second is mean. People who are not given to flattery are apt to be fault-finders.

If a man is often the subject of conversation, he becomes a subject of criticism. If he is our friend, we ought not invariably to speak well of him or else we arouse jealousy and grudge against him; for people, knowing that he is only human, will not believe that he has only good qualities. We must, therefore, concede a little to the adverse criticism of our listeners and point out some of our friend's faults; if we allow him faults which are common and unessential, while extolling his merits, our friend cannot take it in ill part. Toadies are people who praise others in company in the hope of gain. Men are meant to form opinions regarding their fellows and to judge them. Nature has made us judges of our neighbours so that things which are false but are outside the scope of the established legal authority should be arraigned before the court of social opinion. Thus, if a man dishonours some one, the authorities do not punish him, but his fellows judge and punish him, though only so far as it is within their right to punish him and without doing violence to him. People shun him, and that is punishment enough. If that were not so, conduct not punished by the authorities would go altogether unpunished. What then is meant by the enjoinder that we ought not to judge others? As we are ignorant of their dispositions we cannot tell whether they are punishable before God or not, and we cannot, therefore, pass an adequate moral judgment upon them. The moral dispositions of others are for God to judge, but we are competent judges of our own. We cannot judge the inner core of morality: no man can do that; but we are competent to judge its outer manifestations. In matters of morality we are not judges of our fellows, but nature has given us the right to form judgments about others and she also has ordained that we should judge ourselves in accordance with judgments that others form about us. The man who turns a deaf ear to other people's opinion of him is base and reprehensible. There is nothing that happens in this world about which we ought not to form an opinion, and we show considerable subtlety in judging conduct. Those who judge our conduct with exactness are our best friends. Only friends can be quite candid and open with each other. But in judging a man a further question arises. In what terms are we to judge him? Must we pronounce him either good or evil? We must proceed from the assumption that humanity is lovable, and, particularly in regard to wickedness, we ought never to pronounce a verdict either of condemnation or of acquittal. We pronounce such a verdict whenever we judge from his conduct that a man deserves to be condemned or acquitted. But though we are entitled to form opinions about our fellows, we have no right to spy upon them. Everyone has a right to prevent others from watching and scrutinizing his actions. The spy arrogates to himself the right to watch the doings of strangers; no one ought to presume to do such a thing. If I see two people whispering to each other so as not to be heard, my inclination ought to be to get farther away so that no sound may reach my ears. Or if I am left alone in a room and I see a letter lying open on the table, it would be contemptible to try to read it; a right-thinking man would not do so; in fact, in order to avoid suspicion and distrust he will endeavour not to be left alone in a room where money is left lying about, and he will be averse from learning other people's secrets in order to avoid the risk of the suspicion that he has betrayed them; other people's secrets trouble him, for even between the most intimate of friends suspicion might arise. A man who will let his inclination or appetite drive him to deprive his friend of anything, of his fiancée, for instance, is contemptible beyond a doubt. If he can cherish a passion for my sweetheart, he can equally well cherish a passion for my purse. It is very mean to lie in wait and spy upon a friend, or on anyone else, and to elicit information about him from menials by lowering ourselves to the level of our inferiors, who will thereafter not forget to regard themselves as our equals. Whatever militates against frankness lowers the dignity of man. Insidious, underhand conduct uses means which strike at the roots of society because they make frankness impossible; it is far viler than violence; for against violence we can defend ourselves, and a violent man who spurns meanness can be tamed to goodness, but the mean rogue, who has not the courage to come out into the open with his roguery, is devoid of every vestige of nobility of character. For that reason a wife who attempts to poison her husband in England is burnt at the stake, for if such conduct spread, no man would be safe from his wife.

As I am not entitled to spy upon my neighbour, I am equally not entitled to point out his faults to him; and even if he should ask me to do so he would feel hurt if I complied. He knows his faults better than I, he knows that he has them, but he likes to believe that I have not noticed them, and if I tell him of them he realizes that I have. To say, therefore, that friends ought to point out each other's faults, is not sound advice. My friend may know better than I whether my gait or deportment is proper or not, but if I will only examine myself, who can know me better than I can know myself? To point out his faults to a friend is sheer impertinence; and once fault finding begins between friends their friendship will not last long. We must turn a blind eye to the faults of others, lest they conclude that they have lost our respect and we lose theirs. Only if placed in positions of authority over others should we point out to them their defects. Thus a husband is entitled to teach and correct his wife, but his corrections must be well-intentioned and kindly and must be dominated by respect, for if they be prompted only by displeasure they result in mere blame and bitterness. If we must blame, we must temper the blame with a sweetening of love, good-will, and respect. Nothing else will avail to bring about improvement.

NOTE

1. CF. *Babrii fabulae Aesopeae,* ed. O. Cousins, 1897, Fable 59, p. 54.

Is Business Bluffing Ethical?

ALBERT CARR

A respected businessman with whom I discussed the theme of this article remarked with some heat, "You mean to say you're going to encourage men to bluff? Why, bluffing is nothing more than a form of lying! You're advising them to lie!"

I agreed that the basis of private morality is a respect for truth and that the closer a businessman comes to the truth, the more he deserves respect. At the same time, I suggested that most bluffing in business might be regarded simply as game strategy—much like bluffing in poker, which does not reflect on the morality of the bluffer.

I quoted Henry Taylor, the British statesman who pointed out that "falsehood ceases to be falsehood when it is understood on all sides that the truth is not expected to be spoken"—an exact description of bluffing in poker, diplomacy, and business. I cited the analogy of the criminal court, where the criminal is not expected to tell the truth when he pleads "not guilty." Everyone from the judge down takes it for granted that the job of the defendant's attorney is to get his client off, not to reveal the truth; and this is considered ethical practice. I mentioned Representative Omar Burleson, the Democrat from Texas, who was quoted as saying, in regard to the ethics of Congress, "Ethics is a barrel of worms"[1]—a pungent summing up of the problem of deciding who is ethical in politics.

I reminded my friend that millions of businessmen feel constrained every day to say *yes* to their bosses when they secretly believe *no* and that this is generally accepted as permissible strategy when the alternative might be the loss of a job. The essential point, I said, is that the ethics of business are game ethics, different from the ethics of religion.

He remained unconvinced. Referring to the company of which he is president, he declared: "Maybe that's good enough for some businessmen, but I can tell you that we pride ourselves on our ethics. In 30 years not one customer has every questioned my word or asked to check our figures. We're loyal to our customers and fair to our suppliers. I regard my handshake on a deal as a contract. I've never entered into price-fixing schemes with my competitors. I've never allowed my salesmen to spread injurious rumors about other companies. Our union contract is the best in our industry. And, if I do say so myself, our ethical standards are of the highest!"

He really was saying, without realizing it, that he was living up to the ethical standards of the business game—which are a far cry from those of private life. Like a gentlemanly poker player, he did not play in cahoots with others at the table, try to smear their reputations, or hold back chips he owed them.

But this same fine man, at that very time, was allowing one of his products to be advertised in a way that made it sound a great deal better that it actually was. Another item in his product line was notorious among dealers for its "built-in obsolescence." He was holding back from the market a much-improved product because he did not want to interfere with sales of the inferior item it would have replaced. He had joined with certain of his competitors in hiring a lobbyist to push a state legislature, by methods that he preferred not to know too much about, into amending a bill then being enacted.

In his view these things had nothing to do with ethics; they were merely normal business practice. He himself undoubtedly avoided outright falsehoods—never lied in so many words. But the entire organization that he ruled was deeply involved in numerous strategies of deception.

PRESSURE TO DECEIVE

Most executives from time to time are almost compelled, in the interests of their companies or themselves, to practice some form of deception when negotiating with customers, dealers, labor unions, government officials, or even other departments of their companies. By conscious misstatements, concealment of pertinent facts, or exaggeration—in short, by bluffing—they seek to persuade others to agree with them. I think it is fair to say that if the individual executive refuses to bluff from time to time—if he feels obligated to tell the truth, the whole truth, and nothing but the truth—he is ignoring opportunities permitted under the rules and is at a heavy disadvantage in his business dealings.

But here and there a businessman is unable to reconcile himself to the bluff in which he plays a part. His conscience, perhaps spurred by religious idealism, troubles him. He feels guilty; he may develop an ulcer or a nervous tic. Before any executive can make profitable use of the strategy of the bluff, he needs to make sure that in bluffing he will not lose self-respect or become emotionally disturbed. If he is to reconcile personal integrity and high standards of honesty with the practical requirements of business, he must feel that his bluffs are ethically justified. The justification rests on the fact that business, as practiced by individuals as well as by corporations, has the impersonal character of a game—a game that demands both special strategy and an understanding of its special ethics.

The game is played at all levels of corporate life, from the highest to the lowest. At the very instant that a man decides to enter business, he may be forced into a game situation, as is shown by the recent experience of a Cornell honor graduate who applied for a job with a large company:

• This applicant was given a psychological test which included the statement, "Of the following magazines, check any that you have read either regularly or from time to time, and double-check those which interest you most. *Reader's Digest, Time, Fortune, Saturday Evening Post, The New Republic, Life, Look, Ramparts, Newsweek, Business Week, U.S. News & World Report, The Nation, Playboy, Esquire, Harper's, Sports Illustrated.*"

His tastes in reading were broad, and at one time or another he had read almost all of these magazines. He was a subscriber to *The New Republic,* an enthusiast for *Ramparts,* and an avid student of the pictures in *Playboy.* He was not sure whether his interest in *Playboy* would be held against him, but he had a shrewd suspicion that if he confessed to an interest in *Ramparts* and *The New Republic,* he would be thought a liberal, a radical, or at least an intellectual, and his chances of getting the job, which he needed, would greatly diminish. He therefore checked five of the more conservative magazines. Apparently it was a sound decision, for he got the job.

He had made a game player's decision, consistent with business ethics.

A similar case is that of a magazine space salesman who, owing to a merger, suddenly found himself out of a job:

• This man was 58, and, in spite of a good record, his chances of getting a job elsewhere in a business where youth is favored in hiring practice was not good. He was a vigorous, healthy man, and only a considerable amount of gray in his hair suggested his age. Before beginning his job search he touched up his hair with a black dye to confine the gray to his temples. He knew that the truth about his age might well come out in time, but he calculated that he could deal with that situation when it arose. He and his wife decided that he could easily pass for 45, and he so stated his age on his résumé.

This was a lie; yet within the accepted rules of the business game, no moral culpability attaches to it.

THE POKER ANALOGY

We can learn a good deal about the nature of business by comparing it with poker. While both have a large element of chance, in the long run the winner is the man who plays with steady skill. In both games ultimate victory requires intimate knowledge of the rules, insight into the psychology of the other players, a bold front, a considerable amount of self-discipline, and the ability to respond swiftly and effectively to opportunities provided by chance.

No one expects poker to be played on the ethical principles preached in churches. In poker it is right and proper to bluff a friend out of the rewards of being dealt a good hand. A player feels no more than a slight twinge of sympathy, if that, when—with nothing better than a single ace in his hand—he strips a heavy loser, who holds a pair, of the rest of his chips. It was up to the other fellow to protect himself. In the words of an excellent poker player, former President Harry Truman, "If you can't stand the heat, stay out of the kitchen." If one shows mercy to a loser in poker, it is a personal gesture, divorced from the rules of the game.

Poker has its special ethics, and here I am not referring to rules against cheating. The man who keeps an ace up his sleeve or who marks the cards is more than unethical; he is a crook, and can be punished as such—kicked out of the game or, in the Old West, shot.

In contrast to the cheat, the unethical poker player is one who, while abiding by the letter of the rules, finds ways to put the other players at an unfair disadvantage. Perhaps he unnerves them with loud talk. Or he tries to get them drunk. Or he plays in cahoots with someone else at the table. Ethical poker players frown on such tactics.

Poker's own brand of ethics is different from the ethical ideals of civilized human relationships. The game calls for distrust of the other fellow. It ignores the claim of friendship. Cunning deception and concealment of one's strength and intentions, not kindness and openheartedness, are vital in poker. No one thinks any the worse of poker on that account. And no one should think any the worse of the game of business because its standards of right and wrong differ from the prevailing traditions of morality in our society. . . .

WE DON'T MAKE THE LAWS

Wherever we turn in business, we can perceive the sharp distinction between its ethical standards and those of the churches. Newspapers abound with sensational stories growing out of this distinction:

- We read one day that Senator Philip A. Hart of Michigan has attacked food processors for deceptive packaging of numerous products.[2]
- The next day there is a Congressional to-do over Ralph Nader's book, *Unsafe At Any Speed,* which demonstrates that automobile companies for years have neglected the safety of car-owning families.[3]
- Then another Senator, Lee Metcalf of Montana, and journalist Vic Reinemer show in their book, *Overcharge,* the methods by which utility companies elude regulating government bodies to extract unduly large payments from users of electricity.[4]

These are merely dramatic instances of a prevailing condition; there is hardly a major industry at which a similar attack could not be aimed. Critics of business regard such behavior as unethical, but the companies concerned know that they are merely playing the business game.

Among the most respected of our business institutions are the insurance companies. A group of insurance executives meeting recently in New England was startled when their guest speaker, social critic Daniel Patrick Moynihan, roundly berated them for "unethical" practices. They had been guilty, Moynihan alleged, of using outdated actuarial tables to obtain unfairly high premiums. They habitually delayed the hearings of lawsuits against them in order to tire out the plaintiffs and win cheap settlements. In their employment policies they used ingenious devices to discriminate against certain minority groups.[5]

It was difficult for the audience to deny the validity of these charges. But these men were business game players. Their reaction to Moynihan's attack was much the same as that of the automobile manufacturers to Nader, of the utilities to Senator Metcalf, and of the food processors to Senator Hart. If the laws governing their business change, or if public opinion becomes clamorous, they will make the necessary adjustments. But morally they have in their view done nothing wrong. As long as they comply with the letter of the law, they are within their rights to operate their businesses as they see fit.

The small business is in the same position as the great corporation in this respect. For example:

- In 1967 a key manufacturer was accused of providing master keys for automobiles to mail-order customers, although it was obvious that some of the purchasers might be automobile thieves. His defense was plain and straightforward. If there was nothing in the law to prevent him from selling his keys to anyone who ordered them, it was not up to him to inquire as to his customers' motives. Why was it any worse, he insisted, for him to sell car keys by mail, than for mail-order houses to sell guns that might be used for murder? Until the law was changed, the key manufacturer could regard himself as being just as ethical as any other businessman by the rules of the business game.[6]

Violations of the ethical ideals of society are common in business, but they are not necessarily violations of business practices. Each year the Federal Trade Commission orders hundreds of companies, many of them of the first magnitude, to "cease and desist" from practices which, judged by ordinary standards, are of questionable morality but which are stoutly defended by the companies concerned.

In one case, a firm manufacturing a well-known mouthwash was accused of using a cheap form of alcohol possibly deleterious to health. The company's chief executive, after testifying in Washington, made this comment privately:

> We broke no law. We're in a highly competitive industry. If we're going to stay in business, we have to look for profit wherever the law permits. We don't make the laws. We obey them. Then why do we have to put up with this 'holier than thou' talk about ethics? It's sheer hypocrisy. We're not in business to promote ethics. Look at the cigarette companies, for God's sake! If the ethics aren't embodied in the laws by the men who made them, you can't expect businessmen to fill the lack. Why, a sudden submission to Christian ethics by businessmen would bring about the greatest economic upheaval in history!

It may be noted that the government failed to prove its case against him.

LAST ILLUSIONS ASIDE

Talk about ethics by businessmen is often a thin decorative coating over the hard realities of the game:

• Once I listened to a speech by a young executive who pointed to a new industry code as proof that his company and its competitors were deeply aware of their responsibilities to society. It was a code of ethics, he said. The industry was going to police itself, to dissuade constituent companies from wrongdoing. His eyes shone with conviction and enthusiasm.

The same day there was a meeting in a hotel room where the industry's top executives met with the "czar" who was to administer the new code, a man of high repute. No one who was present could doubt their common attitude. In their eyes the code was designed primarily to forestall a move by the federal government to impose stern restrictions on the industry. They felt that the code would hamper them a good deal less than new federal laws would. It was, in other words, conceived as a protection for the industry, not for the public.

The young executive accepted the surface explanation of the code; these leaders, all experienced game players, did not deceive themselves for a moment about its purpose.

The illusion that business can afford to be guided by ethics as conceived in private life is often fostered by speeches and articles containing such phrases as, "It pays to be ethical," or, "Sound ethics is good business." Actually this is not an ethical position at all; it a self-serving calculation in disguise. The speaker is really saying that in the long run a company can make more money if it does not antagonize competitors, suppliers, employees, and customers by squeezing them too hard. He is saying that oversharp policies reduce ultimate gains. That is true, but it has nothing to do with ethics. The underlying attitude is much like that in the familiar story of the shopkeeper who finds an extra $20 bill in the cash register, debates with himself the ethical problem—should he tell his partner?—and finally decides to share the money because the gesture will give him an edge over the s.o.b. the next time they quarrel.

I think it is fair to sum up the prevailing attitude of businessmen on ethics as follows:

We live in what is probably the most competitive of the world's civilized societies. Our customs encourage a high degree of aggression in the individual's striving for success. Business is our main area of competition, and it has been ritualized into a game of strategy. The basic rules of the game have been set by the government, which attempts to detect and punish business frauds. But as long as a company does not transgress the rules of the game set by law, it has the legal right to shape its strategy without reference to anything but its profits. If it takes a long-term view of its profits, it will preserve amicable relations, so far as possible, with those with whom it deals. A wise businessman will not seek advantage to the point where he generates dangerous hostility among employees, competitors, customers, government, or the public at large. But decisions in this area are, in the final test, decisions of strategy, not of ethics.

. . . If a man plans to make a seat in the business game, he owes it to himself to master the principles by which the game is played, including its special ethical outlook. He can then hardly fail to recognize that an occasional bluff may well be justified in terms of the game's ethics and warranted in terms of economic necessity. Once he clears his mind on this point, he is in a good position to match his strategy against that of the other players. He can then determine objectively whether a bluff in a given situation has a good chance of succeeding and can decide when and how to bluff, without a feeling of ethical transgression.

To be a winner, a man must play to win. This does not mean that he must be ruthless, cruel, harsh, or treacherous. On the contrary, the better his reputation for integrity, honesty, and decency, the better his chances of victory will be in the long run. But from time to time every businessman, like every poker player, is offered a choice between certain loss or bluffing within the legal rules of the game. If he is not resigned to losing, if he wants to rise in his company and industry, then in such a crisis he will bluff—and bluff hard.

Every now and then one meets a successful businessman who has conveniently forgotten the small or large deceptions that he practiced on his way to fortune. "God gave me my money," old John D. Rockefeller once piously told a Sunday school class. It would be a rare tycoon in our time who would risk the horse laugh with which such a remark would be greeted.

In the last third of the twentieth century even children are aware that if a man has become prosperous in business, he has sometimes departed from the strict truth in order to overcome obstacles or has practiced the more subtle deceptions of the half-truth or the misleading omission. Whatever the form of the bluff, it is an integral part of the game, and the executive who does not master its techniques is not likely to accumulate much money or power.

NOTES

1. *The New York Times,* March 9, 1967.
2. *The New York Times,* November 21, 1966.
3. New York, Grossman Publishers, Inc., 1965.
4. New York, David McKay Company, Inc., 1967.
5. *The New York Times,* January 17, 1967.
6. Cited by Ralph Nader in "Business Crime," *The New Republic,* July 1, 1967, p. 7.

Thesis: The responsibility of business is success + profit w/i the rules of the game.

Assumptions: Everyone who succeeds in business practices some deception

The Ethics of the institution of business are game-oriented and other than the ethics of the institution of the church.

Ethical problems:

(1) harm may result even if w/i the rules of the game — cf. Stone
(2) question of integrity for individuals
(3) Limits of the law
(4) Problem of dirty hands
(5) Distinction betw/ legal + moral
(6) Corporations do make the laws

PART II

Morality and Corporations

People eat, sleep, vote, love, hate, and suffer guilt. Corporations do none of these. Yet corporations are considered as "persons" under the law and have many of the same rights as humans: to sue, to own property, to conduct business and conclude contracts, freedom of the press, and freedom from unreasonable searches and seizures. Corporations are legal citizens of the state in which they are chartered. They even possess two rights not reserved for humans—unlimited longevity and limited liability. This means that corporations have unlimited charters—they never "die"—and that their shareholders are liable for corporate debts *only* up to the extent of their personal investment.

One of the most stubborn ethical issues surrounding the corporation is not what it should *do,* but how it should be *considered.* What is a corporation? Is it a distinct individual in its own right, or merely an aggregate of individuals, e.g., stockholders, managers, and employees? The answer to this question is crucial for understanding corporations and their activities. We must know, morally speaking, whether a corporation has responsibilities and rights *in addition to* the rights and responsibilities of the aggregate of individuals that make it up. We already know that individual members of a corporation can be held morally responsible. For example, if a chemical engineer intentionally puts a dangerous chemical in a new cosmetic product, he is morally blameworthy. But can we hold the corporation, considered as something distinct from its individual members, morally blameworthy?

On the one hand, the very concept of a corporation seems to involve more than the individual action of specific persons. The corporation is understood to exist even after all its original members are deceased; it is said to "hire" employees or fire them when only a handful of the corporate members are involved in the decision, and it is said to have obligations through its charter that override the desires of its individual members. But even granting that the corporation is a distinct entity such that its actions are not reducible—at least in a straightforward way—to the actions of individuals, does it follow that the corporation has *moral* characteristics that are not reducible to the moral characteristics of its members? Philosophers have addressed this issue by asking whether the corporation is a "moral agent." Rocks, trees, and machines clearly are *not* moral agents. People clearly *are.* What are we to say about corporations?

Whatever the answer to this question, a second immediately follows: namely, *"What should society expect from corporations?"*

The two questions are closely connected. For if we answer the first by concluding that the corporation *is* a moral agent, then we will formulate the second by asking "What is the nature of a corporation's **rights** and **obligations**?" If, on the other hand, we answer the first by denying that the corporation is a moral agent, and hence refuse to ascribe to it any rights or obligations, then we will formulate the second question by asking "What behavior should society expect from the individual persons that make up the corporation, i.e., those who hold its offices, perform its tasks, and construct its rules?" By phrasing the second question this way, we do not attribute moral agency to the corporation but treat it as a powerful, nonmoral entity.

Both the first and second questions have enormous practical and philosophical significance, for if corporations are true moral agents, then we should expect them to develop and manifest a sense of right and wrong, and to possess certain rights, privileges, and responsibilities. But if they are not moral agents, then we must proceed to determine what sorts of entities they really are, in order to discover how best to treat them and what to expect from them. For example, if it is determined that corporations are similar to large machines, then just as any large machine with the capacity to harm society, they must be externally controlled. According to this view we must abandon hope of their exercising genuine moral responsibility.

THE MORAL STATUS OF CORPORATIONS

When discussing whether corporations are moral agents, a good place to begin is with corporate legal history, that is, with the series of legislative acts and court decisions that have defined the corporation's existence. From its beginning in the Middle Ages, the corporation has been subject to differing legal interpretations depending on prevailing historical circumstances. In the Middle Ages, the law did not recognize profit-making ventures as corporations; instead, it granted corporate status only to guilds, boroughs, and the church. In some instances the law decreed that corporations follow strict guidelines; for example, in 1279 the French Statute of Mortmain declared that a corporation's property could not exceed a specified amount. Even hundreds of years after its beginning, the corporation remained subject to strict legal sanctions on the conditions of its charter. As late as the nineteenth century, some U.S. corporations were granted charters only on the condition that they restrict land purchases to a certain geographic location and to a maximum number of acres. Thus corporations were viewed merely as artificial beings, created by the state, and owing their very existence to a decree by the government.

But in the latter part of the nineteenth and the twentieth centuries, especially in the U.S., this view suffered a dramatic reversal. Instead of treating corporations as mere creations of the state, the courts began to see them as natural outcomes of the habits of businesspersons. It saw them as the predictable results of the actions of the businesspersons who, exercising their inalienable right to associate freely with others, gathered together to conduct business and pursue a profit. As such, incorporation came to be seen less as a privilege granted by the state and more as a right to be protected by the state. Chartering a corporation became easier, and government restrictions less severe. Even so, the traditional view of a corporation continues to influence the law. The most accepted legal definition of a corporation remains the one offered by Chief Justice Marshall in 1819: "A corporation," he wrote, "is an artificial being, invisible, intangible, and existing only in the contemplation of law. Being the mere creation of law, it possesses only those properties which the charter of its creation confers upon it. . . ."

Throughout the evolution of corporate law the problem of whether and how to ascribe responsibility to the corporation persisted. In the sixteenth century, the large trading corporations were not themselves held responsible when one ship collided with another; instead the individual boat owners—who participated in the corporation only in order to secure special trading rights—were held individually responsible. By the seventeenth century, the notion of "corporate" responsibility was thoroughly established in the law, but some sticky issues remained. Could a corporation be *criminally* liable? What *rights* if any did corporations share with ordinary persons? In the early twentieth century and again in recent years, U.S. corporations have been charged with homicide—one such case involved the Ford Pinto's exploding gas tank—but in every instance so far, although the court has been willing to impose stiff fines, it has stopped short of entering a guilty homicide verdict.

In 1978 the U.S. Supreme Court delivered a landmark verdict in the case of *First National Bank of Boston* v. *Bellotti,* a case involving the nature of rights granted to corporations. The court's decision is reprinted in this section. The fundamental issue raised is whether a corporation should be allowed the right to free speech even when exercising that right means spending corporate money to promote political causes not directly related to corporate profits. Should corporations have full-fledged first amendment rights to free speech even when that means that they can use their vast financial reserves to support partisan political ends? In a split decision, the Supreme Court decided in favor of recognizing such a right, although the decision itself remains controversial.

Whatever the courts eventually decide about the *legal* status of a corporation, questions about its *moral* status will remain. Two distinct and dramatically opposed moral views on this topic are presented in this section. The first, represented in the articles by contemporary philosophers, Peter French and Kenneth Goodpaster, holds that corporations are moral agents in the sense that they can be attributed moral responsibility more or less on a par with persons. The second, represented in the articles by the contemporary philosopher John Ladd and the organizational theorist Michael Keeley, takes a reverse stand. Ladd and Keeley argue, in different ways, that corporations are not "persons" at all—even of the fictional kind—and hence cannot truly be said to possess rights and responsibilities.

Professor French in his article, "The Corporation As A Moral Person," constructs an argument for corporate moral agency by relying on the nature of a corporation's "internal decision-making structure." Corporations have policies, rules, and decision-making procedures, all of which when considered together qualify them for the status of a moral agent. They can be praised or blamed for such decisions, and their decision-making capacity entails that they are "intentional beings" and have essentially the same responsibilities and rights as ordinary persons. Professor Keeley disagrees. In his article, "Corporations as Non-Persons," he finds it difficult to make sense of talk about corporate "intentions" and "responsibilities" in contrast to the intentions and responsibilities of individual persons in the corporation. Keeley also implies that it is difficult to talk intelligently about the corporation as a single collective entity.

John Ladd, in his well-known article, "Morality and the Ideal of Rationality in Formal Organizations," argues that a corporation is structured to achieve certain goals. But in contrast to French, Ladd argues that because of its structure, a corporation is bound to pursue its goals single-mindedly and cannot, by definition, take morality seriously. It is not consequently a *moral* agent at all, but more like a complicated machine. Kenneth Goodpaster, responding directly to this position, accepts Ladd's definition of a corporation as a goal-pursuing entity, but argues that a corporation is capable of moral responsibility as well, because people working inside the corporation ultimately have control over establishing corporate goals and the manner in which those goals are pursued.

THE MORAL RESPONSIBILITIES OF CORPORATIONS

The second section deals with the difficult issue of what we should hope for in terms of corporate behavior. Whether a corporation is a "moral agent" or not, it must adhere to certain norms of behavior: for example it must not murder or systematically harm others. But beyond specifying bare minimum conditions, what can one say? How can one determine acceptable and unacceptable behavior in corporations?

Thomas Donaldson confronts this question by analyzing the notion of a "social contract" between business and society. In much the same way that most Western democratic governments are justified in terms of a social contract between citizens and government, productive organizations, Donaldson argues, should be seen as participating in a "social contract" between themselves and society. He next spells out the obligations that society has to productive organizations, and, in turn, the obligations that productive organizations have to society.

In the final article in this section, "Developing the Corporate Ethic," the well-known business theorist, Clarence Walton, brings the issue of corporate responsibility down to a concrete level. Proposing what he describes as an ethic of "stewardship" for corporate managers, Walton discusses specific areas in which ethics can be implemented by individual corporate managers.

THE MORAL STATUS OF CORPORATIONS

First National Bank of Boston v. Bellotti

(DECIDED APRIL 26, 1978; U.S. SUPREME COURT)*

National Banking associations and business corporations brought action to challenge the constitutionality of a Massachusetts criminal statute that prohibited them and other business corporations from making contributions or expenditures to influence the outcome of a vote on any question submitted to voters other than questions materially affecting the property, business or assets of the corporation. The case was submitted to a single justice of the Supreme Judicial Court of Massachusetts. Judgment was reserved and the case referred to the full court which upheld the constitutionality of the statute. The corporations appealed, and the Supreme Court, Mr. Justice Powell, held that: ... there was no support in the Constitution for the proposition that expression of views on issues of public importance loses First Amendment protection simply because its source is a corporation that cannot prove that the issues materially affect the corporation's business.

Mr. Justice POWELL delivered the opinion of the Court.

In sustaining a state criminal statute that forbids certain expenditures by banks and business corporations for the purpose of influencing the vote on referendum proposals, the Massachusetts Supreme Judicial Court held that the First Amendment rights of a corporation are limited to issues that materially affect its business, property, or assets. The court rejected appellants' claim that the statute abridges freedom of speech in violation of the First and Fourteenth Amendments. We now reverse.

I

The statute at issue, Mass. Gen. Laws Ann., ch. 55, § 8 (West Supp. 1977), prohibits appellants, two national banking associations and three business corporations, from making contributions or expenditures "for the purpose of ... influencing or affecting the vote on any question submitted to the voters, other than one materially affecting any of the property, business or

*435 U.S. 705 (1978)

assets of the corporation." The statute further specifies that "[n]o question submitted to the voters solely concerning the taxation of the income, property or transactions of individuals shall be deemed materially to affect the property, business or assets of the corporation." A corporation that violates § 8 may receive a maximum fine of $50,000; a corporate officer, director, or agent who violates the section may receive a maximum fine of $10,000 or imprisonment for up to one year, or both.

* * *

[2] The [lower] court framed the principal question in this case as whether and to what extent corporations have First Amendment rights. We believe that the court posed the wrong question. The Constitution often protects interests broader than those of the party seeking their vindication. The First Amendment, in particular, serves significant societal interests. The proper question therefore is not whether corporations "have" First Amendment rights and, if so, whether they are coextensive with those of natural persons. Instead, the question must be whether § 8 abridges expression that the First Amendment was meant to protect. We hold that it does.

A

The speech proposed by appellants is at the heart of the First Amendment's protection.

> "The freedom of speech and of the press guaranteed by the Constitution embraces at the least the liberty to discuss publicly and truthfully all matters of public concern without previous restraint or fear of subsequent punishment . . . Freedom of discussion, if it would fulfill its historic function in this nation, must embrace all issues about which information is needed or appropriate to enable the members of society to cope with the exigencies of their period." Thornhill *v.* Alabama, 310 U.S. 88, 101–102, 60 S.Ct. 736, 744, 84 L.Ed. 1093 (1940).

* * *

[3] As the Court said in Mills *v.* Alabama, 384 U.S. 214, 218, 86 S.Ct. 1434, 1437, 16 L.Ed.2d 484 (1966), "there is practically universal agreement that a major purpose of [the First] Amendment was to protect the free discussion of governmental affairs." If the speakers here were not corporations, no one would suggest that the State could silence their proposed speech. It is the type of speech indispensable to decisionmaking in a democracy, and this is no less true because the speech comes from a corporation rather than an individual. The inherent worth of the speech in terms of its capacity for informing the public does not depend upon the identity of its source, whether corporation, association, union, or individual.

The [lower] court nevertheless held that corporate speech is protected by the First Amendment only when it pertains directly to the corporation's business interests. In deciding whether this novel and restrictive gloss on the First Amendment comports with the Constitution and the precedents of this Court, we need not survey the outer boundaries of the Amendment's protection of corporate speech, or address the abstract question whether corporations have the full measure of rights that individuals enjoy under the First Amendment. The question in this case, simply put, is whether the corporate identity of the speaker deprives this proposed speech of what otherwise would be its clear entitlement to protection. We turn now to that question.

B

[4–6] The [lower] court found confirmation of the legislature's definition of the scope of a corporation's First Amendment rights in the language of the Fourteenth Amendment. Noting that the First Amendment is applicable to the States through the Fourteenth, and seizing upon the observation that corporations "cannot claim for themselves the liberty which the Fourteenth Amendment guarantees," Pierce *v.* Society of Sisters, 268 U.S. 510, 535, 45 S.Ct. 571, 573, 69 L.Ed. 1070 (1925), the court concluded that a corporation's First Amendment rights must derive from its property rights under the Fourteenth.

[7] This is an artificial mode of analysis, untenable under decisions of this Court.

> "In a series of decisions beginning with Gitlow *v.* New York, 268 U.S. 652, 45 S.Ct. 625, 69 L.Ed. 1138 (1925), this Court held that the liberty of speech and of the press which the First Amendment guarantees against abridgment by the federal government is within the *liberty* safeguarded by the Due Process Clause of the Fourteenth Amendment from invasion by state action. That principle has been followed and reaffirmed to the present day." . . .

Freedom of speech and the other freedoms encompassed by the First Amendment always have been viewed as fundamental components of the liberty safeguarded by the Due Process Clause . . .

* * *

Similarly, the Court's decisions involving corporations in the business of communication or entertainment are based not only on the role of the First Amendment in fostering individual self-expression but also on its role in affording the public access to discussion, debate, and the dissemination of information and ideas . . .

* * *

[10, 11] We thus find no support in the First or Fourteenth Amendment, or in the decisions of this Court, for the proposition that speech that otherwise would be within the protection of the First Amendment loses that protection simply because its source is a corporation that cannot prove, to the satisfaction of a court, a material effect on its business or property. The

"materially affecting" requirement is not an identification of the boundaries of corporate speech etched by the Constitution itself. Rather, it amounts to an impermissible legislative prohibition of speech based on the identity of the interests that spokesmen may represent in public debate over controversial issues and a requirement that the speaker have a sufficiently great interest in the subject to justify communication.

* * *

[12, 13] . . . If a legislature may direct business corporations to "stick to business," it also may limit other corporations—religious, charitable, or civic—to their respective "business" when addressing the public. Such power in government to channel the expression of views is unacceptable under the First Amendment. Especially where, as here, the legislature's suppression of speech suggests an attempt to give one side of a debatable public question an advantage in expressing its views to the people, the First Amendment is plainly offended. . . .

In short, the First Amendment does not "belong" to any definable category of persons or entities: It belongs to all who exercise its freedoms.

Mr. Justice WHITE, with whom Mr. Justice BRENNAN and Mr. Justice MARSHALL join, dissenting.

The Massachusetts statute challenged here forbids the use of corporate funds to publish views about referenda issues having no material effect on the business, property, or assets of the corporation. The legislative judgment that the personal income tax issue, which is the subject of the referendum out of which this case arose, has no such effect was sustained by the Supreme Judicial Court of Massachusetts and is not disapproved by this Court today. Hence, as this case comes to us, the issue is whether a State may prevent corporate management from using the corporate treasury to propagate views having no connection with the corporate business. The Court commendably enough squarely faces the issue but unfortunately errs in deciding it. The Court invalidates the Massachusetts statute and holds that the First Amendment guarantees corporate managers the right to use not only their personal funds, but also those of the corporation, to circulate fact and opinion irrelevant to the business placed in their charge and necessarily representing their own personal or collective views about political and social questions. I do not suggest for a moment that the First Amendment requires a State to forbid such use of corporate funds, but I do strongly disagree that the First Amendment forbids state interference with managerial decisions of this kind.

By holding that Massachusetts may not prohibit corporate expenditures or contributions made in connection with referenda involving issues having no material connection with the corporate business, the Court not only invalidates a statute which has been on the books in one form or another for many years, but also casts considerable doubt upon the constitutionality of legislation passed by some 31 States restricting corporate political activity, as well as upon the Federal Corrupt Practices Act.

There is now little doubt that corporate communications come within the scope of the First Amendment. This, however, is merely the starting point of analysis. . . . Indeed, what some have considered to be the principal function of the First Amendment, the use of communication as a means of self-expression, self-realization, and self-fulfillment, is not at all furthered by corporate speech. It is clear that the communications of profitmaking corporations are not "an integral part of the development of ideas, of mental exploration and of the affirmation of self." They do not represent a manifestation of individual freedom or choice. Undoubtedly, as this Court has recognized, see NAACP *v.* Button, 371 U.S. 415, 83 S.Ct. 328, 9 L.Ed.2d 405 (1963), there are some corporations formed for the express purpose of advancing certain ideological causes shared by all their members, or, as in the case of the press, of disseminating information and ideas. Under such circumstances, association in a corporate form may be viewed as merely a means of achieving effective self-expression. But this is hardly the case generally with corporations operated for the purpose of making profits. Shareholders in such entities do not share a common set of political or social views, and they certainly have not invested their money for the purpose of advancing political or social causes or in an enterprise engaged in the business of disseminating news and opinion. In fact, as discussed *infra,* the government has a strong interest in assuring that investment decisions are not predicated upon agreement or disagreement with the activities of corporations in the political arena.

Of course, it may be assumed that corporate investors are united by a desire to make money, for the value of their investment to increase. Since even communications which have no purpose other than that of enriching the communicator have some First Amendment protection, activities such as advertising and other communications integrally related to the operation of the corporation's business may be viewed as a means of furthering the desires of individual shareholders. This unanimity of purpose breaks down, however, when corporations make expenditures or undertake activities designed to influence the opinion or votes of the general public on political and social issues that have no material connection with or effect upon their business, property, or assets. Although it is arguable that corporations make such expenditures because their managers believe that it is in the corporations' economic interest to do so, there is no basis whatsoever for concluding that these views are expressive of the heterogeneous beliefs of their shareholders whose convictions on many political issues are undoubtedly shaped by considerations other than a desire to endorse any electoral or ideological cause which would tend to increase the value of a particular corporate investment. This is particularly true where, as in this case, whatever the belief of the corporate managers may be, they have not been able to demonstrate that the issue involved has any material connection with the corporate business. Thus when a profitmaking corporation contributes to a political candidate this does not further the self-expression or self-fulfillment of its shareholders in the way that expenditures from them as individuals would.

The self-expression of the communicator is not the only value encompassed by the First Amendment. One of its functions, often referred to as the right to hear or receive information, is to protect the interchange of ideas. Any communication of ideas, and consequently any expenditure of funds which makes the communication of ideas possible, it can be argued, furthers the purposes of the First Amendment. This proposition does not establish, however, that the right of the general public to receive communications financed by means of corporate expenditures is of the same dimension as that to hear other forms of expression. . . .

* * *

I recognize that there may be certain communications undertaken by corporations which could not be restricted without impinging seriously upon the right to receive information. In the absence of advertising and similar promotional activities, for example, the ability of consumers to obtain information relating to products manufactured by corporations would be significantly impeded. There is also a need for employees, customers, and shareholders of corporations to be able to receive communications about matters relating to the functioning of corporations. Such communications are clearly desired by all investors and may well be viewed as an associational form of self-expression.

* * *

The governmental interest in regulating corporate political communications, especially those relating to electoral matters, also raises considerations which differ significantly from those governing the regulation of individual speech. Corporations are artificial entities created by law for the purpose of furthering certain economic goals. In order to facilitate the achievement of such ends, special rules relating to such matters as limited liability, perpetual life, and the accumulation, distribution, and taxation of assets are normally applied to them. States have provided corporations with such attributes in order to increase their economic viability and thus strengthen the economy generally. It has long been recognized however, that the special status of corporations has placed them in a position to control vast amounts of economic power which may, if not regulated, dominate not only the economy but also the very heart of our democracy, the electoral process . . .

* * *

This Nation has for many years recognized the need for measures designed to prevent corporate domination of the political process. The Corrupt Practices Act, first enacted in 1907, has consistently barred corporate contributions in connection with federal elections. This Court has repeatedly recognized that one of the principal purposes of this prohibition is "to avoid the deleterious influences on federal elections resulting from the use of money by those who exercise control over large aggregations of capital." . . .

The Corporation as a Moral Person

PETER A. FRENCH

In one of his *New York Times* columns of not too long ago Tom Wicker's ire was aroused by a Gulf Oil Corporation advertisement that "pointed the finger of blame" for the energy crisis at all elements of our society (and supposedly away from the oil company). Wicker attacked Gulf Oil as the major, if not the sole, perpetrator of that crisis and virtually every other social ill, with the possible exception of venereal disease. It does not matter whether Wicker was serious or sarcastic in making his charges (I suspect he was in deadly earnest). I am interested in the sense ascriptions of moral responsibility make when their subjects are corporations. I hope to provide the foundation of a theory that allows treatment of corporations as members of the moral community, of equal standing with the traditionally acknowledged residents: biological human beings, and hence treats Wicker-type responsibility ascriptions as unexceptionable instances of a perfectly proper sort without having to paraphrase them. In short, corporations can be full-fledged moral persons and have whatever privileges, rights and duties as are, in the normal course of affairs, accorded to moral persons.

It is important to distinguish three quite different notions of what constitutes personhood that are entangled in our tradition: the metaphysical, moral and legal concepts. The entanglement is clearly evident in Locke's account of personal identity. He writes that the term "person" is "a *forensic* term, appropriating actions and their merit; and so belongs only to *intelligent agents*, capable of law, and happiness, and misery."[1] He goes on to say that by consciousness and memory persons are capable of extending themselves into the past and thereby become "concerned and *accountable*."[2] Locke is historically correct in citing the law as a primary origin of the term "person." But he is incorrect in maintaining that its legal usage somehow entails its metaphysical sense, agency; and whether or not either sense, but especially the metaphysical, is interdependent on the moral sense, accountability, is surely controversial. Regarding the relationship between metaphysical and moral persons there are two distinct schools of thought. According to one, to be a metaphysical person is to be a moral one; to understand what it is to be accountable one must understand what it is to be an intelligent or a rational agent and vice-versa; while according to the other, being an agent is a necessary but not sufficient condition of being a moral person. Locke holds the interdependence view with which I agree, but he roots both moral and metaphysical persons in the juristic person, which is, I think, wrongheaded. The preponderance of current thinking tends to some version of the necessary pre-condition view, but it does have the virtue of treating the legal person as something apart.

Peter A. French, "The Corporation as a Moral Person," *American Philosophical Quarterly*, 3 (1979), pp. 207–15. Reprinted with permission.

It is of note that many contemporary moral philosophers and economists both take a pre-condition view of the relationship between the metaphysical and moral person and also adopt a particular view of the legal personhood of corporations that effectually excludes corporations *per se* from the class of moral persons. Such philosophers and economists champion the least defensible of a number of possible interpretations of the juristic personhood of corporations, but their doing so allows them to systematically sidestep the question of whether corporations can meet the conditions of metaphysical personhood.[3]

* * *

Many philosophers, including, I think, Rawls have rather uncritically relied upon what they incorrectly perceive to be the most defensible juristic treatment of collectivities such as corporations as a paradigm for the treatment of corporations in their moral theories. The concept of corporate legal personhood under any of its popular interpretations is, I want to argue, virtually useless for moral purposes.

Following many writers on jurisprudence, a juristic person may be defined as any entity that is a subject of a right. There are good etymological grounds for such an inclusive neutral definition. The Latin "*persona*" originally referred to *dramatis personae*, and in Roman law the term was adopted to refer to anything that could act on either side of a legal dispute. [It was not until Boethius' definition of a person: "*Persona est naturae rationabilis individua substantia* (a person is the individual subsistence of a rational nature)" that metaphysical traits were ascribed to persons.] In effect, in Roman legal tradition persons are creations, artifacts, of the law itself, i.e., of the legislature that enacts the law, and are not considered to have, or only have incidentally, existence of any kind outside of the legal sphere. The law, on the Roman interpretation, is systematically ignorant of the biological status of its subjects.

The Roman notion applied to corporations is popularly known as the Fiction Theory. . . .

* * *

The Fiction Theory's major rival in American jurisprudence and the view that does seem to inform Rawls' account is what I shall call "the Legal Aggregate Theory of the Corporation." It holds that the names of corporate bodies are only umbrellas that cover (but do not shield) certain biological persons. The Aggregate Theory treats biological status as having legal priority and corporate existence as a contrivance for purposes of summary reference. (Generally, it may be worth mention, Aggregate Theorists tend to ignore employees and identify corporations with directors, executives and stockholders. The model on which they stake their claim is no doubt that of the primitive partnership.) I have shown elsewhere[4] that to treat a corporation as an aggregate for any purposes is to fail to recognize the key logical differences between corporations and mobs. The Aggregate Theory, then, despite the fact that it has been quite popular in legislatures, courtrooms, and on streetcorners, simply ignores key logical, socio-economic and historical facts of corporate existence. It might prove of some value in clarifying the dispute between Fiction and Aggregate theorists to mention a rather famous case in the English law. (The case is cited by Hallis.) It is that of *Continental Tyre and Rubber Co., Ltd.* vs *Daimler Co. Ltd.* Very sketchily, the Continental Tyre company was incorporated in England and carried on its business there. Its business was the selling of tires made in Germany, and all of its directors were German subjects in residence in Germany, and all but one of its shares were held by German subjects. The case arose during the First World War, and it turned on the issue of whether the company was an English subject by virtue of its being incorporated under the English law and independent of its directors and stockholders, and could hence bring suit in an English court against an English subject while a state of war existed. The majority opinion of The Court of Appeals (5–1) was that the corporation was an entity created by statute and hence was "a different person altogether from the subscribers to the memorandum or the shareholders on the register."[5]

* * *

Underlying all of these interpretations of corporate legal personhood is a distinction, embedded in the law itself, that renders them unhelpful for our purposes. Being a subject of rights is often contrasted in the law with being an "administrator of rights." Any number of entities and associations can and have been the subjects of legal rights. Legislatures have given rights to unborn human beings, they have reserved rights for human beings long after their death, and in some recent cases they have invested rights in generations of the future.[6] Of course such subjects of rights, though they are legal persons, cannot dispose of their rights, cannot administer them, because to administer a right one must be an agent, i.e., able to act in certain ways. It may be only an historical accident that most legal cases are cases in which "the subject of right *X*" and "the administrator of right *X*" are co-referential. It is nowhere required by law, under any of the three above theories or elsewhere, that it be so. Yet, it is possession of the attributes of an administrator of rights and not those of a subject of rights that are among the generally regarded conditions of moral personhood. It is a fundamental mistake to regard the fact of juristic corporate personhood as having settled the question of the moral personhood of a corporation one way or the other.

Two helpful lessons however, are learned from an investigation of the legal personhood of corporations: (1) biological existence is not essentially associated with the concept of a person (only the fallacious Aggregate Theory depends upon reduction to biological referents) and (2) a paradigm for the form of an inclusive neutral definition of a moral person is provided: "a subject of a right." I shall define a moral person as the referent of any proper name or description that can be a non-eliminatable subject of what I shall call (and presently discuss) a responsibility ascription of the second type. The non-eliminatable nature of the subject should be stressed because responsibility and other moral predicates are neutral as regards person and *personum* predication.[7] Though we might say that The Ox-Bow mob should be held responsible for the death of three men, a mob is an example of what I have elsewhere called an aggregate collectivity with no identity over and above that of the sum of the identities of its component membership, and hence to use "The Ox-Bow mob" as the subject of such ascriptions is to make summary reference to each member of the mob. For that reason mobs do not qualify as metaphysical or moral persons.

There are at least two significantly different types of responsibility ascriptions that should be distinguished in ordinary usage (not counting the laudatory recommendation, "He is a responsible lad.") The first-type pins responsibility on someone or something, the who-dun-it or what-dun-it sense. Austin has pointed out that it is usually used when an event or action is thought by the speaker to be untoward. (Perhaps we are most interested in the failures rather than the successes that punctuate our lives.)

The second-type of responsibility ascription, parasitic upon the first, involves the notion of accountability. "Having a responsibility" is interwoven with the notion "Having a liability to answer," and having such a liability or obligation seems to imply (as Anscombe has noted[8]) the existence of some sort of authority relationship either between people or between people and a deity or in some weaker versions between people and social norms. The kernel of insight that I find intuitively compelling, is that for someone

to legitimately hold someone else responsible for some event there must exist or have existed a responsibility relationship between them such that in regard to the event in question the latter was answerable to the former. In other words, "X is responsible for y," as a second-type ascription, is properly uttered by someone Z if X in respect to y is or was accountable to Z. Responsibility relationships are created in a multitude of ways, e.g., through promises, contracts, compacts, hirings, assignments, appointments, by agreeing to enter a Rawlsian original position, etc. The right to hold responsible is often delegatable to third parties; though in the case of moral responsiblility no delegation occurs because no person is excluded from the relationship: moral responsibility relationships hold reciprocally and without prior agreements among all moral persons. No special arrangement needs to be established between parties for anyone to hold someone morally responsible for his acts or, what amounts to the same thing, every person is a party to a responsibility relationship with all other persons as regards the doing or refraining from doing of certain acts: those that take descriptions that use moral notions.

Because our interest is in the criteria of moral personhood and not the content of morality we need not pursue this idea further. What I have maintained is that moral responsibility, although it is neither contractual nor optional, is not a class apart but an extension of ordinary, garden-variety, responsibility. What is needed in regard to the present subject then is an account of the requirements for entry into any responsibility relationship, and we have already seen that the notion of the juristic person does not provide a sufficient account. For example, the deceased in a probate case cannot be held responsible in the relevant way by anyone, even though the deceased is a juristic person, a subject of rights.

A responsibility ascription of the second type amounts to the assertion of a conjunctive proposition, the first conjunct of which identifies the subject's actions with or as the cause of an event (usually an untoward one) and the second conjunct asserts that the action in question was intended by the subject or that the event was the direct result of an intentional act of the subject. In addition to what it asserts it implies that the subject is accountable to the speaker (in the case at hand) because of the subject's relationship to the speaker (who the speaker is or what the speaker is, a member of the "moral community," a surrogate for that aggregate). The primary focus of responsibility ascriptions of the second type is on the subject's intentions rather than, though not to the exclusion of, occasions. Austin wrote: "In considering responsibility, few things are considered more important than to establish whether a man *intended* to do A, or whether he did A intentionally."[9] To be the subject of a responsibility ascription of the second type, to be a party in responsibility relationships, hence to be a moral person, the subject must be at minimum, what I shall call a Davidsonian agent.[10] If corporations are moral persons, they will be non-eliminatable Davidsonian agents.

For a corporation to be treated as a Davidsonian agent it must be the case that some things that happen, some events, are describable in a way that makes certain sentences true, sentences that say that some of the things a corporation does were intended by the corporation itself. That is not accomplished if attributing intentions to a corporation is only a shorthand way of attributing intentions to the biological persons who comprise e.g. its board of directors. If that were to turn out to be the case then on metaphysical if not logical grounds there would be no way to distinguish between corporations and mobs. I shall argue, however, that a *C*orporation's *I*nternal *D*ecision Structure (its CID Structure) is the requisite redescription device that licenses the predication of corporate intentionality.

* * *

Certain events, that is, actions, are describable as simply the bodily movements of human beings and sometimes those same events are redescribable in terms of their upshots, as bringing about something, e.g., (from Austin[11]) feeding penguins *by* throwing them peanuts ("by" is the most common way we connect different descriptions of the same event[12]), and sometimes those events can be redescribed as the effects of some prior cause; then they are described as done for reasons, done in order to bring about something, e.g., feeding the penguins peanuts in order to kill them. Usually what we single out as that prior cause is some desire or felt need combined with the belief that the object of the desire will be achieved by the action undertaken. (This, I think, is what Aristotle meant when he maintained that acting requires desire.) Saying "someone (X) did y intentionally" is to describe an event (y) as the upshot of X's having had a reason for doing it which was the cause of his doing it.

It is obvious that a corporation's doing something involves or includes human beings doing things and that the human beings who occupy various positions in a corporation usually can be described as having reasons for *their* behavior. In virtue of those descriptions they may be properly held responsible for their behavior, *ceteris paribus.* What needs to be shown is that there is sense in saying that corporations and not just the people who work in them, have reasons for doing what they do. Typically, we will be told that it is the directors, or the managers, etc., that really have the corporate reasons and desires, etc., and that although corporate actions may not be reducible without remainder, corporate intentions are always reducible to human intentions.

Every corporation has an internal decision structure. CID Structures have two elements of interest to us here: (1) an organizational or responsibility flow chart that delineates stations and levels within the corporate power structure and (2) corporate decision recognition rule(s) (usually embedded in something called "corporation policy"). The CID Structure is the personnel organization for the exercise of the corporation's power with respect to its ventures, and as such its primary function is to draw experience from various levels of the corporation into a decision-making and ratification process. When operative and properly activated, the CID Structure accomplishes a subordination and synthesis of the intentions and acts of various biological persons into a corporate decision. When viewed in another way, as already suggested, the CID Structure licenses the descriptive transformation of events, seen under another aspect as the acts of biological persons (those who occupy various stations on the organizational chart), to corporate acts by exposing the corporate character of those events. A functioning CID Structure *incorporates* acts of biological persons. For illustrative purposes, suppose we imagine that an event E has at least two aspects, that is, can be described in two non-identical ways. One of those aspects is "Executive *X*'s doing *y*" and one is "Corporation *C*'s doing *z.*" The corporate act and the individual act may have different properties; indeed they have different causal ancestors though they are causally inseparable. (The causal inseparability of these acts I hope to show is a product of the CID Structure, *X*'s doing *y* is not the cause of *C*'s doing *z* nor is *C*'s doing *z* the cause of *X*'s doing *y* although if *X*'s doing *y* causes event *F* then *C*'s doing *z* causes *F* and *vice versa.*)

* * *

Suppose, for illustrative purposes, we activate a CID Structure in a corporation, Wicker's favorite, the Gulf Oil Corporation. Imagine that three executives *X, Y* and *Z* have the task of deciding whether or not Gulf Oil will join a world uranium cartel. *X, Y* and *Z* have before them an Everest of papers that have been prepared by lower echelon executives. Some of the papers will be purely factual reports, some will be contingency plans, some will be formulations of positions developed by various departments, some will outline financial considerations, some will be legal opinions and so on. In so far as these will all have been processed through Gulf's CID Structure system, the personal reasons, if any, individual executives may have had when writing their reports and recommendations in a specific way will have been diluted by the subordination of individual inputs to peer group input even before *X, Y* and *Z* review the matter. *X, Y* and *Z* take a vote. Their taking of a vote is authorized procedure in the Gulf CID Structure, which is to say that under these circumstances the vote of *X, Y* and *Z* can be redescribed as the corporation's making a decision: that is, the event "*XYZ* voting" may be redescribed to expose an aspect otherwise unrevealed, that is quite different from its other aspects e.g., from *X*'s voting in the affirmative. Redescriptive exposure of a procedurally corporate aspect of an event, however, is not to be confused with a description of an event that makes true a sentence that says that the corporation did something intentionally. But the CID Structure, as already suggested, also provides the grounds in its other type of recognitor for such an attribution of corporate intentionality. Simply, when the corporate act is consistent with an instantiation or an implementation of established corporate policy, then it is proper to describe it as having been done for corporate reasons, as having been caused by a corporate desire coupled with a corporate belief and so, in other words, as corporate-intentional.

An event may, under one of its aspects, be described as the conjunctive act "*X* did *a* (or as *X* intentionally did *a*) & *Y* did *a* (or as *Y* intentionally did *a*) & *Z* did *a* (or as *Z* Intentionally did *a*)" (where *a* = voted in the affirmative on the question of Gulf Oil joining the cartel). Given the Gulf CID Structure, formulated in this instance as the conjunction of rules: when the occupants of positions *A, B* and *C* on the organizational chart unanimously vote to do something and if doing that something is consistent with an instantiation or an implementation of general corporate policy and *ceteris paribus,* then the corporation has decided to do it for corporate reasons, the event is redescribable as "the Gulf Oil Corporation did *j* for corporate reasons *f.*" (where *j* is "decided to join the cartel" and *f* is any reason (desire + belief) consistent with basic policy of Gulf Oil, e.g., increasing profits) or simply as "Gulf Oil Corporation intentionally did *j.*" This is a rather technical way of saying that in these circumstances the executives voting is, given its CID Structure, also the corporation deciding to do something, and that regardless of the personal reasons the executives have for voting as they do and even if their reasons are inconsistent with established corporate policy or even if one of them has no reason at all for voting as he does, the corporation still has reasons for joining the cartel; that is, joining is consistent with the inviolate corporate general policies as encrusted in the precedent of previous corporate actions and its statements of purpose as recorded in its certificate of incorporation, annual reports, etc. The corporation's only method of achieving its desires or goals is the activation of the personnel who occupy its various positions. However, if *X* voted affirmatively purely for reasons of personal monetary gain (suppose he had been bribed to do so) that does not alter the fact that the corporate reason for joining the cartel was to minimize competition and hence pay higher dividends to its shareholders. Corporations have reasons because they have interest in doing those things that are likely to result in realization of their established corporate goals regardless of the transient self-interest of directors, managers, etc. If there is a difference between corporate goals and desires and those of human beings it is probably that the corporate ones are relatively stable and not very wide ranging, but that is only because corporations can do relatively fewer things than human beings, being confined in action predominately to a limited socio-economic sphere. The attribution of corporate intentionality is opaque with respect to other possible descriptions of the event in question. It is, of course, in a corporation's interest that its component membership view the corporate purposes as instrumental in the achievement of their own goals. (Financial reward is the most common way this is achieved.)

It will be objected that a corporation's policies reflect only the current goals of its directors. But that is certainly not logically necessary nor is it in practice true for most large corporations. Usually, of course, the original incorporators will have organized to further their individual interests and/or to meet goals which they shared. But even in infancy the melding of disparate interests and purposes gives rise to a corporate long range point of view that is distinct from the intents and purposes of the collection of incorporators viewed individually. Also, corporate basic purposes and policies, as already mentioned, tend to be relatively stable when compared to those of individuals and not couched in the kind of language that would be appropriate to individual purposes. Furthermore, as histories of corporations will show, when policies are amended or altered it is usually only peripheral issues that are involved. Radical policy alteration constitutes a new corporation, a point that is captured in the incorporation laws of such states as Delaware. ("Any power which is not enumerated in the charter and the general law or which cannot be inferred from these two sources is *ultra vires* of the corporation.") Obviously underlying the objection is an uneasiness about the fact that corporate intent is dependent upon policy and purpose that is but an artifact of the socio-psychology of a group of biological persons. Corporate intent seems somehow to be a tarnished illegitimate offspring of human intent. But this objection is another form of the anthropocentric bias. By concentrating on possible descriptions of events and by acknowledging only that the possibility of describing something as an agent depends upon whether or not it can be properly described as having done something (the description of some aspect of an event) for a reason, we avoid the temptation to look for extensional criteria that would necessitate reduction to human referents.

The CID Structure licenses redescriptions of events as corporate and attributions of corporate intentionality while it does not obscure the private acts of executives, directors etc. Although *X* voted to support the joining of the cartel because he was bribed to do so, *X* did not join the cartel, Gulf Oil Corporation joined the cartel. Consequently, we may say that *X* did something for which he should be held morally responsible, yet whether or not Gulf Oil Corporation should be held morally responsible for joining the cartel is a question that turns on issues that may be unrelated to *X*'s having accepted a bribe.

Of course Gulf Oil Corporation cannot join the cartel unless *X* or somebody who occupies position *A* on the organizational chart votes in the affirmative. What that shows, however, is that corporations are collectivities.

That should not, however, rule out the possibility of their having metaphysical status, as being Davidsonian agents, and being thereby full-fledged moral persons.

This much seems to me clear: we can describe many events in terms of certain physical movements of human beings and we also can sometimes describe those events as done for reasons by those human beings, but further we can sometimes describe those events as corporate and still further as done for corporate reasons that are qualitatively different from whatever personal reasons, if any, component members may have for doing what they do.

Corporate agency resides in the possibility of CID Structure licensed redescription of events as corporate-intentional. That may still appear to be downright mysterious, although I do not think it is, for human agency as I have suggested, resides in the possibility of description as well.

Although further elaboration is needed, I hope I have said enough to make plausible the view that we have good reasons to acknowledge the noneliminatable agency of corporations. I have maintained that Davidsonian agency is a necessary and sufficient condition of moral personhood. I cannot further argue that position here (I have done so elsewhere). On the basis of the foregoing analysis, however, I think that grounds have been provided for holding corporations *per se* to account for what they do, for treating them as metaphysical persons *qua* moral persons.

NOTES

1. John Locke, *An Essay Concerning Human Understanding* (1960), Bk. II, Ch. XXVII.
2. Ibid.
3. For a particularly flagrant example see: Michael Jensen and William Meckling, "Theory of the Firm: Managerial Behavior, Agency Costs and Ownership Structure," *Journal of Financial Economics,* vol. 3 (1976), pp. 305–360. On p. 311 they write, "The private corporation or firm is simply one form of legal fiction which serves as a nexus for contracting relationships . . ."
4. "Types of Collectivities and Blame," *The Personalist,* vol. 56 (1975), pp. 160–69, and in the first chapter of my *Foundations of Corporate Responsibility* (forthcoming).
5. "Continental Tyre and Rubber Co., Ltd. vs. Daimler Co., Ltd." (1915), K.B., p. 893.
6. And, of course, in earlier times animals have been given legal rights.
7. See Gerald Massey, "Tom, Dick, and Harry, and All The King's Men," *American Philosophical Quarterly,* vol. 13 (1976), pp. 89–108.
8. G. E. M. Anscombe, "Modern Moral Philosophy," *Philosophy,* vol. 33 (1958), pp. 1–19.
9. J. L. Austin, "Three Ways of Spilling Ink" in *Philosophical Papers* (Oxford, 1970), p. 273.
10. See for example Donald Davidson, "Agency," in *Agent, Action, and Reason,* ed. by Binkley, Bronaugh, and Marras (Toronto, 1971).
11. Austin, p. 275.
12. See Joel Feinberg, *Doing and Deserving* (Princeton, 1970), p. 134f.

Organizations as Non-Persons

MICHAEL KEELEY

As an organizational theorist who looks to philosophers for help on moral questions, I would like to point out an unhelpful development in moral philosophy. This is the suggestion that organizations be considered moral persons for the purpose of analyzing their social responsibilities. The moral-person approach has been advanced, for instance, in recent articles by Peter French and David Ozar,[1] who assume they are building a case for increased corporate accountability. Such a case is curious. Given our sociological heritage, organizational theorists have long viewed corporations as sorts of persons, but this viewpoint has lately been questioned—in part, because of its unattractive social implications.[2] It is now interesting to find out that organizational personhood was not the cause of, but was the solution to, corporate accountability problems all along. I will focus here on the logic of attributing personality to organizations and subsequently comment on the moral disadvantages of this practice.[3]

The practice of ascribing moral agency to corporations has been attacked by others. Both John Ladd and Patricia Werhane, for example, contend that corporations are more like machines than persons or organisms;[4] that is, they are impersonal arrangements for the efficient attainment of particular goals, and moral action contrary to their own ends is simply irrational from an organizational viewpoint. Such arguments are not very convincing, for they grant to organizations the very sort of property around which a theory of moral agency can be built—namely, the property of intentionality. A stronger argument against the moral-person view might be made by showing that organizations have no intentions or goals at all. This will be attempted here.

French's article illustrates the type of mystical move involved in granting organizations status as moral persons. French plausibly argues that to be considered moral persons, organizations must be established as metaphysical, and not simply legal, persons. This, in turn, requires showing that an organization can "intend" its own actions. What is mystical, of course, is the invention of *organizational* intentions, which transform the interaction of individuals into a social being. Organizational theorists have for some time attempted to give a satisfactory account of collective intentions or goals, without clear success.[5] Their failures are relevant to the case for organizational personhood.

To clarify the main issue, it is useful to distinguish three concepts: goals *for* an organization, goals *of* an organization, and consequences *of* an organization. Goals *for* an organization are preferences of people for organizational outcomes (states of affairs brought about through organized behavior). Goals *of* an organization are outcomes intended by the organization itself. Consequences *of* an organization are any outcomes of joint behavior.

Michael Keeley, "Organizations as Non-Persons," *Journal of Value Inquiry,* 15 (1981), pp. 149–55, printed by permission of Martinus Nijhoff Publishers B. V. The Hague, The Netherlands.

Now, it may be possible to identify the first by questioning organizational participants, and it may be possible to identify the third by observing their behavior. But it is not apparent that the second—goals *of* an organization, which are supposed in the social-person view—can be identified by any means. If, in fact, truly *organizational* goals or intentions defy identification, there is not much point pretending that they exist or that organizations resemble persons in any significant way.

At one time, organizational theorists regarded goal identification as unproblematic. Goals were to be found in official documents and the pronouncements of organizational representatives—for instance, in charters, annual reports, and public statements by executives. Such "official goals" are now, however, generally seen to be misleading.[6] They are often put forth to secure societal approval or the commitment of particular participants,[7] and they do not necessarily reflect the true character of organizational operations. Some official goal statements may be harmlessly mythical, incorporating ideals like "Progress is our most important product." Others may be more sinister, for example one touting rehabilitation in a prison which devotes no resources to this purpose. Some corporate reports propose a few modest goals of management. Others claim the organization is fulfilling the dreams of virtually every inhabitant of the globe. In any event, such reports are disputable. Regardless of their scope or authors, goal statements by organizational participants basically describe participants' goals *for* an organization (not necessarily the authors'). More evidence is required that a stated goal is really a goal *of* the organization than the fact that some participants say so.

The usual solution posed to the problem of differentiating goals *of* from goals *for* an organization is to look at actual organizational activities and infer from these what "real" or "operative" goals they support.[8] Along these lines both French and Ladd suggest that one can inspect organizational procedures, which are considered analogous to rules of a game, and derive from these *organizational* intentions. In fact, one cannot. Two different problems are often confused in analyzing organizational activities. The first is to distinguish organizational behavior from non-organizational behavior. The second is to isolate the organizational intent of organizational behavior. A look at operational procedures may help us over the first hurdle, but not the second. Suppose that we observe the actions of organizational participants; we may see a wide variety of regular and occasional performances. Some of these performances we wish to call organizational—e.g., the preparation and transmission of a report to a supervisor. Some we wish to call non-organizational or personal—e.g., a phone call to a spouse regarding dinner plans. We must have a way of distinguishing the two if we are to mark off the organization as a unit of analysis. In many cases (not all) we can make such a distinction by reference to organizational rules or procedures, as reflected in organizational charts, job descriptions, manufacturing specifications, commonly respected customs, and the like. However, while operational procedures may serve to identify organizational behavior, they do not ordinarily establish the organizational *intent* of that behavior or that it has any real organizational intent at all.

To illustrate: consider the game analogy employed by Ladd and

French. If we know the rules of play (i.e., organizational procedures), we can often specify which actions count in the game (i.e., organizational behavior). And usually we can infer from these rules how various participants intend the game to turn out (i.e., goals *for* the organization). But rules of the game do not reveal what the game *itself intends.* In fact, it makes little sense to say that the game itself intends anything. The illogic of inferring organizational intentions from game-like properties is revealed in Ladd's suggestion that the goal of an organization is inherent in its activities, much the same way as the goal of checkmating the king is inherent in the rules of chess.[9] The analogy does not appear to support Ladd's or French's point that organizations have goals of their own. The goal of checkmating in chess is certainly not something *the game* tries or intends to accomplish. Nor is it a shared goal that the participants work together to achieve. Rather, checkmating the black king is a goal for one participant, checkmating the white king the goal of another, and both work toward their separate purposes within the context of mutually agreeable rules. So too in organizations, operative procedures or rules of the game may not themselves entail genuinely organizational goals.

It might be said that I have carried the game analogy too far, that organizational participants do ordinarily cooperate to accomplish common, organizational goals, rather than competitive, personal goals as in chess. French, for instance, contends that in corporations the diverse goals of participants are melded into a long-range, corporate purpose that is distinct from the intentions of participating individuals.[10] In making this claim, French relies heavily on a popular, sociological point: organizations are somehow "more than" aggregates of individuals; they can, in a sense, *act* as coordinated entities. Corporate officers, for example, may commit their firms to courses of action like joining a cartel, which can be described as actions of the corporation and not simply of individuals. This is possibly accurate, but French goes too far in accusing us of "anthropocentric bias" if we do not further grant that such action entails corporate *intent.* He does not show that an alternative, anthropomorphic view of organizational behavior is warranted.

It seems fairly clear that organizations have some collective properties of their own. It is not clear, however, that intentionality is among them. To illustrate: organizations, as systems of human interaction, produce events or consequences that are attributable to the organization—e.g., profits. Consequences of an organization are "more than" the aggregate effects of individual behavior; they are true collective properties in that they occur because of the way people act together and not just because of the type of people who are acting. In other words, though the motives of people influence their behavior, their actual joint behavior (an organization) has consequences independent of their motives. Thus, one might describe the joint production of events or consequences, when individuals act in conformance with organizational procedures, as acts of the organization. From the fact that an organization can so act, in the sense of *producing* an effect, it is a large leap to the claim that it can act in the sense of *intending* an effect. To establish the latter, one must be able to distinguish consequences intended by an organization—goals *of* the organization—from other consequences. This does not seem possible, without resorting to the intentions of participating individuals.

Consider the case of a corporation. Consequences of the organization might include profits, deficits, goods, services, salaries, growth, pollutants, job-induced injuries, racial discrimination, etc. While all may be produced by organizational acts (i.e., behavior consistent with organizational rules or procedures), we usually want to call only some of these "organizational goals." Some others we may want to call "costs" of goal attainment—expenses of rather than reasons for action. But which are goals and which are costs? Unfortunately, operational procedures alone are generally ambiguous in this regard. Certain participants and observers, for instance, may see a manufacturing operation as a profit generator, whose costs include salaries. Others may see this operation as a salary generator, whose costs include profits. Now, *the organization* cannot tell us which is correct. Each position, of course, might be partly correct in that profits and salaries both may be goals. Yet, there is ordinarily no organizational criterion by which to resolve such disputes. As a system of action, an organization appears unable to *itself* prefer one consequence over another (including its own survival). And, so, goal identification appears to depend upon human preferences. What we commonly call "organizational goals" are those potential consequences of organizational behavior which are goals *for* at least some participating individuals—perhaps profits, salaries, and products, but not pollutants or injuries. Neither French nor Ladd nor any organizational theorist, to my knowledge, has offered a criterion for distinguishing organizational goals from a larger set of organizational consequences that is independent of *participant* intentions.

In short, consequences *of* and goals *for* an organization are generally identifiable, while independent goals *of* an organization are not. In order to derive organizational goals from organizational activities, one must assume the former to begin with. This is essentially what French does. His rules of the game, by which organizational behavior is distinguished, turn out to be more than bare descriptions of procedure. They include, for example, "established corporate policy," which involves "statements of purpose as recorded in its certificate of incorporation, annual reports, etc."[11] Actions in line with these are supposedly intended by the corporation. And we are back to square one: official goals, which are simply goals *for* an organization.

As mentioned earlier, official goal statements may be narrow or comprehensive. But, in any case, it is deceptive, I think, to call goals *for* an organization, goals *of* an organization. The latter connotes a certain unanimity that is not usually evident in complex organizations. In small, cohesive groups with few external dependencies, the same goals *for* an organization may be intended by all participants. Yet, such cases are of limited interest. In larger organizations, such as major corporations, goals *for* the organization are diverse and conflicting. And it is frequently important to keep track of *whose* goals one is speaking of—goals *for* shareholders, employees, customers, etc. The collective goal notion over-simplifies organizational analysis.

If one cannot point out the collective analog of individual intent, organizations are strange-looking persons. They don't look much like metaphysical persons, and they don't look much like moral persons. This does not mean, however, that one cannot make moral judgments about organizations. It is still logical, for instance, to argue that, as *social systems* if not persons, organization X is preferable to organization Y on moral grounds. Reconsider the game analogy. While it is odd to ask whether a game is itself behaving responsibly, it is reasonable to ask whether it is fair, right or the like. Possibly one could say that a potentially violent game such as hockey, to the extent that it entails penalties for injurious acts such as tripping, slashing, and fighting, is morally preferable to a similar game which entails no penalties, but allows the participants to inflict unlimited injury on one another to further their own cause. So again in the case of organizations, those which minimize injurious consequences to participants might be preferable on moral grounds.[12] And various sorts of, say governmental, policies may be morally justified in promoting the minimization of aversive organizational consequences.

The image of organization implied here is along lines of a Lockean "trust": organizations are nexes of power and resources that exist to promote the welfare of participating individuals, who have overwhelming claims against the organization. In contrast, the moral-person approach, while assigning responsibilities to organizations, at the same time assigns them inordinate rights to pursue *organizational* welfare. The related image of a Hobbesian Leviathan looms in Peter Drucker's remarks, quoted by French: "[the corporation] must subordinate individual ambitions and decisions to the *needs* of the corporation's welfare and survival."[13] Such subordination is unattractive, but typical in organizational theories incorporating a social-person view. And I think philosophers who try to tack on social responsibilites to this view will justify less corporate accountability than many others would accept. For example, Ozar derives from his moral-person approach the implication that corporations may be excused from moral responsibility under conditions similar to those constituting excuses for persons—if decision makers cannot anticipate the injurious consequences of organizational behavior, if loss of control over organizational processes creates damage, and so forth.[14] One does not have to be a rabid nuclear antagonist to object that significant corporate responsibilities may be trivialized by granting organizations the privilege of such personalized defenses. In sum, the danger of the moral-person approach is that we may give away too much in the way of corporate rights to gain too little in the way of corporate accountability.

NOTES

1. Peter A. French, "The Corporation as a Moral Person," *American Philosophical Quarterly,* 16 (1979):207–15; David T. Ozar, "The Moral Responsibility of Corporations," in Thomas Donaldson and Patricia H. Werhane (eds.), *Ethical Issues in Business* (Englewood Cliffs, NJ: Prentice-Hall, 1979), pp. 294–300.

2. See Michael Keeley, "Organizational Analogy: A Comparison of Organismic and Social Contact Models," *Administrative Science Quarterly,* 25 (1980):337–62.
3. Accountability problems arise with respect to other organized collectivities besides corporations. My remarks will pertain to organizations in general, unless otherwise specified.
4. John Ladd, "Morality and the Ideal of Rationality in Formal Organizations," *The Monist,* 54 (1970): 448–516; Patricia H. Werhane, "Formal Organizations, Economic Freedom and Moral Agency," *Journal of Value Inquiry,* 14 (1980):43–50.
5. See Petro Georgiou, "The Goal Paradigm and Notes Toward a Counter Paradigm," *Administrative Science Quarterly,* 18 (1973): 291–310; Michael Keeley, "A Social-Justice Approach to Organizational Evaluation," *Administrative Science Quarterly,* 23 (1978): 272–92.
6. See Charles Perrow, "The Analysis of Goals in Complex Organizations," *American Sociological Review,* 26 (1961): 854–66; Richard H. Hall, *Organizations,* 2nd ed. (Englewood Cliffs, NJ: Prentice-Hall, 1977), pp. 67–73.
7. As used throughout, "participant" is a broader concept than "member," denoting anyone who interacts in an organizational context. Thus, customers, shareholders, regulators, suppliers, etc., would be included in addition to employees and managers.
8. Hall, *Organizations,* pp. 71 ff.
9. Ladd, "Morality and the Ideal," p. 495.
10. French, "The Corporation," p. 214.
11. Ibid.
12. In this view, problems of organizational responsibility are largely cast as problems of allocating benefits and burdens among organizational participants, as in Keeley, "A Social-Justice Approach."
13. French, "The Corporation," p. 213.
14. Ozar, "The Moral Responsibility." pp. 297–98.

Morality and the Ideal of Rationality in Formal Organizations

JOHN LADD

I. INTRODUCTORY

The purpose of this paper is to explore some of the moral problems that arise out of the interrelationships between individuals and formal organizations (or bureaucracies) in our society. In particular, I shall be concerned with the moral implications of the so-called ideal of rationality of formal organizations with regard to, on the one hand, the obligations of individuals both inside and outside an organization to that organization and, on the

John Ladd, "Morality and the Ideal of Rationality in Formal Organizations," reprinted from the *Monist,* vol. 54, no. 4, with permission of the author and the publisher.

other hand, the moral responsibilities of organizations to individuals and to the public at large. I shall argue that certain facets of the organizational ideal are incompatible with the ordinary principles of morality and that the dilemma created by this incompatibility is one source of alienation in our contemporary, industrial society. The very conception of a formal organization or bureaucracy presents us with an ideological challenge that desperately needs to be met in some way or other.

The term "formal organization" will be used in a more or less technical sense to cover all sorts of bureaucracies, private and public. A distinctive mark of such organizations is that they make a clear-cut distinction between the acts and relationships of individuals in their official capacity within the organization and in their private capacity. Decisions of individual decision-makers in an organization are attributed to the organization and not to the individual. In that sense, they are impersonal. Individual office-holders are in principle replaceable by other individuals without affecting the continuity or identity of the organization. In this sense, it has sometimes been said that an organization is "immortal."

This kind of impersonality, in particular, the substitutability of individuals, is one way in which formal organizations differ from other kinds of social systems, e.g. the family, the community or the nation, which are collectivities that are dependent for their existence on specific individuals or groups of specific individuals and that change when they change. . . .

Social critics, e.g. W. H. Whyte, use phrases like the "smothering of the individual" to describe the contemporary situation created by organizations. It is not my purpose here to decry once more the unhappy condition of man occasioned by his submergence as an individual in the vast social, economic and political processes created by formal organizations. Instead, I shall try to show that the kind of alienation that we all feel and complain about is, at least in part, a logical necessity flowing from the concept of formal organizations itself, that is, it is a logical consequence of the particular language-game one is playing in organizational decision-making. My analysis is intended to be a logical analysis, but one that also has important ethical implications. . . .

Here we may find the concept of a language-game, as advanced by Wittgenstein and others, a useful tool of analysis. The point about a language-game is that it emphasizes the way language and action are interwoven: "I shall call the whole, consisting of language and the actions into which it is woven, the language-game."[1] A language-game is thus more than simply an abstract set of propositions constituting, say, a formal system. The game not only determines what should and what should not be done, but also sets forth the goals and the moves by which they are to be attained. More important even than these, a particular language-game determines how the activities within it are to be conceptualized, prescribed, justified and evaluated. Take as an example what is meant by a "good" move in chess: we have to refer to the rules of chess to determine what a "move" is, how to make one, what its consequences will be, what its objective is and whether or not it is a good move in the light of this objective.[2] Finally, this system of rules performs the logical function of defining the game itself. . . .

If we pursue the game-analogy one step further, we find that there may be even more striking similarities between the language-game of formal organizations and the language-game of other types of games. For instance, the rules and rationale obtaining in most typical games like chess and baseball tend to make the activity logically autonomous, i.e. the moves, defenses and evaluations are made independently of external considerations. In this sense they are self-contained. Furthermore, while playing a game it is thought to be "unfair" to challenge the rules. Sometimes it is even maintained that any questioning of the rules is unintelligible. In any case, there is a kind of sanctity attached to the rules of a game that renders them immune to criticism on the part of those engaged in playing the game. The resemblance of the autonomy of the activity and the immunity of the rules governing the game to the operations of bureaucracies can hardly be coincidental![3]

II. THE CONCEPTS OF SOCIAL DECISION AND SOCIAL ACTION

Let us take as our point of departure Herbert Simon's definition of a formal organization as a "decision-making structure."[4] The central concept with which we must deal is that of a decision (or action) that is attributable to the organization rather than to the individuals who are actually involved in the decisional process. The decision is regarded as the organization's decision even though it is made by certain individuals acting as its representatives. The latter make the decision only for and on behalf of the organization. Their role is, i.e. is supposed to be, impersonal. Such nonindividual decisions will be called *social decisions,* choices or actions. (I borrow the term "social choice" from Arrow, who uses it to refer to a choice made on behalf of a group as distinct from the aggregate of individual choices.)[5]

The officials of an organization are "envisaged as more or less ethically neutral . . . (and) the values to be taken as data are not those which would guide the individual if he were a private citizen. . . ."[6] When the official decides for the organization, his aim is (or should be) to implement the objectives of the organization *impersonally,* as it were. The decisions are made for the organization, with a view to its objectives and not on the basis of the personal interests or convictions of the individual official who makes the decision. This is the theory of organizational decision-making.

One might be tempted to call such organizational decisions "collective decisions," but that would be a misnomer if we take a collective decision to be a decision made by a collection of individuals. Social decisions are precisely decisions (or actions) that are to be *attributed* to the organizations themselves and not to collections of individuals. In practice, of course, the organizational decisions made by officials may actually be collective decisions. But in theory the two must be kept separate; for the "logic" of decisions attributed to organizations is critically different from the "logic" of collective decisions, i.e. those attributed to a collection of individuals.

Underlying the concept of social decisions (choices, actions) as outlined here is the notion that a person (or group of persons) can make decisions that are not his, i.e. are not attributable to him. He makes the decisions on behalf of someone else and with a view to the latter's interest.

not his own. In such cases, we ordinarily consider the person (or group) that acts to be a representative or agent of the person or thing he is acting for. . . .

Accordingly, a social decision, as intended here, would be an action performed by an official as actor but owned by the organization as author. For all the consequences of the decision so made are imputed to the organization and not to the individual decision-maker. The individual decision-making official is not personally bound by the agreements he makes for the organization, nor is he personally responsible for the results of these decisions.

The theory of social decision-making that we are considering becomes even clearer if we examine the theory of organizational authority with which it is conjoined. Formal organizations are hierarchical in structure, that is, they are organized along the principle that superiors issue commands to those below them. The superior exercises authority over the subordinates. . . .

In summary, then, the organizational order requires that its social decisions be attributed to the organization rather than to the individual decision-maker, the "decision is to be made nonpersonally from the point of view of its organization effect and its relation to the organizational purpose,"[7] and the officials, as its agents, are required to abdicate their choice in obedience to the impersonal organizational order.

We now turn to another essential facet of the organizational language-game, namely, that every formal organization must have a goal, or a set of goals. In fact, organizations are differentiated and defined by reference to their aims or goals, e.g. the aim of the Internal Revenue Service is to collect taxes. The goal of most business ventures is to maximize profits, etc. We may find it useful to distinguish between the real and stated goals of an organization. Thus, as Galbraith has pointed out, although the stated goal of large industrial organizations is the maximization of profits, that is a pure myth; their actual, operative goals are the securing of their own survival, autonomy and economic growth.[8] There may, indeed, be a struggle over the goals of an organization, e.g. a power play between officials.[9]

For our present purposes, we may consider the real goal of an organization to be that objective (or set of objectives) that is used as a basis for decision-making, i.e. for prescribing and justifying the actions and decisions of the organization itself, as distinct from the actions and decisions of individual persons within the organization. As such, then, the goal is an essential element in the language-game of a formal organization's activities in somewhat the same way as the goal of checkmating the king is an essential element in the game of chess. Indeed, formal organizations are often differentiated from other kinds of social organizations in that they are "deliberately constructed and reconstructed to seek specific goals."[10]

The logical function of the goal in the organizational language-game is to supply the value premises to be used in making decisions, justifying and evaluating them. "Decisions in private management, like decisions in public management, must take as their ethical premises the objectives that have been set for the organization."[11]

It follows that any considerations that are not related to the aims or goals of the organization are automatically excluded as irrelevant to the organizational decision-making process. This principle of the exclusion of the irrelevant is part of the language-game. It is a logical requirement of the process of prescribing, justifying and evaluating social decisions. Consequently, apart from purely legal considerations, decisions and actions of individual officers that are unrelated to the organization's aims or goals are construed, instead, as actions of those individuals rather than of the organization. If an individual official makes a mistake or does something that fails to satisfy this criterion of social decision, he will be said to have "exceeded his authority," and will probably be sacked or made a vice-president! Again, the point is a logical one, namely, that only those actions that are related to the goal of the organization are to be attributed to the organization; those actions that are inconsistent with it are attributed to the individual officers as individuals. The individual, rather than the organization, is then forced to take the blame for whatever evil results.

Thus, for example, a naval officer who runs his ship aground is court-martialed because what he did was inconsistent with the aims of the naval organization; the action is attributed to him rather than to the Navy. On the other hand, an officer who successfully bombards a village, killing all of its inhabitants, in accordance with the objectives of his organization, is performing a social action, an action that is attributable to the organization and not to him as an individual. Whether or not the organization should take responsibility in a particular case for the mistakes of its officials is a policy decision to be made in the light of the objectives of the organization.

In other words, the concept of a social decision or action is bound up logically with the notion of an organizational aim. The consequence of this co-implication of action and aim is that the notion of an action or decision taken by an organization that is not related to one of its aims makes no sense. It is an unintelligible notion within the language-game of formal organizations. Within that language-game such an action would be as difficult to understand as it would be to understand how a man's knocking over the pieces in a chess game can be part of playing chess.

We finally come to the concept of "rationality," the so-called "ideal of pure rationality."[12] From the preceding observations concerning the organizational language-game, it should be clear that the sole standard for the evaluation of an organization, its activities and its decisions, is its effectiveness in achieving its objectives—within the framework of existing conditions and available means. This kind of effectiveness is called "rationality." Thus, rationality is defined in terms of the category of means and ends. . . .

"Rationality," so construed, is relative, that is, to be rational means to be efficient in pursuing a desired goal, whatever that might be. In the case of organizations, "a decision is 'organizationally' rational if it is oriented to the organization's goals."[13] Rationality is consequently neutral as to "what goals are to be attained."[14] Or to be more accurate, "rationality" is an incomplete term that requires reference to a goal before it is completely intelligible. . . .

Let us return to the organizational language-game. It was observed that within that game the sole standard of evaluation of, e.g. a decision, is the "rational" one, namely, that it be effective in achieving the organization's goal. Hence, any considerations that are taken into account in deliberation about these social decisions and in the evaluation of them are relevant only if they are related to the attainment of the organization's objectives. Let us suppose that there are certain factual conditions that must be considered in arriving at a decision, e.g. the available means, costs, and conditions of feasibility. The determination of such conditions is presumably a matter of empirical knowledge and a subject for empirical investigation. Among these empirical conditions there is a special class that I shall call *limiting operating conditions.* These are conditions that set the upper limits to an organization's operations, e.g. the scarcity of resources, of equipment, of trained personnel, legal restrictions, factors involving employee morale. Such conditions must be taken into account as *data,* so to speak, in organizational decision-making and planning. In this respect information about them is on a par logically with other information utilized in decision-making, e.g. cost-benefit computations.

Now the only way that moral considerations could be relevant to the operations of a formal organization in the language-game that I have been describing is by becoming limiting operating conditions. Strictly speaking, they could not even be introduced as such, because morality is itself not a matter of empirical knowledge. Insofar as morality in the strict sense enters into practical reasoning it must do so as an "ethical" premise, not as an empirical one. Hence morality as such must be excluded as irrelevant in organizational decision-making—by the rules of the language-game. The situation is somewhat parallel to the language-game used in playing chess: moral considerations are not relevant to the decisions about what move to make there either.

Morality enters in only indirectly, namely, as moral opinion, what John Austin calls "positive morality."[15] Obviously the positive morality, laws and customs of the society in which the organization operates must be taken into account in decision-making and planning. The same thing goes for the religious beliefs and practices of the community. A decision-maker cannot ignore them, and it makes no difference whether he shares them or accepts them himself personally. But the determination of whether or not there are such limiting conditions set by positive morality, customs, law, and religion is an empirical matter. Whether there are such limitations is simply a matter of fact and their relevance to the decision-making is entirely dependent upon how they affect the efficiency of the organization's operations.

Social decisions, then, are not and cannot be governed by the principles of morality, or, if one wishes, they are governed by a different set of moral principles from those governing the conduct of individuals as individuals. For, as Simon says: "Decisions in private management, like decisions in public management, must take as their ethical premises the objectives that have been set for the organization."[16] By implication, they cannot take their ethical premises from the principles of morality.

Thus, for logical reasons it is improper to expect organizational conduct to conform to the ordinary principles of morality. We cannot and must not expect formal organizations, or their representatives acting in their official capacities, to be honest, courageous, considerate, sympathetic, or to have any kind of moral integrity. Such concepts are not in the vocabulary, so to speak, of the organizational language-game. (We do not find them in the vocabulary of chess either!) Actions that are wrong by ordinary moral standards are not so for organizations; indeed, they may often be required. Secrecy, espionage and deception do not make organizational action wrong; rather they are right, proper and, indeed, *rational,* if they serve the objectives of the organization. They are no more or no less wrong than, say, bluffing is in poker. From the point of view of organizational decision-making they are "ethically neutral."

Of course, I do not want to deny that it may be in the best interests of a formal organization to pay lip service to popular morality (and religion). That is a matter of public relations. But public relations operations themselves are evaluated and justified on the same basis as the other operations of the organization. The official function of the public relations officer is to facilitate the operations of the organization, not to promote morality. . . .

The upshot of our discussion so far is that actions are subject to two entirely different and, at times, incompatible standards: social decisions are subject to the standard of rational efficiency (utility) whereas the actions of individuals as such are subject to the ordinary standards of morality. An action that is right from the point of view of one of these standards may be wrong from the point of view of the other. Indeed, it is safe to say that our own experience attests to the fact that our actual expectations and social approvals are to a large extent based on a tacit acceptance of a double-standard—one for the individual when he is in his office working for the company and another for him when he is at home among friends and neighbors. Take as an example the matter of lying: nobody would think of condemning Joe X, a movie star, for lying on a TV commercial about what brand of cigarettes he smokes, for it is part of his job. On the other hand, if he were to do the same thing when he is at home among friends, we should consider his action to be improper and immoral. Or again, an individual who, acting in his official capacity, refuses help to a needy suppliant, would be roundly condemned if he were to adopt the same course of action in his private life.

III. THE MORAL RELATIONSHIP OF INDIVIDUALS TO ORGANIZATIONS

It follows from what has already been said that the standard governing an individual's relationship to an organization is likely to be different from the one governing the converse relationship, i.e. of an organization to individuals. The individual, for his part, is supposed to conduct himself in his relationship to an organization according to the same standards that he would employ in his personal relationships, i.e. the standards of ordinary morality. Thus, he is expected to be honest, open, respectful, conscientious, and loyal towards the organization of which he is a member or with which he has dealings. The organization, represented by its officials, can, however, be none of these in return. "Officials are expected to assume an impersonal orientation. . . . Clients are to be treated as cases . . . and subordinates are to be treated in a similar fashion."[17]

The question I now want to explore is whether or not the individual is justified in applying the standard of individual morality to his relations with formal organizations. It will, of course, generally be in the interest of the formal organizations themselves to encourage him to do so, e.g. to be honest, although the organization as such cannot "reciprocate." But we must ask this question from the point of view of the individual or, if you wish, from the moral point of view: what good moral reasons can be given for an individual to assume a moral stance in his conduct and relations with formal organizations, in contradistinction, say, to his conduct and relations with individuals who happen to be employees of such an organization?

The problem, which may be regarded as a question of loyalty and fidelity, puts the age-old problem of authority and obedience in a new light. Authority has become diffused, as I have already pointed out, and the problem of obedience can no longer be treated in terms of the personal relationship of an individual to his sovereign lord. The problem today is not so easily focused on one relationship; for the demands of authority, as represented in modern organizations, are at once more extensive, more pervasive and less personal. The question we face today is, for example, why should I, as an individual, comply with the mass of regulations laid down by an impersonal order, a bureaucratic organization? Why, for example, should I comply with draft-registration procedures? with passport regulations? with income-tax requirements? with mortage, credit, licensing, fair-trade regulations or with anti-trust laws? Or, indeed, has the individual any moral obligation at all to comply with them?[18]

It might be thought that, before trying to answer such questions, we must be careful to distinguish between individuals within an organization, e.g. officials and employees, and those outside it who have dealings with it, e.g. clients and the general public: what each of these classes ought to do is different. Granting that the specific demands placed on individuals in these various categories may be quite different, they all involve the question of authority in one way or another. Hence, for our purposes, the distinction is unimportant. For example, the authority, or the claims to it, of governmental bureaucracies extends far beyond those who are actually in their employ, e.g. the Internal Revenue Service. For convenience, I shall call those who come under the authority of an organization in some capacity or other, directly or indirectly, the *subjects* of the organization. Thus, we are all subjects of the IRS.

Can any moral reasons be given why individual subjects should comply with the decisions of organizations? Or, what amounts to the same thing, what is the basis of the authority of organizations by virtue of which we have an obligation to accept and obey their directives? And why, if at all, do we owe them loyalty and fidelity?

The most obvious answer, although perhaps not the most satisfactory one ethically, is that it is generally expedient for the individual to go along with what is required by formal organizations. If I want a new automobile,

I have to comply with the financing requirements. If I want to avoid being harassed by an internal revenue agent, I make out my income tax form properly. If I want to be legally married, I comply with the regulations of the Department of Public Health. In other words, I comply from practical necessity, that is, I act under a hypothetical imperative.

Still, this sort of answer is just as unsatisfactory from the point of view of moral philosophy as the same kind of answer always has been with regard to political obligation, namely, it fails to meet the challenge of the conscientious objector.

Furthermore, there are many occasions and even whole areas where self-interest is not immediately or obviously involved in which, nevertheless, it makes good sense to ask: why comply? The traditional Lockean argument that our acceptance of the benefits of part of the social and political order commits us morally to the acceptance and conformity with the rest of it rests on the dubious assumption that the social and political order is all of one piece, a seamless web. But when we apply the argument to formal organizations it becomes especially implausible, because there are so many competing claims and conflicting regulations, not to mention loyalties. Not only logically, but as a matter of practicality, it seems obvious that accepting the benefits of one bureaucratic procedure, e.g. mailing letters, does not, from the moral point of view, *eo ipso* bind us to accept and comply with all the other regulations and procedures laid down by the formal organization and, much less, those laid down by formal organizations in general. . . .

In sum, we cannot make compacts with organizations because the standard of conduct which requires that promises be honored is that of individual conduct.[19] It does not and cannot apply to formal organizations. This follows from the fact of a double standard. . . .

I have been able to touch only on some very limited aspects of the relationship of individuals to organizations. I hope, however, that it is now abundantly clear that some sort of crisis is taking place in our moral relationships, and in particular in our conceptions of authority, and that this crisis is due not only to complex historical, psychological and sociological factors, but also to an inherent *logical* paradox in the foundations of our social relations.

IV. THE MORAL RELATIONSHIP OF ORGANIZATIONS TO INDIVIDUALS

For logical reasons that have already been mentioned, formal organizations cannot assume a genuine moral posture towards individuals. Although the language-game of social decision permits actions to be attributed to organizations as such, rather than to the officials that actually make them, it does not contain concepts like "moral obligation," "moral responsibility," or "moral integrity." For the only relevant principles in rational decision-making are those relating to the objectives of the organization. Hence individual officers who make the decisions for and in the name of the organization, as its representatives, must decide solely by reference to the objectives of the organization.

According to the theory, then, the individuals who are officers of an organization, i.e. those who run it, operate simply as vehicles or instruments of the organization. The organizational language-game requires that they be treated as such. That is why, in principle at least, any individual is dispensable and replaceable by another. An individual is selected for a position, retained in it, or fired from it solely on the grounds of efficiency, i.e. of what will best serve the interests of the organization. The interests and needs of the individuals concerned, as individuals, must be considered only insofar as they establish limiting operating conditions. Organizational rationality dictates that these interests and needs must not be considered in their own right or on their own merits. If we think of an organization as a machine, it is easy to see why we cannot reasonably expect it to have any moral obligations to people or for them to have any to it.

For precisely the same reason, the rights and interests of persons outside the organization and of the general public are *eo ipso* ruled out as logically irrelevant to rational organizational decision, except insofar as these rights and interests set limiting conditions to the effectiveness of the organization's operations or insofar as the promoting of such rights and interests constitutes part of the goal of the organization. Hence it is fatuous to expect an industrial organization to go out of its way to avoid polluting the atmosphere or to refrain from making napalm bombs or to desist from wire-tapping on purely moral grounds. Such actions would be irrational.

It follows that the only way to make the rights and interests of individuals or of the people logically relevant to organizational decision-making is to convert them into pressures of one sort or another, e.g. to bring the pressure of the law or of public opinion to bear on the organizations. Such pressures would then be introduced into the rational decision-making as limiting operating conditions. . . .

Since, as I have argued in some detail, formal organizations are not moral persons, and have no moral responsibilities, they have no moral rights. In particular, they have no *moral* right to freedom or autonomy. There can be nothing morally wrong in exercising coercion against a formal organization as there would be in exercising it against an individual. Hence, the other side of the coin is that it would be irrational for us, as moral persons, to feel any moral scruples about what we do to organizations. (We should constantly bear in mind that the officials themselves, as individuals, must still be treated as moral persons with rights and responsibilities attached to them as individuals.) . . .

V. UTILITARIANISM AND ALIENATION

It is abundantly evident that the use of a double standard for the evaluation of actions is not confined to the operations of formal organizations, as I have described them. The double standard for social morality is pervasive in our society. For almost all our social decisions, administrative, political and economic, are made and justified by reference to the "rational" standard, which amounts to the principle that the end justifies the means; and yet as individuals, in our personal relations with one another, we are bound by the ordinary principles of morality, i.e. the principles of obligation, responsibility and integrity. . . .

A great deal more needs to be said about the effects of working from a double standard of morality. In our highly organized (and utilitarian) society, most of us, as individuals, are forced to live double lives, and in order to accommodate ourselves to two different and incompatible standards, we tend to compartmentalize our lives, as I have already pointed out. For the most part, however, the organizational (or utilitarian) standard tends to take over.

Accordingly, our actions as individuals are increasingly submerged into social actions, that is, we tend more and more to use the social standard as a basis for our decisions and to evaluate our actions. As a result, the individual's own decisions and actions become separated from himself as a person and become the decisions and actions of another, e.g. of an organization. They become social decisions, not decisions of the individual. And in becoming social decisions, they are, in Hobbes's terms, no longer "his," they are "owned" by another, e.g. an organization or society.

This is one way of rendering the Marxian concept of alienation. As his actions are turned into social decisions, the individual is alienated from them and is *eo ipso* alienated from other men and from morality. In adopting the administrator's point of view (or that of a utilitarian) and so losing his actions, the individual becomes dehumanized and demoralized. For morality is essentially a relation between men, as individuals, and in losing this relation, one loses morality itself.

VI. CLOSING REMARKS ON THE SOURCE OF THE PARADOX

It is unnecessary to dwell on the intolerable character of the moral schizophrenia in which we find ourselves as the result of the double standard of conduct that has been pointed out. The question is: what can be done about it? The simplest and most obvious solution is to jettison one of the conflicting standards. But which one? The choice is difficult, if not impossible. If we give up the standard of "rationality," e.g. of organizational operations, then we surrender one of the chief conditions of civilized life and progress as well as the hope of ever solving mankind's perennial practical problems, e.g. the problems of hunger, disease, ignorance and overpopulation. On the other hand, if we give up the standard of ordinary moral conduct, then in effect we destroy ourselves as moral beings and reduce our relationships to each other to purely mechanical and materialistic ones. To find a third way out of the dilemma is not only a practical, political and sociological necessity, but a moral one as well. . . .

NOTES

1. Ludwig Wittgenstein, *Philosophical Investigations* (New York: Macmillan Company, 1953), p. 7.
2. These rules are called "constitutive rules" by John Searle. See his *Speech Acts* (Cambridge: The University Press, 1969), Ch. 2, Sec. 5.
3. For further discussion of the game-model and this aspect of rules, see my "Moral and Legal Obligation," in J. Roland Pennock and John W. Chapman, editors, *Political and Legal Obligations, Nomos,* 12 (New York: Atherton Press, 1970).
4. Herbert A. Simon, *Administrative Behavior,* 2nd ed. (New York: Free Press, 1965), p. 9. Hereinafter cited as Simon, AB. For a useful survey of the subject of formal organizations, see Peter M. Blau and W. Richard Scott, *Formal Organizations* (San Francisco: Chandler Publishing Company, 1962). [p.36.] Hereinafter cited as Blau and Scott, FO.
5. See Kenneth Arrow, *Social Choice and Individual Values* (New York: John Wiley, 1951), *passim.*
6. Quoted from A. Bergson by Kenneth Arrow in "Public and Private Values," in *Human Values and Economic Policy,* ed. S. Hook (New York: New York University Press, 1967), p. 14.
7. Quoted from Chester I. Barnard in Simon, AB, p. 203.
8. See John Kenneth Galbraith, *The New Industrial State* (Boston: Houghton Mifflin, 1967), pp. 171–78. Hereinafter cited as NIS.
9. Amitai Etzioni, *Modern Organizations* (Englewood Cliffs, N.J.: Prentice-Hall, 1964), p. 4. Hereinafter cited as MO.
10. Etzioni, MO, p. 3. See also Blau and Scott, FO, p. 5. In a forthcoming article on "Community," I try to show that communities, as distinct from formal organizations, do not have specific goals. Indeed, the having of a specific goal may be what differentiates a *Gesellschaft* from a *Gemeinschaft* in Tönnies' sense. See Ferdinand Tönnies, *Community and Society,* trans. Charles P. Loomis (New York: Harper and Row, 1957), *passim.*
11. Simon, AB, p. 52.
12. "The ideal of pure rationality is basic to operations research and the modern management sciences." Yehezkel Dror, *Public Policymaking Reexamined* (San Francisco: Chandler Publishing Company, 1968), p. 336. Dror gives a useful bibliography of this subject on pp. 336–40.
13. Simon, AB, p. 77.
14. Simon, AB, p. 14.
15. "The name *morality,* when standing unqualified or alone, may signify the human laws which I style positive morality, without regard to their goodness or badness. For example, such laws of the class as are peculiar to a given age, or such laws of the class as are peculiar to a given nation, we style the morality of that given age or nation, whether we think them good or bad, etc." John Austin, *Province of Jurisprudence Determined,* ed. H. L. A. Hart (New York: Noonday Press, 1954), p. 125. The study of positive moralities belongs to what I call "descriptive ethics." See my *Structure of a Moral Code* (Cambridge, Mass: Harvard University Press, 1957).
16. Simon, AB, p. 52.
17. Blau and Scott, FO, p. 34.
18. See my "Moral and Legal Obligation," referred to in note [3].
19. The fact that promising involves an extremely personal relation between individuals is almost universally overlooked by philosophers who discuss promises.

Morality and Organizations

KENNETH GOODPASTER

In what follows, I propose to examine the applicability (and desirability of *rendering* applicable) such notions as 'virtue' and 'moral responsibility' to formal organizational agents (paradigmatically, business corporations and government agencies) in the face of certain conceptual barriers which have been thought to attend such a move. Motivation for such an inquiry stems from several sources. The last decade of American life has witnessed a deep intensification of concern about the quantity and quality of large-scale technological growth, in terms of both social and environmental impact. Clearly the vehicles of this growth have been corporate and bureaucratic agents whose presence in modern society is as ethically mysterious as it is pervasive. Ethics, as traditionally conceived, is a discipline which concentrates on the values and proprieties of individual conduct. That corporate conduct has in fact come to dominate the lives of individuals is only slowly beginning to occur to the moral philosophical community, together with an attendant imperative to accommodate this fact to ethical theory. One important stage in this accommodation process includes a shift in levels of agency (and consequently, moral responsibility or virtue) from the individual to the corporate or organizational decision-maker. On the face of it, what is demanded is a rather straightforward inversion of Plato's avowed methodology in the *Republic.* Instead of taking our cues from the macrocosmic or organizational level in the quest for a deeper understanding of virtue on the microcosmic or individual level, we seem to be faced with the task of searching for clarity about corporate moral responsibility through a close scrutiny of its necessary and sufficient conditions in the lives of ordinary human agents. This is, at least, the strategy that has suggested itself to more than one laborer in the vineyard of "technology and values" including the present writer.[1] Christopher D. Stone, in a recent and important book on law and the corporation has summarized the strategy nicely:

> If people are going to adopt the terminology of 'responsibility' (with its allied concepts of corporate conscience) to suggest new, improved ways of dealing with corporations, then they ought to go back and examine in detail what 'being responsible' entails—in the ordinary case of the responsible human being. Only after we have considered what being responsible calls for in general does it make sense to develop the notion of a corporation being responsible.[2]

Thus the picture which emerges sets a clear, if not widely appreciated and accepted, project: if certain current social and environmental problems are

Paper originally presented at the Bentley College Second National Conference on Business Ethics; reprinted in the *Proceedings of the Second National Conference on Business Ethics,* ed. Michael Hoffman (Waltham, Mass.: Center for Business Ethics, 1977); reprinted by permission of the editor and the author.

related to the conduct of large-scale technological agents, we need to provide both a descriptive-explanatory account of the ethical style of such agents as well as a normative account of what moral responsibility for such agents might amount to. I have elsewhere labeled this double-purpose enterprise "ethical diagnostics"—invoking both the descriptive-explanatory and the therapeutic suggestions of the medical metaphor.[3]

This project (with its strategy) has been challenged, however. Usually the challenge is implicit and subtle, as in the context I shall focus on presently. But sometimes it is overt. Quotations from corporate executives such as the following carry the message:

> The social responsibility of business is to make profits.
>
> The owners of each business enterprise should define the social responsibility of their enterprise as they see fit. This is the only way compatible with the rights of their owners.
>
> I can't believe that social responsibility was ever invented by a businessman; it must have been made up by a sociologist.[4]

The idea that corporate agents should be thought of in the categories of ethical theory at all is what seems to be at stake in these remarks. And the challenge which this provides to the project sketched above is apparent. What should be noted, however, is that though the challenge is significant, it is at least *manageable* in the sense that it represents a difference in viewpoint of a quasiethical sort (sometimes ethical disagreements are actually to be preferred to other sorts!). That is, the disagreement seems to turn on whether we *should* think of or treat organizational agents as morally responsible beings. And we can entertain arguments and counterarguments in an effort to resolve such a disagreement.

But there is a more subtle and deeply rooted challenge to the project to which I propose to devote most of my attention in this essay. It does not come from the business world, but from ethical theory and allied disciplines. And the issue appears *not* to be the *advisability* of construing organizational agents in ethical terms, but rather the very *intelligibility* of doing so. The sort of view I have in mind here is paradigmatically articulated by John Ladd in a penetrating article entitled "Morality and the Ideal of Rationality in Formal Organizations."[5] Ladd's thesis, if I read him correctly, is that there is a logical or conceptual barrier to the project of ethical diagnostics and its moral intent. According to Ladd, if one expects corporate or organizational agents

> . . . to conform to the principles of morality, he is simply committing a logical mistake, perhaps even what Ryle calls a category mistake. In a sense, . . . organizations are like machines, and it would be a category mistake to expect a machine to comply with the principles of morality. By the same token, an official or agent of a formal organization is simply violating the basic rules of organizational activity if he allows his moral scruples rather than the objectives of the organization to determine his decision.[6]

Ladd bases his contention in part on a rather uncompromising account of the ideal of rationality in formal organizations gleaned from organization theorists like Herbert Simon,[7] Chester Barnard,[8] and, more indirectly, Max Weber. Essentially, the picture is that of organizational decision-making involving

(A) Imputation of joint decisions to the organization;

(B) A set of constitutive goals in terms of which the organization is defined and its rationality is assessed; and

(C) The exclusiveness of a means-ends conception of rational decisions in the "language game" of the organization.

And one of the most significant results of the pervasiveness of this organizational standard, in Ladd's view, is a kind of moral schizophrenia which sets in upon participants (and recipients). For standards of moral responsibility are binding on individuals as individuals, whereas the corporate agents in which and toward which individuals operate are (logically) marching to the beat of a nonmoral drummer.

This last point needs expansion, for it contains by implication the other main part of Ladd's basis for his general contention. Besides the account of rationality in formal organizations, there is also an account of the nature of moral responsibility at work in Ladd's discussion which is broadly Kantian in character. Though it is not set out explicitly in the essay under discussion, the reader can piece it together in outline, at least as containing the following elements:

(A') Moral decisions are imputed to the individual agents who are their authors, not to (or from) something else;

(B') Moral responsibility is not (simply?) a matter of pursuing efficiently a goal or set of goals, i.e., it is not essentially instrumental in character; and

(C') Morality involves a conception of rationality in which respect for the integrity and freedom of persons is central.

Thus Ladd embraces the interesting, if controversial, view that standard utilitarian-style approaches to decision-making are, as a matter of logic, incompatible with morally responsible decision-making, at least as it is ordinarily understood. Expediency and moral responsibility are like oil and water.

The upshot, then, in light of the fact that organizations are such an integral part of modern civilized life, is that we find ourselves in a practical, ongoing dilemma which is rooted in a *conceptual* impasse between individual and institutional forms of rational agency.

Now, though much more could and should be said to do justice to Ladd's provocative discussion, perhaps enough has been set out for my present purposes. For if one is reluctant, as I am, to permit the project described at the outset to run aground in the face of what appears to be a challenge to its intelligibility, the alternatives become relatively clear: It would appear that we must either

(1) Abandon Ladd's account of the ideal of rationality in formal organizations, or

(2) Abandon Ladd's implicit views as to the nature of moral responsibility, or

(3) Abandon both (in whole or in part).

The problem is that none of these courses is, in my opinion, easy.

Alternative (1) might seem at first glance to be the most appropriate on several counts. For one thing, it is phrased in terms of an "ideal" of rationality, and the natural response is: *Whose* ideal? After all, if we are simply dealing with certain idiosyncratic conceptions of what it is reasonable for an organization to do, then this should give us no pause in trying to articulate a ("therapeutic") model of what organizations ought to do morally. The problem with this response is that Ladd's account of the ideal of rationality in formal organizations is *not* idiosyncratic, either in terms of popular opinion or in terms of social scientific theories. It undoubtedly represents the dominant model of organizational behavior, both in terms of descriptive-explanatory studies of that behavior and in terms of people's expectations (if not ultimate appraisals) of that behavior.

There is, however, an important respect in which this account is incomplete, and I propose to argue that it is this fact which provides some flexibility in what is otherwise a tense dichotomy between corporate rationality and moral responsibility. In outlining the "ideal" of rationality for formal organizations, Ladd, drawing largely upon H. A. Simon, emphasizes the analogy with game rules (e.g., chess). The constitutive conditions which define what is a 'move' and what is not are compared to the decision-making premises ("organizational goals") which define what is and what is not a genuine organizational decision (as against, say, a personal decision by a member of an organization). But there is a crucial disanalogy here which is not emphasized. It is that, for the most part, game rules are static while organizational premises tend to be more dynamic. In other words, though we are dealing perhaps with differences of degree, the irrelevance of morality to chess is of a different order of magnitude from the irrelevance of morality to organizational rationality. For organizational mandates and goals (the decision-making premises) are subject to constant stress, even evolution, in the presence of complex pressures both from within and from outside the corporate coalition. The limits of willing identification and cooperation among managers, stockholders, workers, customers, and the general public (in the case of private organizations) and legislators, administrators, staff, voters, etc. (in the case of public organizations) result in considerable, though possibly incremental, changes in organizational premises. By contrast, it would be surprising to find such changes in the rules or objectives of chess over time.[9] And the explanation is not hard to discern. Chess, unlike organizational decision-making, is pretty clearly insulated from morally significant impact. My guess is that one could think of limiting cases of game rules which do exhibit developmental characteristics due to their impact on human life (e.g., rules of war, or rules of language or rules of etiquette). But for the most part, the moral irrelevance of constitutive rules varies in direct proportion to the 'artificiality' or 'abstractness' of the games which they constitute. Thus we should expect that the stark separation between organizational rationality and moral responsibility is overstated. Organizational rationality, to be sure, includes a purely 'means-to-ends' component, but the 'ends' which are often taken as 'givens' are rarely taken as unalterable. This being the case, *efficiency* can only exhaust the concept of rationality in formal organizations *if it is also rational for such organizations to abdicate control over the development or change of those ends.* If it is not rational to do this, and I hazard the opinion that it is not, then the ideal of rationality in formal organizations must include more than the efficient pursuit of given or static decision-premises (by analogy with games like chess[10]). It must include criteria for the scrutiny and modification of those premises ('ends') themselves. And it seems less likely that a case can be made for the irrelevance of morality to *these* criteria than for the irrelevance of morality to any *given* premises or ends.

Simon himself seems to me to acknowledge this perception implicitly when he writes:

> . . . although it is correct to say that organization behavior is oriented toward the organization objective, this is not the whole story; for the organization objective itself changes in response to the influence of those for whom the accomplishment of that objective secures personal values.[11]

Thus, though Ladd seems right in interpreting organizational theorists as less sensitive than they might be to the ramifications of controlled adaptation of organizational goals or premises, he goes too far in inferring from remarks about the givenness of organizational goals[12] such conclusions as that:

> —organizational decisions "cannot take their ethical premises from the principles of morality" and
> —"for logical reasons it is improper to expect organizational conduct to conform to the ordinary principles of morality."[13]

What is crucial is that it is an *empirical* question whether the principles of morality find their way into organizational premises, and that the "givenness" of those premises is only a *part* of what is involved in the ideal of rationality for formal organizations.

I conclude, then, that we must enrich the account of rationality for formal organizations to accommodate the phenomenon of controlled adaptation of organizational goals or decision-premises. This modification permits us to conceive of moral principles as candidates for organizational premises, or at least as criteria for the control of those premises, in a way which Ladd's account precludes due to its emphasis on the static "givenness" of those premises. With respect to alternative (1) above, then, it seems unreasonable to abandon Ladd's account altogether, though it seems reasonable to do so in part.

Let us now turn to alternative (2). Here we find difficulties of a procedural sort, since Ladd does not develop explicitly an account of morally responsible decision-making. Determining whether to abandon it in whole or in part, then, is problematic. My strategy will be simply to isolate one feature of the account and suggest that it is overstated as it stands, and then trace the implications of this fact for Ladd's general argument.

As I pointed out earlier (B'), a key element in Ladd's contrast between organizational rationality and morality is the issue of *instrumentality.* As Ladd puts it, instrumental rationality

> ... reduces the relationship between human beings to the category of means to an end, a category in which they do not belong. It makes the only point of a rational action the function that it plays in 'means-ends' chains. The only point of keeping a promise, for instance, is the effect that doing so will have on my ends or the ends of others. This way of looking at rationality reflects what seems to me to be essentially an amoral position, for it reduces morality, which is a matter of the relations between human beings, to what is useful or expedient for some purpose or other.[14]

Now, I have no desire to maintain that a non-instrumentalist conception of moral responsibility is untenable, quite the contrary. But I do wish to point out that there are two importantly different interpretations or versions of what has come to be called "deontological" morality. On the first, consideration of consequences for persons' ends is held to be *relevant* but *insufficient* for morally responsible decision-making, while on the second, such consideration of consequences is held to be *irrelevant* and *unnecessary.*[15] To the extent that Ladd is embracing the latter, more radical, view of morally responsible decision-making, his thesis of incompatibility between morality and organizational rationality is enhanced. To the extent that he is embracing the former, more moderate, view the incompatibility thesis becomes less plausible. For on the moderate view, there is a definite, even essential, place for consequential "means-ends" reasoning in moral decision-making—even if this sort of reasoning does not *exhaust* morality. This observation, joined to my earlier point about the place for controlled adaptation in organizational rationality, begins to complete the picture of a reconciliation where Ladd seems to have seen only conceptual impasse.

The question in the present context, then, becomes: Which of the two general forms of deontological morality is more plausible, if we assume with Ladd that a purely teleological account of morality will not do?[16] It seems to me that we have to answer in favor of the moderate form. The implications of relegating consequences to *irrelevance* are simply intolerable. In terms of Ladd's example of promise-keeping, it is salutary to be reminded that there is more, morally, to our responsibilities in this matter than expediency, but this is no reason for thinking that the effects on persons' ends of keeping or breaking a promise make no moral difference *at all.*[17] The moral ambiguity at work in such slogans as "whatever the consequences" has been too amply demonstrated (to most philosophers) to bear the weight that the radical deontologist wishes to place on it.

I conclude, then, that Ladd's account of the general nature of moral responsibility needs a moderation which is not clearly present, and that with this moderation we again perceive a lessening of the tension between the ideals of organizational rationality and the demands of morality. Thus alternative (2), though too strong, leads us to alternative (3).

The pattern which emerges is as follows. The project of "ethical diagnostics" and its point, the molding of corporate "conscience," appeared to be threatened at the outset by what was claimed to be a logical or conceptual barrier. The ideal of rationality in formal organizations was simply *inconsistent* with the ideal of morally responsible decision-making. On examining Ladd's accounts of the respective ideals, however, I argued that each required modification. Organizational rationality cannot be conceived as *purely* instrumental with no criteria for guiding the development of the goals or premises from which efficiency departs. Nor can moral responsibility be conceived as purely non-instrumental with no attention to the consequences of conduct on the ends or interests of those affected by it (including, I might add, the agent himself). Thus what I claim to have provided so far is rather negative: a kind of *space* for the working out of a solution to our problem. The logical or conceptual barriers to describing and developing formal organizations through moral categories were seen to depend upon unduly strong construals of ideal rationality and ideal morality, respectively. The moderation of these ideals (or better, the clarification of them) relaxes the barriers a bit and allows for the possibility that rationality might be moralized and morality rationalized.

But it is important not to overstate the case. Though perhaps exaggerated, Ladd's approach is a healthy caution to a naive conception of corporate (or organizational) description and reform. There is, in other words, a clear tension between the joint demands of efficiency and adaptation in decision-making, not to mention complications involved in the proper understanding of each demand taken separately. My own view is that this tension (not inconsistency) represents an essential structural feature of rational as well as responsible agency. Both for purposes of empirical analysis and for purposes of reform, our conception of corporate agency (like our conception of individual agency) must reflect the fact that *action* is not simply the mindless pursuit of antecedently given ends. The static model must be replaced by the dynamic one in which action is seen as a mutual accommodation between organism (organization) and environment in which the organism monitors both means and ends. And the monitoring process involves feedback between the agent and the results of his pursuit. Sometimes this feedback will dictate alteration of means; sometimes it will dictate alteration of ends. Rationality in action will depend upon an agent's capacity, among others, to make appropriate adjustments in both areas in an effort to maintain stability and long-term integrity. Whether and in what way an agent engages in this tuning operation is a more important indicator of its conscience or lack of conscience than any given set of goals which it may pursue at any given time. Thus an ethical profile of an organization's decision-making will need to attend not simply to organizational premises, to use Simon's term, but (more importantly) to the *adaptation patterns* which control those premises. In the case of a private organization like a corporation, such goals as profit, growth, market shares, etc., represent a typical corporation's ongoing behavioral premises—but they do not, in themselves, provide us with a picture of the corporation's action-guiding principles in the fuller sense under discussion. To get at these, we need to attend to such features of the organizational structure as:

—information-gathering and processing priorities,
—criteria of management selection, and
—authority relationships between participants.

As with an individual agent, an organizational agent exhibits his ethical commitments as much (perhaps more) in the procedural controls he places on his goal selection as in the goals selected. One of the most difficult (and interesting) tasks of the diagnostician is to isolate the key control variables in a given organization, relating them to patterns of organizational behavior and the results of that behavior.

A natural way in which an organization's goals (premises) might be controlled would be in terms of some *more general or basic* goal such as corporate expansion or community esteem, etc. This might manifest itself in selectivity regarding information-gathering, choice of managers, and degree of centralization of authority. Such a "teleological" organizational ethic might be more or less morally defensible. And there could be combinations of "metagoals" as well. A power company might control its goal selection in terms of both local community satisfaction and company growth.[18]

But the control need not be provided in this way. Indeed, in the end the selection of the metagoals themselves would seem to require criteria of some sort. If an infinite regress is not to be the result, there may well be standards of goal selection of a more formal sort, e.g., law abidingness, justice, acceptability to a certain class or type of persons, etc.

The general implication is that organizational agents (and corporate agents in particular) do exhibit structural features which permit the working out of both a diagnostic and a therapeutic ethical inquiry, once we understand the categorial compatibility (however fragile) between rationality and morality. This is not to say that all formal organizations can be analyzed and modified toward more responsible decision-making without serious disturbance, or even that such modification can be accomplished *at all* in every case. We should not expect more in our interactions with human organizations than we expect in our interactions with human individuals.

However, if we are convinced that modern life with its large-scale technology presents serious problems due to a lack of reflectiveness and responsibility on the part of our more powerful institutions (private and public), and if we are also convinced that our main model for purposes of analysis and reform is the very human person in whose image and likeness those situations are fabricated, then perhaps enough has been said to vindicate the intelligibility (and desirability) of a new task for ethics.

NOTES

1. K. Goodpaster and K. Sayre, "An Ethical Analysis of Power Company Decision-Making," in *Values in the Electric Power Industry,* K. M. Sayre, ed., University of Notre Dame Press (1977), pp. 238–87.
2. Christopher Stone, *Where The Law Ends,* Harper & Row (1975), p. 111.
3. Goodpaster and Sayre, *op. cit.,* p. 280.
4. L. Silk and D. Vogel, *Ethics and Profits,* Simon and Schuster (1976), quoted on p. 138.
5. John Ladd, "Morality and the Ideal of Rationality in Formal Organizations," *The Monist,* Vol. 54 (October 1970), pp. 488–516.
6. Ladd, *op, cit.,* p. 500.
7. H. Simon, *Administrative Behavior* (New York: Free Press, 1965). Third edition now available, 1976.
8. C. Barnard, *The Functions of the Executive* (Cambridge: Harvard University Press, 1938). Also see Barnard's *Forward* to Simon, *op. cit.*
9. I do not mean to suggest that the constitutive rules of chess do not, or have not, undergone evolution. They clearly have. What is important is that this evolution (a) has been very slow since initial formulations of the game and (b) has not been due to the impact of the game or the players on others' lives or well-being (since there is next to no impact here to speak of—which is why chess is "only a game").
10. The other analogy employed by Ladd, the machine, seems to me to clarify the point even more: the picture is of rigid givens, inflexible and unalterable (or at least uncontrollably so), a picture which human organizations exhibit only in superficial ways over short periods of time.
11. Simon, *op. cit.,* p. 114.
12. Remarks like Simon's: "Decisions in private management, like decisions in public management, must take as their ethical premises the objectives that have been set for the organization." (p. 52) My point is that the "setting" is not outside the realm of organizational control.
13. Or even more strongly, Ladd writes: "We cannot and must not expect formal organizations, or their representatives acting in their official capacities, to be honest, courageous, considerate, sympathetic, or to have any kind of moral integrity. Such concepts are not in the vocabulary, so to speak, of the organizational language-game." (Ladd, p. 499)
14. Ladd, p. 515.
15. Cf. W. K. Frankena, *Ethics* (Prentice-Hall, 1973, second edition), Ch. 3.
16. As for the assumption that a purely teleological theory is implausible, too much needs to be said. My opinion, in view of the long history of controversy here, is that the operationalizability of the key *maximandum* for such theories appears inevitably to vary inversely with its plausibility. I suspect that this was Kant's point when he observed in the *Foundations* that the notion of 'happiness' could not sustain an ethic.
17. Cf. Frankena, *op. cit.,* and W. D. Ross, *The Right and the Good* (Oxford, 1930).
18. Goodpaster and Sayre, *op. cit.*

THE MORAL RESPONSIBILITY OF CORPORATIONS

Case Study—Nonenergy Diversification at Mobil Corporation

EARL A. MOLANDER

In June 1974, Mobil Oil Corporation, now an operating unit of Mobil Corporation, announced plans to spend $800 million to acquire a controlling interest in Marcor, parent of Montgomery Ward and Container Corporation. This decision might have been ignored by most observers outside the business community had it not followed severe gasoline and fuel oil shortages and reported first-quarter 1974 earnings for Mobil that were 66 percent higher than those for the same quarter of 1973, profits which Mobil and other oil companies had argued were necessary for new energy exploration and production. A large part of this increase, as management pointed out, resulted from two factors in Mobil's foreign operations over which management had no control: nonrecurring profits following the fourfold increases in Organization of Petroleum Exporting Countries (OPEC) prices, and the relative weakness of the dollar against foreign currencies.

Typical of the outcry from critics of the Marcor acquisition was that of Senator Thomas McIntyre of New Hampshire, who called the move:

> Irresponsibility at its worst. . . . I've lambasted the oil industry before but this decision by the nation's third-largest oil company to spend more than three-fifths of its last year's profits to buy a non-energy enterprise leaves me absolutely outraged.[1]

THE COMPANY

Mobil Corporation was formed in 1976 as a holding company with three principal operating units: Mobil Oil, Montgomery Ward, and Container Corporation. Mobil Oil, whose predecessor was the Standard Oil Company of New York, a part of the Standard Oil Trust, is one of the "Seven Sisters," the seven largest international oil companies. In 1973, Mobil Oil revenues

Case prepared by Earl A. Molander. From *Responsive Capitalism,* by Earl Molander and David Arthur (New York: McGraw-Hill, © 1980), pp. 29–36. Reprinted by permission of McGraw-Hill.

were $12.8 billion and earnings $842.8 million. In 1978, Mobil Corporation revenues were $36.9 billion and earnings $1.1 billion, making Mobil the fourth-largest industrial enterprise in the United States.

Mobil is somewhat unique in that it has less of its own domestic oil than do its major competitors. In 1976, Mobil's domestic production of oil and natural gas liquids accounted for only 48 percent of the oil it refined in the United States, as compared with 73 percent for Exxon and 72 percent for Texaco.[2] Management at Mobil also differed from that of other oil companies. Rather than being run by engineers, Mobil has been managed by people from the financial side of the business.

However, Mobil has an active oil exploration program. From 1964 to 1973, Mobil capital expenditures shifted away from its overseas marketing operations toward exploration and production and toward the United States. Between December 1970 and year-end 1974, Mobil spent over $1 billion for offshore oil leases in the Gulf of Mexico.[3]

In the 1964–1973 period, Mobil's earnings, rate of return, and capital expenditure were not greatly different from the industry as a whole. Earnings in the period immediately prior to the Arab oil boycott and the onset of the energy crisis in 1973 were somewhat depressed in the oil industry. As a result of the devaluation of the dollar in 1973, the company and the industry experienced large earnings increases for 1973.

NONENERGY DIVERSIFICATION

In the mid-1960s, a number of oil companies began to diversify out of the oil business. The rationale behind the move was fivefold:

1. *Supply.* It became apparent to many companies that oil was a dwindling natural resource. There was little expectation of new oil or natural gas discoveries of the magnitude of the previous century.
2. *Demand.* Growth in oil and gas demand was projected to be just over 1 percent a year through 1990.[4] Price increases would take up some of the slack, but it was clearly a slow-growth future.
3. *Political uncertainties in the producing countries.* In the early 1970s, as OPEC began taking over from the Seven Sisters, these companies no longer owned, and therefore could no longer rely on, these crude supplies.
4. *Political uncertainties in the United States.* In the early 1970s, there were a number of threats to the oil companies from the federal government. These included breaking up the vertically integrated companies and blocking industry efforts to explore for oil on the continental shelf.
5. *Stabilizing sales and earnings.* The oil business is subject to cycles, and a move into a business subject to different cycles would help stabilize sales and earnings.

Mobil formally adopted a diversification policy in 1968, primarily because of political uncertainties in the producing countries. According to Mobil Chairman Rawleigh Warner, Jr.,

> I won't say that we could foresee greater involvement by the consuming countries, but it is fair to say we could foresee the greater involvement of the producing countries. That meant a lesser role for us. So we got a policy decision from the board to diversify.[5]

Initially, Mobil studied industries that were capital-intensive and would be a good match for the company's high cash flow. The company had taken some steps to diversify horizontally, moving into petrochemicals and acquiring by bid and purchase some coal (over 3 billion tons by 1974) and oil shale reserves, but acquiring another energy-related company was quite another issue.[6] To avoid conflict with antitrust law, an acquisition within the energy business was ruled out.

MARCOR: A PROSPECTIVE ACQUISITION

From 1968 onward Mobil sifted through various industries. Eventually it began to focus on retailing companies generally and then specifically on Marcor, the company formed by the merger of Montgomery Ward & Company and Container Corporation of America. Lawrence M. Woods, executive vice president in charge of planning and head of a four-person team working on the project, recalls:

> By 1973 we were looking at individual companies. Marcor had turned around —it seemed to have a management that knew what they were about—yet it was not fully priced in the stock market. . . . We knew it was a good investment so we went out and bought 4.5 percent of the stock [in late 1973]. If nothing else, we figured we could get back in the market the money we had spent on the analysis.[7]

As studies of Marcor continued, Mobil became more and more impressed with Marcor and decided to study the company in depth to determine whether to acquire a controlling interest in it. Then came the Arab oil embargo and the production cutbacks of late 1973 and early 1974. The stock market, which was already depressed, plummeted, making Marcor an even more attractive investment.

In spring 1974, the internal study of the possible acquisition of Marcor was completed, and the Mobil board decided to seriously consider making a tender offer for a majority voting position in Marcor.[8] After outside legal opinion confirmed that it would be legal to make the offer, Mobil senior management approached Marcor. After a series of six meetings, officers of the two companies agreed to the general terms of the offer.

On August 12, 1974, Mobil formally tendered an offer for 51 percent of the outstanding common shares of Marcor at $35/share, a premium of $10.25/share. In the view of *Forbes* magazine, this was ". . . enough of a premium to thwart counter-offers and to give several key Marcor men the prospect of a handsome windfall profit on their stock-purchasing plan."[9] Mobil Chairman Warner explained, "We had to put a card on the table not only for management but also for the government, so it could say, 'This isn't all bad.' "[10] To do so, the Mobil tender offer included $70 a share for Marcor's series A preferred stock and an agreement for Mobil to pay $200 million for a new issue of Marcor voting preferred stock. The total cost to Mobil was estimated at $800 million.

Marcor Acquisition Criticized

Criticism of the proposed acquisition came almost immediately. One basis was antitrust. Senator Philip Hart of Michigan, who chaired the Senate Antitrust Subcommittee, argued:

> Hopefully, the Justice Department will move quickly against this merger, or tell Congress whether such a merger constitutes wise public policy . . . [T]here are serious antitrust questions both about a lessening of competition between Marcor and Mobil [in the sale of tires and other auto accessories], and the potential that Mobil, by becoming Marcor's sole supplier, would close out other competitors.[11]

The most heated attack on the Marcor acquisition was the criticism that oil profits were being used to make acquisitions outside the oil business. The attack was led by Senator McIntyre. When the acquisition was first announced in June 1974, McIntyre followed up his criticism noted at the beginning of the case with a charge that:

> The $350 million [the cost of common shares would actually be $500 million] Mobil proposes to spend for controlling shares in Marcor is enough money to build another needed refinery. It is enough money to open several new drilling sites for oil and gas.[12]

Complaints also came from Senators Edward Brooke of Massachusetts and James Abourezk of South Dakota, and Representative Charles Vanik of Ohio who said the proposed acquisition ". . . is simply a way for Mobil Oil to use up embarrassing profits."[13] Congressional critics were quick to remind Mobil that it had defended its rising profits over the preceding year as necessary to finance new exploration for oil and gas.[14]

Even the business media acknowledged that the move raised questions. An article in *Forbes,* glibly entitled "Recycling the Oil Profits, Mobil Style," suggested: "There is talk these days about Arab sheiks buying up the world. They had better move fast. The big oil companies may beat them to it."[15]

When Mobil moved to acquire the Irvine ranch in southern California two years later (they dropped out of a spirited bidding contest the following year when another group topped Mobil's $336.6 million bid by less than $1 million) *Business Week* noted:

> To the oil industry's critics, such diversification is self-indicting. Why, they ask, should the industry and its supporters call for higher prices and profits—supposedly to support greater efforts at finding oil and gas—when the companies are clearly spending more and more money in areas that have nothing to do

with energy? It is a tough question—one that the companies cannot, in fact, answer satisfactorily. But there are some very good reasons why the oil industry is diversifying, few of them incriminating.[16]

Mobil Response

Mobil's own explanation of the Marcor acquisition was in the context of the diversification policy and rationale outlined above. (See letter to shareholders, p. 151.) In a *Forbes* magazine interview, Mobil Chairman Warner explained further:

> The oil business is very different from what we knew five years ago. Governments are interfering. The U.S. Government certainly is. The Federal Energy Administration tells us to whom we must sell our crude and what we can charge. They threaten us with a federal oil company that will have access to the top 20% acreage offshore and be a yardstick to see how effective we are. There are 3,000 bills before Congress, each one of which would do something to the oil industry.[17]

In addition, Warner noted that the Federal Trade Commission was suing Mobil and other oil companies, seeking substantial divestiture of their refineries and pipelines; the Middle Eastern governments were certain to take over 100 percent of the oil concessions there; and the same takeover was possible in Britain and Canada. Said Warner, "I'm not saying all these things are going to happen, but I don't think we are overreacting. We think there's enough going on to put an anchor to windward in the interests of our shareholders."[18]

In explaining why the cash was not being used for new exploration, Warner said:

> The limit of our spending isn't dollars. It's the availability of offshore concessions and the limitations of the people we have. We are looking for oil in 24 countries around the world, and that takes competent people. And it's the availability of rigs, platforms and pipe. It isn't cash or the lack of cash.[19]

On why Mobil chose Marcor, the key for Warner was Montgomery Ward:

> In looking to diversity, we want earnings prospects for better growth in the face of what we saw as future slackening of oil generated volume. We wanted businesses that had different risks, and a consumer franchise if possible. We felt we could buy Ward's earnings stream without dilution to our stockholders.[20]

Warner also told *Business Week:*

> We believe that in the gasoline and oil businesses we are going to see a sharp dropping off in demand growth as a result of increased prices. The retailing business, particularly in soft goods, seemed like a good way to counterbalance that. . . . The stock was undervalued in terms of the job Marcor management had done in turning the company around and solving the great problems at Montgomery Ward.[21]

Letter to Shareholders (Excerpt)

June 28, 1974

To all Mobil shareholders:

As many of you know, Mobil has announced that it is considering the acquisition of a major interest in Marcor Inc., the parent company of Montgomery Ward & Co., Incorporated and Container Corporation of America. . . .

The announcement of what we are considering has understandably raised a number of questions, which I will try to answer for you in this letter.

We have no intention of withdrawing from the oil business, nor in fact even of minimizing our role in oil. The vast majority of our capital and other expenditures will continue to be made in the oil business and in related energy businesses for as long ahead as we can see into the future. We cannot, however, ignore the many charges that have been directed at the oil industry by politicians and some segments of the communications media. . . .

While a diversification investment necessarily lies outside the energy business, we have no intention of becoming a multi-faceted conglomerate. We are considering this step because we are satisfied that this would be a fine investment for your company and one that could, over the years ahead, add immeasurably to the over-all strength of the Mobil organization and thus to your investment in Mobil.

I would like now to address myself to some of the derogatory comments that have been directed at the oil industry and specifically at Mobil. These revolve around such charges as "extortionate" or "obscene" profits, failure to spend enough on oil in the United States, and failure to build enough refining capacity in this country.

In 1973 our net income represented 7.4% of revenues—that is to say, 7.4¢ out of every dollar—and our rate of return on average total assets was 8.5%. In each instance this was the highest figure, by a major factor, in the past 10 years; and in our view these key indices of profitability are neither extortionate nor obscene.

To the charge that we have been investing more money overseas than here, it should be understood that each of the past 10 years has shown a higher percentage of such outlays in the U.S. and Canada than in all the rest of the countries where we have interests. This is true with respect both to capital investments and to exploration expenditures. . . .

It should also be known that your company constructed the most recent large new U.S. refinery in Joliet, Ill., the biggest ever built from scratch in this country. Further, we are now in the process of trying to expand and modernize our refinery at Paulsboro. N.J.

In light of the charges made against us, I cannot help but feel that the Senators and Congressmen who have been attacking the oil industry in general and Mobil in particular would serve their country better by increasing the opportunities and improving the climate for investment in oil than by making what we believe are ill-informed statements and by threatening punitive legislation against oil companies. . . .

Sincerely,

Rawleigh Warner, Jr.
Chairman of the Board

Source: Mobil Corporation, New York, N.Y.

As to the Container Corporation part of Marcor, Warner said:

> There is a kind of an affinity between Container and ourselves: They are timber shy, and we are crude shy. I suppose we were attracted to someone who has had to live by their wits like we have had to do.[22]

Government Investigation

Mobil's formal offer to Marcor shareholders was made on August 12, 1974. Eight days later, Mobil Senior Vice President James Q. Riordan was before a Senate subcommittee explaining the move. He reviewed the company's profit picture, its current and anticipated capital investments in the oil and gas industry, the evolution of its diversification policy, and the specific reasons why the Marcor acquisition was being made. Closing his testimony with a synopsis of recent United States government moves to control oil companies and their activities, Riordan observed:

> It is not the purpose of this testimony to argue the pros and cons of any particular proposed Congressional action, any particular action by a government agency which affects the oil industry, or actions of private groups. The relevant point here is that in Mobil's considered judgment, management cannot ignore the implications of all these challenges and potentially adverse developments both at home and abroad in terms of what they may portend for the future of the company's role in the oil business.
>
> In light of these many developments, the implementation of Mobil's long-established diversification policy continues to be a matter of primary concern. Marcor meets the essential criteria of Mobil's diversification policy—to make a substantial investment unrelated to Mobil's operations in the oil industry.
>
> Mobil's investment in Marcor is grounded in fundamental business considerations. It was not motivated by recent profit levels. It reflects solely a long-range, prudent concern for the best interests of our stockholders.[23]

NOTES

1. As quoted in "A Better Hole" (editorial), *Wall Street Journal,* 24 June 1974, p. 8. Reprinted with permission of the *Wall Street Journal,* © 1974, Dow Jones & Company, Inc. All rights reserved.
2. "What Makes Mobil Run," *Business Week,* 13 June 1977, p. 83.
3. Ibid., p. 84.
4. "Diversification: The New Oil Game," *Business Week,* 24 April 1978, p. 76.
5. "What Makes Mobil Run," p. 82.
6. "Recycling the Oil Profits, Mobil Style," *Forbes,* 15 November 1974, p. 67.
7. "What Makes Mobil Run," p. 82.
8. James Q. Riordan, senior vice president, Mobil Oil Corporation, New York, *Testimony on the Marcor Acquisition before the Senate Select Committee on Small Business, Subcommittee on Government Regulation,* 93rd Cong., 2d Sess., 20 August 1974, p. 3. (Mimeographed.)
9. "Recycling the Oil Profits," p. 67.

10. Ibid.
11. "Mobil Formally Sets Marcor Bid," *Wall Street Journal,* 13 August 1974, p. 9. Reprinted with permission of the *Wall Street Journal,* © 1974, Dow Jones & Company, Inc. All rights reserved.
12. "Mobil's Plan to Buy Marcor Control Fuels Congressional Fire," *Wall Street Journal,* 20 June 1974, p. 5. Reprinted with permission of the *Wall Street Journal,* © 1974, Dow Jones & Company, Inc. All rights reserved.
13. Ibid.
14. Ibid.
15. "Recycling the Oil Profits," p. 66.
16. "What Makes Mobil Run," p. 80.
17. "Recycling the Oil Profits," p. 66.
18. Ibid.
19. Ibid., p. 67.
20. "Big Oil's Move into Retailing," *Chain Store Age Executive,* September 1976, p. 32.
21. "What Made Mobil Buy into Marcor," *Business Week,* 29 June 1974, p. 29.
22. Ibid.
23. Testimony by James Q. Riordan, pp. 4–5.

Constructing a Social Contract for Business

THOMAS DONALDSON

In a speech to the Harvard Business School in 1969, Henry Ford II stated:

> The terms of the contract between industry and society are changing . . . Now we are being asked to serve a wider range of human values and to accept an obligation to members of the public with whom we have no commercial transactions.

The "contract" to which Henry Ford referred concerns a corporation's *indirect* obligations. It represents not a set of formally specified obligations, but a set of binding, abstract ones. A social contract for business, if one exists, is not a typewritten contract in the real world, but a metaphysical abstraction not unlike the "social contract" between citizens and government that philosophers have traditonally discussed. Such a contract would have concrete significance, for it would help to interpret the nature of a corporation's indirect obligations—ones which are notoriously slippery.

The aim of this essay is to discover a corporation's indirect obligations by attempting to clarify the meaning of business's so-called "social contract." The task is challenging. Although people speak frequently of such a contract, few have attempted to specify its meaning.

A good starting point is the so-called "social contract" that philosophers have spoken of between society and the state. This political contract has usually been viewed as a theoretical means for justifying the existence of the state. Philosophers have asked, "Why should people let a government exist at all?" in other words, "Why should people prefer to have a government control much of their actions—to impose taxes, raise armies, and punish criminals—instead of having no government at all?" They never doubted for a moment the need for a state, but they believed raising such questions would clarify not only the justification for the state's existence, but also the reciprocal obligations between the state and its citizens. If a government began to abuse its citizenry, to trample on its rights or to diminish social welfare, then according to such philosophers it had broken the tenets of the social contract and could be overthrown. Such a theory in the hands of the seventeenth-century English philosopher John Locke, provided much of the theoretical support for the American Revolution and design of the Declaration of Independence and the U.S. Constitution.

The political social contract provides a clue for understanding the contract for business. If the political contract serves as a justification for the existence of the state, then the business contract by parity of reasoning should serve as the justification for the existence of the corporation.

Thus, crucial questions are: Why should corporations exist at all? What is the fundamental justification of their activities? How can we measure their performance and say when they have achieved their fundamental purpose? Consider a case involving General Motors and the production of automobiles. The automobiles that General Motors produced during the 1950s and 1960s all had noncollapsible steering wheels (called by Ralph Nader "ram-rodding" steering wheels), and evidence indicated that they contributed to hundreds of thousands of highway deaths. But General Motors and other auto manufacturers kept them on the cars anyway, claiming the added expense of collapsible steering wheels would reduce car sales and profits. Their claim may well have been true. However, by refusing to install safer steering wheels, had they failed to achieve a fundamental corporate mission? Had they violated a tenet of an implied social contract between them and society? Or had they just attended to business—although in a way which had unfortunate consequences for society? To answer these questions, we must first know what justifies General Motors' existence.

It is reasonable to look for a fundamental purpose, or set of purposes, that justifies corporate existence. Doing so makes conceptual sense, despite the fact one would never look for what justifies, say, human existence. Corporations, unlike humans, are artifacts, which is to say *we* create them. We *choose* to create corporations and we might choose either not to create them or to create different entities. Corporations thus are like political states in their need for justification.

One might attempt to justify corporate existence by appealing to corporate productivity: to the automobiles, irons, tools, clothing, and medical equipment corporations create. Because society demands such items, it seemingly also requires the corporations that produce them. Adam Smith, the eighteenth-century Scottish philosopher, emphasizes productivity when he justifies a set of economic practices through their contribution to the wealth of nations. But although productivity is surely a crucial piece in the puzzle of corporate justification, it fails to provide a full solution. To say that an organization produces wealth for society is not sufficient to justify it from a moral perspective, since morality encompasses the entire range of human welfare. To say something produces wealth is to say something morally good about it—assuming that wealth is counted as a human good—but it fails to tell us what else the thing does, or how its process of creation affects society. Consider the example of a nuclear power reactor. To say that a nuclear reactor generates electricity is to say something good about it, but it fails to consider the reactor in the context of the possibility of melt-downs, the storage of nuclear waste, the costs of alternative production, and so forth. (This is true even if we suppose that ultimately nuclear reactors are fully justified.) The logic of the problem of corporate justification is similar. To achieve a complete moral picture of a corporation's existence, we must consider not only its capacity to produce wealth, but the full range of its effects upon society.

Before we attempt to spell out the terms of the social contract, a prior issue must be settled; namely, *who* are the parties to the contract? So far we have spoken of a contract between society and business, but the concepts of "business" and "society" are vague. Let us stipulate that "business" refers to *productive organizations,* i.e., ones where people cooperate to produce at least one specific product or service. Productive organizations would include corporations (of the productive sort), but would also include government owned businesses, large business partnerships, and productive firms in socialist countries.

By attempting to find the moral underpinnings of all productive organizations, we will indirectly be searching for the moral underpinnings of corporations, since virtually all corporations are productive organizations. Once the moral underpinnings of productive organizations are known, it will be possible to answer from a moral perspective the question: Why does Exxon exist? Or, speaking more precisely, it will be possible to answer this question when Exxon is considered *as a member of the class of productive organizations.*

The term "society" is similarly vague. It might refer to the aggregate of individuals who make up society, or to something over and above the sum of those individuals. For clarity, let us stipulate that the contract is between productive organizations and *individual members of society,* not between productive organizations and some supra-individual, social entity.

The simplest way of understanding the social contract is in the form: "We (the members of society) agree to do *X,* and you (the contracting organizations) agree to do *Y*." Applying this form to General Motors (or any productive organization) means that the task of a social contract argument is to specify *X*, where *X* refers to the obligations of society to productive organizations, and to specify *Y*, where *Y* refers to the obligations of productive organizations to society.

It is relatively easy in this context to specify *X*, because what productive organizations need from society is:

1. Recognition as a single agent, especially in the eyes of the law.
2. The authority: (a) to own or use land and natural resources, and (b) to hire employees.

It may appear presumptuous to assume that productive organizations must be warranted by society. Can one not argue that any organization has a *right* to exist and operate? That they have this right *apart* from the wishes of society? When asking such questions, one must distinguish between claims about rights of mere organizations and claims about rights of organizations with special powers, such as productive organizations. A case can be made for the unbridled right of the Elks Club, whose members unite in fraternal activities, to exist and operate (assuming it does not discriminate against minorities or women); but the same cannot be said for Du Pont Corporation, which not only must draw on existing stores of mineral resources, but must find dumping sites to store toxic chemical by-products. Even granted that people have an inalienable right to form and operate organizations, and even granted that this right exists apart from the discretion of society, the productive organization requires special status under the law and the opportunity to use society's resources: two issues in which every member of society may be said to have a vested interest.

Conditions 1 and 2 are obviously linked to each other. In order for a productive organization to use land and hire employees (conditions of 2), it must have the authority to perform those acts as if it were an individual agent (the condition of 1). The philosophical impact of 1 should not be exaggerated. To say that productive organizations must have the authority to act as individual agents is not necessarily to affirm that they are abstract, invisible persons. Rather it is a means of stating the everyday fact that productive organizations must, for a variety of purposes, be treated as individual entities. For example, a corporation must be able to hire new employees, to sign contracts, and to negotiate purchases without getting the O.K. from *all* its employees and stockholders.

Defining the *Y* side of the contract is as difficult as defining the *X* side is easy. It is obvious that productive organizations must be allowed to exist and act. But it is not obvious precisely why societies should allow them to exist, that is, what specific benefits society should hope to gain from the bargain. What specific functions should society expect from productive organizations? What obligations should it impose? Only one assumption can be made readily: that the members of society should demand at a minimum that the benefits from authorizing the existence of productive organizations outweigh the detriments of doing so. This is nothing other than the expectation of all voluntary agreements: that no party should be asked to conclude a contract which places him or her in a position worse than before.

To specify society's terms for the social contract, let us return to a traditional device in social contract theory, the device of imagining society *without* the institution that is being analyzed. In short, let us consider society without productive organizations, in a "state of nature." Instead of the traditional state of nature where people live without government, we shall consider a state where people live without *productive organizations.* To avoid confusing this state with the traditional ones, let us call it the "state of individual production." Thus, the strategy involves:

1. Characterizing conditions in a state of individual production (without productive organizations).
2. Indicating how certain problems are remedied by the introduction of productive organizations.
3. Using the reasons generated in the second step as a basis for specifying a social contract between society and its productive organizations.

The details must be spelled out. How are we to imagine the state of individual production? What people occupy it? Are they selfish? Charitable? How do they labor?

At a minimum the people in the state of individual production should be imagined as having "economic interests," i.e., as being people for whom it is desirable to have some things or services produced by human labor. Under such a definition almost any human would qualify, except perhaps ascetics or persons who prefer death to life. Thus, the people envisioned by the present strategy are ordinary, economically interested persons who have not yet organized themselves, or been organized, into productive organizations.

Should they be imagined as purely egoistic, wanting only to satisfy their own selfish interests, or as purely benevolent, wanting only to satisfy the interests of others? In the real world both characterizations are extreme —ordinary people are neither devils nor saints—and thus is suggested the strategy of assuming the same about people in the state of individual production. Let us adopt this strategy; if the contract has application to ordinary people, it will help to keep ordinary people in mind.[1]

To imagine a state of individual production, i.e., without productive organizations, is to imagine a society in which individuals produce and work alone. It is to imagine society without factories, banks, hospitals, restaurants, or railroads, since all these organizations, as well as many others, count as productive organizations, that is, they are organizations in which people cooperate to produce at least one specific product or service. (For our purposes, noneconomic factors such as family structure, religious attitudes, and educational interests shall be disregarded.) Now in such a state we may imagine any level of technology we wish. The only crucial fact is that people produce *individually.*

THE TERMS OF THE CONTRACT

Two principal classes of people stand to benefit or be harmed by the introduction of productive organizations: (1) people who consume the organizations' products, i.e., consumers; and (2) people who work in such organizations, i.e., employees. The two classes are broadly defined and not mutually exclusive. "Consumer" refers to anyone who is economically interested; hence virtually anyone qualifies as a consumer. "Employee" refers to anyone who contributes labor to the productive process of a productive organization, including managers, laborers, part-time support personnel, and (in corporations) members of the board of directors.

Consumers

From the standpoint of our hypothetical consumers, productive organizations promise to *enhance the satisfaction of economic interests.* That is to say, people could hope for the introduction of productive organizations to better satisfy their interests for shelter, food, entertainment, transportation, health care, and clothing. The prima facie benefits for consumers include:

1. *Improving efficiency* through:
   a. Maximizing advantages of specialization.
   b. Improving decision-making resources.
   c. Increasing the capacity to use or acquire expensive technology and resources.
2. *Stabilizing levels of output and channels of distribution.*
3. *Increasing liability resources.*

Each benefit needs explanation.

The first benefit, improving efficiency, is the special excellence of productive organizations. Productive organizations tend to generate products that are equal or better in quality and price, with lower expenditures of human labor, than is possible in the state of individual production. Let us examine a few of the reasons for this remarkable capacity.

1A. **Maximizing the advantages of specialization.** Adam Smith's well-known thought-experiment in the *Wealth of Nations* provides ready evidence for the truth that two can often be more efficient than one. He showed that in the production of pins, one person working alone could account for a mere handful of pins, whereas in a system of first-order specialization—where one cuts the wire, another points the wire, and so on—the proportionate share of pins per worker increases dramatically. The same is true today. To produce clocks, erasers, and antibiotics efficiently, an enormous degree of cooperative specialization is required: the mere existence of products like the Space Shuttle owes itself to such specialization. Economists agree that many products are further subject to *economies of scale;* that is, their efficient production is dependent not only upon cooperative specialization, but on a certain level of it. Because of this factor, a company like American Motors may be too small to compete successfully with General Motors in the production of automobiles.

1B. **Improving decision-making resources.** Productive organizations share with individual persons the tendency to err in decision-making. Despite this, such organizations have decision-making advantages. First, they can utilize the ongoing talents of people with different backgrounds. Thus, a decision by Westinghouse, Inc., to manufacture a new appliance may call on the knowledge of chemists, accountants, engineers, and marketing specialists. One person could never possess such knowledge.

Second, they can increase information storage. In the same way a person can collect and remember information on a small scale, organizations do so on a large scale. Productive organizations can have superhuman memories: some corporations have libraries larger than those in universities.

1C. **Increasing the capacity to use and acquire expensive technology and resources.** This advantage is nearly self-evident. All other things being equal, two or more people will have greater financial resources than one; hence productive organizations can make capital expenditures on a larger scale than single individuals. Often the use of large, expensive equipment is important not only for increasing production, but for generating higher quality production, since expensive equipment is frequently necessary to improve productive efficiency.

2. **Stabilizing levels of output and channels of distribution.** The imaginary inhabitants of our state of individual production stand to benefit by the merging of individual craftsmen into organizations which are relatively stable, and whose level of output and pattern of distribution are relatively constant. Individual craftsmen are subject to illness, psychological problems, and the need for rest. For example, to rely on an individual mail carrier for the delivery of one's mail is riskier than depending on a large postal organization. Individuals must sleep, eat, and rest, but a large postal organization never sleeps, never eats—it even grows larger at Christmas.

3. **Increasing liability resources.** Under this heading are grouped the benefits that consumers reap because organizations, in contrast to individuals, have "deep pockets." In short, they are better able to compensate injured consumers. In the late 1970's Ford Motor Company was forced by the courts to compensate victims of the Ford Pinto's exploding gas tank. Because of design defects, the Pinto's tank was prone to ignite when hit from behind. The money paid by Ford to victims (and relatives of victims) was astounding; it ran into the millions of dollars. Although few productive organizations are as large as Ford, it remains true that organizations are better able to back their products with financial resources than individuals.

Employees

These, then, are the prima facie benefits from introducing productive organizations for consumers. But productive organizations should also be viewed from the standpoint of their effects on people as workers, that is, from the standpoint of their effects upon individual laborers and craftsmen in the state of individual production who opt to work for productive organizations.

It is not difficult to discover certain prima facie benefits, such as the following:

1. Increasing income potential (and the capacity for social contributions).
2. Diffusing personal liability.
3. Adjusting personal income allocation.

1. **Increasing income potential and capacity for social contributions.** This benefit follows immediately from the earlier fact that second-order-cooperative specialization increases productive efficiency. The person, like Smith's hypothetical pin maker, who joins others in the production of pins is able to make many times more pins than he would alone. This increase also represents an increase in his chance to receive a higher income.

2. **Diffusing personal liability.** A second prima facie benefit from the standpoint of workers lies in the capacity of an organization to diffuse liability, or in short, to insure the individual against the risk of massive compensation demands. A worker in the state of individual production who sells faulty, dangerous products is morally liable for the damages her product causes. But the extent of this liability can exceed her capacity to pay. Therefore she stands to gain by working with others in a productive organization, for it then becomes the productive organization, not she, who assumes ultimate liability.

3. **Adjusting personal income allocation.** The increased resources of the productive organization allow the worker to participate in an income-allocation scheme which is detached from the vicissitudes of his capacity to produce, and which is more closely tied to his actual needs. The vicissitudes of the worker's capacity include occasional illness, disabling accidents, and a tendency to lose speed and strength as he ages. Yet his needs persist and sometimes even increase in the face of these vicissitudes. The employee can work harder when he is healthy: but he needs as much money, and sometimes more, when he is ill. The worker may not be able to produce more when he is 50 than when he was 20, but if he marries and has a family his need for income may be greater at 50. When the worker joins a productive organization, the organization can allocate personal income according to a scheme more equitable for him and everyone else.

These prima facie benefits to the worker may be added to the prima facie consumer benefits discussed earlier. Together they constitute a set of reasons which rational people living in a state of individual production might use to justify the introduction of productive organizations. Indeed, if some such set of prima facie benefits did *not* exist, then people would be foolish to introduce such organizations; there would be nothing to gain.

It now becomes possible in light of this analysis to begin the task of specifying the general character of a hypothetical social contract. From the standpoint of society, the goal of a productive organization may be said to be *to enhance the welfare of society through a satisfaction of consumer and worker interests.* In turn, each of the prima facie benefits that we have discussed can be construed as specific terms of the social contract.

Minimizing Drawbacks:

An obvious question arises. If people in the state of individual production must agree upon the terms of the social contract, and if these terms directly relate to the task of enhancing society's welfare, then why stop with maximizing prima facie benefits? Why not also minimize prima facie drawbacks? John Locke employed a similar strategy in structuring his political social contract; he not only specified the positive goals of government, but, recognizing government's tendency to abuse privilege, also saw fit to specify certain pitfalls that government must avoid. Are there prima facie drawbacks from introducing productive organizations as well?

Our imaginary consumer stands to benefit because productive organizations, along with the technology they encourage, improve productivity and put more shoes, clothing, electricity, and automobiles on the market. But there is an unwanted consequence of which twentieth-century consumers are painfully aware: increased production tends to deplete natural resources while increasing pollution. More shoes, clothing, electricity, and automobiles require more leather, cotton, coal, and iron. The world has a finite supply. Moreover, the amazing machines so well adapted to productive organizations—the gas engines, the coal furnaces, and the nuclear reactors—all generate by-products which render the environment less fit for human life.

The problem of the increased pollution and depletion of natural resources is more obvious than a second problem, namely the diffusion of individual moral responsibility which sometimes occurs in productive organizations. In the state of individual production, consumers buy their goods from the individual craftsman who stands behind his product, or at least if he does not, the consumers know where to find him. When the cobbler sells a pair of shoes to John Doe and the shoes fall apart, he must confront Doe face to face. Contrast this situation with that of productive organizations, in which workers never see the consumer. To the employee, the consumer is faceless, and the employee's level of psychic accountability tends to lower along with a rise in consumer anonymity. The employee is responsible for his behavior, but to his superior, not to the customer; and his superior sometimes is more apathetic than he. In extreme instances the employee may participate in a form of rebellion unknown to the independent craftsman: "industrial sabotage," where workers retaliate against management by intentionally damaging products.

While speaking of potential drawbacks of productive organizations, one must also acknowledge that the political power of productive organizations is sometimes used to enhance individual interests. Such power sometimes is used to secure favors from government which damage both consumer interests and the interests of the general public. Organizations can receive favors which bolster monopoly power and aggravate inefficiency, as when the railroads in the United States in the late nineteenth century used government grants and privileges to develop a stranglehold on public transportation. Organizations can also use power to divert government expenditures from consumer items to items that actually harm the consumers' interests. In Germany prior to World Wars I and II, for example, large munitions manufacturers used their political influence to increase taxation, and thus decrease consumers' buying power, for massive purchases of cannons, tanks, fighter planes, and warships. Undeniably, from the overall standpoint of the German public, these purchases were disastrous.

From the perspective of consumers these problems represent potential drawbacks often associated with the introduction of productive organizations. But drawbacks also exist for employees.

Workers in the state of individual production possess a few obvious advantages. For one, they are close to the product and able to take pride in their own creations and the fact that their hands were responsible for the lamp, the soap, or the shirt being sold. But workers in productive organizations are typically removed from the product. They can be, in the words of Marx, "alienated" in a way that blocks their very capacity for self-realization. During World War II the U.S. aircraft manufacturers discovered that alienation was hampering production. Production was shown to increase when the draftsmen, riveters, and sheetmetal workers were taken to *see* the finished product they had worked on—the airplane itself.

In addition to possible alienation and loss of pride, the worker may also suffer from losing control over the design of the product and of his or her work structure. Whereas the individual craftsman can structure her hours and conditions to suit herself, the organizational worker must suit the needs of the overall organization. A man or woman working on an assembly line is powerless to improve the design of the product, and equally powerless to change the design of the work process. The look of the product, the speed of the conveyor belt, and even the number of steps to perform the task all have been determined by others, who are frequently strangers to the worker. Seldom even does the worker have control over safety arrangements or levels of in-plant pollutants.

The increased capacity of productive organizations (over individuals) to use large, expensive technology and massive resources reveals on the other side a decreased capacity of the workers to control their lives. They must adapt to the machines. If a machine operates most efficiently at a certain pace, then the worker must, like the spool boys of the nineteenth-century cotton industry, hurry to meet that pace. In such cases it is as if the machine were controlling the person instead of the person controlling the machine. Similarly, the increased efficiency which results from specialization reveals, on its reverse, the monotony of the simple task repeated thousands of times. The man who knocked the struts into place on the wheels of Henry Ford's Model T was far more efficient than the old craftsman who built a carriage from the bottom up. But the Ford worker knocked struts in place on wheels every minute of every working day.

These prima facie *drawbacks* may be seen as reasons for *not* introducing productive organizations. Unless the prima facie benefits discussed earlier outweigh these prima facie drawbacks, no contract will be concluded because rational people will not choose a lesser over a greater good. And if the benefits outweigh the drawbacks, it follows that in order maximally to enhance welfare, productive organizations should both pursue positive goals and minimize negative ones. Thus, using our discussion as a basis for this list of negative goals, we have:

From the standpoint of *consumers,* productive organizations should minimize:

1. Pollution and the depletion of natural resources.
2. The destruction of personal accountability.
3. The misuse of political power.

From the standpoint of *workers* productive organizations should minimize:

1. Worker alienation.
2. Lack of worker control over work conditions.
3. Monotony and dehumanization of the worker.

The social contract sketched out requires, then, that productive organizations maximize goods and minimize evils relative to consumer and worker welfare. But how, from a moral point of view, should the inevitable trade-offs be made between maximizing and minimizing, and between consumer interests and worker interests? For example, a corporate decision may impair worker interests while at the same time enhancing consumer interests. Consider the age-old trade-off between higher salaries and lower consumer prices. If coffee workers are paid higher salaries, then coffee drinkers pay higher prices. Conversely, if doctors are paid lower salaries, then the patients pay lower prices. These trade-offs are common not only in the area of salaries, but in many others as well.

How would the rational inhabitants of our state of individual production answer this question? Because the contract specifies that the function of productive organizations is to enhance the welfare of society, our inhabitants might choose a utilitarian standard for making trade-offs, that is, a standard that would specify that organizational policies or action should aim for *the greatest good for the greatest number.* On the other hand, they might prefer a nonutilitarian, or deontological standard, which would specify that *organizational action should accord with general policies or rules which could be universalized for all productive organizations* (i.e., which society would want all productive organizations to adopt).

Whatever the standard—and it must be acknowledged that determining the standard is difficult—two things seem certain. First, society does acknowledge that trade-offs often must be made. Society could not reasonably expect productive organizations to maximize worker interests come what may, say by adopting the policy of paying workers the absolute maximum possible at a given time, for to do so would grossly neglect consumers. If General Motors expended every bit of its resources on employees, the result for society would be catastrophic. Similarly, the consumer must not receive all the attention. Such a policy would result in poor working conditions, low salaries, and frustrated workers (no matter how satisfied employees might be in their life as consumers).

Because trade-offs must be made, it remains logically possible that people in the state of individual production would choose to introduce productive organizations and to establish the social contract, even when they expected either worker interests or consumer interests to be less satisfied than in the state of nature—so long as *overall* welfare were enhanced. In other words, the inhabitants might believe that, on balance, people as workers stand to lose from the introduction of productive organizations, and that potential alienation, loss of control, and other drawbacks make the overall condition of the worker worse than before. But if the benefits to people as consumers fully *overshadowed* these drawbacks, we should still expect the contract to be enacted.

There is a caveat which has application to the overall contract. People would make a trade-off of the kind just discussed only on the condition that it did not violate certain minimum standards of justice, however these are specified. For example, they would refuse to enact the contract if they knew that the existence of productive organizations would systematically reduce a given class of people to an inhuman existence, subsistence poverty, or enslavement. Although the contract might allow productive organizations to undertake actions requiring welfare trade-offs, it would prohibit organizational acts of injustice. It might allow productive organizations to institute layoffs under certan conditions, say, to block skyrocketing production costs; here, worker welfare would be diminished while consumer welfare would be enhanced. But it is another matter when companies commit gross injustices in the process—for example, if they lie to workers, telling them that no layoffs are planned merely to keep them on the job until the last minute. Similarly, it is another matter when organizations follow discriminatory hiring policies, refusing to hire blacks or women, in the name of "consumer advantage." These are clear injustices of the kind that society would want to prohibit as a condition of the social contract. We may infer, then, that a tenet of the social contract will be that productive organizations are to remain within the bounds of the general canons of justice.

Determining what justice requires is a notoriously difficult task. The writings of Plato, Aristotle, and more recently, John Rawls, have shed considerable light on this subject, but unfortunately we must forgo a general discussion of justice here. At a minimum, however, the application of the concept of justice to productive organizations implies *that productive organizations avoid deception or fraud, that they show respect for their workers as human beings, and that they avoid any practice that systematically worsens the situation of a given group in society.* Despite the loud controversy over what justice means, most theorists would agree that justice means at least this much for productive organizations.

Our sketch of a hypothetical social contract is now complete. By utilizing the concept of rational people existing in a state of individual production, we have indicated the terms of a contract which they would require for the introduction of productive organizations. The questions asked in the beginning were: Why should corporations exist at all? What is the fundamental justification for their activities? How can we measure their performance, to say when they have performed poorly or well? A social contract helps to answer these questions. Corporations considered as productive organizations exist to enhance the welfare of society through the satisfaction of consumer and worker interests, in a way which relies on exploiting corporations' special advantages and minimizing disadvantages. This is the *moral foundation* of the corporation when considered as a productive organization.

It is well to notice that the social contract does not specify additional obligations or rights which *corporations* have in contrast to *productive organizations* in general. The social contract justifies corporations as *productive organizations,* not as *corporations.* Presumably, then, further reasons remain to be discovered for society's establishing a certain type of productive organization, such as the corporation—with limited liability, stockholder ownership, and its other characteristics. The important task of discovering those reasons, however, must wait for another occasion. Our development of the social contract has fallen short of a full moral comprehension of corporations, but it has secured a solid footing in an equally important area: comprehending the moral underpinnings of productive organizations.

We have seen that the productive organization cannot be viewed as an isolated moral entity unconstrained by the demands of society, for its very reason for existing lies with its capacity to satisfy certain social interests. Productive organizations, whether U.S. corporations or not, are subject to moral evaluations which transcend the boundaries of the political systems that contain them. When an organization, in the United States or elsewhere, manufactures a product that is inherently dangerous, or when it pushes its employees beyond reasonable limits, it deserves moral condemnation: the organization has failed to live up to a hypothetical contract—a contract between itself and society.

When Henry Ford II referred to the social contract, he left the term "social contract" undefined. This essay has attempted to sharpen the focus of what such a contract might mean, and thereby clarify the content of a corporation's societal obligations. The social contract expresses the underlying conviction that corporations exist to serve more than themselves. This conviction emerges in the speeches of businesspeople as well as in the writings of philosophers. It is the conviction expressed by the inventor of the Model T, the grandfather of Henry Ford II, when he said: "For a long time people believed that the only purpose of industry is to make a profit. They were wrong. Its purpose is to serve the general welfare."[2]

NOTES

1. Some social contract theorists, e.g., Thomas Hobbes and John Rawls, have adopted a different approach, preferring to emphasize people's self-interested tendencies in the state of nature. This view has some definite advantages, since

one can say "Even self-interested people will agree to such and such a principle," and, in turn, one's argument gains a persuasive edge. Rawls does not literally assume that people are egoists, but he does assume that they wish to maximize their possession of primary goods. But in the present instance, no compelling reasons exist for representing people to be worse than they are, and one good reason does exist for representing them to be as they are: the presence of even ordinary (i.e., non-self-interested) motives can help clarify the conditions of the social contract.

2. Quoted in David Ewing, *Freedom Inside the Organization,* (New York: McGraw-Hill, 1977), p. 65.

Developing the Corporate Ethic

CLARENCE WALTON

My question—how may the corporate ethic be understood—was stimulated by a comment, made by one executive to the effect that some corporations are still addicted to a jungle ethic. For such enterprise the guiding precept seems to be this: get what you can, when you can, and by any means available under the law. Business is a competitive game not to be played according to the Marquess of Queensbury rules. While this ethical precept of the "robber baron" days may be sustained by some enterprises in some industries, it tends to be less evident in more mature organizations. Yet differences persist in how executives are expected to perform on behalf of their enterprise when they are in competition with others. It is to these differences that the following comments are addressed.

The nation is made up of thousands of firms each struggling for a place in the economic sun of profitability. To assure profits it must compete successfully, but new management views firms' obligation to other competitors, including labor unions, as critical to the moral tone of the company and the society. How should an enterprise interpret the fiduciary role to its employees? Basically, two quasi-philosophic answers can be given. Either the fiduciary role is to be informed by a *representationalist* ethic or it is to be informed by a *stewardship* ethic. Under the representationalist ethic, the executive operates under a clear guideline: get the best possible result for the constituency you represent. If, in the process of bargaining, your adversary or competitor makes a mistake, take enough advantage of the error to avoid risk to your own position. Next time around your adversary will have learned to behave more wisely and act more firmly on behalf of the constituency he represents.

This essay orginally was part of a longer essay "The Executive Ethic: View from the Top," by Clarence Walton in The American Assembly, *The Ethics of Corporate Conduct,* ed. Clarence Walton (Englewood Cliffs, N.J.: Prentice Hall Inc., 1977). Reprinted by permission of the author and the American Assembly, Columbia University.

Opposed to this is a *stewardship* ethic based on the postulate that managers have an obligation to guard, preserve and enhance the value of the enterprise *for the good of all touched by it.* When Reginald Jones took over the top job at General Electric he convened a conference of 300 top executives in January of 1973 to outline the corporation's and his own philosophy. He called it stewardship, by which he meant that executives are responsible for the assets of others, the economic well-being of employees, precious resources of the nation, and obligations to a world in need.

How is a stewardship ethic revealed? Not long ago, one corporate executive faced a dramatic issue whose resolution depended on how the fiduciary role was to be interpreted. A decision had been made at headquarters to close an obsolete nineteenth-century mill in New England, and the job of resolving termination issues was left to local management and to local labor leaders. When the final signed agreement reached by these two parties was forwarded to corporate headquarters there was, in the words of the president, a sense of being "appalled at the gross injustice that had been done to the workers." Under a representationalist ethic the company would have quietly bemoaned the injustice, pocketed the gains, and hoped that in future negotiations the asking price by labor would not be too high. But the ethical failure was clearly the union's.

What actually happened was the reverse. Taking careful steps not to embarrass either local management or local union leaders, the president arranged an ingenious and circuitous device which permitted the unions to reappeal the issue. Immediately upon the appeal, headquarters became directly involved in providing counsel and advice so that a far more equitable termination arrangement was arrived at. A stewardship ethic brought results that were unlikely of attainment under a representationalist moral code.

Once the basic philosophy for the fiduciary role has been determined, the task of promulgation, education, overseeing, and sanctioning becomes critical. In this, the example of IBM provides useful perspectives. T. J. Watson, who started the enterprise on the high road of success, had come to run the Computer Tabulating Recording Company when he was fired, at age forty, by John Patterson of National Cash Register. What the elder Watson expressed as a business philosophy strikes many as a simple restatement of the Puritan ethic. His son, Thomas Watson, Jr., continued the tradition by saying—aloud and often—that the company's philosophy contained three simple beliefs: respect for the individual, producing the best customer service in the world, and product excellence.

As a result of these oft-stated beliefs, there developed not only a moral *tone* for the organization but mechanisms for translating the concepts into operational realities. Job security, good wages, retirement benefits, educational opportunities, growth through advancement, the famous open-door policy for handling grievances—all were practical steps taken to demonstrate that the individual was respected. And despite a reputation for sobersidedness, IBM deliberately sought out the "wild ducks." The words were drawn from Soren Kierkegaard's story of a man on the New Zealand coast who spent hours watching wild ducks fly south in great flocks. Out of compassion, he took to feeding them in a nearby pond. Soon some of the ducks no longer bothered to fly south and wintered on what he fed. Kierkegaard's moral: you can make wild ducks tame but you can never make tame ducks wild. Said Mr. Watson: "We are convinced that every business needs its wild ducks and in IBM we try not to tame them."

What is true for Watson's company is true for Stuart and Quaker Oats. Personal development and advancement, quality products, the highest ethical and moral standards are among the stated first principles. Perlmutter put it simply for Supermarkets General: "I believe firmly that my job is to make work satisfying, rewarding, challenging—and yes, enjoyable." And the list could be extended. The point is that formation of a corporate philosophy and its clear articulation by top management are essential in promoting the moral tone.

* * *

[A] presumption [exists] that certain improvements in corporate behavior, which are expected by the general public, must come from top management. Whether the presumption is justified depends on which of the following questions is judged to be the correct one: "Have I any right to try to make persons in my organization different from what they are?" or "Have I any right to withhold myself and my beliefs in a changing value climate from helping that change take place in directions consistent with—and supportive of—my ethical beliefs?" By the very nature of their assignments, managers should favor, circumspectly, the second question because they know instinctively that top executives are renewal-stimulators. When they cease to renew and when they cease to stimulate they forfeit leadership. Janus-like, managers look *inward* to the moral fiber of those who make up the organization and *outward* to the marketplace—and beyond.

THE INWARD LOOK

The Individual

Because nothing is more precious than the individual personality, nothing is more presumptuous than a business organization behaving like a "mother" corporation. Yet there are instances when the enterprise exercises such pressure on the individual that indifference to personal problems so engendered is itself ethically dubious. There are . . . frequent comments on the price paid by executives in terms of family relationships. Yet relatively few corporations sponsor seminars for husbands and wives which seek to probe, in an ethically and psychologically sophisticated way, that delicate family-company interlock. It was once said of one large corporation that its procedure of personnel transfers made stable family life almost an impossibility. Another possibility for exploration by the ethical corporation might be the whole issue of value formation. Karl Jung reported that in psychoanalyzing American and European patients, he was constantly amazed by the differences between the two and concluded that Americans suffer from a particular type of alienation not found on the Continent. That alienation, concluded Jung, was due to the fact that Americans are a hyphenated people —white men living in a land with an "Indian soul." Jung's conclusion, lacking definitive proof, nevertheless provides interesting insights for introspections of ourselves. Are we aware of the rich diversity of our own value systems? Does that diversity enrich or enfeeble the individual psyche? Should companies care?

My point is not that the business enterprise should serve as psychologist-psychoanalyst-confessor-doctor-teacher but, rather, that in the present context, an ethical enterprise is drawn into areas heretofore untouched and should form its ethical policy or guidelines only after exploring a large range of possibilities that seem currently of little interest.

The Ethical Process

If the foregoing represent areas where the corporation will move gingerly, there are others where ethical demands for accountability may be met more effectively. And accountability attaches itself to the non-skilled worker, to top management and to the board itself.

While enterprises are moving rapidly to establish ethical guidelines or codes of conduct for their own firms, such guidelines appear to have been established without much input from the worker who is directly affected. Management has operated on the old Weberian theory of "pyramid authority" where critical decisions are made by the top and imposed upon subordinates. Given the present *consensual* climate, . . . one has to consider methods whereby middle management and other employees can be involved in formulating such codes—especially as these relate directly to the individual's special area of responsibility. The process could be long and expensive; it could also be rich and rewarding.

The process could take various forms and the following is merely suggestive. Sensitive issues which affect substantially certain kinds of work could be discussed by groups of managers engaged in that work and their conclusions sent to top management for review. It would be salutary if, then, top management returned the proposed guidelines with its observations to the lower organizational level for further critique and comment. In all cases final authority would rest with top management and/or the board. But process itself is part of the ethical content, and an individual feels more accountable when there has been opportunity to participate in stipulating the rules which determine his or her behavior.

One other area teases the imagination with new possibilities, and that is a further use of the open-door policy. Companies which employ this technique allow a subordinate who has a grievance to go over the head of his immediate superior—and to the very top, if necessary. Why restrict the open-door policy exclusively to grievances? Might not the same technique be extended to include cases where a subordinate knows he has done something unethical and simply wishes to get it off his chest? In present circumstances he simply watches, waits and hopes. There is no incentive to clear the ethical deck and considerable incentive to play it safe. But, absent serious crime, the open door could be used to encourage employees to unload some of their problems, under assurances that the penalty would not be dismissal. A totally different ethical climate could evolve. Top management would have to concede greater powers of discretion to mid-managers and they, in turn, would carry a heavier burden to determine the sanction, to protect the individual's confidence, and to decide how much ought to be reported.

The Board

While management is responsible for performance the board is ultimately responsible for policy. The present spate of criticisms tends, strangely enough, to ignore the boards themselves. Three questions are germane: (1) How should the board operate? (2) Who should sit on the board? (3) What restraints should the board put upon itself?

To the first question, the former Columbia dean, Courtney Brown, has written persuasively that corporations are not simply economic organizations but quasi-polities as well and, therefore, require some checks and balances. Drawing on his rich experiences on many important boards, Brown concluded that the functions of the chief executive officer and the board chairman should be separated and that each should report directly to the board.

While each might entertain, at times, different views of appropriate policy responses, the board would be better informed and better able to perform its essential functions when major policy questions arise.

The second question touches on the *composition of a modern board.* Various suggestions for a "public" representative, when related to widespread interest in more cosmopolitan memberships, signify a new force in public values. A corporation can wait—and be acted upon. Or it can act—and act upon itself and the society. It should act.

The first criterion for choice obviously must be competence. But beyond competence (and this term itself is subject to diverse meanings) are other needs. A good board should enlist individuals of rich experiences in business and in unions, in government and in education, in the performing-literary arts and the media. But no one should go on a board without rigorous indoctrination and education by other board members and by top management. The new board member must have a genuine understanding of the enterprise for which he is asked to assume so much responsibility. One may truly question the ethics of a corporation which recruits to the board persons of high intelligence and integrity but with indifferent knowledge of the characteristics of the industry, and makes no effort to correct their deficiency.

In carrying out board duties corporations might profitably watch a trend in university governance whereby board members are regularly assigned to a different school within the institution. The presumption is that each board member would learn more through a special assignment and that the dean of a given school would, in turn, have ready access to one seat of authority. There are problems, of course. Communication channels could become clogged by biased information, innuendo, and rumor. But here again the good judgment of the board would have to be relied upon to sift truth from fiction.

In more direct relationship to ethical behavior, Theodore Purcell, citing the examples set by General Mills, General Electric, and Pitney-Bowes, has suggested, in the May 1975 *Management Review,* the appointment of corporate-ethics specialists to identify generic questions of an ethical nature that should be asked routinely along with the usual legal, financial, and marketing questions. A strategic planner asks what would the firm's market share be if certain actions are taken. Will it run afoul of antitrust laws? The ethics advocate might want to know how a given decision will affect the right of employees, or the long-run general welfare of the cities or countries where plants are located. He might develop the company ethical code and encourage ethics seminars for managers. All this calls for an ethics director who is a strong and able manager and who has the backing of his chief executive officer. The CEO will be a prime force in the success or failure of the ethical advocacy idea.

Taking on a larger array of duties raises a significantly new question, namely, the number of boards upon which any individual can efficiently serve. Corporations might wish to examine two things: (1) the practicability of limiting the number of directorates held, and (2) the establishment of regular annual review processes of the director's activities elsewhere to preclude conflict-of-interest problems and any slippage in the performance of duties.

The Professionals

The liberal sprinkling of accountants and lawyers on boards can create especially sensitive moral problems. Take the case of the lawyer. Not so long ago it was discovered that some Philadelphia law firms had developed a practice of permitting personal injury lawyers to acquire interest in their client's causes by providing monthly support for the injured plaintiff and by paying doctor bills. Such lawyers resisted any settlement that did not handsomely repay their interest in the outcome of the case. A clamor for change produced reforms. But the problem caused when a lawyer acquires an interest in the securities of a corporate client has rarely come to public notice. The insider position gives the attorney special opportunities for special gains. While suggestions have been made that law firms should not permit a member to invest in a client's securities except with the approval of the firm's executive committee, this is only one side of the coin. The corporation has an obligation to protect itself and may actually disagree sharply with the decision of the law firm's executive committee. Furthermore, it is not uncommon for a big law firm to have two partners giving advice to clients who oppose one another in litigation. While the corporate client has a moral stake in procedures—even when approved by the lawyer's code—one rarely hears the issue discussed publicly.

Another question has been raised regarding the rights of an attorney to represent a client when, in his own conscience, he is strongly opposed to the position espoused by the corporation he is called upon to represent. In most cases the lawyer and the corporation seem to want it both ways, that is, to retain the association and to mute the differences through subtle compromises. One might ask whether a more honest policy would call for the corporation not to employ lawyers who do not really share their views; at a minimum, might not corporations ask aloud whether the law firm is honest with itself and with its client when it elects to represent a corporation with which it has substantial differences? A good rule might simply be this: no outside accountants and no lawyers with their own practice on the board. When the enterprise needs professional advice let it pay for it. Yet the proposal may represent overkill. If, therefore, accountants and lawyers stay on boards they surely must be aware that public opinion finds it hard to understand how, in the bribery cases, management could disburse sums reaching seven or eight figures without the professionals' knowledge—and possibly help. It is not hyperbole to state that a regular reading of the *United States Law Week* brings up enough incidents to warrant concern by corporations that client-professional relationships also need monitoring. Are the fees regularly analyzed for fairness and accuracy? Are the communications channels between enterprise and law firm understood?

Astronomical legal fees are ultimately paid by customers or stockholders; inordinately long periods of time given to a case by government lawyers are paid by taxpayers. Always there is the excuse that justice cannot be hurried. True enough. But the other side of the coin is that justice can be deliberately delayed by a calculated strategy on either side. . . .

There are other concerns. Enterprises having large defense contracts with government have to be very careful in using lawyers who have come from recent government employment. The law profession shows a strange ineptitude in coming to grips with this problem. One might normally think that a lawyer would disqualify himself from any transaction by his corporate client where his former public office is involved. Indeed, as one looks at corporate codes and senses the concern of enterprises to avoid exploiting proprietary information from an employee coming from another company —as well as to protect its own proprietary data—one is struck by the apparent indifference of both corporations and the law profession to meet squarely this problem of the lawyer's revolving door. If that profession does not move, should corporations prohibit lawyers from preparing applications or briefs to be used in appeals before regulatory agencies where the lawyer has recently had important connections? A District of Columbia proposal to bar a lawyer who has left a government agency from participating for a five-year period in any transaction with that agency has caused a furor. One might confidently predict the proposal will not be sustained. No extensive recapitulation is necessary to emphasize the dangers of present practices.

Unlike lawyers who are expected to play advocacy roles for their clients, accountants are presumed to act in the public interest; a further presumption in the public mind is that the profession is governed by rather precise mathematical rules which offer little room for personal judgment or deviations. In point of fact there exists a rather flexible "consultation" ethic which gives room for moral evasion. In a *Saturday Review* article of November 1, 1975, Professor Abraham Briloff of Baruch College illustrated this point by recalling the role of accountants toward firms promoting recreational land development in Florida, Arizona and California. By entering on the books, essentially as payments in full, customer pledges to pay for lots over the next decade it was made to appear that the developers were earning a fantastic profit. While this incident may be exceptional Briloff insisted that the leeway offered to accountants in determining the value of inventories on hand, plant depreciation or good-will is so ample that the "great book" called Generally Accepted Accounting Procedures can permit two plus two to equal some rather unexpected sums.

Recent court cases (Continental Vending, National Student Marketing and Penn Central) have combined to curb this sort of behavior but Briloff feels that the "Big Eight" in accounting maintain an oligopolistic stranglehold on the American Institute of Certified Public Accountants. Only they can bring voluntary reform. The Professor insisted that unless the AICPA especially stop serving as a trade association and playing the role of ostrich regarding transgressions of those within the power structure government regulation is inevitable.

THE OUTWARD LOOK

If *accountability* is the key word for assessing managers within a company, *performance* is the key word when it comes to their company's behavior in the market place. Performance itself is influenced by the economic goals established, the philosophy which permeates it and, when it surfaces as a major issue of conflict, obligations to the existing organization or to the stockholders.

Goal-Setting

So far as goal-setting is concerned, Fred Allen said a good place to start is with sensible sales and profit objectives so that subordinates will not feel inordinate pressure to make unrealistic objectives and to take an "anything goes" attitude. The same thinking was revealed by Fletcher Byrom, Koppers' chairman, when he said that profit and capital growth may determine the quality of performance but they can never be viewed as ends in themselves. The philosophy which animates the performance ethic is critical.

Strategic planners are primarily concerned with the impact of their decision on market shares and on antitrust laws. Might not the corporation routinely ask—as Purcell has suggested—that in addition to the usual legal, financial, and marketing questions, ethical questions be raised: How will the proposed action affect the rights of employees? The welfare of the community? The moral tone of society itself?

Three examples—A few examples illustrate how the performance ethic is shaped by an underlying philosophy. When Marx Toys was a subsidiary of Quaker Oats it returned an especially good profit on the sale of toy machine guns. It was an item which did not depend on seasonal demand, was easy to manufacture and distribute, was desired by retailers because of its rapid turnover—and obviously sought by youngsters. When the question of violence was raised as an ethical issue there was a tendency for some to heed the plea that nothing be changed. Here was a "hot item." In the face of strong consumer demand, someone would sell the product anyhow; further, no one really had assessed the reliability of evidence that use of the toy adversely affected child behavior. But the company, not wishing to engage in anything that might be suspect in so serious a matter, withdrew. An interesting question arises: If Quaker Oats decided to stay in the toy gun market would it have been unethical? If the answer is yes, what are the ethical implications for others—and for society at large? In an analogous situation, Milton Perlmutter reported that Supermarkets General had received occasional requests from distributors of pornographic literature which could be sold, so the vendor argued, safely within an "adult" area of the store. But management refused flatly such overtures—even though the profit margin was substantial.

Ethical sensitivity appears in other guises. For example, in the IBM guidelines a fictional story was told regarding a new product which, for security purposes, was developed under the code name CRUSH—an anacronym for Calculating Regressions Under Standard Hypotheses. It was expected that the program product, when announced, would compete very favorably with the successful program marketed by a smaller enterprise. But IBM said that the code itself was inappropriate because it could be interpreted as an intention to "crush the competition."

Proposed mergers—Often a very vexatious ethical question occurs when a board member or an executive is torn between loyalty to stockholders' interest and loyalty to the present organizational format. It has sometimes been noted how difficult this is for a responsible corporate officer who feels the merger would be good for share-holders and that management's resistance was due to self-interest. Handling proposed merger issues *is* becoming more ethically sensitive. It becomes doubly so when one management group accuses the other of raiding expeditions.

Are there ways to resolve the issue other than inflated rhetoric, name-calling, media bombardment and the like? The day may not be far off when such issues will be resolved in some kind of public forum before both stockholder groups. Suppose a debate were carried over educational television during a sufficient time frame before five knowledgeable external jurors, and further, suppose that when the debate were concluded the jurors would make their assessments known to the stockholders *before* they voted on the issue. Each management would retain the right to sustain—or withdraw—from the original positions but the conclusions would be reached after genuine full disclosure. Far-fetched? So was the thought of unions in 1875 and so was the thought of reaching the moon in 1940.

THE LARGER SOCIETY

Advocacy and Criticism

Meanwhile, as inner corporate restructuring is considered, corporate executives will likely be concerned with the shape and nature of the American society. If Lodge's prediction . . . comes true and government activity actually increases, what is the proper ethical posture for corporations *qua* corporations? Should corporate resources be used to shape public policy? Mobil Oil has acted positively to run a series of advertisements during the 1977 energy crisis which criticized short-sighted public policy. Some congressmen were upset and publicly criticized Mobil. But the corporation stuck to its guns. But advocacy is not easy. Professor Milton Friedman remarked that

> if you are a businessman at the head of a great corporation you would think three times before you spoke out on major public issues. You would look over your left shoulder and see the IRS getting ready to come and audit your accounts and you would look over your right shoulder and see the Department of Justice standing only too ready to launch an antitrust suit against you. And then, if you have more shoulders than two, you would ask what the FTC is going to do about the products you produce, and what is the Safety Council going to do about this and that and other things. You are not free to speak if you are in this position.

Silence means forfeiture of the game. There are areas where the business community is ethically obligated to speak out and take a stand. The operation of regulatory agencies is one. Regulators must be vigorous in defense of public interests, but motives are not always above reproach. Should a prosecuting agency be obliged to pay costs in some cases of obviously egregious judgment when the government loses a case? Such a practice would discipline the crusading ardor of bureaucrats who see "winning a big one" as the way to fame and power. It could equally result in an overly cautious approach. The point is not that the answer is provided but, rather, that the problem exists. There has been widespread negative criticism. There have been less constructive approaches.

Universities are another important agency. Presumed to be the critics of society, they themselves are hypersensitive to external criticism of the type mounted by Max Ways. When David Packard, William Simon and Henry Ford III criticized some faculty's hostility to free enterprise (or the Ford Foundation for its operations) the result was a volley of angry retorts from the academic community. Yet it seems to me that in the marketplace of ideas, the businessman has a role to play and that in his commitment to democratic government and to free enterprise he had better take his stand at this critical moment. Playing it safe tactically may be playing it wrong ethically.

Intermediate Organizations

Should business seek to assist in building other intermediate organizations created to improve the moral tone of business behavior? Carl Madden has censured professional schools of business for being too cautious in dealing with ethical problems. But Harvard's Robert Ackerman recently expressed a rather common view when he said that

> the literature on ethics and corporate social responsibilities began to be so full of rhetoric and so void of sensitivity to the problems of managing the large corporation that I fully intended to let the matter drop. Then one afternoon that 1971 summer, a proposition came into focus that I had only dimly perceived before: the difficulty corporations were having in satisfying their social critics might lie precisely in the organizational innovations that had permitted them to cope effectively with diversifications and competitive conditions. Ironically, the genius of American business might be flawed, not because of dubious intentions or its interests in profits, but because it could not implement responses to social change with sufficient speed and competence.

Certainly since that date the Harvard Business Faculty has been very active in exploring the role of ethics in corporate affairs.

There is a new movement within universities that might well commend themselves to positive support by business and the following note is appended to suggest the growing range of possibilities. The proposition offered here is that if business has often found faculties hostile toward them, they could support autonomous centers that refrain from ideological warfare against free enterprise yet criticize those whose own behavior tends to subvert the values of that system. Examples come to mind.

The University of Virginia has attempted to develop greater ethical sensitivity through its School of Business and under the leadership of Stuart Shepherd. Fred Allen of Pitney-Bowes and Fletcher Byrom of Koppers are spearheading efforts to bring other new organizations into being.

In January 1977 The Catholic University of America announced a new Center for Organizational Ethics. Funded by seed money from the National Endowment for the Humanities, the Center plans to tackle initially four major projects:

1. *Concept-building* which provides ethical responses to imperatives brought on by ecology, consumerism, minority claims, third-world views and the like.
2. *Case-writing* not only for use in professional schools of business but for use in liberal arts courses as well.
3. *Comparative analyses* of professional codes to determine common assumptions, explore differences, and to contrast them with practices in other countries. For example: conflicts of interest seem to have significantly different meanings to accountants and lawyers in America and both differ from prescribed professional behavior in England.

4. *Counselors-for-Business*—a project which, because of its novel nature, requires additional explanation.

Drawing on the experiences of the Hague International Court of Justice, plans are under way to create a distinguished panel of experts from business and law, moral theology and social science, government and journalism, etc., who would be on call to review different ethical issues as these arise. A "jury" of four or five of them could, with adequate staff help, issue advisory opinions on certain problems which come to light. Such opinions would, therefore, add the force of external moral suasion. Successful performance over a period of time would bring to it a greater recognition by courts and Congress—and by business itself. Further if a corporation is taxed by a particularly vexatious issue, the center could—providing no clear violations of the law are involved—offer opinions on request and on a confidential basis which management is free to accept or reject. Help in assessing guidelines could come and, very importantly, the whole state of the art could be advanced. Will these distinguished counselors be a success? The answer is as ambiguous as the project is risky. Ideally, the center should be eventually so successful that it would be no longer needed.

"Life is not so simple" marks the beginning of ethical wisdom. When life has become so complex that it literally spews forth problems, we have great difficulty—and great opportunity. Seizing the opportunity is the current challenge. Yet harvesting creative ideas and noble thoughts comes infrequently in history. Vintage years are scarce. But they do occur: 1685 was a vintage year for music when Bach, Scarlatti and Handel were born; 1776 was a vintage year for freedom because of Thomas Jefferson, Adam Smith and Richard Arkwright.

Will the future bring vintage years for corporate ethics? Interesting question, *n'est-ce pas?*

PART III

Property, Profit and Justice

Issues about money and economics are often connected to those of ethics and values. If a friend borrows five dollars and later refuses to repay it, then the issue quickly becomes an ethical one—we say the friend really *should* repay the money. At higher levels of economics, ethical issues also play an important role. For example, to decide how society can best distribute wealth, one must know what ethical standards distinguish fair from unfair distributions. Thus it is not surprising that two well-known economists, Adam Smith and Karl Marx (both of whom are discussed in this section), actually began their careers as philosophers.

Two of the most volatile issues in economics have ethical implications: the importance of the profit motive and society's treatment of private property. The pursuit of profit and the existence of private property are said by some economists to be the foundation of a free society. The eighteenth-century philosopher John Locke argued that each person has a natural *right* to own property. However, others argue that the profit motive and private property cannot be ethically justified because they result in labor abuses, unfair income distribution, monopolistic practices, and misuse of the environment.

A third issue involving both economic matters and ethical and political concerns is the nature of justice. For example, is there such a thing as a just distribution of wealth, resources, and opportunities in society? Can moral reasons be given to show that some people *ought* to have more of these and others less?

TRADITIONAL THEORIES ABOUT PROFIT AND PROPERTY

The Profit Motive

It is not uncommon today to hear of a person or corporation condemned for being greedy. Such an attitude, which questions the morality of emphasizing profit and monetary gain, is not new. If anything, the modern period is one in which people are more accepting of economic pursuits than at other times in history. Before the nineteenth century, hoarding wealth and lending money for profit were targets of intense criticism.

The greatest defender of the profit motive was the eighteenth-century philosopher-economist Adam Smith. Today, nearly 200 years after Smith presented his ideas in *The Wealth of Nations* (excerpts of which are presented in this section), his name is almost synonymous with the defense of the free market (*laissez-faire*) economic system. However, Smith did not believe that economic gain was man's most noble goal; rather he agreed with his professor of moral philosophy, Francis Hutcheson, who claimed that benevolence, not self-interest, was humanity's most noble motive. But in contrast to his teacher, Smith asserted that human good could—at least within the marketplace—follow from the free pursuit of self-interest. In the most famous quotation from *The Wealth of Nations,* he says:

> It is not from the benevolence of the butcher, the brewer, or the baker that we expect our dinner, but from their regard of their own interest. We address ourselves not to their humanity, but to their self-love and never talk to them of our own necessities, but of their advantage.

Thus Smith emphasized the way in which pursuing one's own economic self-interest in the free marketplace could enhance public welfare. Smith believed the world was designed so that people pursuing their own selfish economic ends will tend to generate, in the absence of governmental intervention, great public good. He calls this special tendency the "invisible hand," a tendency that guides each person's pursuit of self-interest into a pattern of healthy competition—which, in turn, yields high quality products at the lowest possible prices. It has been said that Smith showed people how a "private vice" can be transformed into a "public virtue."

Criticisms of the Invisible Hand

By the time of the Industrial Revolution in the early nineteenth century, Smith's ideas dominated economic theory. Interestingly, many of the emerging social patterns of that era were justified by appealing to his philosophy. The increased specialization, the reduction of quotas and tariffs, and the increased reluctance to allow government to regulate business—all these were justified by appealing to Smith's *Wealth of Nations.* Smith himself, however, did not live to see the changes; nor did he live to see some of the human misery which became commonplace during the Industrial Revolution. Labor was poorly paid, working conditions were deplorable and working hours were very long. And one of the most depressing aspects of it was child labor in the factories where children often worked for sixteen hours a day, six days a week in order to add to a family's meager income.

Many witnesses of the Industrial Revolution were persuaded that the economic system itself was to blame for these problems. The German philosopher and economist Karl Marx argued that the "free market" Smith had championed was little more than a convenient fiction for capitalist property owners. Whereas Smith had praised the competitive market because of its ability to generate better products at lower prices, Marx argued that in the marketplace workers themselves were considered as mere commodities available to factory owners at the lowest possible wages. Indeed, he believed that the pressures of the marketplace would force the worker, who could not refuse to work without starving, to accept wages barely above a subsistence level. Meanwhile the owner of the means of production, the capitalist, could exploit the worker by using his labor and then selling the worker's product at a profit to himself. Marx identified the difference between the costs of production, including wages, and the selling price of the product as "surplus value." For Marx, then, *profits* always meant exploitation of the worker by the capitalist; and whenever technology develops, the economic gap between the capitalist and the worker must widen further, because technology makes products more efficiently with less human labor, thus promoting unemployment and lower wages.

In the selections taken from *Economic and Philosophic Manuscripts of 1844,* Marx outlines his influential theory of alienation, in which he asserts that the worker in capitalistic society is separated from, and deprived of, his very own labor. When the worker is forced to work for the capitalist he is also forced to give the capitalist what most belongs to the worker—his own work. The factory employee toils away producing items which the factory owner shall eventually sell, and he feels no connection to the product he produces; rather, he has been *alienated* from the effects of his labor. Thus, through the concept of alienation Marx offers a fundamental condemnation of the modern capitalistic economic system.

At the same time that Marx was developing his criticisms of capitalism, another and equally dramatic development was taking place. In 1858, the English naturalist Charles Darwin published his monumental work on evolution, *The Origin of the Species.* Darwin argued, in short, (1) that organisms in the biological kingdom had evolved from simple to more complex species; and (2) that during this process organisms less adaptable to the environment did not survive, whereas more adaptable ones flourished. Darwin himself expressly stated that his ideas applied only to the biological kingdom, but many thinkers used his principles to examine social and economic issues. The resulting theory of society, which was popularized by Herbert Spencer and industrialists such as Andrew Carnegie (whose article, "Wealth," is reproduced in this section), was known as Social Darwinism.

Social Darwinism was to have its effect on issues with which Adam Smith and Karl Marx dealt, but in point of fact it agreed with neither view. The Social Darwinists argued that the Industrial Revolution was an example of social evolution from simple societies to complex communities. In the evolution of a capitalistic industrial system, then, some individuals may suffer, but the system itself makes a great contribution to human welfare since it weeds out the unsuccessful, weak competitors and allows the tougher ones to flourish. Thus, both the marketplace and nature work according to the very same iron laws. Those who can, survive, and those who cannot, perish. In this way, the thesis of Social Darwinism was used to justify the profit motive, which for the Social Darwinist simply represents the essential motivating force in the struggle for economic survival. Unfortunately, the entire theory of Social Darwinism was also used in the nineteenth century as a justification for deplorable working conditions and massive economic inequalities.

We see, then, how issues in this section of Part III center on questions of human motivation, the nature of people, and the best economic system for society. Interestingly enough, all these questions are interrelated. For example, the ethical question of when, if at all, it is best for people to be motivated by profit is directly connected to the question of what kind of nature is common to human beings. For if it is true, as some have argued, that people *must* and will pursue their own self-interest because of their very nature, then it can be argued, as Smith does, that the pursuit of self-interest in the form of economic gain is often morally justified. In a similar fashion, both these issues are tied to that of which economic structure is best for society. If people are naturally self-interested, and if it is right that profit should be pursued in the marketplace, then perhaps society needs an economic system which acknowledges and reflects these facts. On the other hand, one may argue that the pursuit of self-interest should be avoided, and that no economic system should encourage people to be selfish if one believes that society is thereby harmed.

The case study, "Abbott Laboratories: Marketing Infant Formula in the Third World," illustrates both the positive and the negative features of a free self-interested pursuit of profit in the marketplace. Abbott, like the Nestle Corporation, markets powdered infant formula to developing nations. Critics of this activity argue that because of its misuse by uninformed mothers the infant formula is a contributor to the deaths of thousands of babies. The case deals with Abbott's evaluation of these sales both from the standpoint of corporate profits, and from that of the effects of infant formula misuse in the Third World.

Private Ownership

Another important issue is that of public versus private ownership, an issue which is closely connected to that of the profit motive. A common argument used by those who criticize private property deals with motives. They argue that the elimination of private property makes it impossible for people to pursue wealth, and thus discourages them from acting from a bad motive, i.e., the profit motive. However, many arguments made both for and against private ownership can be examined apart from this point of view. Among these is the classical and ingenious argument in favor of private property offered by the eighteenth-century English philosopher, John Locke.

Locke believed that human beings have a fundamental right to own private property, and the basic premises which establish this right can be found in the selection from his *Second Treatise on Government.* Even today these arguments are commonly used in defending the right to own property. Locke asserts what he claims is a truism: namely, that in the absence of any formally structured society, i.e., in the "state of nature," all people may be said to *own their own bodies.* Moreover, all people living in such a state may be said also to possess the *right* to own their own bodies. It was upon this seemingly obvious premise that Locke rested his defense. Because if one admits that one has the right to own one's body, then it follows that one owns the actions of that body, or in other words, one's own labor. Finally, one also owns, and has a right to own, the things with which one mixes one's labor. For example, if in the state of nature a person picks fruit from wild bushes, then that person may be said to own that fruit. And if we admit that property may be freely traded, given, and accumulated, then we have the beginning of the basis for solid justification of vast ownership of capital and land.

In sharp contrast to Locke's seemingly benign defense, Karl Marx argues that private property is actually an institution which perpetuates the class struggle. He believes that it is likely that no such "state of nature" as Locke described ever existed, and he tries to give an accurate historical account of the evolution of the institution of private property. In the selections from *The Communist Manifesto,* Marx tries to show how, at every stage in a struggle for private property, one class succeeds in exploiting another. Thus, he argues that the institution of private property in a capitalistic economic system is nothing other than the means by which the privileged class, i.e., the capitalists or bourgeoisie, exploits the class of the less privileged, i.e., the workers.

We should remind ourselves that the immediate question confronting most people in the Western world is probably not whether to adopt a purely communistic or a purely free market form of economy. Of more immediate practical significance is the question of *how much* of society's goods and services should be placed in public ownership. How important is it, for example, that certain of society's economic institutions remain in the hands of private ownership? Can businesses which are privately owned contribute as much to the public welfare as those which are publicly owned? Is it possible for the latter, like the post office or public utilities, to violate basic human rights and freedoms? In this context the case "Plasma International" raises the question of the good or bad effects of allowing the market to distribute goods and services—especially when the good is a human necessity, like blood.

PROFIT AND PROPERTY: MODERN DISCUSSIONS

One of the most outspoken critics of public ownership in the twentieth century is the economist Milton Friedman. Strongly opposing Marx, Friedman argues that the maintenance of the economic institution of private property is necessary to ensure basic political rights and freedoms. In his article, "The Social Responsibility of Business Is to Increase Its Profits," Friedman denies the claim that businesses have obligations to society over and above their obligation to make a profit. In the spirit of Adam Smith, Friedman believes that the free market works best, and makes its greatest contribution, when companies compete for the consumers' business and for the maximization of profits. Consequently, says Friedman, if a company were to make social responsibility a primary goal it would be failing in its duty—and hence, ironically would not be fulfilling its real "social responsibility." The social responsibility of a corporate manager is simply to maximize profits on behalf of the corporation's owners, the shareholders.

Friedman strongly objects to placing society's major economic institutions in public ownership. Not only would the competitive marketplace be undermined, thus resulting in poorer products and services for the consumer, but a basic freedom would be denied insofar as the government would be interfering with the right to own property. In other of his writings, Friedman even argues that certain institutions that are now public, such as the post office and national parks, should be turned over to private investors.

How seriously one takes either Friedman's arguments, or ones asserting the opposite—that the railroads, oil industry, etc. should become publicly owned—will hinge on how seriously one takes the arguments of Locke and Marx. Is Locke correct in arguing that there is a natural right to private property? And how does his argument relate to Marx's claim that private property makes it possible for one class to exploit another?

In the case study, "The Chrysler Corporation," the issue of the role of government in assisting private enterprise is raised. Should the government have helped Chrysler through its financial crises? Or should government stay out of the affairs of private business?

Friedman's proposal for a free market has received widespread attention in the 1980s as a potential solution to our economic problems. But the proposal has also been sharply criticized. Joan Robinson, a noted British economist, argues that a free market (laissez-faire) theory is inconsistent because it cannot reconcile its ideals of free trade, competition, stable prices and full employment unless there is government intervention. Thus free market theory seems to be self-defeating.

Some contemporary thinkers challenge the Lockean notion of property on which Friedman relies. In a reading included in this section, George Cabot Lodge contends that the Lockean notion of private property is no longer faithful to contemporary property relationships. Lodge notes the disintegration of the absolute right to private property and suggests that this disintegration has occurred both because the courts have systematically weakened property rights for the sake of public interest, and because corporations have "dispersed ownership" by selling shares of stock. Locke's notion of private ownership had given way to a broader sense of community where basic human claims to survival, a decent standard of living, and a clean environment override traditional property claims. The result, in brief, is a reevaluation not only of private property, but of labor rights and the traditional ideas of freedom and responsibility.

JUSTICE

The subject of social justice, both for traditional and modern philosophers, is directly connected to economics and ethical theory. For example, one subcategory of justice that is a principle topic in this section, namely, "distributive justice," concerns the issue of how, and according to what principle, the society's goods *should* be distributed. Although justice is a fundamental concept, its scope is not broad enough to include all ethical and political goods. Thus, no matter how desirable it may be to have justice established in society, we must acknowledge other goods also worth having, such as benevolence and charity. Justice refers to a minimal condition which should exist in a good society, a condition that traditionally has been interpreted as "giving each individual his due."

This notion of justice, however, requires further clarification, as illustrated by the following story: Once a group of soldiers found themselves defending a fort against an enemy. The soldiers were in desperate need of water, and the only source was 200 yards from the fort in enemy territory. Courageously a small group sneaked outside the fort, filled their canteens with water, and returned safely. After showing the water to their fellow soldiers, the successful adventurers proposed that it should be distributed in accordance with the principles of justice. Since justice requires distribution on the basis of merit, they said, they themselves should get the water because they risked their lives in obtaining it. There was considerable disagreement. Although agreeing that justice requires distribution on the basis of deserving characteristics, a different group of soldiers, which had been longest without water, claimed they deserved it more because they *needed* it more than the others. After all, they were the thirstiest. And still a different group, agreeing with the same general principle of justice, argued that *everyone* deserved *equal* amounts of the water because all human beings, considered generally, have equal worth. The moral, obviously, is that an adequate concept of justice must specify the particular characteristic or set of characteristics which, when possessed by human beings, will serve as the basis for "giving each person his due."

Although the subject of distributive justice is a popular topic among modern philosophers, some claim that the mere idea is prejudicial and controversial. If a society's goods are to be distributed, then doesn't this imply the existence of a distributing agency (such as the government) to enforce certain principles of distribution, thus taking away from those who have more than they deserve and giving to those who have less? Yet it can be argued that the very existence of such a process violates basic principles of individual liberty because it denies individuals the opportunity to engage freely in the transactions of goods. In this way it is maintained that distributive, and redistributive, practices necessitate the violation of basic liberties and freedoms, and therefore that no willful distribution can itself be just.

The fundamental issue of individual liberty, along with questions about the right of government to interfere with such liberty, are found in F. A. Hayek's essay, "The Principles of a Liberal Social Order." As one of the best-known defenders in the twentieth century of a free and unregulated social order, Hayek is anxious to distinguish the kind of society in which the free actions of individuals combine to yield a "spontaneous" social order from the kind of closed, regulated society in which the social order is a consequence of design. It is only in a spontaneous social order, Hayek believes, that individual liberty can be meaningful. As soon as one begins to demand that a certain order must be imposed (for example, that people should receive goods and services in proportion to their needs), then it becomes necessary to abolish the spontaneous social order and to institute strong government control—both of which open the door to totalitarian practices. Hayek admits that a free society does not always yield a direct correspondence between personal merit or need and the distribution of goods and services; yet he emphatically denies that such a correspondence can be brought about without sacrificing an even more important political value, namely, an open society which protects individual liberty. Thus Hayek is one of the foremost advocates of spontaneous social order as the foundation for a just society, and his views have had a significant impact upon other well-known modern theorists, such as John Hospers and Robert Nozick.

Another modern writer presented in this section, John Rawls, also considers questions of justice and the social order. In contrast to Hayek, Rawls believes that the idea of distributive justice can be coordinated with principles of individual rights and liberties. He argues that a just society is one in which agreements are freely made and in which no one is left out and deserving people are not short-changed. Rawls argues that a just society is based on two principles: (1) " . . . each person engaged in an institution or affected by it has an equal right to the most extensive liberty compatible with a like liberty for all. . . ." and (2) " . . . inequalities as defined by the institutional structure . . . are arbitrary unless it is reasonable to expect that they will work out to everyone's advantage and provided that the positions and offices to which they attach or from which they may be gained are open to all." Thus Rawls is not arguing that in a just society things would be structured so as to give all people an equal number of goods, e.g., money, education, or status; and he allows that some people may have a great deal more than others. However, in order for a society to be just, such inequalities are only acceptable if their existence is to the advantage of the least fortunate as well as to everyone else. Rawls further specifies that no form of distribution in any society is just unless it satisfies the first condition of justice: freedom. Rawls's article, "Distributive Justice," excerpts of which are presented in this section, first appeared in 1967 and is a precursor of his influential book, *A Theory of Justice,*[1] in which he more fully develops the views presented here.

NOTE

1. John Rawls, *A Theory of Justice* (Cambridge, Mass.: Harvard University Press, 1971).

TRADITIONAL THEORIES OF PROPERTY AND PROFIT

Case Study—Abbott Laboratories: Marketing Infant Formula In The Third World

EARL A. MOLANDER

On December 10, 1978, Abbott Laboratories received notification that the Religious of Jesus and Mary, a Catholic order holding 100 shares of Abbott stock, would present to company shareholders at the upcoming annual meeting a proposal to establish a review committee to oversee the company's promotion of infant formula in developing nations. The proposal submitted read in part:

> WHEREAS medical testimony before the U.S. Senate linked higher levels of infant mortality and disease to bottle feeding in unsanitary and poverty conditions,
>
> WHEREAS expert testimony also confirmed that promotion practices of infant formula and milk companies encourage women to abandon breast-feeding in favor of expensive commerical preparations and feeding bottles,
>
> WHEREAS the management of Abbott/Ross has shown concern for the misuses inherent in marketing baby formula in environments characterized by lack of income, education, sanitation and medical care,
>
> THEREFORE BE IT RESOLVED that the shareholders request the Board of Directors to establish an Infant Formula Review Committee having the following structures, function and duties.. . .

THE COMPANY

Abbott Laboratories is a diversified multinational manufacturer of pharmaceutical, hospital, and health care products headquartered in Chicago, Illinois. In 1977, total Abbott sales were $1.24 billion, of which 33 percent were in 160 countries overseas.

Abbott, through its Ross Laboratories division (hereafter referred to as Abbott/Ross), and the Mead Johnson division of Bristol-Myers dominate

From "Abbott Laboratories Puts Restraints on Marketing Infant Formula in the Third World," in *Responsive Capitalism.* Earl A. Molander, ed. (New York: McGraw-Hill Book Company, © 1980), pp. 264–83. Reprinted with permission of the publisher.

the United States infant formula industry with 55 and 35 percent of the market, respectively. Overseas, Abbott/Ross faces stiff competition from Mead Johnson, the Wyeth Laboratories division of American Home Products, and numerous foreign producers. In that part of the overseas infant formula market that is in the developing countries (estimated by Abbott to be about $350 million), Abbott/Ross's market share is only 6 percent. The market in the developing countries is dominated by Nestlé of Switzerland with an estimated 60 percent of all sales.

INFANT FORMULAS: HISTORY[1]

For various physiological and psychological reasons, a small percentage of mothers (variously estimated at between 5 and 20 percent) are unable to provide sufficient breast milk for their newborn infants.[2] (This number rises substantially if the mother is malnourished, in which case the volume of breast milk, not the quality, decreases.) Still other mothers prefer not to breast-feed, either for reason of convention, because they work, or for personal reasons.

Until the Industrial Revolution, virtually all infants were breast-fed. In limited instances a natural mother's breast-feeding failure was compensated for by the employment of wet nurses. Nevertheless, infant mortality was high. There were attempts at artificially feeding, usually using spouted pots of pottery, pewter, or silver, but in almost all instances the infant eventually died.

Around 1800 the invention of mass-produced glass bottles fitted with nipples of various sorts improved the infant survival rate, but it was not until the late nineteenth and early twentieth centuries that three developments made widescale success with bottle-feeding possible: (1) development of safer water supplies and sanitary standards for handling and storing milk; (2) further development of easily cleansed and sterilized bottles and nipples; and (3) alteration of the curd tension of milk through processing to make it more digestible by the infant.

To meet the growing demand for a high-grade infant formula which could as closely as possible approximate a mother's breast milk and be fed to an infant with a nippled bottle, in the 1920s, the company that in 1964 became the Ross Laboratories division of Abbott developed Similac, a product made from skim milk, lactose, and other ingredients.

Even with the development of breast-feeding alternatives, into the 1940s two-thirds of newborn infants in the United States were still breast-fed. Beginning in the late 1940s, breast-feeding became unpopular with many mothers, almost exclusively for reasons of convention. Many infants were bottle-fed with a preparation of evaporated cow's milk, sometimes with carbohydrates added, diluted with water. This feeding was supplemented with cod liver oil for vitamin D and fruit juice for ascorbic acid, the only significant vitamin deficiencies associated with bottle-feeding. With this change went an increased demand for infant formula.

The percentage of women choosing to initiate breast-feeding remained nearly constant at 22 percent from the early 1950s to the early

1970s. However, in the mid-1970s breast-feeding enjoyed a resurgence to where approximately 50 percent of mothers of newborn infants in 1978 were choosing to breast-feed.

CRITICISM OF OVERSEAS MARKETING PRACTICES

For reasons which would eventually become a question of considerable debate among health officials, infant formula manufacturers, and their critics, many mothers in developing countries, especially in urban areas, began to move away from traditional breast-feeding practices and feed their babies with bottles. Among the breast milk substitutes were infant formula, powdered cow's milk (millions of pounds of dried skim milk were donated to developing countries as a part of United States food aid programs), and various mixtures of indigenous foods.

In the late 1960s, health officials in developing countries began to note symptoms of malnutrition and diarrhea in bottle-fed babies, a syndrome that has come to be called "bottle illness." Certain health officials drew a direct connection between this syndrome and the promotional practices of infant formula companies, although in the majority of infant morbidity and mortality cases the contents of the bottle were other than infant formula. These health officials were led by Dr. Derrick B. Jelliffe, then head of the Caribbean Food and Nutrition Institute in Jamaica, who labeled the syndrome "commerciogenic malnutrition."[2]

One consequence of abandonment of breast-feeding and its replacement with bottle-fed infant formula was a loss of protective antibodies from breast milk. Far more serious, however, were the potential misuses of the infant formula by the Third World mother, including: (1) dilution with impure water, and (2) incorrect dilution. Although insufficient dilution was sometimes a problem, a more serious concern was overdilution, brought on either by failure to understand directions or by a desire to "stretch" the formula because of its substantial price (as high as 25 to 40 percent) relative to family income.

Serious concern regarding the effect of prepared infant formula products on infant nutrition and breast-feeding practices in the Third World was first brought to the attention of Abbott/Ross and other infant formula firms by Dr. Jelliffe in 1970 at a meeting in Bogota, Colombia, sponsored by the United Nations (UN). At the meeting, Dr. Jelliffe presented his charges that infant morbidity and mortality in general were linked in a significant way to the promotion and use of commercial formulas and recommended they be withdrawn from the developing countries entirely. While some of the medical and nutritional experts in attendance agreed with his charges, others took strong exception to them.

A second group of health experts, led by Dr. Fernando Monkeberg, director of the Institute of Nutrition and Food Technology at the University of Chile, took the position that more serious problems would exist if the infant formula alternative were not available. This group argued that while breast-feeding appeared to be declining, particularly in urban centers, this phenomenon was largely independent of prepared infant formula promotion. Further, the group insisted that data on morbidity and mortality had to be examined as part of a much larger picture that included maternal nutrition, sanitation, access to health care, purchasing power, education, lactation failure due to family disruption, urbanization with subsequent life style changes, etc.[3]

The two groups agreed that there was a legitimate need for alternatives to breast-feeding. They also agreed that the use of any type of breast milk supplement or alternative can create problems when combined with poor sanitation, poverty, impure water, or misinformation. But the groups disagreed substantially on the impact of the availability and promotion of infant formulas on a perceived decline in breast-feeding in the developing countries.

At the time of the 1970 Bogota meeting, most infant formula manufacturers were promoting their products through (1) the mass media—including radio, television, newspaper, and billboards; (2) samples given to health care professionals for free distribution to new mothers; and (3) "mothercraft" nurses, company employees who promoted the product in hospitals and the home. Because Abbott/Ross was a pharmaceutical and health care products firm that traditionally has marketed its products, including infant formula, directly to health care professionals, its infant formula marketing in the developing countries was concentrated originally in sales calls on health care professionals. By contrast, the majority of its competitors were food products companies, like Nestlé, experienced in direct consumer promotion and relying heavily on consumer advertising.

From 1970 to 1973, Abbott/Ross participated in a series of international meetings studying the infant nutrition issue, many under the sponsorship of the United Nations Protein Advisory Group (PAG). These meetings culminated in a 1973 PAG report in which the UN group declared, "It is urgent that infant formulas be developed and introduced to satisfy the special needs of infants who are not breast-fed."[4] The report was also critical of current industry promotion practices, however, and laid down specific "Recommendations to Industry" regarding how infant formulas should be marketed in the Third World.

In order to establish better control over its international sale of infant formula, in the spring of 1974, Abbott/Ross published its own "Code of Marketing Ethics for Developing Countries," the first in the infant formula industry. Following the PAG guidelines, Abbott's code prohibited mass-media marketing and emphasized the need for advice from health care professionals to help the new mother with the choice of whether to breast-feed and the choice among competing infant formulas. (The most recent edition of the code, which contains substantial changes from the first code, is presented as Appendix 1.)

INTERNATIONAL COUNCIL OF FOOD INDUSTRIES

Abbott/Ross, after inaugurating its own code of marketing ethics, joined several other companies in an effort to unite all the infant formula companies in adopting a uniform marketing code. This effort eventually led to the founding of the International Council of Infant Food Industries (ICIFI).

A meeting of ICIFI in November 1975 led to the formulation of an industrywide code of ethical conduct. Dave Cox, president of Ross Laboratories, recalled the meeting in Geneva, Switzerland:

> At the meeting, I posed nine minimum conditions under which I thought this problem [criticism of the industry] would be resolved and not get bigger. And I was voted down 8–1 on all of them. I offered to compromise on all of these nine criteria except media promotion to parents, but still could not reach accord with the other companies.[5]

Having failed to resolve so basic an issue, Abbott/Ross opted not to become a member of ICIFI.[6]

INFANT FORMULA MARKETING BECOMES A PUBLIC CONTROVERSY

In 1974, public awareness of the infant formula marketing issue increased dramatically when a Swiss citizens' action organization, Arbeitsgruppe Dritte Welt (Third World Working Group), published a pamphlet entitled *Nestlé Kills Babies*. In response, Nestlé filed a libel suit against the group. Although the group was convicted of the charge and paid small fines, the suit and trial had the effect of drawing worldwide attention to the infant formula companies.

From 1975 onward, articles about the infant formula controversy began to appear with increasing frequency in various United States publications. Many carried striking titles such as, "Baby Formula Abroad: Exporting Infant Malnutrition"; "Bottle Babies: Death and Business Get Their Market"; "Nestlé's Latest Killing in the Bottle Baby Market"; and "The Bottle Baby Scandal: Milking the Third World for All It's Worth."[7]

In these articles, the charges made by Dr. Jelliffe in Bogota in 1970 were reiterated. (At this point, Dr. Jelliffe had become head of the Division of Population, Family, and International Health in the UCLA School of Public Health and was a leading academic critic of infant formula promotion.) In many instances, the charges were placed in the context of generalized criticism of multinational expansion into the Third World.

INTERNAL REORGANIZATION

As the criticism of infant formula promotion practices grew, Dave Cox, president of Ross, hired Tom McCollough to deal exclusively with this problem. At one time, McCollough had been a vice president with the company. Following a number of positions with the Urban Coalition and various civil rights activities, McCollough had left Ross in 1970 to pursue a new career in educational administration. But in early 1976, Dave Cox persuaded McCollough to return to Ross where he could apply his broad business experience and familiarity with public policy and social conflict to the infant formula issue.

In June 1976, Abbott/Ross formed a permanent work team under the direction of Tom McCollough to study infant nutrition, formula, breastfeeding, and related matters in the Third World. The work team, which now includes a nutritionist, an anthropologist, a medical information specialist, and a pediatric consultant, operates in close cooperation with the Abbott international division and corporate headquarters. The team's role is to "recommend corporate policy change; undertake educational programs for breastfeeding in developing nations; monitor medical, nutritional and social research being conducted around the world related to infant feeding and breastfeeding; and publish monographs and position papers as data emerge."[8] . . .

UNITED STATES GOVERNMENT INVOLVEMENT

In early 1977, the United States government became involved in the infant formula issue. The Committee on International Relations of the House of Representatives issued a report encouraging the promotion of breast-feeding in developing nations. In May 1978, Senator Edward Kennedy's Subcommittee on Health and Scientific Research of the Senate Human Resources Committee held hearings on the sale and promotion of infant formula in developing countries. Witnesses included representatives of the four leading manufacturers—Abbott/Ross, Bristol-Myers, American Home Products, and Nestlé—Dr. Jelliffe, and other experts on infant nutrition in developing countries, and representatives from the various special interest groups which had participated in the stockholder actions against Abbott/Ross and other manufacturers, led by Leah Margulies, director of the Interfaith Center on Corporate Responsibility's infant formula campaign.

Expert and interest group testimony tended to treat the industry as a whole, only occasionally differentiating among the practices of the individual firms. When firms were cited, Nestlé received far and away the greatest amount of criticism, followed by Bristol-Myers and American Home Products. As a firm, Abbott/Ross received essentially no specific accusations.

In her testimony, Ms. Margulies was particularly critical of the marketing codes of the manufacturers, arguing,

> [T]he codes . . . are weak, and . . . legitimize the very practices that we think ought to be stopped. The codes codify how to give out free samples, instead of stopping the free samples. The codes will say that a nurse should have a company insignia on and maybe not be in white uniform, rather than stopping the nurses.[9]

In his testimony, Dr. Jelliffe reviewed the four principal arguments against bottle-fed formulas and in favor of breast-feeding:

1. Economics—the burden which infant formula purchases places on an already poor family.
2. Prevention of infection—the antibodies carried in breast milk.
3. Nutrition—more reliable and better nutrients for the infant.
4. Child spacing and population control—because of the reduced risk of pregnancy to the breast-feeding mother.[10]

Dr. Jelliffe also agreed with Ms. Margulies on the industry's ethical codes, noting: "[T]he chances of them being carried out in the periphery, where the man on the spot is judged by the sales that he makes, are very slight indeed, in my opinion."[11]

In their testimony, prepared statements, and subsequent communications to the subcommittee, Abbott/Ross and the other firms disputed some of the testimony of the expert and interest group witnesses. Nutritional experts from Abbott's Ross Division presented a review of the literature on infant-feeding practices in the Third World which suggested that infant formula products had made, and would continue to make, a contribution to infant health and survival. These experts disputed the charge that the availability of infant formula products was a major factor inhibiting the breast-feeding decision of Third World mothers. They also argued that nearly all available data dealt with "bottle-feeding," and not specifically infant formula.

The hearings concluded without any promise of forthcoming legislative proposals. However, Kennedy asked the World Health Organization to convene a conference where issues could be explored in depth. The conference was scheduled for October 1979. . . .

THE PROBLEM OF RELIABLE DATA

In trying to resolve the complexities of the infant formula promotion issue, one is confronted with very little hard data to support either the contentions of the critics or the defense from industry. There are a number of questions on which the data problem is acute:

1. What is the quantitative impact of (*a*) free samples and (*b*) commercial promotion on the decision of a mother to breast-feed?
2. Given the sociopsychological factors in lactation, what is the effect of consumer promotion on the ability of mothers to lactate?
3. What fraction of the morbidity and mortality of infants in the developing countries is attributable to misuse of infant formula, and what fraction to maternal malnutrition, environmental conditions, and the use of other than infant formula—indigenous foods of various kinds—in bottle-feeding.?

Critics cite a number of studies which they contend support their view.[12] But a close scrutiny shows the conclusions to be inferential in many instances. For example, in testifying at the Kennedy hearing, Dr. Manuel Carballo wrote:

> While no attempt has been made in this study to correlate patterns of breast feeding with the type and degree of marketing of industrially processed infant foods, it appears significant that in two of the settings where mothers were provided with free samples of milk there was also a marked low incidence of breast feeding. Similarly the extent to which knowledge about brand products has extended into urban poor and rural communities, and the diverse network of distribution channels utilized in the marketing and distribution of infant foods, would also seem significant. The possible association of these practices with patterns of breast feeding cannot be overlooked.[13]

Industry spokespersons have tended to insist that the critics' contentions be subjected to rigorous analysis. But for critics like Sister Marilyn Uline, this is a weak defense:

> I have ambivalent feelings about what constitutes hard data. What is acknowledged as hard data by industry is that which can be subjected to the rigid canons of social science. For me hard data is doctors in the Third World changing their attitudes toward infant formula marketing. If the evidence convinces them, it convinces me.[14]

Tom McCollough recognizes that the absence of solid data both to support the critics' view and support the industry's defense is a problem:

> When our work team was first formed, Dave Cox told me he wanted me to do research. We surveyed the literature and very quickly found there was a paucity of good data on infant feeding practices, especially related to infant formula. So we visited overseas sites to try to learn first hand about industry practices and talk to local health care officials and pediatricians. These field visits confirmed not only the absence of good data but the difficulty of doing good studies, especially longitudinal studies, in the fluid world of a developing nation.[15]

To deal with this problem, Abbott/Ross is funding a number of projects to study infant formula feeding practices and their health effects for the baby. These studies include a major field study in the Caribbean designed and conducted by Dr. Judith Gussler, a cultural anthropologist and Ross employee working exclusively on this issue. To monitor the research activities of others and the actions and pronouncements of industry critics, Abbott/Ross has a medical information specialist. Further, Abbott/Ross has commissioned a major study to review all the available literature and information on the subject.

SUMMATION

In spite of these efforts, the 1979 Abbott annual meeting was again the stage for a shareholder's resolution on infant feeding in the Third World. For the infant formula industry, the controversy has expanded, not abated, and has led to boycott of Nestlé products in the United States and numerous shareholder resolutions at all three major American infant formula manufacturers, including Abbott/Ross.

In 1979, the industry was confronted not just by Interfaith Center but also by the Infant Formula Action Coalition (INFACT), formed in Minneapolis in early 1977 to deal exclusively with the infant formula issue. In the period since its formation, INFACT has organized regional councils throughout the country and has forged alliances with a number of other activist groups, notably the World Hunger Coalition and the social action movements of organized mainline church denominations. Currently, INFACT is coordinating the Nestlé boycott while ICCR concentrates its efforts on the American corporations manufacturing infant formula in which they own stock.

This amorphous but well-connected coalition of infant formula critics has made for a less-than-predictable environment for the companies involved. The Abbott shareholder resolution introducing this case study is a classic example of that unpredictability.

For nearly four years, Abbott/Ross had interacted with Sister Marilyn Uline, the representative of the Adrian Dominican Sisters, and other ICRI/ICCR representatives in Chicago. Late in 1978, Abbott/Ross executives met with this group and INFACT representatives for a frank discussion of differences and recent corporate decisions. The meeting was marked by candor and a cooperative spirit. No shareholder resolution was mentioned to Abbott/Ross, leading the company to believe none would be introduced at the 1979 annual meeting. Subsequent communication between the Chicago group and the company encouraged Abbott/Ross executives in this view, although they were never told specifically that there would be no resolution. Nevertheless, some ICCR members felt that a resolution should be submitted and, seeing none from the Chicago group arranged for one to be submitted from Maryland (the Religious of Jesus and Mary).

The resolution thus came as an unpleasant surprise to Abbott/Ross. In Tim McCollough's view:

> The shareholder action raises a new question, however, and that is of legitimate negotiation and interaction between the critics and the corporation. If the perceived, authorized agents cannot be counted on, and any dissident member can circumvent the system, is it worth interacting at all if no agreements can be forged?
>
> It's disappointing to see supposedly sophisticated, liberal critics playing zero sum games. They know that "win-win" strategies are possible, but seem not to have the will or skill to make them work.[16]

APPENDIX 1: CODE OF MARKETING ETHICS FOR DEVELOPING COUNTRIES WITH REFERENCE TO INFANT FEEDING (REVISED, WINTER 1977), EXCERPTED

Restricted Promotion Of Infant Formula Products

1. We believe that unsupervised, direct promotion of infant feeding products to mothers can unjustly impel them to make decisions concerning the care and nutrition of their babies for which they may lack adequate medical or nutritional knowledge.

   Therefore, we do not advertise our products through general circulation magazines, directories, newspapers, radio, television, billboards, and other public mass media. We believe that no communication to the general public should encroach in any way on the responsibility of health care professionals to provide guidance as their judgment and experience dictate.

2. We do not encourage use of our products where private purchase would impose a financial hardship on the family, or where inadequate facilities for preparation constitute a hazard in infant health. We represent the cost of infant feeding accurately so that professional personnel can better advise mothers according to their economic status.

3. If any contact with mothers is made, either written or oral, it must be with the explicit agreement of a health care professional, so that the responsibility for that contact rests with the profession. If a company representative at any time is permitted to talk with mothers, in hospitals, health clinics, or maternity centers, that permission must be granted in writing, and a non-Abbott health care professional present.

   To help ensure that our infant feeding products are directed only to mothers who need and can afford them and have the capability to prepare them properly and to encourage professional guidance on their use, product samples are supplied only to professional health care personnel at their request. Visiting mothers in their homes is not allowed, even though requested by a health care professional.

4. We employ experienced and professionally knowledgeable company representatives who understand local needs. They are thoroughly taught the preference and value of breastfeeding, the knowledge and proper application of our products, and the influence of social pressures that can lead to unwise purchases and practices by those who cannot afford to buy infant formula.

   They are schooled to perform their duties in a professional manner and with integrity. Deception and other unethical practices are expressly forbidden. Specifically, any implication that our employees are members of a hospital, clinic, or maternity center staff is contrary to company policy. Even in the case of female employees who are qualified nurses, nurses uniforms are not to be worn. Nurses are reimbursed through adequate salary, not sales commission. The activities of our representatives must be coordinated with those of medical professionals responsible for infant and mother care. They may, under the supervision of responsible health care personnel, furnish "genuine" out-reach services in support of infant care instructions and counselling provided by the clinic, hospital or maternity center, but without any attempt to incur obligation for such services.

5. Our product label and printed instructions, in addition to stressing the importance of breastfeeding, will emphasize the need for accurate, proper proportions in preparing the formula. Pictographs as well as the written word will be included in appropriate languages.

6. While restricting our promotion to health care professionals, we will direct additional company resources to aid their overall mission by providing communications on current health care developments, and by providing them with nonproduct related services for distribution to mothers to:
   (a) encourage breastfeeding
   (b) promote good overall nutritional practices
   (c) improve infant and child care
   (d) improve sanitation

7. Further, to insure that the letter and spirit of this revised and strengthened Code of Marketing Ethics is followed, we will distribute it widely in developing countries to appropriate health care agencies and personnel. We invite those directly responsible for infant care in the developing world to report any current deviation from this Code by our employees or distributors. Unless proscribed by law, we will terminate any distributor who does not follow the Code. The company has devised internal procedures and policy to maintain ongoing surveillance of our marketing practices in these nations.

We recognize the variation that exists between countries as to state of development, economic resources and availability of trained health personnel and want our activities in all countries to conform to the spirit and letter of this Code.

NOTES

1. Much of this history is drawn from H. F. Meyer, *Infant Foods and Feeding Practice* (Springfield, Ill.: Charles C. Thomas, 1960), especially chap. 1.
2. Quoted in Barbara Garson, "The Bottle Baby Scandal: Milking the Third World for All It's Worth," *Mother Jones,* December 1977, p. 33.
3. *Marketing and Promotion of Infant Formula in the Developing Nations, Hearings before the Senate Committee on Human Resources, Subcommittee on Health and Scientific Research*, 95th Cong., 2d Sess., 1978, report by David O. Cox, president of the Ross Division of Abbott Laboratories, pp. 198–99.
4. United Nations, Protein-Calorie Advisory Group, "Promotion of Special Foods (Infant Formula and Processed Protein Foods) for Vulnerable Groups," PAG Statement No. 23, 18 July 1972, revised November 1973.

5. Interview with Dave Cox, president, Ross Laboratories, Columbus, Ohio, 2 February 1979.
6. "Infant Formula in Third World," *Commitment* (Abbott house organ), Spring 1976, p. 12.
7. Leah Margulies, "Baby Formula Abroad: Exporting Infant Malnutrition," *Christianity and Crisis*, 10 November 1975, pp. 264–67; Leah Margulies, "Bottle Babies: Death and Business Get Their Market," *Business & Society Review*, Spring 1978, pp. 43–49; Douglas Clement, "Nestlé's Latest Killing in the Bottle Baby Market," *Business & Society Review,* Summer 1978, pp. 60–64; Barbara Garson, "Bottle Baby Scandal," pp. 33–40.
8. Quoted in "Abbott Program Supports Breastfeeding," *Commitment,* Summer 1977, p. 7.
9. *Marketing and Promotion of Infant Formula in the Developing Nations, Hearings before the Senate Committee on Human Resources, Subcommittee on Health and Scientific Research,* 95th Cong., 2d Sess., 1978, p. 39.
10. Ibid., pp. 68–69.
11. Ibid., pp. 248–81.
12. See for example, T. Greiner, *The Promotion of Bottle Feeding by Multinational Corporations: How Advertising and the Health Professions Have Contributed,* Publication 2 (Ithaca, N. Y.: Cornell International Nutrition Monograph Series, 1975); T. Greiner, *Regulation and Education: Strategies for Solving the Bottle Feeding Problem*, Publication 4 (Ithaca, N. Y.: Cornell International Nutrition Monograph Series, 1977); and *U.S. Senate Hearings*, 95th Cong., 2d Sess., 23 May 1978, statement of Dr. Manuel Carballo, scientist, maternal and child health, division of family health of the World Health Organization, pp. 103–115.
13. *U.S. Senate Hearings*, p. 112.
14. Interview with Sister Marilyn Uline, Adrian Dominican Sisters, Chicago, Ill., 1 February 1979.
15. Interview with Tom McCollough, research specialist, Third World, Ross Laboratories, Columbus, Ohio, 2 February 1979.
16. Letter from Tom McCollough, Ross Laboratories, Columbus, Ohio, to the author, 14 March 1979.

Boycott Nestle News

JUNE, 1981

WORLD HEALTH ASSEMBLY CASTS STRONG VOTE TO CONTROL FORMULA PROTECTION: U.S. STANDS ALONE IN OPPOSITION

Victory! On May 21, 1981 the World Health Assembly (WHA) of the United Nations voted overwhelmingly in favor of the International Code of Marketing for Breastmilk Substitutes with the U.S. government casting the *only* "no" vote out of 122 countries voting. While we have occasion to rejoice in this decision by such a reputable group of international health experts, we must also recognize that the Reagan Administration vote is shameful to us as Americans and has isolated us from the world health community. The

Code is clearly a victory for all people concerned about stopping infant formula promotion and saving babies' lives. Although it is not binding, it is a clear statement of principles and a mandate from the WHA to member nations to examine infant formula practices in their own nations and enact legislation accordingly.

The Reagan Administration's vote did not go unnoticed. Reacting in opposition to the vote, two senior officials of the U.S. Agency for International Development (AID) resigned their posts. Dr. Stephen Joseph, a pediatrician and the highest ranking medical professional at the agency and Eugene Babb, the deputy assistant administrator for food and nutrition argued that the U.S. government was "swayed by the self-interest argument of the infant formula lobby." The Reagan vote was cast to protect the $1.4 billion worldwide formula market—at the expense of infant lives.

THE NESTLE BOYCOTT MUST GO ON!

The Reagan vote on the Code is a clear indication that we cannot depend on the U.S. government to voice opposition to continued promotion. As concerned Americans we must let our voices be heard: by other nations (particularly Third World nations), by the industry (particularly by the industry leader, Nestle) and by the U.S. government. Never before has so much attention been given to what we have known for a decade to be a widespread and preventable health hazard. It is *crucial* that we all ensure that the issue continues to receive the attention it deserves. *ACTION BY ALL OF US IS URGENTLY NEEDED!!!*

Case Study— Plasma International

T. W. ZIMMERER AND P. L. PRESTON

The Sunday headline in the Tampa, Florida, newspaper read:

Blood Sales Result in Exorbitant Profits for Local Firm

The story went on to relate how the Plasma International Company, headquartered in Tampa, Florida, purchased blood in underdeveloped countries for as little as 45[1] cents a pint and resold the blood to hospitals in the United States and South America. A recent disaster in Nicaragua produced scores

"Plasma International," case prepared by T. W. Zimmerer and P. L. Preston, reprinted from *Business and Society,* ed. Robert D. Hay, Edmund R. Gray, and James E. Gates (Cincinnati, Ohio: South-Western Publishing Co., 1976). Reprinted with permission from the publisher and authors.

of injured persons and the need for fresh blood. Plasma International had 10,000 pints of blood flown to Nicaragua from West Africa and charged the hospitals $75 per pint, netting the firm nearly three quarters of a million dollars.

As a result of the newspaper story, a group of irate citizens, led by prominent civic leaders, demanded that the City of Tampa, and the State of Florida, revoke Plasma International's licenses to practice business. Others protested to their congressmen to seek enactment of legislation designed to halt the sale of blood for profit. The spokesperson was reported as saying, "What kind of people are these—selling life and death? These men prey on the needs of dying people, buying blood from poor, ignorant Africans for 45 cents worth of beads and junk, and selling it to injured people for $75 a pint. Well, this company will soon find out that the people of our community won't stand for their kind around here."

"I just don't understand it. We run a business just like any other business; we pay taxes and we try to make an honest profit," said Sol Levin as he responded to reporters at the Tampa International Airport. He had just returned home from testifying before the House Subcommittee on Medical Standards. The recent publicity surrounding his firm's activities during the recent earthquakes had once again fanned the flames of public opinion. An election year was an unfortunate time for the publicity to occur. The politicians and the media were having a field day.

Levin was a successful stockbroker when he founded Plasma International Company three years ago. Recognizing the world's need for safe, uncontaminated, and reasonably priced whole blood and blood plasma, Levin and several of his colleagues pooled their resources and went into business. Initially, most of the blood and plasma they sold was purchased through store-front operations in the southeast United States. Most of the donors were, unfortunately, men and women who used the money obtained from the sale of their blood to purchase wine. While sales increased dramatically on the base of an innovative marketing approach, several cases of hepatitis were reported in recipients. The company wisely began a search for new sources.

Recognizing their own limitations in the medical-biological side of the business they recruited a highly qualified team of medical consultants. The consulting team, after extensive testing, and a worldwide search, recommended that the blood profiles and donor characteristics of several rural West African tribes made them ideal prospective donors. After extensive negotiations with the State Department and the government of the nation of Burami, the company was able to sign an agreement with several of the tribal chieftains.

As Levin reviewed these facts, and the many costs involved in the sale of a commodity as fragile as blood, he concluded that the publicity was grossly unfair. His thoughts were interrupted by the reporter's question: "Mr. Levin, is it necessary to sell a vitally needed medical supply, like blood, at such high prices especially to poor people in such a critical situation?" "Our prices are determined on the basis of a lot of costs that we incur that the public isn't even aware of," Levin responded. However, when reporters pressed him for details of these "relevant" costs, Levin refused any further comment. He noted that such information was proprietary in nature and not for public consumption.

NOTE

1. Prices have been adjusted in this article to allow for inflation occurring since the article was written (eds.).

Benefits of the Profit Motive

ADAM SMITH

BOOK I

OF THE CAUSES OF IMPROVEMENT IN THE PRODUCTIVE POWERS OF LABOR AND OF THE ORDER ACCORDING TO WHICH ITS PRODUCE IS NATURALLY DISTRIBUTED AMONG THE DIFFERENT RANKS OF THE PEOPLE

Chapter I
Of The Division Of Labor

The greatest improvement in the productive powers of labor, and the greater part of the skill, dexterity, and judgment with which it is anywhere directed, or applied, seem to have been the effects of the division of labor. . . .

To take an example, therefore, from a very trifling manufacture; but one in which the division of labor has been very often taken notice of, the trade of the pin-maker; a workman not educated to this business (which the division of labor has rendered a distinct trade), nor acquainted with the use of the machinery employed in it (to the invention of which the same division of labor has probably given occasion), could scarce, perhaps, with his utmost industry, make one pin in a day, and certainly could not make twenty. But in the way in which this business is now carried on, not only the whole work is a peculiar trade, but it is divided into a number of branches, of which the greater part are likewise peculiar trades. One man draws out the wire, another straights it, a third cuts it, a fourth points it, a fifth grinds it at the top for receiving the head; to make the head requires two or three distinct operations; to put it on is a peculiar business, to whiten the pins is another;

From Adam Smith, *The Wealth of Nations*, Books I and IV (1776; rpt. Chicago: University of Chicago Press, 1976).

it is even a trade by itself to put them into the paper; and the important business of making a pin is, in this manner, divided into about eighteen distinct operations, which in some manufactories, are all performed by distinct hands, though in others the same man will sometimes perform two or three of them. I have seen a small manufactory of this kind where ten men only were employed, and where some of them consequently performed two or three distinct operations. But though they were very poor, and therefore but indifferently accommodated with the necessary machinery, they could, when they exerted themselves, make among them about twelve pounds of pins in a day. There are in a pound upwards of four thousands pins of a middling size. Those ten persons, therefore, could make among them upwards of forty-eight thousand pins in a day. Each person, therefore, making a tenth part of forty-eight thousand pins, might be considered as making four thousand eight hundred pins in a day. But if they had all wrought separately and independently, and without any of them having been educated to this peculiar business, they certainly could not each of them have made twenty, perhaps not one pin in a day; that is, certainly, not the two hundred and fortieth, perhaps not the four thousand eight hundredth part, of what they are at present capable of performing in consequence of a proper division and combination of their different operations.

In every other art and manufacture, the effects of the divisions of labor are similar to what they are in this very trifling one; though in many of them, the labor can neither be so much subdivided, nor reduced to so great a simplicity of operation. The division of labor, however, so far as it can be introduced, occasions, in every art, a proportionable increase of the productive powers of labor. . . .

This great increase of the quantity of work, which in consequence of the division of labor, the same number of people are capable of performing, is owing to three different circumstances: first, to the increase of dexterity in every particular workman; secondly, to the saving of the time which is commonly lost in passing from one species of work to another; and lastly, to the invention of a great number of machines which facilitate and abridge labor, and enable one man to do the work of many.

First, the improvement of the dexterity of the workman necessarily increases the quantity of the work he can perform; and the division of labor, by reducing every man's business to some one simple operation and by making this operation the sole employment of his life, necessarily increases very much the dexterity of the workman. A common smith, who, though accustomed to handle the hammer, has never been used to make nails, if upon some particular occasion he is obliged to attempt it, will scarce, I am assured, be able to make about two or three hundred nails in a day, and those too very bad ones. A smith who has been accustomed to make nails, but whose sole or principal business has not been that of a nailer, can seldom with his utmost diligence make more than eight hundred or a thousand nails in a day. I have seen several boys under twenty years of age who had never exercised any other trade but that of making nails, and who, when they exerted themselves, could make, each of them, upwards of two thousand three hundred nails in a day. The making of a nail, however, is by no means one of the simplest operations. The same person blows the bellows, stirs or mends the fire as there is occasion, heats the iron, and forges every part of the nail: In forging the head too he is obliged to change his tools. The different operations into which the making of a pin or of a metal button is subdivided, are all of them much more simple; and the dexterity of the person, of whose life it has been the sole business to perform them, is usually much greater. The rapidity with which some of the operations of those manufactures are performed exceeds what the human hand could, by those who had never seen them, be supposed capable of acquiring.

Secondly, the advantage which is gained by saving the time commonly lost in passing from one sort of work to another is much greater than we should at first view be apt to imagine it. It is impossible to pass very quickly from one kind of work to another, that is carried on in a different place, and with quite different tools. A country weaver who cultivates a small farm must lose a good deal of time in passing from his loom to the field, and from the field to his loom. When the two trades can be carried on in the same workhouse, the loss of time is no doubt much less. It is even in this case, however, very considerable. . . .

Thirdly, and lastly, every body must be sensible how much labor is facilitated and abridged by the application of proper machinery. . . .

. . . A great part of the machines made use of in those manufactures in which labor is most subdivided were originally the inventions of common workmen, who, being each of them employed in some very simple operation, naturally turned their thoughts toward finding out easier and readier methods of performing it. Whoever has been much accustomed to visit such manufacturers must frequently have been shown very pretty machines which were the inventions of such workmen in order to facilitate and quicken their own particular part of the work. In the first fire-engines, a boy was constantly employed to open and shut alternately the communication between the boiler and the cylinder, according as the piston either ascended or descended. One of those boys, who loved to play with his companions, observed that, by tying a string from the handle of the valve which opened this communication to another part of the machine, the valve would open and shut without his assistance, and leave him at liberty to divert himself with his play-fellows. One of the greatest improvements that has been made upon this machine, since it was first invented, was in this manner the discovery of a boy who wanted to save his own labor. . . .

It is the great multiplication of the productions of all the different arts, in consequence of the division of labor, which occasions, in a well-governed society, that universal opulence which extends itself to the lowest ranks of the people. Every workman has a great quantity of his own work to dispose of beyond what he himself has occasion for; and every other workman being exactly in the same situation, he is enabled to exchange a great quantity of his own goods for a great quantity, or, what comes to the same thing, for the price of a great quantity of theirs. He supplies them abundantly with what they have occasion for, and they accommodate him as amply with what he has occasion for, and a general plenty diffuses itself through all the different ranks of the society. . . .

Chapter II
Of the Principle Which Gives Occasion To The Division Of Labor

This division of labor, from which so many advantages are derived, is not originally the effect of any human wisdom which foresees and intends that general opulence to which it gives occasion. It is the necessary, though very slow and gradual, consequence of a certain propensity in human nature which has in view no such extensive utility: the propensity to truck, barter, and exchange one thing for another.

. . .In almost every other race of animals each individual, when it is grown up to maturity, is entirely independent, and in its natural state has occasion for the assistance of no other living creature. But man has almost constant occasion for the help of his brethren, and it is in vain for him to expect it from their benevolence only. He will be more likely to prevail if he can interest their self-love in his favor, and show them that it is for their own advantage to do for him what he requires of them. Whoever offers to another a bargain of any kind, proposes to do this. Give me that which I want, and you shall have this which you want, is the meaning of every such offer; and it is in the manner that we obtain from one another the far greater part of those good offices which we stand in need of. It is not from the benevolence of the butcher, the brewer, or the baker, that we expect our dinner, but from their regard to their own interest. We address ourselves, not to their humanity but to their self-love, and never talk to them of our own necessities but of their advantages. Nobody but a beggar chooses to depend chiefly upon the benevolence of his fellow-citizens. Even a beggar does not depend upon it entirely. The charity of well-disposed people, indeed, supplies him with the whole fund of his subsistence. But though this principle ultimately provides him with all the necessaries of life which he has occasion for, it neither does nor can provide him with them as he has occasion for them. The greater part of his occasional wants are supplied in the same manner as those of other people, by treaty, by barter, and by purchase. With the money which one man gives him he purchases food. The old clothes which another bestows upon him he exchanges for other old clothes which suit him better, or for lodging, or for food, or for money, with which he can buy either food, clothes, or lodging, as he has occasion.

As it is by treaty, by barter, and by purchase that we obtain from one another the greater part of those mutual good offices which we stand in need of, so it is this same trucking disposition which originally gives occasion to the division of labor. In a tribe of hunters or shepherds a particular person makes bows and arrows, for example, with more readiness and dexterity than any other. He frequently exchanges them for cattle or for venison with his companions; and he finds at last that he can in this manner get more cattle and venison than if he himself went to the field to catch them. From a regard to his own interest, therefore, the making of bows and arrows grows to be his chief business, and he becomes a sort of armorer. Another excels in making the frames and covers of their little huts or movable houses. He is accustomed to be of use in this way to his neighbors, who reward him in the same manner with cattle and with venison till at last he finds it his interest to dedicate himself entirely to this employment, and to become a sort of house carpenter. In the same manner a third becomes a smith or a brazier; a fourth a tanner or dresser of hides or skins, the principal part of the clothing of savages. And thus the certainty of being able to exchange all that surplus part of the produce of his own labor, which is over and above his own consumption, for such parts of the produce of other men's labor as he may have occasion for, encourages every man to apply himself to a particular occupation, and to cultivate and bring to perfection whatever talent or genius he may possess for that particular species of business.

The difference of natural talents in different men is, in reality, much less than we are aware of; and the very different genius which appears to distinguish men of different professions, when grown up to maturity, is not upon many occasions so much the cause as the effect of the division of labor. The difference between the most dissimilar characters, between a philosopher and a common street porter, for example, seems to arise not so much from nature as from habit, custom, and education. When they came into the world, and for the first six or eight years of their existence, they were, perhaps, very much alike, and neither their parents nor play-fellows could perceive any remarkable difference. About that age, or soon after, they come to be employed in very different occupations. The difference of talents comes then to be taken notice of, and widens by degrees, till at last the vanity of the philosopher is willing to acknowledge scarce any resemblance. But without the disposition to truck, barter, and exchange, every man must have procured to himself every necessary and conveniency of life which he wanted. All must have had the same duties to perform, and the same work to do, and there could have been no such difference of employment as could alone give occasion to any great difference of talents. . . .

BOOK IV

Chapter II

Every individual is continually exerting himself to find out the most advantageous employment for whatever capital he can command. It is his own advantage, indeed, and not that of the society, which he has in view. But the study of his own advantage, naturally, or rather necessarily, leads him to prefer that employment which is most advantageous to the society. . . .

As every individual, therefore, endeavours as much as he can both to employ his capital in the support of domestic industry, and so to direct that industry that its produce may be of the greatest value, every individual necessarily labors to render the annual revenue of the society as great as he can. He generally, indeed, neither intends to promote the public interest, nor knows how much he is promoting it. By preferring the support of domestic to that of foreign industry, he intends only his own security: and by directing that industry in such a manner as its produce may be of the greatest value, he intends only his own gain, and he is in this, as in many other cases, led by an invisible hand to promote an end which was no part of his intention. Nor is it always the worse for the society that it was no part of it. By pursuing his own interest he frequently promotes that of the society more effectually than when he really intends to promote it. I have never known much good done by those who affected to trade for the public good. It is an affectation, indeed, not very common among merchants, and very few words need be employed in dissuading them from it.

The Justification of Private Property

JOHN LOCKE

. . . God, who hath given the world to men in common, hath also given them reason to make use of it to the best advantage of life and convenience. The earth and all that is therein is given to men for the support and comfort of their being. And though all the fruits it naturally produces, and beasts it feeds, belong to mankind in common, as they are produced by the spontaneous hand of nature; and nobody has originally a private dominion exclusive of the rest of mankind in any of them as they are thus in their natural state; yet being given for the use of men, there must of necessity be a means to appropriate them some way or other before they can be of any use or at all beneficial to any particular man. The fruit or venison which nourishes the wild Indian, who knows no enclosure, and is still a tenant in common, must be his, and so his, i.e., a part of him, that another can no longer have any right to it, before it can do any good for the support of his life.

Though the earth and all inferior creatures be common to all men, yet every man has a property in his own person; this nobody has any right to but himself. The labor of his body and the work of his hands we may say are properly his. Whatsoever, then, he removes out of the state that nature hath provided and left it in, he hath mixed his labor with, and joined to it something that is his own, and thereby makes it his property. It being by him removed from the common state nature placed it in, it hath by this labor something annexed to it that excludes the common right of other men. For this labor being the unquestionable property of the laborer, no man but he can have a right to what that is once joined to, at least where there is enough, and as good left in common for others.

He that is nourished by the acorns he picked up under an oak, or the apples he gathered from the trees in the wood, has certainly appropriated them to himself. Nobody can deny but the nourishment is his. I ask, then, When did they begin to be his—when he digested, or when he ate, or when he boiled, or when he brought them home, or when he picked them up? And

From John Locke, *Second Treatise on Government* (1764; rpt, New York: MacMillan, 1956).

'tis plain if the first gathering made them not his, nothing else could. That labor put a distinction between them and common; that added something to them more than nature, the common mother of all, had done, and so they became his private right. And will anyone say he had no right to those acorns or apples he thus appropriated, because he had not the consent of all mankind to make them his? Was it a robbery thus to assume to himself what belonged to all in common? If such a consent as that was necessary, man had starved, notwithstanding the plenty God had given him. We see in commons which remains so by compact that 'tis the taking any part of what is common and removing it out of the state nature leaves it in, which begins the property; without which the common is of no use. And the taking of this or that does not depend on the express consent of all the commoners. Thus the grass my horse has bit, the turfs my servant has cut, and the ore I have dug in any place where I have a right to them in common with others, become my property without the assignation or consent of anybody. The labor that was mine removing them out of that common state they were in, hath fixed my property in them. . . .

It will perhaps be objected to this, that if gathering the acorns, or other fruits of the earth, etc., makes a right to them, then anyone may engross as much as he will. To which I answer, Not so. The same law of nature that does by this means give us property, does also bound that property too. "God has given us all things richly" (I Tim. vi. 17), is the voice of reason confirmed by inspiration. But how far has He given it us? To enjoy. As much as anyone can make use of any advantage of life before it spoils, so much he may by his labor fix a property in; whatever is beyond this, is more than his share, and belongs to others. Nothing was made by God for man to spoil or destroy. And thus considering the plenty of natural provisions there was a long time in the world, and the few spenders, and to how small a part of that provision the industry of one man could extend itself, and engross it to the prejudice of others—especially keeping within the bounds, set by reason, of what might serve for his use—there could be then little room for quarrels or contentions about property so established.

But the chief matter of property being now not the fruits of the earth, and the beasts that subsist on it, but the earth itself, as that which takes in and carries with it all the rest, I think it is plain that property in that, too, is acquired as the former. As much land as a man tills, plants, improves, cultivates, and can use the product of, so much is his property. He by his labor does as it were enclose it from the common. Nor will it invalidate his right to say, everybody else has an equal title to it; and therefore he cannot appropriate, he cannot enclose, without the consent of all his fellow-commoners, all mankind. God, when He gave the world in common to all mankind, commanded man also to labor, and the penury of his condition required it of him. God and his reason commanded him to subdue the earth, i.e., improve it for the benefit of life, and therein lay out something upon it that was his own, his labor. He that, in obedience to this command of God, subdued, tilled, and sowed any part of it, thereby annexed to it something that was his property, which another had no title to, nor could without injury take from him.

Nor was this appropriation of any parcel of land, by improving it, any prejudice to any other man, since there was still enough and as good left; and more than the yet unprovided could use. So that in effect there was never the less left for others because of his enclosure for himself. For he that leaves as much as another can make use of, does as good as take nothing at all. Nobody could think himself injured by the drinking of another man, though he took a good draught, who had a whole river of the same water left him to quench his thirst; and the case of land and water, where there is enough of both, is perfectly the same.

God gave the world to men in common; but since He gave it them for their benefit, and the greatest conveniences of life they were capable to draw from it, it cannot be supposed He meant it should always remain common and uncultivated. He gave it to the use of the industrious and rational (and labor was to be his title to it), not to the fancy or covetousness of the quarrelsome and contentious. He that had as good left for his improvement as was already taken up, needed not complain, ought not to meddle with what was already improved by another's labor; if he did, it is plain he desired the benefit of another's pains, which he had no right to, and not the ground which God had given him in common with others to labor on, and whereof there was as good left as that already possessed, and more than he knew what to do with, or his industry could reach to.

It is true, in land that is common in England, or any other country where there is plenty of people under Government, who have money and commerce, no one can enclose or appropriate any part without the consent of all his fellow-commoners: because this is left common by compact, i.e., by the law of the land, which is not to be violated. And though it be common in respect of some men, it is not so to all mankind; but is the joint property of this country, or this parish. Besides, the remainder, after such enclosure, would not be as good to the rest of the commoners as the whole was, when they could all make use of the whole, whereas in the beginning and first peopling of the great common of the world it was quite otherwise. The law man was under was rather for appropriating. God commanded, and his wants forced him, to labor. That was his property, which could not be taken from him wherever he had fixed it. And hence subduing or cultivating the earth, and having dominion, we see are joined together. The one gave title to the other. So that God, by commanding to subdue, gave authority so far to appropriate. And the condition of human life, which requires labor and materials to work on, necessarily introduces private possessions.

The measure of property nature has well set by the extent of men's labor and the conveniency of life. No man's labor could subdue or appropriate all, nor could his enjoyment consume more than a small part; so that it was impossible for any man, this way, to entrench upon the right of another or acquire to himself a property to the prejudice of his neighbor, who would still have room for as good and as large a possession (after the other had taken out his) as before it was appropriated. Which measure did confine every man's possession to a very moderate proportion, and such as he might appropriate to himself without injury to anybody in the first ages of the world, when men were more in danger to be lost, by wandering from their company, in the then vast wilderness of the earth than to be straitened for want of room to plant in. . . .

And thus, without supposing any private dominion and property in Adam over all the world, exclusive of all other men, which can no way be proved, nor any one's property be made out from it, but supposing the world, given as it was to the children of men in common, we see how labor could make men distinct titles to several parcels of it for their private uses, wherein there could be no doubt of right, no room for quarrel.

Nor is it so strange, as perhaps before consideration it may appear, that the property of labor should be able to overbalance the community of land. For it is labor indeed that puts the difference of value on everything; and let anyone consider what the difference is between an acre of land planted with tobacco or sugar, sown with wheat or barley, and an acre of the same land lying in common without any husbandry upon it, and he will find that the improvement of labor makes the far greater part of the value. I think it will be but a very modest computation to say that of the products of the earth useful to the life of man nine-tenths are the effects of labor; nay, if we will rightly estimate things as they come to our use, and cast up the several expenses about them—what in them is purely owing to nature, and what to labor—we shall find that in most of them ninety-nine hundreths are wholly to be put on the account of labor. . . .

From all which it is evident that, though the things of nature are given in common, yet man, by being master of himself and proprietor of his own person and the actions or labor of it, had still in himself the great foundation of property; and that which made up the great part of what he applied to the support or comfort of his being, when invention and arts had improved the conveniences of life, was perfectly his own, and did not belong in common to others.

Thus labor, in the beginning, gave a right of property, wherever anyone was pleased to employ it upon what was common, which remained a long while the far greater part, and is yet more than mankind makes use of. Men at first, for the most part, contented themselves with what unassisted nature offered to their necessities; and though afterwards, in some parts of the world (where the increase of people and stock, with the use of money, had made land scarce, and so of some value), the several communities settled the bounds of their distinct territories, and by laws within themselves, regulated the properties of the private men of their society, and so, by compact and agreement, settled the property which labor and industry began—and the leagues that have been made between several states and kingdoms, either expressly or tacitly disowning all claim and right to the land in the other's possession, have, by common consent, given up their pretenses to their natural common right, which originally they had to those countries; and so have, by positive agreement, settled a property amongst themselves in distinct parts of the world—yet there are still great tracts of ground to be found which, the inhabitants thereof not having joined with the rest of mankind in the consent of the use of their common money, lie waste, and more than the people who dwell on it do or can make use of, and so still lie in common; though this can scarce happen amongst that part of mankind that have consented to the use of money.

The greatest part of things really useful to the life of man, and such as the necessity of subsisting made the first commoners of the world look after, as it doth the Americans now, are generally things of short duration, such as, if they are not consumed by use, will decay and perish of themselves: gold, silver, and diamonds are things that fancy or agreement have put the value on more than real use and the necessary support of life. Now of those good things which nature hath provided in common, everyone hath a right, as hath been said, to as much as he could use, and had a property in all he could effect with his labor—all that his industry could extend to, to alter from the state nature had put it in, was his. He that gathered a hundred bushels of acorns or apples had thereby a property in them; they were his goods as soon as gathered. He was only to look that he used them before they spoiled, else he took more than his share, and robbed others; and, indeed, it was a foolish thing, as well as dishonest, to hoard up more than he could make use of. If he gave away a part to anybody else, so that it perished not uselessly in his possession, these he also made use of; and if he also bartered away plums that would have rotted in a week, for nuts that would last good for his eating a whole year, he did no injury; he wasted not the common stock, destroyed no part of the portion of goods that belonged to others, so long as nothing perished uselessly in his hands. Again, if he would give his nuts for a piece of metal, pleased with its color, or exchange his sheep for shells, or wool for a sparkling pebble or a diamond, and keep those by him all his life, he invaded not the right of others; he might heap up as much of these durable things as he pleased, the exceeding of the bounds of his just property not lying in the largeness of his possessions, but the perishing of anything uselessly in it.

And thus came in the use of money—some lasting thing that men might keep without spoiling, and that, by mutual consent, men would take in exchange for the truly useful but perishable supports of life.

And as different degrees of industry were apt to give men possessions in different proportions, so this invention of money gave them the opportunity to continue and enlarge them; for supposing an island, separate from all possible commerce with the rest of the world, wherein there were but a hundred families—but there were sheep, horses, and cows, with other useful animals, wholesome fruits, and land enough for corn for a hundred thousand times as many, but nothing in the island, either because of its commonness or perishableness, fit to supply the place of money—what reason could anyone have there to enlarge his possessions beyond the use of his family and a plentiful supply to its consumption, either in what their own industry produced, or they could barter for like perishable useful commodities with others? Where there is not something both lasting and scarce, and so valuable to be hoarded up, there men will not be apt to enlarge their possessions of land, were it never so rich, never so free for them to take; for I ask, what would a man value ten thousand or a hundred thousand acres of excellent land, ready cultivated, and well stocked too with cattle, in the middle of the inland parts of America, where he had no hopes of commerce with other parts of the world, to draw money to him by the sale of the product? It would not be worth the enclosing, and we should see him give up again to the wild common of nature whatever was more than would supply the conveniences of life to be had there for him and his family.

Thus in the beginning all the world was America, and more so than that is now, for no such thing as money was anywhere known. Find out something that hath the use and value of money amongst his neighbors, you shall see the same man will begin presently to enlarge his possessions.

But since gold and silver, being little useful to the life of man in proportion to food, raiment, and carriage, has its value only from the consent of men, whereof labor yet makes, in great part, the measure, it is plain that the consent of men have agreed to a disproportionate and unequal possession of the earth—I mean out of the bounds of society and compact; for in governments the laws regulate it; they having, by consent, found out and agreed in a way how a man may rightfully and without injury possess more than he himself can make use of by receiving gold and silver, which may continue long in a man's possession, without decaying for the overplus, and agreeing those metals should have a value.

And thus, I think, it is very easy to conceive without any difficulty how labor could at first begin a title of property in the common things of nature, and how the spending it upon our uses bounded it; so that there could then be no reason of quarrelling about title, nor any doubt about the largeness of possession it gave. Right and conveniency went together; for as a man had a right to all he could employ his labor upon, so he had no temptation to labor for more than he could make use of. This left no room for controversy about the title, nor for encroachment on the right of others; what portion a man carved to himself was easily seen, and it was useless, as well as dishonest, to carve himself too much, or take more than he needed.

Alienated Labour

KARL MARX

We shall begin from a *contemporary* economic fact. The worker becomes poorer the more wealth he produces and the more his production increases in power and extent. The worker becomes an ever cheaper commodity the more goods he creates. The *devaluation* of the human world increases in direct relation with the *increase in value* of the world of things. Labour does not only create goods; it also produces itself and the worker as a *commodity,* and indeed in the same proportion as it produces goods. . . .

All these consequences follow from the fact that the worker is related to the *product of his labour* as to an *alien* object. For it is clear on this presupposition that the more the worker expends himself in work the more powerful becomes the world of objects which he creates in face of himself, the poorer he becomes in his inner life, and the less he belongs to himself. It is just the same as in religion. The more of himself man attributes to God the less he has left in himself. The worker puts his life into the object, and his life then belongs no longer to himself but to the object. The greater his activity, therefore, the less he possesses. What is embodied in the product of his labour is no longer his own. The greater this product is, therefore, the more he is diminished. The *alienation* of the worker in his product means not only that his labour becomes an object, assumes an *external* existence, but that it exists independently, *outside himself,* and alien to him, and that it stands opposed to him as an autonomous power. The life which he has given to the object sets itself against him as an alien and hostile force.

. . . the worker becomes a slave of the object; first, in that he receives an *object of work,* i.e. receives *work,* and secondly, in that he receives *means of subsistence.* Thus the object enables him to exist, first as a *worker* and secondly, as a *physical subject.* The culmination of this enslavement is that he can only maintain himself as a *physical subject* so far as he is a *worker,* and that it is only as a *physical subject* that he is a worker. . . .

What constitutes the alienation of labour? First, that the work is *external* to the worker, that it is not part of his nature; and that, consequently, he does not fulfill himself in his work but denies himself, has a feeling of misery rather than well-being, does not develop freely his mental and physical energies but is physically exhausted and mentally debased. The worker, therefore, feels himself at home only during his leisure time, whereas at work he feels homeless. His work is not voluntary but imposed, *forced labour.* It is not the satisfaction of a need, but only a *means* for satisfying other needs. Its alien character is clearly shown by the fact that as soon as there is no physical or other compulsion it is avoided like the plague. External labour, labour in which man alienates himself, is a labour of self-sacrifice, of mortification. Finally, the external character of work for the worker is shown by the fact that it is not his own work but work for someone else, that in work he does not belong to himself but to another person. . . .

We arrive at the result that man (the worker) feels himself to be freely active only in his animal functions—eating, drinking and procreating, or at most also in his dwelling and in personal adornment—while in his human functions he is reduced to an animal. The animal becomes human and the human becomes animal.

Eating, drinking and procreating are of course also genuine human functions. But abstractly considered, apart from the environment of human activities, and turned into final and sole ends, they are animal functions.

We have now considered the act of alienation of practical human activity, labour, from two aspects: (1) the relationship of the worker to the *product of labour* as an alien object which dominates him. This relationship is at the same time the relationship to the sensuous external world, to natural objects, as an alien and hostile world; (2) the relationship of labour to the *act of production* within *labour.* This is the relationship of the worker to his own activity as something alien and not belonging to him, activity as suffering (passivity), strength as powerlessness, creation as emasculation, the *personal* physical and mental energy of the worker, his personal life (for what is life but activity?), as an activity which is directed against himself, independent of him and not belonging to him. This is *self-alienation* as against the above-mentioned alienation of the *thing.*

We have now to infer a third characteristic of *alienated labour* from the two we have considered.

Man is a species-being not only in the sense that he makes the community (his own as well as those of other things) his object both practically and theoretically, but also (and this is simply another expression for the same thing) in the sense that he treats himself as the present, living species, as a *universal* and consequently free being.[1]

Species-life, for man as for animals, has its physical basis in the fact that man (like animals) lives from inorganic nature, and since man is more universal than an animal so the range of inorganic nature from which he lives is more universal. . . . The universality of man appears in practice in the universality which makes the whole of nature into his inorganic body: (1) as a direct means of life; and equally (2) as the material object and instrument of his life activity. Nature is the inorganic body of man; that is to say nature, excluding the human body itself. To say that man *lives* from nature means that nature is his *body* with which he must remain in a continuous interchange in order not to die. The statement that the physical and mental life of man, and nature, are interdependent means simply that nature is interdependent with itself, for man is a part of nature.

Since alienated labour: (1) alienates nature from man; and (2) alienates man from himself, from his own active function, his life activity; so it alienates him from the species. It makes *species-life* into a means of individual life. In the first place it alienates species-life and individual life, and secondly, it turns the latter, as an abstraction, into the purpose of the former, also in its abstract and alienated form.

For labour, *life activity, productive life,* now appear to man only as *means* for the satisfaction of a need, the need to maintain his physical existence. Productive life is, however, species-life. It is life creating life. In the type of life activity resides the whole character of a species, its species-character; and free, conscious activity is the species-character of human beings. Life itself appears only as a *means of life.*

The animal is one with its life activity. It does not distinguish the activity from itself. It is *its activity.* But man makes his life activity itself an object of his will and consciousness. He has a conscious life activity. It is not a determination with which he is completely identified. Conscious life activity distinguishes man from the life activity of animals. Only for this reason is he a species-being. Or rather, he is only a self-conscious being, i.e. his own life is an object for him, because he is a species-being. Only for this reason is his activity free activity. Alienated labour reverses the relationship, in that man because he is a self-conscious being makes his life activity, his *being,* only a means for his *existence.*

The practical construction of an *objective world,* the *manipulation* of inorganic nature, is the confirmation of man as a conscious species-being, i.e. a being who treats the species as his own being or himself as a species-being . . .

It is just in his work upon the objective world that man really proves himself as a *species-being.* This production is his active species-life. By means of it nature appears as *his* work and his reality. The object of labour is, therefore, the *objectification of man's species-life:* for he no longer reproduces himself merely intellectually, as in consciousness, but actively and in a real sense, and he sees his own reflection in a world which he has constructed. While, therefore, alienated labour takes away the object of production from man, it also takes away his *species-life,* his real objectivity as a species-being, and changes his advantage over animals into a disadvantage in so far as his inorganic body, nature, is taken from him.

Just as alienated labour transforms free and self-directed activity into a means, so it transforms the species-life of man into a means of physical existence.

Consciousness, which man has from his species, is transformed through alienation so that species-life becomes only a means for him. (3) Thus alienated labour turns the *species-life of man,* and also nature as his mental species-property, into an *alien* being and into a *means* for his *individual existence.* It alienates from man his own body, external nature, his mental life and his *human* life. (4) A direct consequence of the alienation of man from the product of his labour, from his life activity and from his species-life, is that *man* is *alienated* from other *men.* When man confronts himself he also confronts *other* men. What is true of man's relationship to his work, to the product of his work and to himself, is also true of his relationship to other men, to their labour and to the objects of their labour.

In general, the statement that man is alienated from his species-life means that each man is alienated from others, and that each of the others is likewise alienated from human life.

Human alienation, and above all the relation of man to himself, is first realized and expressed in the relationship between each man and other men. Thus in the relationship of alienated labour every man regards other men according to the standards and relationships in which he finds himself placed as a worker.

We began with an economic fact, the alienation of the worker and his production. We have expressed this fact in conceptual terms as *alienated labour,* and in analysing the concept we have merely analysed an economic fact. . . .

The *alien* being to whom labour and the product of labour belong, to whose service labour is devoted, and to whose enjoyment the product of labour goes, can only be *man* himself. If the product of labour does not belong to the worker, but confronts him as an alien power, this can only be because it belongs to *a man other than the worker.* . . .

Thus, through alienated labour the worker creates the relation of another man, who does not work and is outside the work process, to this labour. The relation of the worker to work also produces the relation of the capitalist (or whatever one likes to call the lord of labour) to work. *Private property* is, therefore, the product, the necessary result, of *alienated labour,* of the external relation of the worker to nature and to himself.

Private property is thus derived from the analysis of the concept of *alienated labour;* that is, alienated man, alienated labour, alienated life, and estranged man.

We have, of course, derived the concept of *alienated labour (alienated life)* from political economy, from an analysis of the *movement of private property.* But the analysis of this concept shows that although private property appears to be the basis and cause of alienated labour, it is rather a consequence of the latter, just as the gods are *fundamentally* not the cause but the product of confusion of human reason. At a later stage, however, there is a reciprocal influence.

Only in the final state of the development of private property is its secret revealed, namely, that it is on one hand the *product* of alienated labour, and on the other hand the *means* by which labour is alienated, *the realization of this alienation. . . .*

Just as *private property* is only the sensuous expression of the fact that man is at the same time an *objective* fact for himself and becomes an alien and non-human object for himself; just as his manifestation of life is also his alienation of life and his self-realization a loss of reality, the emergence of an *alien* reality; so the positive supersession of private property, i.e. the *sensuous* appropriation of the human essence and of human life, of objective man and of human *creations,* by and for man, should not be taken only in the sense of *immediate,* exclusive *enjoyment,* or only in the sense of *possession* or *having.* Man appropriates his manifold being in an all-inclusive way, and thus as a whole man. All his *human* relations to the world—seeing, hearing, smelling, tasting, touching, thinking, observing, feeling, desiring, acting, loving—in short, all the organs of his individuality, like the organs which are directly communal in form, are in their objective action (their *action in relation to the object*) the appropriation of this object, the appropriation of human reality. The way in which they react to the object is the confirmation of *human reality.* It is human effectiveness and human *suffering,* for suffering humanly considered is an enjoyment of the self for man.

Private property has made us so stupid and partial that an object is only *ours* when we have it, when it exists for us as capital or when it is directly eaten, drunk, worn, inhabited, etc., in short, *utilized* in some way. But private property itself only conceives these various forms of possession as *means of life,* and the life for which they serve as means is the life of *private property* —labour and creation of capital.

The supersession of private property is, therefore, the complete *emancipation* of all the human qualities and senses. It is such an emancipation because these qualities and senses have become *human,* from the subjective as well as the objective point of view. The eye has become a *human* eye when its *object* has become a *human,* social object, created by man and destined for him. The senses have, therefore, become directly theoreticians in practice. They relate themselves to the thing for the sake of the thing, but the thing itself is an *objective human* relation to itself and to man, and vice versa. Need and enjoyment have thus lost their *egoistic* character and nature has lost its mere *utility* by the fact that its utilization has become *human* utilization. . . .

NOTE

1. In this passage Marx reproduces Feuerbach's argument in *Das Wesen des Christentums.*

The Communist Manifesto

KARL MARX AND FRIEDRICH ENGELS

I. BOURGEOIS AND PROLETARIANS

The history of all hitherto existing society is the history of class struggles.

Freeman and slave, patrician and plebeian, lord and serf, guildmaster and journeyman, in a word, oppressor and oppressed, stood in constant opposition to one another, carried on an uninterrupted, now hidden, now open fight, a fight that each time ended, either in a revolutionary reconstitution of society at large, or in the common ruin of the struggling classes.

In the earlier epochs of history, we find almost everywhere a complicated arrangement of society into various orders, a manifold gradation of social rank. In ancient Rome we have patricians, knights, plebeians, slaves; in the Middle Ages, feudal lords, vassals, guildmasters, journeymen, apprentices, serfs; and in almost all of these particular classes, again, other subordinate gradations.

The modern bourgeois society that has sprouted from the ruins of feudal society has not done away with class antagonisms. It has only established new classes, new conditions of oppression, new forms of struggle in place of the old ones.

Our epoch, the epoch of the bourgeoisie, shows, however, this distinctive feature: it has simplified the class antagonisms. Society as a whole is more and more splitting up into two great hostile camps, into two great classes directly facing each other: *bourgeoisie* and *proletariat.*

From the serfs of the Middle Ages sprang the chartered burghers of the earliest towns. From these burghers the first elements of the bourgeoisie were developed.

The discovery of America, the rounding of the Cape, opened the fresh ground for the rising bourgeoisie. The East-Indian and Chinese markets,

From Karl Marx and Friedrich Engels, *The Communist Manifesto,* trans. Samuel Moore (New York: Washington Square Press, 1934); reprinted by permission of the publisher.

the colonization of America, trade with the colonies, the increase in the means of exchange and in commodities generally, gave to commerce, to navigation, to industry, an impulse never before known, and thereby, to the revolutionary element in the tottering feudal society, a rapid development.

The feudal system of industry, under which industrial production was monopolized by closed guilds, now no longer sufficed for the growing wants of the new markets. The manufacturing system took its place. The guildmasters were pushed on one side by the manufacturing middle class; division of labor between the different corporate guilds vanished in the face of division of labor in each single workshop.

Meanwhile the markets kept on growing; demand went on rising. Manufacturing no longer was able to keep up with this growth. Then, steam and machinery revolutionized industrial production. The place of manufacture was taken by the giant, *modern industry;* the place of the industrial middle class, by industrial millionaires, the leaders of whole industrial armies, the modern bourgeois.

Modern industry has established the world market, for which the discovery of America paved the way. This market has given an immense development to commerce, to navigation, to communication by land. This development has, in its turn, reacted on the extension of industry; and in proportion as industry, commerce, navigation, railways extended, in the same proportion the bourgeoisie developed, increased its capital, and pushed into the background every class handed down from the Middle Ages.

We see, therefore, how the modern bourgeoisie is itself the product of a long course of development, of a series of revolutions in the modes of production and of exchange. . . .

The need of a constantly expanding market for its products chases the bourgeoisie over the whole surface of the globe. It must nestle everywhere, settle everywhere, establish connections everywhere.

The bourgeoisie has through its exploitation of the world market given a cosmopolitan character to production and consumption in every country. To the great chagrin of reactionaries, it has drawn from under the feet of industry the national ground on which it stood. All old-established national industries have been destroyed or are daily being destroyed. They are dislodged by new industries, whose introduction becomes a life and death question for all civilized nations, by industries that no longer work up indigenous raw material, but raw material drawn from the remotest zones; industries whose products are consumed, not only at home, but in every quarter of the globe. In place of the old wants, satisfied by the productions of the country, we find new wants, requiring for their satisfaction the products of distant lands and climates. In place of the old local and national seclusion and self-sufficiency, we have intercourse in every direction, universal inter-dependence of nations. And as in material, so also in intellectual production. The intellectual creations of individual nations become common property. National one-sidedness and narrow-mindedness become more and more impossible, and from the numerous national and local literatures, there emerges a world literature.

The bourgeoisie, by the rapid improvement of all instruments of production, by the immensely facilitated means of communications, draws all, even the most backward, nations into civilization. The cheap prices of its commodities are the heavy artillery with which it batters down all Chinese walls, with which it forces the underdeveloped nations' intensely obstinate hatred of foreigners to capitulate. It compels all nations, on pain of extinction, to adopt the bourgeois mode of production; it compels them to introduce what it calls civilization into their midst, *i.e.,* to become bourgeois themselves. In one word, it creates a world in its own image.

The bourgeoisie has subjected rural areas to the rule of cities. It has created enormous cities, has greatly increased the urban population as compared with the rural, and has thus rescued a considerable part of the population from the idiocy of rural life. Just as it has made the country dependent on the cities, so has it made barbarian and semi-underdeveloped countries dependent on the civilized ones, nations of peasants on nations of bourgeois, the East on the West.

The bourgeoisie keeps more and more doing away with the scattered state of the population, of the means of production, and of property. It has agglomerated population, centralized means of production, and has concentrated property in a few hands. The necessary consequence of this was political centralization. Independent, or but loosely connected, provinces with separate interests, laws, governments, and systems of taxation became lumped together into one nation, with one government, one code of laws, one national class-interest, one frontier, and one customs-tariff.

The bourgeoisie, during its rule of scarcely one hundred years, has created more massive and more colossal productive forces than have all preceding generations together. Subjection of Nature's forces to man, machinery, application of chemistry to industry and agriculture, steam-navigation, railways, electric telegraphs, clearing of whole continents for cultivation, canalization of rivers, whole populations conjured out of the ground—what earlier century had even a presentiment that such productive forces slumbered in the lap of social labor?

We see then: the means of production and of exchange, on whose foundation the bourgeoisie built itself up, were generated in feudal society. At a certain stage in the development of these means of production and of exchange, the conditions under which feudal society produced and exchanged, the feudal organization of agriculture and manufacturing industry, in one word, the feudal relations of property became no longer compatible with the already developed productive forces; they became so many fetters. They had to be burst asunder; they were burst asunder.

Into their place stepped free competition, accompanied by a social and political constitution adapted to it, and by the economical and political sway of the bourgeois class.

A similar movement is going on before our own eyes. Modern bourgeois society with its relations of production, of exchange and of property, a society that has conjured up such gigantic means of production and of exchange, is like the sorcerer, who is no longer able to control the powers of the subterranean world which he has called up by his spells. For many decades now the history of industry and commerce has been but the history of the revolt of modern productive forces against modern conditions of production, against the property relations that are the conditions for the existence of the bourgeoisie and of its rule. It is enough to mention the commercial crises that by their periodical return put on trial, each time more threateningly, the existence of the entire bourgeois society. In these crises a great part not only of the existing products, but also of the previously created productive forces, are periodically destroyed. In these crises there breaks out an epidemic that, in all earlier epochs, would have seemed an absurdity—the epidemic of overproduction. Society suddenly finds itself put back into a state of momentary barbarism; it appears as if a famine, a universal war of devastation had cut off the supply of every means of subsistence; industry and commerce seem to be destroyed; and why? Because there is too much civilization, too much means of subsistence, too much industry, too much commerce. The productive forces at the disposal of society no longer tend to further the development of the conditions of bourgeois property; on the contrary, they have become too powerful for these conditions, by which they are fettered, and so soon as they overcome these fetters, they bring disorder into the whole of bourgeois society, endanger the existence of bourgeois property. The conditions of bourgeois society are too narrow to comprise the wealth created by them. And how does the bourgeoisie get over these crises? On the one hand by enforced destruction of a mass of productive forces; on the other, by the conquest of new markets, and by the more thorough exploitation of the old ones. That is to say, by paving the way for more extensive and more destructive crises, and by diminishing the means whereby crises are prevented.

The weapons with which the bourgeoisie felled feudalism to the ground are now turned against the bourgeoisie itself.

But not only has the bourgeoisie forged the weapons that bring death to itself; it has also called into existence the men who are to wield those weapons—the modern working class—the proletarians.

In proportion as the bourgeoisie, *i.e.,* capital, is developed, in the same proportion is the proletariat, the modern working class, developed—a class of laborers, who live only so long as they find work, and who find work only so long as their labor increases capital. These laborers, who must sell themselves piecemeal, are a commodity, like every other article of commerce, and are consequently exposed to all the vicissitudes of competition, to all the fluctuations of the market.

Owing to the extensive use of machinery and to division of labor, the work of the proletarians has lost all individual character, and, consequently, all charm for the workman. He becomes an appendage of the machine, and it is only the most simple, most monotonous, and most easily acquired knack that is required of him. Hence, the cost of production of a workman is restricted, almost entirely, to the means of subsistence that he requires for his maintenance, and for the propagation of his race. But the price of a commodity, and therefore also of labor, is equal to its cost of production. In proportion, therefore, as the repulsiveness of the work increases, the wage decreases. What is more, in proportion as the use of machinery and division of labor increases, in the same proportion the burden of toil also increases, whether by prolongation of the working hours, by increase of the work exacted in a given time or by increased speed of the machinery, etc.

Modern industry has converted the little workshop of the patriarchal master into the great factory of the industrial capitalist. Masses of laborers, crowded into the factory, are organized like soldiers. As privates of the industrial army they are placed under the command of a perfect hierarchy of officers and sergeants. Not only are they slaves of the bourgeois class, and of the bourgeois state; they are daily and hourly enslaved by the machine, by the foreman, and, above all, by the individual bourgeois manufacturer himself. The more openly this despotism proclaims gain to be its end and aim, the more petty, the more hateful, and the more embittering it is. . . .

But with the development of industry the proletariat not only increases in number; it becomes concentrated in greater masses, its strength grows, and it feels that strength more. The various interests and conditions of life within the ranks of the proletariat are more and more equalized, in proportion as machinery obliterates all distinctions of labor, and nearly everywhere reduces wages to the same low level. The growing competition among the bourgeoisie, and the resulting commercial crises, make the wages of the workers ever more fluctuating. The unceasing improvement of machinery, ever more rapidly developing, makes their livelihood more and more precarious; the collisions between individual workmen and individual bourgeoisie take more and more the character of collisions between two classes. Thereupon the workers begin to form combinations (trade unions) against the bourgeoisie; they club together in order to keep up the rate of wages; they found permanent associations in order to make provision beforehand for these occasional revolts. Here and there the contest breaks out into riots.

From time to time the workers are victorious, but only for a time. The real fruit of their battles lies not in the immediate result, but in the ever-expanding union of the workers. This union is helped by the improved means of communication that are created by modern industry and that place the workers of different localities in contact with one another. It was just this contact that was needed to centralize the numerous local struggles, all of the same character, into one national struggle between classes. But every class struggle is a political struggle. And that union, to attain which the burghers of the Middle Ages, with their miserable highways, required centuries, the modern proletarians, thanks to railways, achieve in a few years. . . .

Hitherto, every form of society has been based, as we have already seen, on the antagonism of oppressing and oppressed classes. But in order to oppress a class, certain conditions must be assured to it under which it can, at least, continue its slavish existence. The serf, in the period of serfdom, raised himself to membership in the commune, just as the petty bourgeois, under the yoke of feudal absolutism, managed to develop into a bourgeois. The modern laborer, on the contrary, instead of rising with the progress of industry, sinks deeper and deeper below the conditions of existence of his own class. He becomes a pauper, and pauperism develops more rapidly than population and wealth. And here it becomes evident that the bourgeoisie is unfit any longer to be the ruling class in society, and to impose its conditions of existence upon society as an overriding law. It is unfit to rule because it is incompetent to assure an existence to its slave within his slavery, because it cannot help letting him sink into such a state, that it has to feed him, instead of being fed by him. Society can no longer live under this bourgeoisie, in other words, its existence is no longer compatible with society.

The essential condition for the existence, and for the sway of the bourgeois class, is the formation and augmentation of capital; the condition for capital is wage labor. Wage labor rests exclusively on competition between the laborers. The advance of industry, whose involuntary promoter is the bourgeoisie, replaces the isolation of the laborers, due to competition, by their revolutionary combination, due to association. The development of modern industry, therefore, cuts from under its feet the very foundation on which the bourgeoisie produces and appropriates products. What the bourgeoisie, therefore, produces, above all, is its own grave-diggers. Its fall and the victory of the proletariat are equally inevitable.

II. PROLETARIANS AND COMMUNISTS

. . . .All property relations in the past have continually been subject to historical change consequent upon the change in historical conditions.

The French Revolution, for example, abolished feudal property in favor of bourgeois property.

The distinguishing feature of communism is not the abolition of property generally, but the abolition of bourgeois property. But modern bourgeois private property is the final and most complete expression of the system of producing and appropriating products that is based on class antagonisms, on the exploitation of the many by the few.

In this sense, the theory of the Communists may be summed up in the single phrase: Abolition of private property.

We Communists have been reproached with the desire of abolishing the right of personally acquiring property as the fruit of a man's own labor, which property is alleged to be the groundwork of all personal freedom, activity and independence.

Hard-won, self-acquired, self-earned property! Do you mean the property of the petty artisan and of the small peasant, a form of property that preceded the bourgeois form? There is no need to abolish that; the development of industry has to a great extent already destroyed it, and is still destroying it daily.

Or do you mean modern bourgeois private property?

But does wage labor create any property for the laborer? Not a bit. It creates capital, *i.e.,* that kind of property that exploits wage labor, and that cannot increase except upon condition of begetting a new supply of wage labor for fresh exploitation. Property, in its present form, is based on the antagonism of capital and wage labor. Let us examine both sides of this antagonism.

To be a capitalist, is to have not only a purely personal, but a social *status* in production. Capital is a collective product, and only by the united action of many members, nay, in the last resort, only by the united action of all members of society, can it be set in motion.

Capital is, therfore, not a personal, it is a social power.

When, therefore, capital is converted into common property, into the property of all members of society, personal property is not thereby transformed into social property. It is only the social character of the property that is changed. It loses its class character.

Let us now take wage labor.

The average price of wage labor is the minimum wage, *i.e.,* that quantum of the means of subsistence, which is absolutely requisite to keep the laborer in bare existence as a laborer. What, therefore, the wage laborer appropriates by means of his labor, merely suffices to prolong and reproduce a bare existence. We by no means intend to abolish this personal appropriation of the products of labor, an appropriation that is made for the maintenance and reproduction of human life, and that leaves no surplus wherewith to command the labor of others. All that we want to do away with is the miserable character of this appropriation, under which the laborer lives merely to increase capital, and is allowed to live only in so far as the interest of the ruling class requires it.

In bourgeois society, living labor is but a means to increase accumulated labor. In communist society, accumulated labor is but a means to widen, to enrich, to promote the existence of the laborer.

In bourgeois society, therefore, the past dominates the present; in communist society the present dominates the past. In bourgeois society capital is independent and has individuality, while the living person is dependent and has no individuality.

And the abolition of this state of things is called by the bourgeoisie, abolition of individuality and freedom! And rightly so. The abolition of bourgeois individuality, bourgeois independence, and bourgeois freedom is undoubtedly aimed at.

By freedom is meant, under the present bourgeois conditions of production, free trade, free selling and buying.

But if selling and buying disappears, free selling and buying disappears also. This talk about free selling and buying, and all the other "brave words" of our bourgeoisie about freedom in general, have a meaning, if any, only in contrast with restricted selling and buying, with the fettered traders of the Middle Ages, but have no meaning when opposed to the communistic abolition of buying and selling, of the bourgeois conditions of production, and of the bourgeoisie itself.

You are horrified at our intending to do away with private property. But in your existing society, private property is already done away with for nine-tenths of the population; its existence for the few is solely due to its non-existence in the hands of those nine-tenths. You reproach us, therefore, with intending to do away with a form of property, the necessary condition for whose existence is the nonexistence of any property for the immense majority of society.

In one word, you reproach us with intending to do away with your property. Precisely so; that is just what we intend.

From the moment when labor can no longer be converted into capital, money, or rent, into a social power capable of being monopolized, *i.e.,* from the moment when individual property can no longer be transformed into bourgeois property, into capital, from that moment, you say, individuality vanishes.

You must, therefore, confess that by "individual" you mean no other person than the bourgeois, than the middle-class owner of property. This person must, indeed, be swept out of the way, and made impossible.

Communism deprives no man of the power to appropriate the products of society; all that it does is to deprive him of the power to subjugate the labor of others by means of such appropriation.

It has been objected that upon the abolition of private property all work will cease, and universal laziness will overtake us.

According to this, bourgeois society ought long ago to have gone to the dogs through sheer idleness; for those of its members who work, acquire nothing, and those who acquire anything, do not work. The whole of this objection is but another expression of the tautology: that there can no longer be any wage labor when there is no longer any capital.

Wealth

ANDREW CARNEGIE

This article is one of the clearest attempts to justify Social Darwinism. Written in 1889, it defends the pursuit of wealth by arguing that society is strengthened and improved through the struggle for survival in the marketplace. Interestingly, it was written by one of the world's wealthiest men, Andrew Carnegie, who came to the United States as a poor immigrant boy and quickly rose to enormous power. He began his career as a minor employee in a telegraph company, but emerged in a few years as superintendent of the Pennsylvania Railroad. After the Civil War he entered the iron and steel business, and by 1889 he controlled eight companies which he eventually consolidated into the Carnegie Steel Corporation. Shortly before he died, he merged the Carnegie Steel Corporation with the United States Steel Company.

Carnegie took seriously the task of managing his vast fortune, and he made use of many of the ideas which are presented in the following article. He gave generously to many causes, including public libraries, public education, and the development of international peace.

The problem of our age is the proper administration of wealth, so that the ties of brotherhood may still bind together the rich and poor in harmoni-

First published in the *North American Review,* June 1889.

ous relationship. The conditions of human life have not only been changed, but revolutionized, within the past few hundred years. In former days there was little difference between the dwelling, dress, food, and environment of the chief and those of his retainers. The Indians are today where civilized man then was. When visiting the Sioux, I was led to the wigwam of the chief. It was just like the others in external appearance, and even within the difference was trifling between it and those of the poorest of his braves. The contrast between the palace of the millionaire and the cottage of the laborer with us today measures the change which has come into civilization.

This change, however, is not to be deplored, but welcomed as highly beneficial. It is well, nay essential, for the progress of the race, that the houses of some should be homes for all that is highest and best in literature and art, and for all the refinements of civilization, rather than that none should be so. Much better this great irregularity than universal squalor. Without wealth there can be no Maecetions. When these apprentices rose to be masters, there was little or no change in their mode of life, and they, in turn, educated in the same routine succeeding apprentices. There was, substantially, social equality, and even political equality, for those engaged in industrial pursuits had then little or no political voice in the State.

But the inevitable result of such a mode of manufacture was crude articles at high prices. Today the world obtains commodities of excellent quality at prices which even the generation preceding this would have deemed incredible. In the commercial world similar causes have produced similar results, and the race is benefited thereby. The poor enjoy what the rich could not before afford. What were the luxuries have become the necessaries of life. The laborer has now more comforts than the farmer had a few generations ago. The farmer has more luxuries than the landlord had, and is more richly clad and better housed. The landlord has books and pictures rarer, and appointments more artistic, than the King could then obtain.

The price we pay for this salutary change is, no doubt, great. We assemble thousands of operatives in the factory, in the mine, and in the counting-house, of whom the employer can know little or nothing, and to whom the employer is little better than a myth. All intercourse between them is at an end. Rigid Castes are formed, and, as usual, mutual ignorance breeds mutual distrust. Each Caste is without sympathy for the other, and ready to credit anything disparaging in regard to it. Under the law of competition, the employer of thousands is forced into the strictest economies, among which the rates paid to labor figure prominently, and often there is friction between the employer and the employed, between capital and labor, between rich and poor. Human society loses homogeneity.

The price which society pays for the law of competition, like the price it pays for cheap comforts and luxuries, is also great; but the advantages of this law are also greater still, for it is to this law that we owe our wonderful material development, which brings improved conditions in its train. But, whether the law be benign or not, we must say of it, as we say of the change in the conditions of men to which we have referred: It is here; we cannot evade it; no substitutes for it have been found; and while the law may be sometimes hard for the individual, it is best for the race, because it insures the survival of the fittest in every department. We accept and welcome, therefore, as conditions to which we must accommodate ourselves, great inequality of environment, the concentration of business, industrial and commercial, in the hands of a few, and the law of competition between these, as being not only beneficial, but essential for the future progress of the race. Having accepted these, it follows that there must be great scope for the exercise of special ability in the merchant and in the manufacturer who has to conduct affairs upon a great scale. That this talent for organization and management is rare among men is proved by the fact that it invariably secures for its possessor enormous rewards, no matter where or under what laws or conditions. The experienced in affairs always rate the MAN whose services can be obtained as a partner as not only the first consideration, but such as to render the question of his capital scarcely worth considering, for such men soon create capital; while, without the special talent required, capital soon takes wings. Such men become interested in firms or corporations using millions; and estimating only simple interest to be made upon the capital invested, it is inevitable that their income must exceed their expenditures, and that they must accumulate wealth. Nor is there any middle ground which such men can occupy, because the great manufacturing or commercial concern which does not earn at least interest upon its capital soon becomes bankrupt. It must either go forward or fall behind: to stand still is impossible. It is a condition essential for its successful operation that it should be thus far profitable, and even that, in addition to interest on capital, it should make profit. It is a law, as certain as any of the others named, that men possessed of this peculiar talent for affairs, under the free play of economic forces, must, of necessity, soon be in receipt of more revenue than can be judiciously expended upon themselves, and this law is as beneficial for the race as the others.

Objections to the foundations upon which society is based are not in order, because the condition of the race is better with these than it has been with any others which have been tried. Of the effect of any new substitutes proposed we cannot be sure. The Socialist or Anarchist who seeks to overturn present conditions is to be regarded as attacking the foundation upon which civilization itself rests, for civilization took its start from the day that the capable, industrious workman said to his incompetent and lazy fellow, "If thou dost not sow, thou shalt not reap," and thus ended primitive Communism by separating the drones from the bees. One who studies this subject will soon be brought face to face with the conclusion that upon the sacredness of property civilization itself depends—the right of the laborer to his hundred dollars in the savings bank, and equally the legal right of the millionaire to his millions. To those who propose to substitute Communism for this intense Individualism the answer, therefore, is: The race has tried that. All progess from that barbarous day to the present time has resulted from its displacement. Not evil, but good, has come to the race from the accumulation of wealth by those who have the ability and energy that produce it. But even if we admit for a moment that it might be better for the race to discard its present foundation, Individualism—that it is a nobler ideal that man should labor, not for himself alone, but in and for a brotherhood of his fellows, and share with them all in common, realizing Swedenborg's idea of Heaven, where, as he says, the angels derive their happiness, not from laboring for self, but for each other—even admit all this, and a sufficient answer is, This is not evolution, but revolution. It necessitates the changing of human nature itself—a work of aeons, even if it were good to change it, which we cannot know. It is not practicable in our day or in our age. Even if desirable theoretically, it belongs to another and long-succeeding sociological stratum. Our duty is with what is practicable now; with the next step possible in our day and generation. It is criminal to waste our energies in endeavoring to uproot, when all we can profitably or possibly accomplish is to bend the universal tree of humanity a little in the direction most favorable to the production of good fruit under existing circumstances. We might as well urge the destruction of the highest existing type of man because he failed to reach our ideal as to favor the destruction of Individualism, Private Property, the Law of Accumulation of Wealth, and the Law of Competition; for these are the highest results of human experience, the soil in which society so far has produced the best fruit. Unequally or unjustly, perhaps, as these laws sometimes operate, and imperfect as they appear to the Idealist, they are nevertheless, like the highest type of man, the best and most valuable of all that humanity has yet accomplished.

We start, then, with a condition of affairs under which the best interests of the race are promoted, but which inevitably gives wealth to the few. Thus far, accepting conditions as they exist, the situation can be surveyed and pronounced good. The question then arises—and, if the foregoing be correct, it is the only question with which we have to deal—What is the proper mode of administering wealth after the laws upon which civilization is founded have thrown it into the hands of the few? And it is of this great question that I believe I offer the true solution. It will be understood that *fortunes* are here spoken of, not moderate sums saved by many years of effort, the returns from which are required for the comfortable maintenance and education of families. This is not *wealth,* but only *competence,* which it should be the aim of all to acquire.

. . .Indeed, it is difficult to set bounds to the share of a rich man's estate which should go at his death to the public through the agency of the state, and by all means such taxes should be graduated, beginning at nothing upon moderate sums to dependents, and increasing rapidly as the amounts swell, until of the millionaire's hoard, as of Shylock's at least

> "——The other half
> Comes to the privy coffer of the state."

This policy would work powerfully to induce the rich man to attend to the administration of wealth during his life, which is the end that society should always have in view, as being that by far most fruitful for the people. Nor need it be feared that this policy would sap the root of enterprise and render men less anxious to accumulate, for to the class whose ambition it is to leave great fortunes and be talked about after their death, it will attract more attention, and, indeed, be a somewhat nobler ambition to have enormous sums paid over to the state from their fortunes.

There remains, then, only one mode of using great fortunes; but in this we have the true antidote for the temporary unequal distribution of wealth, the reconciliation of the rich and the poor—a reign of harmony—another ideal, differing, indeed, from that of the Communist in requiring only the further evolution of existing conditions, not the total overthrow of our civilization. It is founded upon the present most intense individualism, and the race is prepared to put it in practice by degrees whenever it pleases. Under its sway we shall have an ideal state, in which the surplus wealth of the few will become, in the best sense, the property of the many, because administered for the common good, and this wealth, passing through the hands of the few, can be made a much more potent force for the elevation of our race than if it had been distributed in small sums to the people themselves. Even the poorest can be made to see this, and to agree that great sums gathered by some of their fellow-citizens and spent for public purposes, from which the masses reap the principal benefit, are more valuable to them than if scattered among them through the course of many years in trifling amounts.

The best uses to which surplus wealth can be put have already been indicated. Those who would administer wisely must, indeed, be wise, for one of the serious obstacles to the improvement of our race is indiscriminate charity. It were better for mankind that the millions of the rich were thrown into the sea than so spent as to encourage the slothful, the drunken, the unworthy. Of every thousand dollars spent in so-called charity today, it is probable that $950 is unwisely spent; so spent, indeed, as to produce the very evils which it proposes to mitigate or cure. A well-known writer of philosophic books admitted the other day that he had given a quarter of a dollar to a man who approached him as he was coming to visit the house of his friend. He knew nothing of the habits of this beggar; knew not the use that would be made of this money, although he had every reason to suspect that it would be spent improperly. This man professed to be a disciple of Herbert Spencer; yet the quarter-dollar given that night will probably work more injury than all the money which its thoughtless donor will ever be able to give in true charity will do good. He only gratified his own feelings, saved himself from annoyance—and this was probably one of the most selfish and very worst actions of his life, for in all respects he is most worthy.

In bestowing charity, the main consideration should be to help those who will help themselves; to provide part of the means by which those who desire to improve may do so; to give those who desire to rise the aids by which they may rise; to assist, but rarely or never to do all. Neither the individual nor the race is improved by alms-giving. Those worthy of assistance, except in rare cases, seldom require assistance. The really valuable men of the race never do, except in cases of accident or sudden change. Every one has, of course, cases of individuals brought to his own knowledge where temporary assistance can do genuine good, and these he will not overlook. But the amount which can be wisely given by the individual for individuals is necessarily limited by his lack of knowledge of the circumstance connected with each. He is the only true reformer who is as careful and as anxious not to aid the unworthy as he is to aid the worthy, and perhaps, even more so, for in alms-giving more injury is probably done by rewarding vice then by relieving virtue.

Thus is the problem of Rich and Poor to be solved. The laws of accumulation will be left free; the laws of distribution free. Individualism will continue, but the millionaire will be but a trustee for the poor; intrusted for a season with a great part of the increased wealth of the community, but administrating it for the community far better than it could or would have done for itself. The best minds will thus have reached a stage in the development of the race in which it is clearly seen that there is no mode of disposing of surplus wealth creditable to thoughtful and earnest men into whose hands it flows save by using it year by year for the general good. This day already dawns. But a little while, and although, without incurring the pity of their fellows, men may die sharers in great business enterprises from which their capital cannot be or has not been withdrawn, and is left chiefly at death for public uses, yet the man who dies leaving behind him millions of available wealth, which was his to administer during life, will pass away "unwept, unhonored, and unsung," no matter to what uses he leaves the dross which he cannot take with him. Of such as these the public verdict will then be: "The man who dies thus rich dies disgraced."

Such, in my opinion, is the true Gospel concerning Wealth, obedience to which is destined some day to solve the problems of the Rich and the Poor, and to bring "Peace on earth, among men Good-Will."

PROPERTY AND PROFIT: MODERN DISCUSSIONS

Case Study—Chrysler in Chaos

JULIA VITULLO-MARTIN

General Motors Chairman Thomas A. Murphy summed up the businessman's view of the Chrysler problem when he said, "In my judgment, there's never been a viable business that has lacked for financing." If Chrysler is viable—what business analysts call a going concern—then it should have access to private capital and no need to resort to public financing. If it's not a going concern, no amount of federal intervention will save the dying company. In fact, any financing is just squandered money.

Murphy holds the traditional, hard-line, free enterprise position: Competition is the discipliner of corporate life, shoving aside the weak and the unworthy while rewarding the strong and the profitable. Take away this discipline by shoring up the weak with artificial, government intervention and you destroy the foundation of American business. And after paying that destructive price, you will get nothing in return, because the troubled company will go under as soon as federal help is withdrawn.

Like most such debates, the Chrysler debate has been disorderly, with side issues taking center stage, grabbing the audience's attention, while the important issues remain in the wings. The central question is: Is Chrysler a going concern facing several serious, but temporary, problems that can be overcome with outside help? Or is it a mortally wounded company whose frenetic, last-minute movements—interpreted by would-be federal financiers as evidence of life—are actually its death throes? One cannot decide what the federal government should do about Chrysler until this question is answered.

But distinguishing between a going and a failing concern is the whole trick in banking, and finance is littered with lenders who haven't been able to tell one from the other. The abandonment of Chrysler by most of its 250 bankers here and abroad does not by itself mean that Chrysler's case is hopeless. The bankers could be wrong—history shows they often are—but their desertion of Chrysler puts the burden on the company to prove that it deserves public financing and will use the financing properly (and, ironi-

Julia Vitullo-Martin, "Chrysler in Chaos: Is the Company Beyond Repair?" *Saturday Review,* January 19, 1980, reprinted by permission.

cally, profitably) to restore the company's economic health. (The Senate Banking Committee's ever-skeptical chairman, Senator William Proxmire, began a day of Chrysler hearings by noting that "the commercial banks . . . most familiar with Chrysler's financial picture show a curious reluctance to commit themselves to providing any increased credit" to Chrysler even *with* federal guarantees. That is indeed reluctance. Proxmire went on to muse, "Either the banks know something Secretary Miller doesn't know, or they are passing up a golden opportunity to do some profitable business.")

Chrysler has not been able to refute its bankers' misgivings. Indeed, as the evidence and arguments against bailing out Chrysler pile up, it becomes distressingly clear that Chrysler cannot explain how it would use the federal guarantees to convert itself from the moribund company it now is to the going concern it wants to become. Its problems seem insurmountable.

First, Chrysler's profit margin on each car sold has traditionally been the lowest in the industry. Last year's profit of $200 per car was $100 less than Ford's and $400 less than GM's. Chrysler explains that because the company is so small—one third of GM's size and one half of Ford's—it has not been able to take advantage of the economies of scale in design, engineering, or production that General Motors and Ford enjoy. Take engine design, for example. Designing and building a four-cylinder engine line costs $500 million. Because the line is highly automated, it can run 24 hours a day, costing GM half as much per car to produce its 600,000 cars as Chrysler spends on 300,000. Chrysler's size prevents it from building many components for itself, with the result that 68¢ of its sales dollar goes to outside suppliers, versus 61¢ for Ford and 51¢ for GM. Indeed, Chrysler's smallness has greatly exacerbated its troubles in the last 10 years, as federal regulators have pursued the auto industry relentlessly, imposing standards that have cost Chrysler twice as much—$620 per car on 1.7 million cars—as GM's $340 on each of its 6 million cars.

In response, critics like Ralph Nader and Proxmire hoot. Federal regulations, they say, saved Chrysler's neck. For years Chrysler had made reckless decisions at every turn: building big cars when Americans wanted little cars, producing gas guzzlers right before the gas shortage hit and persisting with them long after, and manufacturing inefficient and unattractive cars when consumers were insisting on efficiency and style. Federal regulations forced the company—kicking and screaming—to make small cars, which have turned out to be Chrysler's best sellers.

Second, Chrysler gets more severely battered by recessions and the consequent drop in sales than the Big Two because it sells a disproportionate number of cars to blue-collar workers, who in turn are disproportionately hurt by recessions. Critics grant the point, but say that Chrysler has increased its problems by building cars on speculation rather than following the usual industry practice of building cars only to dealers' orders. As a result, the company has built up enormous inventories accompanied by onerous carrying costs. Last year their inventory of 80,000 unsold cars and trucks cost the company $700 million in lost revenue—as well as a staggering $2 million a week for storage. (And this is only the Chrysler

Corporation's central inventory. It doesn't include the 355,000 vehicles Chrysler dealers had languishing in their showrooms at the close of fiscal 1979).

Third, in the late 1960s, both because the company was small (and getting smaller in relation to the Big Two) and because it was so undiversified and subject to recessions, Chrysler decided to concentrate on its acquisitions overseas, leaving the fight over the domestic market to GM and Ford. (Its domestic share had fallen from 26 percent of the market in 1946 to 9 percent today.) The decision proved disastrous. With the exception of its profitable and well-managed Mexican subsidiary, its foreign acquisitions produced nothing but staggering losses. Cash, management talent, and flexibility were drained from the Detroit operation, throwing the entire company woefully out of balance. By the time Chrysler started selling off its unprofitable foreign operations in the mid-Seventies, it was doing so at panic prices because it was so desperate for cash.

Fourth, Chrysler had financed its expansion abroad at the expense of its operations at home. Old plants were left to rot. Worse, Chrysler decided not to build a new plant to produce engines for what turned out to be its most popular car, the Omni, but instead to buy engines from Volkswagen, which could sell it only 300,000 a year. Chrysler's miscalculation of the public's demand for Omnis cost it sales of about 60,000 cars that it couldn't deliver because it had no engines. By then, the company's cash needs were so voracious that it laid off much of its engineering and design staff in 1975, leading to costly design errors over the next few years. But pressing as its cash needs were, they did not stop the company from paying stockholders' dividends until August 1979.

Thus has Walter Chrysler's company, once renowned for its engineering innovations, fallen on the hardest of times. The company that produced the first streamlined car, invented "fluid drive" (which became automatic transmission), power brakes, power steering, and power-operated convertible tops—all for the moderately priced car—has seen its ability to control its financial destiny eroded almost to zero. This disastrous state of affairs would lead one to conclude that Chrysler is not a going concern, cannot make it with or without federal financing, and would be best left alone to die a quick, but dignified death.

Why should the company be saved? *Not* because it deserves to be saved. Even its current chairman, Lee A. Iacocca, admits that 50 to 70 percent of Chrysler's problems are its own fault—due to its own disgraceful mismanagement.

The only argument for saving Chrysler is that its demise would have a severe and lasting effect on the national economy. The U.S. Treasury (part of the executive branch) claims that the effect would be a $2.75 billion loss to the Treasury in revenues, unemployment and welfare payments. Chrysler employs 140,000 workers here and in Canada and claims that if it were shut down, 200,000 to 300,000 workers would lose their jobs, and the government would be out $1 billion in taxes formerly paid by those workers.

Those figures are preposterous, assuming shutdown of all Chrysler facilities. That's not what would happen.

Under bankruptcy, the company would have two choices: either reorganize and continue operating under the new Chapter XI of the federal bankruptcy law or close down and sell off all its assets to pay its debts. With either option, it would probably sell some assets to other auto companies, most likely, foreign companies. This selling off of assets would clearly be disruptive and unpleasant for both the national and various local economies —but not on the mythic scale that Treasury has been promulgating. (The most troubling problem for the Carter administration would be that the reorganization would shut down older plants in the already declining industrial Snowbelt.)

Which brings us back to the federal government and its place in any rescue of Chrysler. If the federal government bails Chrysler out, it will become Chrysler's lead creditor, and thus responsible for deciding what Chrysler must do to strengthen its assets and reduce its liabilities. Many conservatives oppose federal aid to Chrysler because they don't want to see the federal government intervene in the internal affairs of a corporation. But that is the government's legitimate role as senior creditor: to ensure that the debtor institutes procedures and policies that will enable him to repay his debt.

The Carter administration has shown no inclination to take its oversight role seriously. It has taken no steps to ensure that Chrysler, which has been teetering on the brink of disaster for years, will be able to turn itself around.

Certainly this is not the first time the federal government has become the creditor to private debt. It has cosigned $1 out of every $12 in private loans outstanding in this country. By the end of last year, it had $254 billion in loan guarantees outstanding, and $130 billion in direct loans. Most of that credit backs homes and farms, but federal credit has also been used to rescue whole industries (shipbuilding), private companies (Lockheed), and even cities (New York). Those precedents form a moral basis for Chrysler's pleas, while outlining the federal government's past roles.

Looking at the federal precedents, most observers would probably assume that the case most similar to Chrysler's is Lockheed's. In 1970 Lockheed faced a cash-flow crisis because of catastrophic cost overruns on a government contract and the bankruptcy of one of its major suppliers. Lockheed didn't want to default on the contract, but without a cash loan it couldn't met its obligations—like fulfilling its navy shipbuilding contracts and completing the L-1011 commercial jet plane. Though cash poor, Lockheed was a fundamentally sound company, with assured future revenues from government contracts but with very serious short-run problems that could be overcome with temporary help. (Lockheed paid off the loans handily in 1977—a year ahead of schedule.)

A somewhat closer case to Chrysler's is that of New York City, the most recent and the largest of the individual federal rescues. The difference between New York and Chrysler are obvious. New York City is a government, existing under federal protection and sufferance. Even those who condemn New York City for its past profligacy can hardly deny that the city's continuance is "clothed with the public interest," to borrow the legal phrase. The city performs necessary public services that the federal government has an interest in protecting. The same cannot be said of Chrysler, a profit-making company which produces a consumer product that consumers themselves have rejected.

But put aside these differences and look at New York City and Chrysler for the basic similarities between these very large failing entities. In the early Seventies, both were behaving like poor credit risks. The city showed all the symptoms of a company in trouble: While its revenue base was flattening out, it continued to increase expenditures, doubling its expense budget between 1965 and 1972, and expanded its functions and its work force. To economize, the city spent modest capital funds to build a few new facilities, cut maintenance of existing facilities, and used substantial capital funds for operating expenses. As early as the mid-Sixties, the city began amassing mountains of short-term debt. Enticed by the financial reports put out by the city and happy with the bargain returns, investors continued to buy city notes.

Chrysler was following much the same pattern. Even though its net sales more than doubled from $5.8 billion in 1969 to $13.6 billion in 1978, inflation negated almost all of the increase. Financially, the company was at a standstill. It spent erratically on maintenance and repairs, clearly deferring maintenance to conserve cash and waiting until 1976 to begin an urgently needed plant renewal program. Chrysler masked its problems by expanding into new markets abroad, generating a false sense of energy and cash flow, when the company was overextended and cash poor. Through it all, it issued sanguine annual reports.

What finally triggered Chrysler's financial crisis is what triggered the crises for its predecessors at the federal trough (including New York City): cash flow. Chrysler just did not have enough money on hand to pay its regular bills, which have been piling up at the rate of $100 million a month, while its revenues have been steadily declining. It was particularly damaged by last spring's Iranian crisis, which drove consumers away from gas-guzzling recreational vehicles, a market Chrysler dominated.

Before approaching the federal government, Chrysler tried the conventional (and less publicly damaging) step of going to its bankers, who denied the company further credit, just as New York's bankers had refused the city in 1975. Both Chrysler and New York needed cash to continue operating in the short run while staving off demands by major creditors for payments. Once a company or a city ceases operation, major bankers will knock on the door, demanding immediate payment of any past loans or bills —remember, the entire American business world runs on temporary credit —and cash for any future supplies. In a crisis triggered by lack of cash, such new demands would push the debtor into bankruptcy. Underlying and fueling the cash crisis is the lenders' loss of faith in the ability of the borrower to repay his debts. At this stage, the lenders have a couple of choices. They can decide that the borrower is so financially weak that he can't be rescued; they will then refuse further credit, cut their losses, and get out as best they can. Or they can decide that with new credit to solve the cash problems and new creditors to spread the risk, they will be able to recoup their loans.

Since the risk is now very high, the creditors and the company will look around for new partners eager to see the bankrupt entity solvent. Such partners might be employees and their pension funds (a very important source of capital in America today), shareholders, the state, or the federal government.

Rejected by its bankers ("All bankers are thieves and goniffs," said a city official at a similar stage), Chrysler turned to Washington. A sensible move. As the world's fourteenth largest industrial corporation, Chrysler is in the big leagues of capital. As the holder of one of the greatest concentrations of capital in the world, the federal government is an obvious lender. If Congress rejects Chrysler, it will not be for lack of capital.

Chrysler is not just asking Washington for capital, however. It is asking the federal government, in effect, to be its lead banker because commercial bankers have refused the role. As lead banker, Washington not only puts itself in for the highest stake—$1.5 billion in loan guarantees—but also assumes the major role in putting together the rest of the financing package. And that private package will have at least equal federal participation.

No one, after all, ever seriously thought that $1.5 billion in financing would be enough for Chrysler. To put the request in perspective, compare Chrysler's numbers to New York City's. The city had a budget of just over $12 billion in 1975, when it was asking for seasonal (short-term) loans to ease its gigantic cash flow problems. It had accumulated $4.5 billion in short-term debt that it couldn't possibly pay off in one year. Indeed, even without paying off the debt, it couldn't meet its operating expenses without incurring more debt, which is how the trouble began. Washington agreed to give the city $2.3 billion in seasonal loans.

The city said, thank you, that should solve the problem. But it didn't. Three years later the city again approached Washington, asking this time for long-term loans on top of the seasonal. Long-term loans represented an enormous escalation in risk for the creditor. After much haranguing, Washington agreed to $1.65 billion in long-term loan guarantees, if the other local partners—banks, pension funds, insurance companies, the state of New York—could work out a package to provide a total of $4.5 billion long-term over four years.

Chrysler's operating budget is not very far out of line with the city's. The company's financing arm has $1.2 billion in unsecured short-term debt coming due. The company itself has used up its entire $4.8 billion in credit lines. To turn itself around, Chrysler needs to get its hands on enough capital to sustain itself while developing new products, retooling old plants, and learning to manufacture crucial component parts (like engines) that it has been buying elsewhere. Loan guarantees of $1.5 billion will not begin to fulfill these needs. Chrysler knows it; its bankers know it. Surely the federal government must know it. As Citibank Chairman Walter Wriston told the Senate, even if Chrysler got all the loans being discussed in the late fall of 1979, there was a "very reasonable chance" that the company's health could not be repaired. Chairman John McGillicuddy of Manufacturer's Hanover (Chrysler's agent bank) was even blunter: "We don't lend money in circumstances where we don't have the expectation that we will be repaid. And at this point in time, this is where Chrysler Corporation is."

The financing package will require not only additional credit from reluctant private partners, but other elements:

• Some creditors will have to forgo calling debt that is due, especially the creditor who holds the debt that triggered the crisis. (Chrysler has been in technical default for months on $800 million. The banks temporarily waived payment.)

• Longer-term creditors must agree to restructure debt that's not yet due, if it's clear that the company will be unable to pay it off when it comes due. This is crucial since the company has a great deal of old, long-term debt coming due within the next few years. The debt may have been long-term when it was incurred 15 years ago, but its due date makes it short-term in the refinancing.

• The most important strategic element in the process is the lead banker's drive for unanimity. All creditors must agree to defer collection. Many a company has gone into bankruptcy because all but one creditor has agreed—and the one recalcitrant creditor broke the agreement. The most dramatic recent example is Cleveland, which defaulted when the Cleveland Trust demanded payment, pushing the city over the brink.

Chrysler's bankers, however, are not even close to unanimity. They are still very much in the squabbling stage. With one eye on his bankers, Chrysler Chairman Lee Iacocca testified in front of the House Banking subcommittee that the federal loan guarantees would be "almost overshadowed by the importance of the government's vote of confidence needed to keep our present creditors in line." Chrysler, for example, barely got the required two-thirds vote of its bankers to waive loan covenants requiring the company to keep on hand $600 million in working capital. Since such covenants involve principles more than cash, they indicate just how much trouble Chrysler will have when it gets down to negotiating more costly items.

All this is very grim. But a company facing bankruptcy does have some leverage over its creditors: The creditors want their money back, and only the company can give it to them. Creditors usually agree to some kind of debt restructuring plan because they fear that without the restructuring, they'll be paid nothing at all or much less than the full amount. Fear makes them cooperative.

Fear does not, however, make them friendly. Their continued involvement with a debtor they would like to repudiate usually provokes them to demand that new controls be put on the company's internal management, that costs—including labor—be cut, that assets be sold for cash, and that unprofitable operations be severed.

The whole point of a bankrupt company's asking for new credit is to use that credit to buy time to turn the company around. The point of a creditor's extending the credit is to ensure that the company uses the time properly. The process is a painful one—not just because punitive credit principles say that a bankrupt company should pay for its mistakes, but also because the company, coerced by its creditors, must do things it had been unwilling to do voluntarily.

Neither Chrysler nor its creditors wants to face the sacrifices each must make. But if the federal government bails out the Chrysler Corporation, it also bails out the workers, the bankers, the shareholders, the seven states in which Chrysler plants are located, and the corporation's suppliers. Justice—and credit principles—demand that all of them give up something to save the bankrupt entity.

That's exactly what happened in New York City's case: New York City workers agreed to a wage freeze; the bankers agreed not to call debt that was due, while extending other debt far into the future; city businesses and residents bore raises in six already high corporate and personal income taxes; the state of New York extended an $800 million seasonal loan accompanied by substantial new aid; individual city noteholders were given the choice of exchanging the notes for new bonds or just not being paid for a year.

This is not happening in the Chrysler case. Iacocca got a few minor agreements from creditors, most of whom are closing out old lines of credit while refusing any new ones. The company has negotiated a much-praised, but bad, contract with the United Auto Workers that ignored the big issues of productivity and absenteeism—issues that should be dealt with now—while only *deferring* the large raises that will increase labor costs at the other two auto companies by one-third over three years to $20 an hour. Nor has the state of Michigan done anything other than lobby Washington for federal aid. It has made no serious proposals to sacrifice anything. And all of this is happening to the sickest company in a sick industry. As the *Economist* pointed out recently: The American car market is in a tailspin. Ford has been badly damaged and expects a $1 billion deficit this year in domestic operations. GM looks much sounder, although some analysts are saying it, too, will face a domestic gap.

Centuries of credit practices have taught creditors a firm, inviolable principle: Credit can only help the company that knows how to help itself. If in its newest foray into the world of private credit, the federal government ignores this principle, it will have on its hands not only the stricken Chrysler—for which it will be perpetually responsible—but many others as well.

That there will be others lining up for federal aid and guarantees is undeniable. And what principles will the federal government cite to turn them away? The government has abandoned the traditional principles of the marketplace—after all, if any company has ever deserved the market's harsh judgment Chrysler did—and cannot in the future use market principles to deny to a small company what it so generously yielded to a giant. Worse, ailing giants, starting with Ford and followed by U.S. Steel, may soon be in line behind Chrysler. The $11 billion U.S. Steel Corporation has lost $902 million over the last five years and is now closing plants and laying off some 13,000 workers to cut future losses. Chrysler has not made a single argument for federal intervention that would not apply equally fairly to Ford and U.S. Steel. Further, Wall Street is dizzy with rumors of unpublicized corporate troubles and collapses across the country. The federal government has put itself on a dangerous path, which will lead it straight to the 6,000 annual bankrupt companies that will ask no more than to be treated like Chrysler. Having aided the one, can it reject all the others?

Case Study—Give Us a Chance To Compete

LEE A. IACOCCA

Everybody these days is an expert on automobile imports. We welcome the debate, but some of the ivory-tower stuff I've been reading lately needs an answer. I read that if our government does anything at all to reduce the flood of Japanese cars into this country, it will stand as a violation of the sacred principles of free trade, and will take away the basic right of all Americans to buy anything they want, no matter where it's produced.

The fact is that they don't have that right now, nor does any nation on earth grant it to its people—especially when it devastates a basic domestic industry and puts hundreds of thousands out of work.

Everybody misses that point. There is something wrong when Americans are laid off and the Japanese are working overtime. There is something wrong when this nation pays $2 billion in special welfare (the Trade Readjustment Allowance) so we can all buy Japanese cars. There is something wrong when they can ship cars here but we can't ship cars there.

The answer is not tariffs or a trade war. And it certainly is not more of what we have now. The answer is a little voluntary recovery time so we can get back on our feet and compete head to head with anybody in the world.

Oil: Let's face the fact that the automobile industry is in trouble largely on account of U.S. Government actions such as keeping the price of gasoline artificially low, and piling on regulations that are costly to comply with. But it is not a fact that a cold-turkey withdrawal from every kind of government intervention is necessarily good for the industry's health.

It is important to remember that the government changed the oil-price rules in the middle of the game, throwing us all into a five-year, $80 billion rebuilding program. That's how long it takes and that's how much it costs to convert to a whole new fleet of smaller, fuel-efficient cars that will offset the overnight doubling of gasoline prices.

We can complete that transition and meet the market. But we can't stay alive in the meantime if our market is handed over to an importer who lives by the rules of one-way trade. I know the conventional wisdom says that the Japanese simply work harder for less pay, taking breaks only to sing the company song—with the result that the U.S. buyer gets cheaper cars.

The fact is that the Japanese give their car makers a tax break on the cars they ship into this country. Through this tax break alone, a Japanese car that sells for about $7,000 in Japan can be sold in this country for about $6,300. Try doing that with one of our cars over there. The price doubles.

Japan has given the stiff-arm to U.S. cars for the last twenty years. In addition to a variety of hidden trade barriers, they slap a 20 per cent "indirect" commodity tax on cars sold in Japan—a tax that is scheduled to increase to 22.5 per cent in May.

That's not free trade. That's a one-way street that has created an annual trade deficit with Japan of $11.2 billion on cars and trucks alone, and has cost us $2 billion a year in TRA payments to laid-off workers.

The rest of the world won't have that. *No other country gives imported vehicles a tax-related price advantage over its own.* The Common Market countries hang a 10.8 per cent tariff on imported cars, plus a value-added tax ranging from 13 per cent in Germany to 33 per cent in France.

We're the only country that says: let them in, the more the better! As a result, the United States leads all industrialized nations in the size of its trade deficits, the number of workers unemployed and the number of large corporations in basic industries fighting for their lives.

Some people argue that restricting the number of Japanese cars sold in this country would hype the price of U.S. cars. That's just not so. We sell cars in a very tough market. We had competitive pricing over here long before the first boatload of Japanese cars docked in California. And we'll continue to have it in the future.

Others argue that cutting down the flood of Japanese cars would help only the workers in Detroit. Do we still have to be reminded that the automobile industry accounts for one out of every six jobs across the country? Not just the jobs of autoworkers, but hundreds of thousands of jobs in America's basic industries: steel, iron, rubber, aluminum, glass, machine tools, plastics and electronics. Thousands of small companies—suppliers and dealers—depend on the auto industry.

Free Enterprise: They're all sick, and they need help. The help should come in the form of a voluntary marketing agreement to hold imports to 1977–78 levels for two or three years. After that, take the gloves off. Free enterprise forever. We can compete. Yankee ingenuity is still alive and well. But we do need time to get up off the canvas and catch our breath.

Import restraint is not the full answer to the industry's problems. A lower prime rate would be even better. But it is time for a little common sense. We ought to ask the Japanese to voluntarily limit the number of cars they ship here while our nation's largest industry gets back on its feet. If we don't, I think we'll face a demand by the people for a much more restrictive and damaging system of import controls from which we can never retreat.

Evidently President Reagan thinks so, too. Last fall, when he visited Detroit, I stood beside him when he said: "There is a place where government can be legitimately involved—and this is where I think government has a role that has been shirked so far, and that is, to convince the Japanese that, in one way or another and in their own best interest, the deluge of their cars into the United States must be slowed while our industry gets back on its feet."

I think the man meant what he said. And he does have a way of cutting through the philosophical baloney. It's time for the rest of us to leave the ivory tower too. Like all Americans, the people in the auto industry want a fair shot at keeping their jobs. I think they ought to have that chance.

The Social Responsibility of Business Is To Increase Its Profits

MILTON FRIEDMAN

When I hear businessmen speak eloquently about the "social responsibilities of business in a free-enterprise system," I am reminded of the wonderful line about the Frenchman who discovered at the age of 70 that he had been speaking prose all his life. The businessmen believe that they are defending free enterprise when they declaim that business is not concerned "merely" with profit but also with promoting desirable "social" ends; that business has a "social conscience" and takes seriously its responsibilities for providing employment, eliminating discrimination, avoiding pollution and whatever else may be the catchwords of the contemporary crop of reformers. In fact they are—or would be if they or anyone else took them seriously—preaching pure and unadulterated socialism. Businessmen who talk this way are unwitting puppets of the intellectual forces that have been undermining the basis of a free society these past decades.

The discussion of the "social responsibilities of business" are notable for their analytical looseness and lack of rigor. What does it mean to say that "business" has responsibilities? Only people can have responsibilities. A corporation is an artificial person and in this sense may have artificial responsibilities, but "business" as a whole cannot be said to have responsibilities, even in this vague sense. The first step toward clarity to examining the doctrine of the social responsibility of business is to ask precisely what it implies for whom.

Presumably, the individuals who are to be responsible are businessmen, which means individual proprietors or corporate executives. Most of the discussion of social responsibility is directed at corporations, so in what follows I shall mostly neglect the individual proprietors and speak of corporate executives.

In a free-enterprise, private-property system, a corporate executive is an employee of the owners of the business. He has direct responsibility to his employers. That responsibility is to conduct the business in accordance with their desires, which generally will be to make as much money as possible while conforming to the basic rules of the society, both those embodied in law and those embodied in ethical custom. Of course, in some cases his employers may have a different objective. A group of persons might establish a corporation for an eleemosynary purpose—for example, a hospital or a school. The manager of such a corporation will not have money profit as his objectives but the rendering of certain services.

From *New York Times Magazine,* September 13, 1970.

In either case, the key point is that, in his capacity as a corporate executive, the manager is the agent of the individuals who own the corporation or establish the eleemosynary institution, and his primary responsibility is to them.

Needless to say, this does not mean that it is easy to judge how well he is performing his task. But at least the criterion of performance is straightforward, and the persons among whom a voluntary contractual arrangement exists are clearly defined.

Of course, the corporate executive is also a person in his own right. As a person, he may have many other responsibilities that he recognizes or assumes voluntarily—to his family, his conscience, his feelings of charity, his church, his clubs, his city, his country. He may feel impelled by these responsibilities to devote part of his income to causes he regards as worthy, to refuse to work for particular corporations, even to leave his job, for example, to join his country's armed forces. If we wish, we may refer to some of these responsibilities as "social responsibilities." But in these respects he is acting as a principal, not an agent; he is spending his own money or time or energy, not the money of his employers or the time or energy he has contracted to devote to their purposes. If these are "social responsibliities," they are the social responsibilities of individuals, not of business.

What does it mean to say that the corporate executive has a "social responsibility" in his capacity as businessman? If this statement is not pure rhetoric, it must mean that he is to act in some way that is not in the interest of his employers. For example, that he is to refrain from increasing the price of the product in order to contribute to the social objective of preventing inflation, even though a price increase would be in the best interests of the corporation. Or that he is to make expenditures on reducing pollution beyond the amount that is in the best interests of the corporation or that is required by law in order to contribute to the social objective of improving the environment. Or that, at the expense of corporate profits, he is to hire "hardcore" unemployed instead of better qualified available workmen to contribute to the social objective of reducing poverty.

In each of these cases, the corporate executive would be spending someone else's money for a general social interest. Insofar as his actions in accord with his "social responsibility" reduce returns to stockholders, he is spending their money. Insofar as his actions raise the price to customers, he is spending the customers' money. Insofar as his actions lower the wages of some employees, he is spending their money.

The stockholders or the customers or the employees could separately spend their own money on the particular action if they wished to do so. The executive is exercising a distinct "social responsibility," rather than serving as an agent of the stockholders or the customers or the employees, only if he spends the money in a different way than they would have spent it.

But if he does this, he is in effect imposing taxes, on the one hand, and deciding how the tax proceeds shall be spent, on the other.

This process raises political questions on two levels: principle and consequences. On the level of political principle, the imposition of taxes and the expenditure of tax proceeds are governmental functions. We have established elaborate constitutional, parliamentary and judicial provisions to control these functions, to assure that taxes are imposed so far as possible in accordance with the preferences and desires of the public—after all, "taxation without representation" was one of the battle cries of the American Revolution. We have a system of checks and balances to separate the legislative function of imposing taxes and enacting expenditures from the executive function of collecting taxes and administering expenditure programs and from the judicial function of mediating disputes and interpreting the law.

Here the businessman—self-selected or appointed directly or indirectly by stockholders—is to be simultaneously legislator, executive and jurist. He is to decide whom to tax by how much and for what purpose, and he is to spend the proceeds—all this guided only by general exhortations from on high to restrain inflation, improve the environment, fight poverty and so on and on.

The whole justification for permitting the corporate executive to be selected by the stockholders is that the executive is an agent serving the interests of his principal. This justification disappears when the corporate executive imposes taxes and spends the proceeds for "social" purposes. He becomes in effect a public employee, a civil servant, even though he remains in name an employee of a private enterprise. On grounds of political principle, it is intolerable that such civil servants—insofar as their actions in the name of social responsibility are real and not just window-dressing—should be selected as they are now. If they are to be civil servants, then they must be elected through a political process. If they are to impose taxes and make expenditures to foster "social" objectives, then political machinery must be set up to make the assessment of taxes and to determine through a political process the objectives to be served.

This is the basic reason why the doctrine of "social responsibility" involves the acceptance of the socialist view that political mechanisms, not market mechanisms, are the appropriate way to determine the allocation of scarce resources to alternative uses.

On the grounds of consequences, can the corporate executive in fact discharge his alleged "social responsibilities"? On the one hand, suppose he could get away with spending the stockholders' or customers' or employees' money. How is he to know how to spend it? He is told that he must contribute to fighting inflation. How is he to know what action of his will contribute to that end? He is presumably an expert in running his company —in producing a product or selling it or financing it. But nothing about his selection makes him an expert on inflation. Will his holding down the price of his product reduce inflationary pressure? Or, by leaving more spending power in the hands of his customers, simply divert it elsewhere? Or, by forcing him to produce less because of the lower price, will it simply contribute to shortages? Even if he could answer these questions, how much cost is he justified in imposing on his stockholders, customers, and employees for this social purpose? What is his appropriate share and what is the appropriate share of others?

And, whether he wants to or not, can he get away with spending his stockholders', customers' or employees' money? Will not the stockholders fire him? (Either the present ones or those who take over when his actions in the name of social responsibility have reduced the corporation's profits and the price of its stock.) His customers and his employees can desert him for other producers and employers less scrupulous in exercising their social responsibilities.

This facet of "social responsibility" doctrine is brought into sharp relief when the doctrine is used to justify wage restraint by trade unions. The conflict of interest is naked and clear when union officials are asked to subordinate the interest of their members to some more general purpose. If the union officials try to enforce wage restraint, the consequence is likely to be wildcat strikes, rank-and-file revolts and the emergence of strong competitiors for their jobs. We thus have the ironic phenomenon that union leaders—at least in the U.S.—have objected to Government interference with the market far more consistently and courageously than have business leaders.

The difficulty of exercising "social responsibility" illustrates, of course, the great virtue of private competitive enterprise—it forces people to be responsible for their own actions and makes it difficult for them to "exploit" other people for either selfish or unselfish purposes. They can do good—but only at their own expense.

Many a reader who has followed the argument this far may be tempted to remonstrate that it is all well and good to speak of Government's having the responsibility to impose taxes and determine expenditures for such "social" purposes as controlling pollution or training the hard-core unemployed, but that the problems are too urgent to wait on the slow course of political processes, that the exercise of social responsibility by businessmen is a quicker and surer way to solve pressing current problems.

Aside from the question of fact—I share Adam Smith's skepticism about the benefits that can be expected from "those who affected to trade for the public good"—this argument must be rejected on grounds of principle. What it amounts to is an assertion that those who favor the taxes and expenditures in question have failed to persuade a majority of their fellow citizens to be of like mind and that they are seeking to attain by undemocratic procedures what they cannot attain by democratic procedures. In a free society, it is hard for "evil" people to do "evil," especially since one man's good is another's evil.

I have, for simplicity, concentrated on the special case of the corporate executive, except only for the brief digression on trade unions. But precisely the same argument applies to the newer phenomenon of calling upon stockholders to require corporations to exercise social responsibility (the recent G.M. crusade for example). In most of these cases, what is in effect involved is some stockholders trying to get other stockholders (or customers or employees) to contribute against their will to "social" causes favored by the activists. Insofar as they succeed, they are again imposing taxes and spending the proceeds.

The situation of the individual proprietor is somewhat different. If he acts to reduce the returns of his enterprise in order to exercise his "social responsibility," he is spending his own money, not someone else's. If he wishes to spend his money on such purposes, that is his right, and I cannot see that there is any objection to his doing so. In the process, he, too, may impose costs on employees and customers. However, because he is far less likely than a large corporation or union to have monopolistic power, any such side effects will tend to be minor.

Of course, in practice the doctrine of social responsibility is frequently a cloak for actions that are justified on other grounds rather than a reason for those actions.

To illustrate, it may well be in the long-run interest of a corporation that is a major employer in a small community to devote resources to providing amenities to that community or to improving its government. That may make it easier to attract desirable employees, it may reduce the wage bill or lessen losses from pilferage and sabotage or have other worthwhile effects. Or it may be that, given the laws about the deductibility of corporate charitable contributions, the stockholders can contribute more to charities they favor by having the corporation make the gift than by doing it themselves, since they can in that way contribute an amount that would otherwise have been paid as corporate taxes.

In each of these—and many similar—cases, there is a strong temptation to rationalize these actions as an exercise of "social responsibility." In the present climate of opinion, with its widespread aversion to "capitalism," "profits," and "soulless corporation" and so on, this is one way for a corporation to generate goodwill as a by-product of expenditures that are entirely justified in its own self-interest.

It would be inconsistent of me to call on corporate executives to refrain from this hypocritical window-dressing because it harms the foundations of a free society. That would be to call on them to exercise a "social responsibility"! If our institutions, and the attitudes of the public make it in their self-interest to cloak their actions in this way, I cannot summon much indignation to denounce them. At the same time, I can express admiration for those individual proprietors or owners of closely held corporations or stockholders of more broadly held corporations who disdain such tactics as approaching fraud.

Whether blameworthy or not, the use of the cloak of social responsibility, and the nonsense spoken in its name by influential and prestigious businessmen, does clearly harm the foundations of a free society. I have been impressed time and again by the schizophrenic character of many businessmen. They are capable of being extremely far-sighted and clear-headed in matters that are internal to their businesses. They are incredibly short-sighted and muddle-headed in matters that are outside their businesses but affect the possible survival of business in general. This short-sightedness is strikingly exemplified in the calls from many businessmen for wage and price guidelines or controls or income policies. There is nothing that could do more in a brief period to destroy a market system and replace it by a centrally controlled system than effective governmental control of prices and wages.

The short-sightedness is also exemplified in speeches by businessmen on social responsibility. This may gain them kudos in the short run. But it helps to strengthen the already too prevalent view that the pursuit of profits is wicked and immoral and must be curbed and controlled by external forces. Once this view is adopted, the external forces that curb the market will not be the social consciences, however highly developed, of the pontificating executives; it will be the iron fist of Government bureaucrats. Here, as with price and wage controls, businessmen seem to me to reveal a suicidal impulse.

The political principle that underlies the market mechanism is unanimity. In an ideal free market resting on private property, no individual can coerce any other, all cooperation is voluntary, all parties to such cooperation benefit or they need not participate. There are no values, no "social" responsibilities in any sense other than the shared values and responsibilities of individuals. Society is a collection of individuals and of the various groups they voluntarily form.

The political principle that underlies the political mechanism is conformity. The individual must serve a more general social interest—whether that be determined by a church or a dictator or a majority. The individual may have a vote and say in what is to be done, but if he is overruled, he must conform. It is appropriate for some to require others to contribute to a general social purpose whether they wish to or not.

Unfortunately, unanimity is not always feasible. There are some respects in which conformity appears unavoidable, so I do not see how one can avoid the use of the political mechanism altogether.

But the doctrine of "social responsibility" taken seriously would extend the scope of the political mechanism to every human activity. It does not differ in philosophy from the most explicitly collectivist doctrine. It differs only by professing to believe that collectivist ends can be attained without collectivist means. That is why, in my book "Capitalism and Freedom," I have called it a "fundamentally subversive doctrine" in a free society, and have said that in such a society, "there is one and only one social responsibility of business—to use its resources and engage in activities designed to increase its profits so long as it stays within the rules of the game, which is to say, engages in open and free competition without deception or fraud."

What Are the Rules of the Game?

JOAN ROBINSON

The neo-classical heritage still has a great influence, not only on the teaching of economics but in forming public opinion generally, or at least in providing public opinion with its slogans. But when it comes to an actual issue, it has nothing concrete to say. Its latter-day practitioners take refuge

Joan Robinson, "What Are the Rules of the Game?" from *Economic Philosophy* (London: C. A. Watts and Co., Ltd., 1962), pp. 126–48. Reprinted with permission.

in building up more and more elaborate mathematical manipulations and get more and more annoyed at anyone asking them what it is that they are supposed to be manipulating.

In so far as economic doctrines have an influence on the choice of objectives for national policy, on the whole it is obscurantist rather than helpful.

The *utility* concept purports to look behind the "veil of money" but *utility* cannot be measured, while money values can, and economists have a bias in favour of the measurable like the tanner's bias in favour of leather.

The very fallacies that economics is supposed to guard against, economists are the first to fall into. Their central concept, National Income, is a mass of contradictions. Consumption, for instance, is customarily identified with sale of consumers' goods, and a high rate of "consumption" is identified with a high standard of life. But consumption, in the plain meaning of the term, in the sense that it is connected with the satisfaction of natural wants, does not take place at the moment when goods are handed over the counter, but during longer or shorter periods after that event. This time-dimension is completely left out of the figures. It is left out not because anyone denies its importance but because of the mere difficulty of catching it in a statistical net.

Fashion in clothes is a kind of sport where non-material values enter in, though on utilitarian principles the pain of many losers probably outweighs the pleasure of the few winners. However that may be, in goods whose purpose is to provide material satisfaction, durability is a great gain; if the time-dimension of consumption falls as the quantity-dimension of sales rises, it is a serious error to take the latter as a measure of changes in the standard of life.

Again, according to the doctrine of *utility*, goods are assumed to satisfy wants that exist independently of them. It was for this reason that goods were held to be a Good Thing. It is by no means obvious that goods which carry their own wants with them, through cunning advertisement, are a Good Thing. Surely we should be quite as well off without the goods and without the wants? This is the kind of question that, very naturally, is painfully irritating to National-Income statisticians. (National-Income studies are, of course, extremely valuable in their proper sphere, that is, in measuring changes in output, as an indication of business activity, and changes in productivity as a measure of efficiency.)

The great point of the *utility* theory was to answer Adam Smith's question about water and diamonds—to distinguish *total utility* which is supposed to measure satisfaction and *marginal utility* which is measured by price. The opportunity to buy a commodity, compared with a situation in which it does not exist, may offer an advantage to consumers which is in no way measured by the sums actually spent on it. Yet in National-Income accounting, goods have to be entered in terms of their exchange values, not their *utilities.* This would be a matter only for philosophical speculation were it not that policy is affected by propaganda for the standard of life as it appears in the figures, and there is a continuous and systematic pressure for goods with a sales value against those which are free. The fight that has to be put up, for instance, to keep wild country from being exploited for money profit is made more difficult because its defenders can be represented as standing up for "non-economic" values (which is considered soft-headed, foolish and unpatriotic) though the economists should have been the first to point out that *utility,* not money, is economic value and that the *utility* of goods is not measured by their prices.

The *laissez-faire* bias that still clings around orthodoxy also helps to falsify true values. When Keynes (in his "moderately conservative" mood) maintained that, provided overall full employment is guaranteed "there is no objection to be raised against the classical analysis of the manner in which private self-interest will determine what in particular is produced,"[1] he had forgotten that in an earlier chapter he had written "There is no clear evidence from experience that the investment policy which is socially advantageous coincides with that which is most profitable."[2] At that point he was considering the bias of private enterprise in favour of quick profits. There is still more fundamental bias in our economy in favour of products and services for which it is easy to collect payment. Goods that can be sold in packets to individual customers, or services that can be charged for at so much per head, provide a field for profitable enterprise. Investments in, say, the layout of cities, cannot be enjoyed except collectively and are not easy to make any money out of; while negative goods, such as dirt and noise, can be dispensed without any compensation being required.

When you come to think of it, what can easily be charged for and what cannot, is just a technical accident. Some things, such as drainage and street lighting, are so obviously necessary that a modicum is provided in spite of the fact that payment has to be collected through the rates, but it is only the most glaring necessities that are met in this way, together with some traditional amenities, like flower-beds in the parks, that are felt to be necessary to municipal self-respect.

Funds for investment in profitable concerns are very largely provided out of the profits made on past investments. When we buy a packet of goods we pay the costs of producing it (including a return to the lenders of the finance that has gone into equipment for making it) and a bit extra as well, which goes to undistributed profits to finance more investments. In many cases the price also includes a contribution to taxes to be spent on general administration, social services, interest on the national debt, defence, and so forth. The difference between profit margins and indirect taxes, in terms of their economic functioning, is not at all clear cut; one is no more and no less a "burden" than the other. The difference between them is that the outlay of profit margins on dividends, amenities or profitable investment, under nominal control of the shareholders, is in the hands of boards of directors, while the outlay of rates and taxes is in the hands of city corporations and government departments, under nominal control of the electorate. The idea that one is necessarily more "economic" than the other has no foundation except in ideological prejudice.

Professor Galbraith depicts the situation in America, where both the output of saleable goods and the neglect of nonsaleable services are even more extreme than here—

> The family which takes its mauve and cerise, air-conditioned, power-steered, and power-braked car out for a tour passes through cities that are badly paved, made hideous by litter, blighted buildings, bill-boards, and posts for wires that should long since have been put underground. They pass on into a countryside that has been rendered largely invisible by commercial art. (The goods which the latter advertise have an absolute priority in our value system. Such aesthetic considerations as a view of the countryside accordingly come second. On such matters we are consistent.) They picnic on exquisitely packaged food from a portable icebox by a polluted stream and go on to spend the night at a park which is a menace to public health and morals. Just before dozing off on an air-mattress, beneath a nylon tent, amid the stench of decaying refuse, they may reflect vaguely on the curious unevenness of their blessings.[3]

We have not quite reached that stage here, but we are well on the way.

Some interpretations of employment policy take it for granted that private enterprise investment should always be given the first claim on resources and public investment should take up the slack. Thus "public works" should be undertaken when private investment appears to be going into a slump and slackened off again when private investment picks up.

It was all very well for Lloyd George and Keynes to advocate clearing the slums and widening the roads purely as a means of giving work, because the official orthodoxy was opposed to doing anything, but now it does not seem to make much sense that we have to wait for a slump to get these jobs done. It is possible to argue that private investment is helpful to exports, that we cannot afford to clear the slums until our industry is in better shape, and that exports cannot flourish unless profitable industry as a whole is flourishing. That is a logical argument though not necessarily convincing. But the argument that public investment, however beneficial, must be less eligible from a national point of view than any private investment, merely because it is public, has no logical basis; it is just a hang-over from *laissez-faire* ideology.

To take another example, Keynes maintained (when he allowed his mind to stray over long-run problems) that investment steadily maintained at full-employment levels would soon saturate all useful demands for capital equipment, and require a reduction of the rate of interest to vanishing point. But he did not lament it; he looked forward to it as the beginning of an age of civilized life. The "vulgar Keynesians" took it up in another sense. They turned the prospective drying up of profitable investment opportunities into the "stagnation thesis." The stagnationists, instead of welcoming the prospect of a period when saving would have become unnecessary, high real wages would have reduced the rate of profit to vanishing point, and technical progress could be directed to lightening toil and increasing leisure, regard its approach as a menace. This, of course, is a perfectly reasonable point of view if the aim of economic life is held to be to provide a sphere for making profits. Satiation of material wants is bad for profits. But this does not go very well with the usual claim that the private enterprise system is justified by its power to meet wants.

In practice employment policy is not based on any particular theory but follows the line of least resistance. Public investment is the easiest thing to cut when restriction appears to be called for, and private consumption the pleasantest thing to boost when a stimulus is needed. From the point of view of planning socially beneficial investment it is usually: Heads I win and tails you lose.

Not only is the system distorted by its bias towards investing in what happens to be profitable, but even within that sphere there is no reason to expect the profit motive to lead to a well balanced pattern of investment. This has always been a weak point in the neo-classical system. The doctrine that, under conditions of free competition, given resources are used to yield maximum satisfaction, applies essentially to an equilibrium position. It can be demonstrated only by assuming that an equilibrium exists and showing that a *departure* from it would be harmful (it also has to assume, of course, that the distribution of income is somehow what it ought to be) . . .

By the same token, where an industry is in control of a monopoly, wise planning for the future dictates reserve in responding to an increase in demand. Surplus capacity is the great evil to be avoided. The stronger the monopoly, the more cautious it will be, and if, by always remaining in the rear of demand, it can make a seller's market permanent, so much the better.

In a world in which some industries are much easier to enter than others, there is a systematic distortion in the pattern of investment, which is something over and above the general instability that employment policy is designed to control, over and above mistakes in forecasting which are liable to occur in any system, and over and above the misdirection of investment through speculative influences, which Keynes referred to when he said that "When the capital development of a country becomes a by-product of the activities of a Casino, the job is likely to be ill done."[4]

All this would be true even if the distribution of income and wealth were accepted as fair and reasonable. In a modern democracy that is far from being the case. Through political channels—the tax system and social services—we are continually pushing against the distribution of income that our economic system throws up.

The pressure is haphazard and often ineffective (the difference between our highly progressive tax system on paper and our highly regressive system of tax avoidance in reality is sufficiently notorious). The effort at redistribution has no particular philosophy behind it and there does not seem to be any rational criterion for the point at which to draw the line; it sways to and fro (though not very far) as the balance of political pressures shifts. . . .

Edgworth, . . . and many after him, took refuge in the argument that we do not really know that greater equality would promote greater happiness, because individuals differ in their capacity for happiness, so that, until we have a thoroughly scientific hedonimeter, "the principle 'every man, and every woman, to count for one,' should be very cautiously applied."[5]

Many years ago, this point of view was expressed by Professor Harberier: "How do I know that it hurts you more to have your leg cut off than it hurts me to be pricked by a pin?" It seemed at the time that it would have been more telling if he had put it the other way round.

Such arguments are getting rather dangerous nowadays, for though we shall presumably never have a hedonimeter whose findings would be unambiguous, the scientific measurement of pain is fairly well developed, and it would be very surprising if a national survey of the distribution of susceptibility to pain turned out to have just the same skew as the distribution of income.

If the question is once put: Would a greater contribution to human welfare be made by an investment in capacity to produce knick-knacks that have to be advertised in order to be sold or an investment in improving the health service? it seems to me that the answer would be only too obvious; the best reply that *laissez-faire* ideology can offer is not to ask the question.

It is possible to defend our economic system on the ground that, patched up with Keynesian correctives, it is, as he put it, the "best in sight." Or at any rate that it is not too bad, and change is painful. In short, that our system is the best system that we have got.

Or it is possible to take the tough-minded line that Schumpeter derived from Marx. The system is cruel, unjust, turbulent, but it does deliver the goods, and, damn it all, it's the goods that you want.

Or, conceding its defects, to defend it on political grounds—that democracy as we know it could not have grown up under any other system and cannot survive without it.

What is not possible, at this time of day, is to defend it, in the neo-classical style, as a delicate self-regulating mechanism, that has only to be left to itself to produce the greatest satisfaction for all.

But none of the alternative defences really sounds very well. Nowadays, to support the *status quo,* the best course it just to leave all these awkward problems alone.

To descend from questions of universal and of national policy to the internal operation of the system, let us ask what rules of the game are accepted nowadays for various players in an industrial economy.

What about Trade Unions? According to strict *laissez-faire* doctrine they used to be placed on a par with monopolies. The free operation of market forces would secure for each group of workers their marginal net product, and a Trade Union, by forcing the wage above its equilibrium level, would cause unemployment, just as a monopolist restricts sales by keeping up prices.

In some ways the most striking novelty in Keynesian doctrine was that (abstracting from effects on foreign trade) an all-around reduction in wages would not reduce unemployment and would actually be likely to increase it.

At the same time "imperfect competition" had come into fashion and discredited the idea that market forces can be relied upon to establish the equality of wages with the value of marginal products, so that even on its own waters the old orthodoxy could not keep afloat.

Nowadays it is pretty generally agreed that Trade Unions do not introduce an element of monopoly into the system but constitute rather what Professor Galbraith[6] has christened a "countervailing power" to cancel the element of monopoly which inevitably exists on the employer's side of the wage bargain. At the same time the employer's side, at least in big business, has learned to accept the Trade Unions and on the whole, apart from occasional flurries, to co-exist with them fairly amicably.

The new doctrine, however, cuts both ways. A rising tendency of money wage rates is necessary to keep monopoly in check but if it goes too fast it does no good to the workers and is a great nuisance to everyone else.

Experience of the vicious spiral in the years of high employment has demonstrated this clearly enough, as an overall truth. But it remains the duty of each Trade Union individually to look after the interests of its own members. To appeal to any one Union to exercise public spirit and refrain from wage demands is appealing to it to betray its trust. An appeal to organized labour as a whole to exercise restraint is naturally regarded with the deepest suspicion as long as profits are not restrained.

Here there has been a spectacular breakdown in the doctrine that the pursuit of self-interest by each promotes the good of all.

The old theory *assumed* full employment and stable prices. Now history has called its bluff. Where is the mechanism that will establish such a situation? The old rules of the game have become unplayable and badly need to be revised.

What about the other side of the bargain? Is it the proper thing for employers to resist wage demands? Not long ago a lockout in the printing trade reduced the British Press to silence, played havoc with publishing business and ruined a number of small local printers. Afterwards the employers claimed credit for having saved the public, at serious loss to themselves, from the greater rise in wages that they would have had to concede if they had settled without a fight.[7] Do we agree in feeling grateful and congratulating them on their public spirit? or do we regret the loss of production and the general ill-will that followed the dispute? Orthodox doctrine cannot help us.

And what about prices? The old theory that they are settled by competition could not survive the long buyer's market of the inter-war period, and the theories of imperfect and monopolistic competition have left mere chaos in their wake. The business man's theory (which has been taken up by some economists) that prices are governed by costs is no more helpful; it is quite impossible to define the cost, including a proper contribution to overheads, depreciation and "a fair and reasonable profit," for any particular batch of output of any particular commodity. Some formula or other for allocating costs can be found that will justify any price, within reason, that a firm finds it convenient to charge.

The businessman's theory, in any case, is evidently not intended to be taken literally, for, with a few exceptions, they do not show any alacrity in reducing prices when costs fall.

All that orthodox theory tells us is that in conditions of perfect competition prices fall with costs and that in conditions of oligopoly they very likely do not. Does theory tell us that it would be a Good Thing if firms acted *as though* there was perfect competition, and brought prices down? . . .

Then again, there is the question of the durability of commodities, referred to above. Suppose that a manufacturer has discovered a way, without extra cost, to make his products more durable. Should he adopt this method, so as to benefit his customers, or should he rather consider the danger of satisfying their demands and reducing the market for replacements? Would he not be well advised to turn his research workers on to find a less durable material, provided that it can be made to look as attractive and is not much more costly? Here the doctrine that the most profitable is the most socially beneficial course of conduct hits an awkward snag.

Then again, what about dividend policy? There is a strong propensity in human nature, which has not been explained (perhaps a clue might be found in the instincts of animals that live in packs) for the individual to cotton on to any kind of group of which he finds himself a member, and to develop patriotism for it.

Nation, race, church, city, evoke loyalty. Marx never got round to writing the chapter on class. Class loyalty, in vulgar Marxism, is presented as a form of egoism, but it is not so; it often demands the sacrifice of the immediate interest of an individual. . . .

The entity which evokes this loyalty is the firm as such. The shareholders (apart from those foundation members who are identified with the firm) are regarded more or less on a par with creditors and it is a disagreeable necessity to part with the firm's earnings to satisfy them.

Devotion to the firm as such points to a high rate of self-financing, except in the case of boards of very large companies which want from time to time to make big new issues. They pay out dividends, and seek to keep up the market price of shares, not because they are acting in the interests of the shareholders, but because this is the best way to raise more capital for the firm that they serve.

On this question of distributing profits, what is proper behavior? Some economists are against self-finance because it spoils the marginal theory. Investment goes where profits happen to have been earned and investments of a relatively low marginal productivity may be pushed by old firms while new ones with very high marginal productivity cannot get finance. Much better, they argue, to distribute profits and let all firms go to the market. But of money that has once been paid out, perhaps 10 per cent will be saved and made available for reinvestment, whereas 100 per cent of retained profits are reinvested. Is the superior quality of external finance great enough to outweigh such a large difference in quantity?

Management (for Management with a large M is also an entity with its own point of view) is all against this doctrine and regards reinvestment as the main justification for profits. The idea that the motive for industry is the pursuit of profit is resented as dastardly slander. It is quite the other way around: industry is the motive for the pursuit of profit.

In a now forgotten manifesto signed by a hundred and twenty businessmen, which was issued during the war, we find this credo set forth: Industry (Industry with a big I)—

> has a three-fold public responsibility, to the public which consumes its products, to the public which it employs, and to the public which provides the

> capital by which it operates and develops . . . The responsibility of those directing Industry is to hold a just balance between the varying interests of the public as consumers, the staff and workmen as employees, and the stockholders as investors, and to make the highest possible contribution to the well-being of the nation as a whole.[8]

This sounds pompous and arrogant. Who gave these fellows the right to determine the distribution of the National Income and what super-human wisdom do they claim directs them to distribute it aright? Yet there is a great deal of truth in the view that the power to allocate resources and distribute income has in fact been placed in their hands. To the list of interests which they have to balance should be added, first of all, boards of directors, and secondly, in a vague and more diffused way, that solidarity with their colleagues in an industry which nowadays so much softens the edge of competition, and solidarity with Industry as such—that is with the class to which they belong. But the high-mindedness is not all just a publicity stunt to recommend their class to the rest of us. There is a large element, in the patriotism which attaches a manager to his firm, of a desire for a good reputation and a good conscience. Even when it is hypocritical, hypocrisy—the homage which vice pays to virtue—is much to be preferred to cynicism. The modern capitalist is hardly recognizable in Marx's portrait of the ruthless exploiter, squeezing every drop of surplus out of the sweat of the workers.

Keynes in one of his optimistic moods spoke of the tendency of big business to socialize itself.[9] Nowadays Management (the kind with a big M) likes to see itself as a kind of public service.

All this has been much damaged lately by a violent kick-back of old-fashioned profit-seeking capitalism. The legal fiction that firms belong to their shareholders has been taken up to knock high-minded, gentlemanly Management over the head. Once more some economists, clinging to the old orthodoxy, welcome the take-over bidder on the grounds that what is profitable must be right, conceding to the profits of financial manipulations the halo that once belonged to the "reward of Enterprise." Those who hold that the proper purpose of industry is to pay dividends must welcome the pressure being put upon boards of directors to offer counter-bribes to their shareholders.

Which side should we be on? Is the gentlemanly public spirit of Management too often a cloak for gentlemanly ease and long weekends? Will the exaltation of the shareholders make managers cynical and Trade Unions aggressive, and face us once more with sharp questions which have been muffled in the comfortable woolly-mindedness of the Welfare State?

Another question on which orthodoxy has led us into great confusion is monopoly. Generally, in the orthodox scheme, monopoly is a Bad Thing. Professor Knight has been known to attack the U.S. anti-trust laws as an illegitimate interference with the freedom of the individual, but for most economists competition is absolutely essential to the justification of *laissez faire;* it is competition which equates the margins, distributes resources so as to maximize *utility* and generally makes the whole scheme work.

But competition, surely, is the main cause of monopoly? How can it be that to lower prices, expand markets, undersell rivals, is a Good Thing, but that the firm that succeeds in overcoming these difficulties and remains in possession of the field is a wicked monopolist? The objection to restrictive practices, and the main justification for the present campaign against them, is that they restrain competition and keep inefficient producers going. If the campaign succeeds, competition, driving out the inefficient, will create more monopolies. Is that what we want? And if not, what *do* we want? What are the rules of the game? . . .

Perhaps all this seems negative and destructive. To some, perhaps, it even recommends the old doctrines, since it offers no "better 'ole" to go to. The contention of this essay is precisely that there is no "better 'ole."

The moral problem is a conflict that can never be settled. Social life will always present mankind with a choice of evils. No metaphysical solution that can ever be formulated will seem satisfactory for long. The solutions offered by economists were no less delusory than those of the theologians that they displaced.

All the same we must not abandon the hope that economics can make an advance towards science, or the faith that enlightenment is not useless. It is necessary to clear the decaying remnants of obsolete metaphysics out of the way before we can go forward. . . .

NOTES

1. *General Theory,* pp. 378–9.
2. *Ibid.*, p. 157.
3. *The Affluent Society,* pp. 186–7.
4. *General Theory,* p. 159.
5. *Mathematical Psychics,* p. 81.
6. See *American Capitalism.*
7. See *The Times,* 1st September 1959. Letter from J. Brooke-Hunt.
8. *A National Policy for Industry,* 1942.
9. *Essays in Persuasion,* p. 314.

The New Property

GEORGE CABOT LODGE

The Lockean ideology attached supreme importance to property rights as a means to fulfilling the values of survival, justice, and self-respect. We have seen that by the term "property," Locke meant both body and estate, and that by "estate" he meant essentially land or clearly owned artifacts; and that he regarded the sole role of the state as being the protection of property, a man's body and estate. He was speaking for a clientele who owned property and were anxious to keep it from the king. For them, property was the means to political and economic independence, the guarantor of freedom. Those who did not own property, those who had sold even their bodies through wage labor, were so deprived of independence as to be incapable of voting freely and, therefore, were made ineligible to vote. In early America, property was widely diffused—nearly everyone had a reasonable chance to own some. (Slaves were, of course, excepted, being property themselves. In fact, slavery was justified in part because of the enormous power of property rights as an idea in America.)

After a period in which the corporation was seen as the creation of a legislature for the fulfillment of a specific community need, the idea of individual property rights came to make the corporation legitimate. Time and again this right was used to protect the corporation as an individual against the intervention of the state. And although the ownership of the corporation became more and more diffused until it was nothing but a myth, the idea of property was maintained, its unreality ignored in the name of efficiency and growth.[1] Today, the concept of private property when applied to the large public corporation is so obscure as to be nearly useless for legitimization. At the same time, uncertainty about the definition of efficiency and the acceptability of growth deprive these two notions of their old force.

The beginning of the disintegration of the idea of property rights in America can be set in the year 1877, when Chief Justice Morrison R. Waite found in *Munn* v. *Illinois*[2] that property "affected with a public interest" ceases to be purely private. Waite employed this concept to justify state regulation of rates charged by a private warehouse. The doctrine was taken further in 1934 in *Nebbia* v. *New York,*[3] when the Supreme Court found that the state could intervene whenever the public needed protection in the name of community need. It is hard to improve on the much earlier statement of the problem of private property rights versus the public interest made by Chief Justice Shaw in Massachusetts in 1839:

> It is difficult, perhaps impossible, to lay down any general rule, that would precisely define the power of the government in the acknowledged right of eminent domain. It must be large and liberal, so as to meet the public exigencies, and it must be so limited and constrained, as to secure effectually the rights of citizens; and it must depend, in some instances, upon the nature of the exigencies as they arise, and the circumstances of individual cases.[4]

The continuing disintegration of property rights as a legitimizing idea today is rooted in two factors: the changes that have come about in the nature of the American community (Shaw's "public exigencies"), and the continued dispersion of "ownership" of some 2,000 large publicly held corporations which account for something like 70–80 per cent of the nation's corporate assets.[5] As the right to property gives way, a new idea is taking its place—the communitarian right of all members to survival, to income, to health, education, green space, natural beauty, and so on. It is not that the right to property need be abolished or that it is evil. It can continue to be appropriate in some settings, including most of the nation's several million small and clearly proprietary enterprises. But it has lost its dominant place as the prime guarantor and arbiter of human rights. In particular, it has lost its utility with respect to the large nonproprietary corporation.

The transformation is observable in several key areas. In the first place, technology has opened access to new sectors of our universe in which the traditional notions of property rights and ownership are simply irrelevant. Outer space and the seabed, for example, are defined by international law as "the common province of mankind" and "the common heritage of mankind," respectively.[6] No person, no corporation, no state may own these areas. They belong to all; they are of "the commons."

In the second place, scarce resources are coming to be placed in the public domain. We are increasingly aware of the scarcity of vital commodities: clean air to breathe, pure water to drink, fertile soil, natural beauty, fuel for energy, and perhaps food to eat. In the name of survival, these resources are moving inexorably beyond property into a new cradle of legitimacy composed of two related ideas: community need, and harmony between man and nature.

Examples of this transformation in new law are abundant, none more dramatic than the National Environmental Protection Act and the Clean Air Act. In 1972, for example, a land developer began construction of a high-rise apartment building on a small plot of land near Mammoth Lake in the High Sierras of California. Residents sued to halt the construction even though it was on private land. It offended the environment, they said. The case worked its way to the California Supreme Court, and in a 6–1 decision the court ruled in favor of the residents. In consequence, state and local governments now must make environmental-impact studies and expose them to public scrutiny before they can approve private construction projects which may have a significant impact on the environment. The California decision meant that citizens can sue to halt any such project that is not accompanied by such a study. According to the attorney who represented the Mammoth Lake residents, the California court decision was "the first time that any U.S. law has given citizens the right to participate directly in private land-use decisions before they are made." A number of land development and housing companies are in a quandary about what to do. "I think they want to put the builders out of business," said Gene Meyers, executive vice president of Levitt United.[7]

In much the same vein a federal task force on land use, headed by Laurance S. Rockefeller, advised President Nixon in 1973 that henceforth "development rights" on private property must be regarded as resting with the community rather than with property owners:

> There is a new mood in America. Increasingly, citizens are asking what urban growth will add to the quality of their lives. They are questioning the way relatively unconstrained piecemeal urbanization is changing their communities, and are rebelling against the traditional processes of government and the market place which they believe have inadequately guided development in the

> past ... They are measuring new development proposals by the extent to which environmental criteria are satisfied.[8]

Even with declining fertility rates, the report said, the nation's population will keep growing until well into the twenty-first century. It put present growth at the rate of 27,000 new households a week. The Constitution guarantees these families the right to move about freely, a fact that caused the task force to raise some long-range questions. May not the "new mood" force this attribute of individualism to change, in the face of community need? May it not be necessary for every level of government, covering every locality, to plan its growth, to provide for open space, proper housing, and the rest? And may this not require that communities establish population ceilings? Specifically, the report urged that all levels of government engage in buying up land for public uses and adopt strict regulations governing the use of privately held land. It observed that the states have the power to do this, "but must overcome a tradition of inactivity."

The strength of this tradition cannot be underestimated. Colorado Springs, for example, is a heavenly place nestled beneath the majesty of the Rocky Mountains on the edge of the Great Plains. Recently, its population has been growing by leaps and bounds, with industrial sprawl marring its perimeters. Youths abound, and there is insufficient work for them to do; vandalism is high. The community is running out of water and inversion makes the air foul on certain days. It is turning from heaven to hell before the stricken eyes of its business and civic leaders. I spoke to those leaders in 1972 about their ideology, which is as near to pure Lockeanism as one is likely to find in America today. They heard me out and shuffled silently from the hall. Later, in the hotel bar, I met the city manager who had heard the speech. He told me, "You're right. We have to plan as a community, but every time I suggest it, they call me a socialist or something worse." Others from the hall joined us in the bar. Relaxed, they lamented their plight, the waywardness of their children, the decline of what they had held dear. I made my speech again; this time the ideological barriers were more permeable. Since then, even Colorado Springs has begun to plan—its Lockeanism eroded by crisis.

In April 1974, the Environmental Protection Agency, acting under the National Environmental Protection Act, moved indirectly to limit the population size of Ocean County, New Jersey. An official of the EPA said, "We intend to do this all over the country." The EPA ruled that the national pollution standards set by the act required a total population of no more than 250,000 in sixteen municipalities of the county. It sought to enforce this ruling by refusing to grant the Ocean County Sewage Authority either the required discharge permit or federal funds to build a system which would serve a larger population.[9]

In the third place, mass urbanization has undermined the traditional theory of private domain. The old ideas simply fade, slowly but surely, as increasing numbers of people pay rent in vast complexes where ownership guarantees none of the political, social, and economic independence described by Locke and formerly provided by the family farm or business. The old idea of property is powerless to prevent the deterioration of low-cost housing blocs; already the federal government owns large tracts of faltering or abandoned inner-city housing. In 1972, for example, the Department of Housing and Urban Development found itself the reluctant owner of 5,000 single-family homes in Detroit's wasteland; the situation is as bad in other cities.[10] Cities and neighborhoods within cities are communities, and can only function if they are treated as such. But this requires entirely different ideological foundations, an entirely new collective consciousness.

In the fourth place, there has been a shift in the nature and function of work and in the means that workers have to fulfillment and self-respect. Of primary importance here is the fact that virtually all members of the American community now have at least a theoretical right that would have been unthinkable as recently as fifty years ago: the right, in effect, to survive. Along with this go other rights of community membership—to a minimum income, to health services, even to entertainment as in public television. (And further rights derive from membership in certain communities, such as IBM or AT&T, Oregon or Los Angeles.) The definition of survival has now become disconnected from work, being guaranteed by the community.

This has several important implications for the idea of property rights. The right to survive as a right of membership is obviously more important than property rights. And the idea of one's body being one's property, which was so central to Lockean individualistic thought, loses force.

Other factors have eroded the old notion of labor as a man's use of his own body. Today, labor increasingly means skill, knowledge, education, and organization. These are not owned by anybody; they are the product of the community. Further, as Robert L. Heilbroner has put it: "In the advanced capitalist nations, new elites based on science and technology are gradually displacing the older elites based on wealth."[11] At the same time, other wealth-producing factors such as resources and capital are becoming less clearly "owned" and of decreasing importance compared with the intangibles of knowledge and organization.

The ascendancy of community-created labor resources, coupled with the communitarian guarantee of survival and the decline in the legitimacy of property rights—and thus in the old basis of managerial authority—is having profound organizational effects. There need be no top or bottom in the managerial hierarchy; there must merely be a gradient of different skills and roles. Authority can derive from a variety of sources, which may have nothing to do with property . . . And because the number, size, and importance of organizations (particularly the corporation) are growing, the terms of membership in those organizations are of increasing concern. Once, private ownership of his labor conferred a degree of individual independence upon a worker, even if it was only his body that he owned. But the worker today is increasingly compelled to function in a large organization in which any rights he may have depend upon his locus there and upon his dedication to the organization's goals.

Charles Reich has stated the dilemma well:

> When status and relationships to organizations replace private property, the result is a change in the degree of independent sovereignty enjoyed by the individual. Private property gave each person a domain in which he could be independent, and it enabled him to tell the rest of the world to go fly a kite. But a person whose "property" consists of a position in an organization is tied to the fate of the organization; if the organization goes down he goes with it.[12]

This redefinition of property plays havoc with some profoundly traditional notions of individual incentive and responsibility. As Aristotle wrote:

> that which is common to the greatest number has the least care bestowed upon it. Every one thinks chiefly of his own, hardly at all of the common interest, and only when he is himself concerned as an individual. For besides other considerations, everybody is more inclined to neglect the duty which he expects another to fulfil; as in families many attendants are often less useful than a few.[13]

Western man has seemed to husband best that which is his. Furthermore, we derive important psychological satisfaction from owning something, even though it be but a knick-knack. Surely this trait in our culture will not wither soon; nonetheless, we must adjust it to the new concept of place in the communitarian order.

Other cultures have succeeded in reaching a solution here. In Japan, for example, the common interest has always been placed above that of the individual. Indeed, the individual achieves fulfullment only insofar as he contributes to his family, to his village, to the greater Japan. Centuries of cultural development and environmental adaptation have created this ideology—if a break in the dike around your rice paddy causes a flood in mine, our individual interests become inseparable from our common interest and the latter must prevail. Tightly delimited in resources, the Japanese have consequently produced a radically different ideology and radically different institutions from the United States or the West in general. As we move into an era of communitarianism, we can see that these institutions are functioning in many ways more effectively than ours. The role of the state and its relationship to business, for example, have given Japan a substantial edge in its strategic planning in the world economy. But the difficulty of moving away from our Western bias is as great as the seeming inevitability of such a movement.

Finally, the 2,000 or so largest corporations in America, which control most of the nation's corporate assets, have over the years detached themselves from the old idea of property. Even when managers cling to it for legitimacy, what authority they have derives from their place in a hierarchy of uncertain legitimacy. Since large corporations have obvious potential power and influence, this uncertainty renders them vulnerable to charges of abuse and conspiracy. Whether or not their power and influence are in fact abusive or conspiratorial, their estrangement from the old bases of legitimacy makes them suspect. The problem is heightened when the community is unclear or inexplicit about what it expects of corporations.

Myth has it that a share of General Motors, for example, is philosophically as important as a share in the ownership of the corporation. The myth, however, is empty of reality. A share of GM is nothing more than a claim on income and is generally disposed of if a share of IBM pays more. The claim that the shareholders elect the board of directors which in turn controls the "hired hands" of management is vapid. Myles Mace, in his study of corporate boards of directors, quotes one typical executive vice president:

> Management creates policies. We decide what course we are going to paddle our canoe in. We tell our directors the direction of the company and the reasons for it. Theoretically, the board has a right of veto, but they never exercise it . . . We communicate with them. But they are in no position to challenge what we propose to do.[14]

So management appoints the board and the board endorses management in a mystical, self-perpetuating process, which albeit efficient, is plainly illegitimate.[15] We were willing to live with the illegitimacy as long as efficiency and growth were of overriding importance, but now that other factors have called into question the previously uncounted costs of growth, our willingness is evaporating. The individual components of corporate America—what Galbraith calls the planning system—are too large and powerful to be left to themselves; and collectively, in the complexes these organizations have formed with each other and in the economic sectors they dominate, they have become political forces to be reckoned with on the very largest scale. No one can doubt that the intentions of the utility industry, the oil industry, the automobile industry, and the communications industry have become matters of national concern politically and socially, as well as economically. Yet although in fact these are vast industrial complexes, the terms in which they regard themselves are frequently individualistic and proprietary.

Even in the equity markets that serve these industries, the trend from the individual to the collective is apparent and sweeping. Investors in the equity markets, theoretically the owners of the corporations, are increasingly unidentifiable as individuals to whom the ownership of corporations could conceivably be attached. "Like the curator of the National Zoo," said G. Bradford Cook, when he retired as chairman of the Securities and Exchange Commission, "I feel constrained to warn: The individual investor has acquired the status of an endangered species."[16] The place of the individual investor has been taken by huge organizations whose ownership is also extremely obscure: mutual funds, insurance companies, pension funds, and bank trust departments. Whereas such groups accounted for only 35 per cent of the dollar value of New York Stock Exchange trading volume in 1963, the percentage is well over 70 today. This development has changed and perhaps profoundly threatened capital market structures; John C. Whitehead, a Goldman, Sachs partner, asserts that institutional dominance has endangered the market's valuation capability and demolished its liquidity: "We can look forward in another decade to complete dominance of our markets and of our corporations by a relatively small handful of institutions—the kind of industrial society that currently exists in Europe and Japan."[17]

This phenomenon of gigantism is having an interesting side effect on the innovation and enterprise which historically have been the handmaidens of the traditional ideology. Because the big institutions show market interest in relatively few stocks, newer and smaller companies are finding it increasingly difficult to go public at all. The vulnerability of our system to the acquisitiveness of the giants can be sensed in the example of Morgan Guaranty, which in 1972 owned more common stock than any other institution on earth—$2 billion worth of IBM, $1.1 billion of Kodak, and $500 million or more of Avon, Sears, and Xerox.[18] Taken together, all these factors have thoroughly confused our original notions of the role of the publicly held corporation and eroded its legitimacy. Ideologically, it has become a mere collection of persons and matter with considerable potential power—political and social as well as economic—floating dangerously in a philosophic limbo. If it survives, as it probably will, it has to be made legitimate. The only questions are how and by whom. The issues surrounding these questions fall into two categories:

1. Those having to do with the external relationships between the corporate collective and the communities which it affects.
2. Those having to do with the internal structure of the organization and thus with managerial authority and collective discipline.

NOTES

1. James Willard Hurst, *The Legitimacy of the Business Corporation in the Law of the United States, 1780–1970* (Charlottesville: The University Press of Virginia, 1970), pp. 234–53.
2. *Munn* v. *Illinois,* 94 U.S. 113 (1877).
3. *Nebbia* v. *New York,* 291 U.S. 502 (1934).
4. J. Shaw, *per curiam, Boston Water Power Co.* v. *Boston and Worcester Railroad,* 3 Pick, 360 (1839). Quoted in Harry N. Scheiber, "The Road to *Munn*: Eminent Domain and the Concept of Public Purpose in the State Courts," *Perspectives in American History,* vol. v, (1971): 399.
5. In 1968, the United States contained about 1.6 million profit-seeking corporations. Forty-three % of those possessed assets of less than $50,000 and 94% had assets of less than $1 million. On the other hand, 1,900 companies, constituting 0.13% of the corporate population, had assets of $100 million or more and held about 60% of total corporate assets. This concentration of assets in large publicly owned firms whose shares are traded on the stock exchanges has been increasing steadily since World War II. Neil Jacoby has estimated that 10,000 of the 1.6 million corporations have stock which is publicly traded—Neil H. Jacoby, *Corporate Power and Social Responsibility* (New York: The Macmillan Co., 1973), pp. 28, 49, and 179. Jacoby used data from *Statistics of Income: Corporation Returns 1965* (Washington D.C.: U.S. Government Printing Office, 1965), pp. 4–5; Betty Bock, *Concentration, Oligopoly and Profit: Concept and Data* (New York: The Conference Board, 1972).

6. Elisabeth Mann Borgese, "The Promise of Self Management," *The Center Magazine,* June 1972.
7. Earl C. Gottschalk, Jr., "Guarding the Land," *Wall Street Journal,* Oct. 9, 1972.
8. Quoted in Gladwin Hill, "Authority to Develop Land Is Termed a Public Right," *The New York Times,* May 30, 1973.
9. U.S. Environmental Protection Agency, Region II, "Conclusions and Recommendations on the Central Service Area Sewage Project of Ocean County, New Jersey," April 1974.
10. John Herbers, "U.S. Now Big Landlord in Decaying Inner City," *The New York Times,* Jan. 2, 1972.
11. Robert L. Heilbroner in *The New York Times Magazine,* as quoted in John K. Galbraith, *Economics and the Public Purpose* (Boston: Houghton Mifflin Co., 1973), p. 81.
12. Charles Reich, *The Greening of America* (New York: Random House, Inc., 1970), p. 111.
13. Aristotle, *Politics,* Book II, 1261b, in Benjamin Jowett, *The Politics of Aristotle* (Oxford, England: The Clarendon Press, 1885), p. 30.
14. Myles L. Mace, "The President and the Board of Directors," *Harvard Business Review,* March–April 1972, p. 41.
15. The fact that the courts are holding directors increasingly liable for the sins of managers does not really help the legitimacy problem, even though it has probably increased the wariness of directors. The amount of liability insurance sold to directors and officers has increased from practically nothing to more than $1 billion—"The Law: Trouble for the Top," *Forbes,* Sept. 1, 1968, p. 23.
16. *Business Week,* June 2, 1973, pp. 58 and 59.
17. In Japan, equity capital is rarely more than 25% of the corporation's total capitalization. Management controls companies with virtually no interference from stockholders. Ultimate control lies with the company's bank. The bank has no vote, but the company's dependence on the bank gives it what a Japanese manager once described as the "power of irresistible persuasion." Banks in turn are heavily influenced by government. See Peter F. Drucker, "Global Management," *Challenge to Leadership* (New York: The Free Press, 1973), p. 240.
18. *Business Week,* June 2, 1973, p. 59.

JUSTICE

Case Study—International Computer Sales

LAURA NADEL AND HESH WIENER

Would you sell a computer to Hitler?

You remember Hitler. He maimed, tortured and killed millions of people. They were, as far as he was concerned, enemies of the state. That, he felt, was enough.

Some people escaped. But imagine if Hitler had had a computer to keep track of his victims and intended victims. Log in. Type GIVE ME THE NAMES OF 20 JEWS AND 30 CATHOLICS IN BERLIN. And . . . but why go on? Hitler died a long time ago. These things don't happen any more. Or do they?

There are countries on this earth with governments so cruel that you can't find words to condemn their actions. And these governments carry out their missions, it seems, with the aid of computers. American computers.

In Chile, Uruguay, Argentina, or Brazil, an agent of the secret police can come to your door and ask you detailed questions about one of your friends—or even about someone you hardly know. If you do not answer satisfactorily, you may be threatened or taken away.

If you are taken away by the secret police, you may be tortured. According to the United Nations report, you could be hung upside down in a vat of urine or forced to eat vomit until your memory improves. If it doesn't, what follows will make you wish you had drowned in the tank in which you were hanging. You may be told that your loved ones will be treated even more harshly, although you probably can't imagine what more harshly means.

Like all modern police forces, secret police agencies have the latest in crime information systems, as sophisticated as their governments can afford. For example, according to a knowledgeable refugee, the Chilean government's computer systems store complete information about "the opposition, those considered leftists or suspects. The computer has all the facts." In South America, such systems are running on American Computers—the United States is the technological supplier of choice in this hemisphere.

The American computer manufacturers that supply Latin American governments with computers say they are not aware that their machines are used by the secret police. But they do concede that it is not possible for them to control how their machines are used by their customers. Most vendors say that they can not take responsibility for the ultimate use to which their products are put.

"We are in a position similar to a car manufacturer," says IBM's director of information, Dan Burnham. "If General Motors sells you a car, and you use it to kill someone, that doesn't make General Motors responsible.

"Once the manufacturer sells the automobile, there's no guarantee it won't be used to commit a crime."

Control Data Corp.'s vice president Roger G. Wheeler, speaking for that company, concedes the responsibility of a manufacturer, especially a manufacturer of computers of awesome capacity. CDC, alone among American mainframe vendors, has a corporate policy governing the sale of its machines.

"Our own sense of responsibility," says Wheeler, "would not permit us to provide a computer system for any purpose that abridges human rights and dignity."

Asked whether IBM has a similar policy, Dan Udell, an IBM public relations officer, said that "IBM's official policy is to act in accordance with U.S. national policy in dealing with all countries."

IBM has substantial interests in Latin America. In Brazil, for example, IBM's factory in Sao Paulo makes System 370s. In Argentina, IBM builds high-speed line printers. In Uruguay, IBM has an enormous service bureau and data center. In Chile, IBM has no plants but does have a data center in Santiago.

It is in Santiago that the DINA, Chile's secret police, is headquartered. In the old offices of the Pan American Bank, an eight-story building, the DINA directors oversee their work. Sources say that there are computers in this building, computers of American manufacture, which may well be linked to other DINA offices and police organizations by Chile's sophisticated tele-communications complex.

Communications links in Chile include a modern ITT telephone system said to be as good as any in the United States, an extensive microwave network for long distance communications, satellite links, and government radio channels. These facilities enable the DINA to keep in touch with its more specialized offices.

On Jose Arietta street, on the outskirts of the Chilean capital, is a building officially known as Villa Grimaldi, commonly called the Palace of Laughter. It is here that victims of the secret police may be taken for torture. Ultimately, victims are sent to concentration camps or prisons, of which there are many in Chile. Villa Grimaldi, according to United Nations sources, has extensive communications equipment.

The use of computers by the secret police in Chile was first brought to public attention by the National Council of Churches. Reports received by the council indicated that an American computer was destined to become a tool of the DINA.

NCC representatives went to an IBM shareholders' meeting on April 28, 1975, with the hope that they could halt IBM's planned installation of a 370/145 at the University of Chile in Santiago. They claimed that the system would be used by the police agencies of that country, not the university.

"The Chileans did purchase a 145," IBM's Burnham explains, "and they told us they weren't doing it for intelligence purposes." IBM decided to trust the Chileans.

"If I was the Chilean military junta, I wouldn't put my computer in the University of Chile," reasons Burnham. However, he says, he does "understand the generals have taken over the university."

The National Council of Churches is more definite on this issue than any IBM spokesman. William Wipfler, the Latin-American director of NCC feels that IBM does indeed have a responsibility in this matter.

"We called the attention of IBM to the repeated violations of human rights in Chile and asked them to reconsider their plans to install the 145."

The National Council of Churches backed their pleas with proxies totaling 200,000 shares of IBM stock.

"The question is not whether they would sell computers to Hitler," says Wipfler, "but whether they would sell gas chambers to Hitler. Either way you're giving him weapons. When you know who Hitler is, you can't pretend you don't know what he's doing with your equipment."

Frank Cary, IBM chairman, spoke at the 1975 meeting in response to the church group's protest.

"We don't think the installation of a computer on the campus of the University of Chile has any sinister implications at all."

Sinister, according to Washington journalist Tom Mechling, is hardly the word. "The University of Chile would be a real Machiavellian place to put the things. On the basis of what I've learned from extremely reliable sources, I'm very much convinced that that computer is being used for name, rank, and serial number. These people who say they can't know what it's being used for suffer the Eichmann syndrome. They claim they're only carrying out orders."

But IBM did send Dan Udell down to Santiago.

"We checked it out in detail. It's used for payroll, for processing student aptitude tests, for enrollment statistics and applications to college. To the best of our knowledge there are no other applications."

Perhaps the 145 at the University of Chile is not used by the secret police. But there is another, more direct link between the university and the Chilean secret police, a link typical of those that connect various Chilean institutions.

The leading computer service bureau in Chile is ECOM (for Empressa Nacional de Computacion), an organization that provides extensive computer support to the government. This relationship is a long-standing one, according to a Chilean refugee now living in England. But, our source indicates, that relationship now includes computer support for DINA operation.

The president of ECOM is Rene Peralta, a former official of the Chilean Navy. He is also the former head of computation at the University of

Chile, the very organization now training people in the use of a 370/145. The chairman of ECOM is an active general in the Chilean Army.

Our source claims that the systems at ECOM include modern powerful American computers. The services provided by ECOM include teleprocessing—the software there is capable of running database applications.

On May 20, 1975, General Pinochet, head of Chile's military junta, dedicated a 370/145 at the Technical University. This computer has been linked to other campuses by telex lines, according to Chilean sources.

The Technical University system is one of several shared by the Chilean Association of University Computing Centers. Among the members of this association are the University of Chile, Catholic University, University of Concepcion, and ECOM.

Today, the Technical University is headed by Army Colonel Reyes. Commenting on this, an informed exile said "interrelationships between the universities and the military are natural" in Chile.

In addition to Peralta, there is another figure whose name comes up whenever computers and repression in Chile is discussed. He is Patricio Leniz, a former civil engineer who, according to informed sources, was a key software man on the computer projects of the DINA.

Patricio Leniz is the brother of Fernando Leniz, former minister of the military junta ruling Chile. Fernando Leniz is also the former chairman of *El Mercurio,* Chile's right-wing newspaper.

Further substantiation of the DINA's use of computers comes from refugees' accounts of mass arrests in Chile. Those rounded up surrender their identification cards which are quickly processed. Suspects are separated from the detainees and ID cards are soon returned to those free. The rapid checking of names against police files requires an online computer facility. Other stories from individuals detained by police corroborate the rapid checking of dossiers.

IBM is not the only American manufacturer that sells computers to Chile. Burroughs also sells machines there. Neil Jackson, Burroughs director of communications, said that the Chileans have one older machine which Burroughs sold them in 1970. This, he points out, was three governments ago.

Jackson's statement conflicts with a report that there are Burroughs mainframes at the Technical University, the Catholic University and at the government's service bureau, ECOM.

Jackson stated that "Burroughs's official policy is that we never comment on the political affairs of any of the 120 countries with which we do business, including our own."

Suppose a B3500 is now used for police purposes? "Obviously we hope it's not," said Jackson. "We're not aware of any use by any of our customers for any purposes that violate human rights."

Refugees from other Latin-American police states also tell of the use of computer printouts during interrogations to cross-check data provided by detainees. According to these exiles, dossiers are shared among the police forces of Argentina, Chile, Uruguay, and Brazil.

The most detailed report of the use of computer-generated information during a police interrogation comes from a clergyman. He entered

Uruguay and was picked up by the police there for questioning. During the ordeal the police tried to get him to talk about a Catholic priest they were investigating.

When detained for questioning, the clergyman was presented with a computer printout describing the details of the career of his colleague. On the printout were all the addresses at which the sought-after priest had lived, his salary at each point in his career, his telephone numbers and his relations with other Catholics in Uruguay .

The interrogated clergyman said that the most incredible thing about the questioning was that, as far as he could tell, the man the police sought had never been in Uruguay.

This printout, a church spokesman claims, could not have been stolen from the personnel files of the Catholic church, it must have come from some police computer system. Police in Latin America, he said, keep close tabs on many priests.

The idea of using computing equipment to support police activities in Latin America has been promoted by the United States government. During the early years of this decade the Agency for International Development (AID) provided South American police forces with weapons, training, and data processing equipment under its "public safety" programs.

In the AID document describing U.S. assistance to the government of Venezuela, contract 529-11-710-022, U.S. officials report that "The technical groundwork has been laid for the country's public safety agencies, through electronic data processing and related processes, to pool their identification and intelligence data in a central location for more efficient coordination and rapid distribution of relevant facts and leads."

AID's Office of Public Safety, in a report on its assistance to Brazilian authorities, specifically lists IBM systems among police equipment shipped to that country.

Is this practice continuing? An AID official said that that agency no longer provides police equipment to Latin states. But AID does "provide computers to Chile."

The computers are included with moneys earmarked for activities other than "public safety." An AID official said that a recent grant for agriculture included a "computer component." He added that there is no practical way for AID personnel in Washington to check on the ultimate use to which such a computer is put. Informed sources state that the Chilean Institute of Agriculture building in Calle Belgrado, Santiago, is a center of communications for the DINA.

Evidence that Latin American authorities use computers for repression is abundant. Yet there seems to be no way for either computer manufacturers or humane government to halt this activity.

What little hope there is for a change in these practices may lie with the United Nations, a body limited to persuasive power.

The United Nations has been concerned about the possible use of computers as an aid to police in dictatorships. The proposed United Nations code of ethics states:

"It would seem imperative for computer experts to have some training in human rights concepts and in certain aspects of the law.

"In computer based decision-making, the computer user should bear in mind the need to protect and promote the rights of the individual."

Can the United Nations actually halt the use of computers by police states? Can it prevent automation of "the final solution?"

"The U.N. has no methods of enforcing its principles," says Leonore Hooley, a United Nations human rights officer.

"We operate on the principle of nonintervention in the internal affairs of countries."

Meanwhile, the Chilean government published a booklet last year. It is entitled "Universities and Development" and is written by Sergio Maldonado. In that booklet is a statement about a familiar figure:

> Hitler, a politician of the highest rank, knew how to majestically interpret the aspirations of the German people at the propitious moment. In a short time, he was able to raise them up so they could regain their place among world powers.

GERMAN SYSTEM PROTECTS PEOPLE

The most sensibly designed police information system in the world is Berlin's criminal police information network. This recently installed system uses special hardware and software to protect the rights of citizens while it speeds police and court work.

When an arrest is made, the arresting officer is required to enter relevant data on a workstation terminal at his local precinct house. But before he can log on the system, the officer must insert his machine-readable identification card into a reader.

Only when complete and correct data is presented at the terminal will it be forwarded to a central system which again checks for errors and creates or updates a file which automatically produces documents for the police force. Later, reports are generated for prosecutors and jurists should court action be necessary.

A detective making an inquiry about a suspect must follow a similar procedure. The officer's identification card is checked against records to assure that the action is within the officer's jurisdiction.

An illegal action is detected by the system which also produces summary reports of proper as well as improper activities for review by police authorities. Further, data can be made available to defense attorneys and other appropriate parties during the preparation of legal case or during an actual trial. No party can receive data beyond that mandated by law.

The terminals, which have hardwired programs, were built by Nixdorf Computer. They contain a special processor, printers, identification card readers and communications hardware. The mainframe that guards the data base is Siemens system. Training for all users is performed by the police personnel.

There are currently 79 of the Nixdorf terminals online, and many more can be accommodated as needed. The mainframe can be altered, too, because the terminal is intelligent enough to match any new protocols that might be established.

While the system was installed to cut the amount of paperwork officers must complete in the course of dealing with routine crimes, the approach taken by the police of Berlin demonstrates that an effective criminal information system can also be designed to insure justice, security, and accuracy. It is expected that the Berlin system will be adopted by other police forces in Germany and in other countries as well.

Case Study—Who Has First Claim on Health Care Resources?

ROBERT M. VEATCH

State Bill 529 calls for the establishment of community-based homes for the care and education of the mentally retarded. The bill provides one home for every fifteen persons presently institutionalized in four state institutions for the mentally retarded at a cost of $55.8 million. The estimated costs for the new care for the present population of 7,600 will be $70 million a year.

The bill was introduced by Representative John Sheehan who spoke in favor of it. He painted a dismal picture of antiquated institutions bereft of basic human necessities or amenities. Thousands of human beings, many unclothed, spend their lives huddled in dark, drab rooms, where they are supervised by an overworked staff, many of whom have no professional training. Sheehan, who has the support of the parents' organization, the State Department of Mental Health, the local ACLU, and the religious leadership, concluded his case by pleading, "Justice requires that we extend this token contribution to these citizens, burdened by physical and psychological suffering, and by the degradation of our society's past inhumanity to its fellow humans."

Representative James Hudson and Dr. Robert Simmons, while emphasizing their concern for care of the retarded, spoke in opposition to the bill. Representative Hudson, noting that he was elected representative of all the citizens in his district, argued that he had an obligation to examine the alternative uses for the $14 million in additional funds called for by the bill. But first, he pointed out that the new total sum of $70 million equalled 1.5 percent of the state's budget, a budget raised by all its citizens, while the institutionalized population equalled only one-tenth of one percent of the

Robert M. Veatch, "Who Has First Claim on Health Care Resources?" *Hastings Center Report,* August 1975, reprinted by permission of the Hastings Center.

state's population. The proposed increase of $14 million could buy hot lunches for all the state's school children; it could also provide job training for productive members of society. Hudson argued that the fairest thing to do would be to spread the money evenly among those who would be productive. "Our task as legislators," he concluded, "must be to serve the greatest good of the greatest number."

Dr. Simmons, as a physician, argued that the money could be used more efficiently in providing health care for three groups: normal or more nearly normal children (thousands of whom could be reached for every mentally retarded child), those potentially engaged in productive labor, and pregnant women. He showed that much mental retardation can be eliminated through prenatal diagnosis which he estimated to cost $200 per case for Down's syndrome compared to $60,000 for each institutionalized child. Even allowing that some of the institutionalized retarded might be gainfully employed if they were in high-quality, community-based homes, the savings from spending the funds on detection rather than on more expensive forms of institutionalized care are enormous.

The legislative committee must now make its decision on the bill.

Case Study—Cat Scan

In a typical governmental response to a problem of its own making, Congress in 1974 entered into the business of health planning to try to reduce medical costs that were being inflated by badly designed Medicare and Medicaid programs. One feature of the scheme required hospitals to obtain "certificates of need" from a "Health Systems Agency" in order to make any sizable capital investment.

While the HSAs were theoretically controlled by local citizens, many in practice became tools of state and federal health bureaucrats. One of the outcomes was a limitation on use of some of the more expensive forms of medical technology, even where there were clearly demonstrated cost, and life, saving benefits. One such device was the complex machine commonly known as the CT or "CAT" scanner, which uses a computer and X-rays to formulate "pictures" of the internal organs of the body.

Doctors find this machine invaluable, particularly for diagnosing diseases and injuries affecting the brain. When health planners denied them to some hospitals, doctors in some cases raised the $500,000 on their own, installing what the bureaucrats chose to call "fugitive scanners" near hospitals for lifesaving diagnostic work.

One hospital that was, until this year, denied a CAT scanner was Harlem Hospital Center, a big New York municipal facility. Health planners ruled that doctors there could use scanners in nearby hospitals, but for

"Death in Harlem," *Wall Street Journal,* Monday June 8, 1981, p. 18. Reprinted by permission of *The Wall Street Journal,*

various reasons, either because patients were too ill or the equipment not free when needed, the use of CAT scans by Harlem Hospital doctors was sharply limited.

Three doctors at the hospital have just published an article in the New England Journal of Medicine detailing the effects of this, based on a retrospective analysis of hospital records for 1979.

Their conclusion:

> "Lack of a CT scanner at Harlem Hospital led to prolonged hospitalization, discharge without adequate diagnosis and probably in some cases morbidity and mortality. We do not claim that all or even most of the 163 medical and surgical patients who were thought to need CT, but who died without it, would have survived had it been available. Autopsies were infrequent. Individual analysis of these cases, however, raises the possibility of treatable lesions detectable only with CT—a possibility that was regarded with considerable anxiety during each patient's hospitalization."

The Harlem case is but one more example of the risks of bureaucrat-controlled medicine. The Reagan administration has proposed to phase out federal funding of Health Systems Agencies, leaving it up to state and local groups to decide whether they are worthwhile. Federal administration of Professional Standards Review Organizations, set up to monitor whether doctors are wasting hospital resources, also is slated for phase-out.

Both efforts are being resisted in Congress, naturally. But the Harlem experience tells us that in this one area, the loss of decision-making power by local professionals and boards can be a matter of life and death.

Distributive Justice

JOHN RAWLS

We may think of a human society as a more or less self-sufficient association regulated by a common conception of justice and aimed at advancing the good of its members.[1] As a co-operative venture for mutual advantage, it is characterized by a conflict as well as an identity of interests. There is an identity of interests since social co-operation makes possible a better life for all than any would have if everyone were to try to live by his own efforts; yet at the same time men are not indifferent as to how the greater benefits produced by their joint labours are distributed, for in order to further their own aims each prefers a larger to a lesser share. A conception of justice is

From John Rawls, "Distributive Justice," *Philosophy, Politics, and Society,* 3rd series, ed. by Peter Laslett and W. G. Runciman (Basil Blackwell, Oxford; Barnes & Noble Books, Totowa, N. J., 1967). Reprinted by permission of the author.

a set of principles for choosing between the social arrangements which determine this division and for underwriting a consensus as to the proper distributive shares.

Now at first sight the most rational conception of justice would seem to be utilitarian. For consider: each man in realizing his own good can certainly balance his own losses against his own gains. We can impose a sacrifice on ourselves now for the sake of a greater advantage later. A man quite properly acts, as long as others are not affected, to achieve his own greatest good, to advance his ends as far as possible. Now, why should not a society act on precisely the same principle? Why is not that which is rational in the case of one man right in the case of a group of men? Surely the simplest and most direct conception of the right, and so of justice, is that of maximizing the good. This assumes a prior understanding of what is good, but we can think of the good as already given by the interests of rational individuals. Thus just as the principle of individual choice is to achieve one's greatest good, to advance so far as possible one's own system of rational desires, so the principle of social choice is to realize the greatest good (similarly defined) summed over all the members of society. We arrive at the principle of utility in a natural way: by this principle a society is rightly ordered, and hence just, when its institutions are arranged so as to realize the greatest sum of satisfactions.

The striking feature of the principle of utility is that it does not matter, except indirectly, how this sum of satisfactions is distributed among individuals, any more than it matters, except indirectly, how one man distributes his satisfactions over time. Since certain ways of distributing things affect the total sum of satisfactions, this fact must be taken into account in arranging social institutions; but according to this principle the explanation of common-sense precepts of justice and their seemingly stringent character is that they are those rules which experience shows must be strictly respected and departed from only under exceptional circumstances if the sum of advantages is to be maximized. The precepts of justice are derivative from the one end of attaining the greatest net balance of satisfactions. There is no reason in principle why the greater gains of some should not compensate for the lesser losses of others; or why the violation of the liberty of a few might not be made right by a greater good shared by many. It simply happens, at least under most conditions, that the greatest sum of advantages is not generally achieved in this way. From the standpoint of utility the strictness of common-sense notions of justice has a certain usefulness, but as a philosophical doctrine it is irrational.

If, then, we believe that as a matter of principle each member of society has an inviolability founded on justice which even the welfare of everyone else cannot override, and that a loss of freedom for some is not made right by a greater sum of satisfactions enjoyed by many, we shall have to look for another account of the principles of justice. The principle of utility is incapable of explaining the fact that in a just society the liberties of equal citizenship are taken for granted, and the rights secured by justice are not subject to political bargaining nor to the calculus of social interests. Now, the most natural alternative to the principle of utility is its traditional rival, the theory of the social contract. The aim of the contract doctrine is precisely to account for the strictness of justice by supposing that its principles arise from an agreement among free and independent persons in an original position of equality and hence reflect the integrity and equal sovereignty of the rational persons who are the contractees. Instead of supposing that a conception of right, and so a conception of justice, is simply an extension of the principle of choice for one man to society as a whole, the contract doctrine assumes that the rational individuals who belong to society must choose together, in one joint act, what is to count among them as just and unjust. They are to decide among themselves once and for all what is to be their conception of justice. This decision is thought of as being made in a suitably defined initial situation one of the significant features of which is that no one knows his position in society, nor even his place in the distribution of natural talents and abilities. The principles of justice to which all are forever bound are chosen in the absence of this sort of specific information. A veil of ignorance prevents anyone from being advantaged or disadvantaged by the contingencies of social class and fortune; and hence the bargaining problems which arise in everyday life from the possession of this knowledge do not affect the choice of principles. On the contract doctrine, then, the theory of justice, and indeed ethics itself, is part of the general theory of rational choice, a fact perfectly clear in its Kantian formulation.

Once justice is thought of as arising from an original agreement of this kind, it is evident that the principle of utility is problematical. For why should rational individuals who have a system of ends they wish to advance agree to a violation of their liberty for the sake of a greater balance of satisfactions enjoyed by others? It seems more plausible to suppose that, when situated in an original position of equal right, they would insist upon institutions which returned compensating advantages for any sacrifices required. A rational man would not accept an institution merely because it maximized the sum of advantages irrespective of its effect on his own interests. It appears, then, that the principle of utility would be rejected as a principle of justice, although we shall not try to argue this important question here. Rather, our aim is to give a brief sketch of the conception of distributive shares implicit in the principles of justice which, it seems, would be chosen in the original position. The philosophical appeal of utilitarianism is that it seems to offer a single principle on the basis of which a consistent and complete conception of right can be developed. The problem is to work out a contractarian alternative in such a way that it has comparable if not all the same virtues.

In our discussion we shall make no attempt to derive the two principles of justice which we shall examine; that is, we shall not try to show that they would be chosen in the original position.[2] It must suffice that it is plausible that they would be, at least in preference to the standard forms of traditional theories. Instead we shall be mainly concerned with three questions: first, how to interpret these principles so that they define a consistent and complete conception of justice; second, whether it is possible to arrange the institutions of a constitutional democracy so that these principles are satisfied, at least approximately; and third, whether the conception of distributive shares which they define is compatible with common-sense notions of justice. The significance of these principles is that they allow for the strictness of the claims of justice; and if they can be understood so as to yield a consistent and complete conception, the contractarian alternative would seem all the more attractive.

The two principles of justice which we shall discuss may be formulated as follows: first, each person engaged in an institution or affected by it has an equal right to the most extensive liberty compatible with a like liberty for all; and second, inequalities as defined by the institutional structure or fostered by it are arbitrary unless it is reasonable to expect that they will work out to everyone's advantage and provided that the positions and offices to which they attach or from which they may be gained are open to all. These principles regulate the distributive aspects of institutions by controlling the assignment of rights and duties throughout the whole social structure, beginning with the adoption of a political constitution in accordance with which they are then to be applied to legislation. It is upon a correct choice of a basic structure of society, its fundamental system of rights and duties, that the justice of distributive shares depends.

The two principles of justice apply in the first instance to this basic structure, that is, to the main institutions of the social system and their arrangement, how they are combined together. Thus, this structure includes the political constitution and the principal economic and social institutions which together define a person's liberties and rights and affect his life-prospects, what he may expect to be and how well he may expect to fare. The intuitive idea here is that those born into the social system at different positions, say in different social classes, have varying life-prospects determined, in part, by the system of political liberties and personal rights, and by the economic and social opportunities which are made available to these positions. In this way the basic structure of society favours certain men over others, and these are the basic inequalities, the ones which affect their whole life-prospects. It is inequalities of this kind, presumably inevitable in any society, with which the two principles of justice are primarily designed to deal.

Now the second principle holds that an inequality is allowed only if there is reason to believe that the institution with the inequality, or permitting it, will work out for the advantage of every person engaged in it. In the case of the basic structure this means that all inequalities which affect life-prospects, say the inequalities of income and wealth which exist between social classes, must be to the advantage of everyone. Since the principle applies to institutions, we interpret this to mean that inequalities must be to the advantage of the representative man for each relevant social position; they should improve each such man's expectation. Here we assume that it is possible to attach to each position an expectation, and that this expectation is a function of the whole institutional structure: it can be raised and lowered by reassigning rights and duties throughout the system. Thus the expectation of any position depends upon the expectations of the others, and these in turn depend upon the pattern of rights and duties established by the basic structure. But it is not clear what is meant by saying that inequalities must be to the advantage of every representative man. . . .

[One] . . . interpretation [of what is meant by saying that inequalities must be to the advantage of every representative man] . . . is to choose some social position by reference to which the pattern of expectations as a whole is to be judged, and then to maximize with respect to the expectations of this representative man consistent with the demands of equal liberty and equality of opportunity. Now, the one obvious candidate is the representative man of those who are least favoured by the system of institutional inequalities. Thus we arrive at the following idea: the basic structure of the social system affects the life-prospects of typical individuals according to their initial places in society, say the various income classes into which they are born, or depending upon certain natural attributes, as when institutions make discriminations between men and women or allow certain advantages to be gained by those with greater natural abilities. The fundamental problem of distributive justice concerns the differences in life-prospects which come about in this way. We interpret the second principle to hold that these differences are just if and only if the greater expectations of the more advantaged, when playing a part in the working of the whole social system, improve the expectations of the least advantaged. The basic structure is just throughout when the advantages of the more fortunate promote the well-being of the least fortunate, that is, when a decrease in their advantages would make the least fortunate even worse off than they are. The basic structure is perfectly just when the prospects of the least fortunate are as great as they can be.

In interpreting the second principle (or rather the first part of it which we may, for obvious reasons, refer to as the difference principle), we assume that the first principle requires a basic equal liberty for all, and that the resulting political system, when circumstances permit, is that of a constitutional democracy in some form. There must be liberty of the person and political equality as well as liberty of conscience and freedom of thought. There is one class of equal citizens which defines a common status for all. We also assume that there is equality of opportunity and a fair competition for the available positions on the basis of reasonable qualifications. Now, given this background, the differences to be justified are the various economic and social inequalities in the basic structure which must inevitably arise in such a scheme. These are the inequalities in the distribution of income and wealth and the distinctions in social prestige and status which attach to the various positions and classes. The difference principle says that these inequalities are just if and only if they are part of a larger system in which they work out to the advantage of the most unfortunate representative man. The just distributive shares determined by the basic structure are those specified by this constrained maximum principle.

Thus, consider the chief problem of distributive justice, that concerning the distribution of wealth as it affects the life-prospects of those starting out in the various income groups. These income classes define the relevant representative men from which the social system is to be judged. Now, a son of a member of the entrepreneurial class (in a capitalist society) has a better prospect than that of the son of an unskilled labourer. This will be true, it seems, even when the social injustices which presently exist are removed and the two men are of equal talent and ability; the inequality cannot be done away with as long as something like the family is maintained. What, then, can justify this inequality in life-prospects? According to the second principle it is justified only if it is to the advantage of the representative man who is worst off, in this case the representative unskilled labourer. The inequality is permissible because lowering it would, let's suppose, make the working man even worse off than he is. Presumably, given the principle of open offices (the second part of the second principle), the greater expectations allowed to entrepreneurs has the effect in the longer run of raising the life-prospects of the labouring class. The inequality in expectation provides an incentive so that the economy is more efficient, industrial advance proceeds at a quicker pace, and so on, the end result of which is that greater material and other benefits are distributed throughout the system. Of course, all of this is familiar, and whether true or not in particular cases, it is the sort of thing which must be argued if the inequality in income and wealth is to be acceptable by the difference principle.

We should now verify that this interpretation of the second principle gives a natural sense in which everyone may be said to be made better off. Let us suppose that inequalities are chain-connected: that is, if an inequality raises the expectations of the lowest position, it raises the expectations of all positions in between. For example, if the greater expectations of the representative entrepreneur raises that of the unskilled labourer, it also raises that of the semi-skilled. Let us further assume that inequalities are close-knit: that is, it is impossible to raise (or lower) the expectation of any representative man without raising (or lowering) the expectations of every other representative man, and in particular, without affecting one way or the other that of the least fortunate. There is no loose-jointedness, so to speak, in the way in which expectations depend upon one another. Now, with these assumptions, everyone does benefit from an inequality which satisfies the difference principle, and the second principle as we have formulated it reads correctly. For the representative man who is better off in any pair-wise comparison gains by being allowed to have his advantage, and the man who is worse off benefits from the contribution which all inequalities make to each position below. Of course, chain-connection and close-knitness may not obtain; but in this case those who are better off should not have a veto over the advantages available for the least advantaged. The stricter interpretation of the difference principle should be followed, and all inequalities should be arranged for the advantage of the most unfortunate even if some inequalities are not to the advantage of those in middle positions. Should these conditions fail, then, the second principle would have to be stated in another way.

It may be observed that the difference principle represents, in effect, an original agreement to share in the benefits of the distribution of natural talents and abilities, whatever this distribution turns out to be, in order to alleviate as far as possible the arbitrary handicaps resulting from our initial starting places in society. Those who have been favoured by nature, whoever they are, may gain from their good fortune only on terms that improve the well-being of those who have lost out. The naturally advantaged are not to gain simply because they are more gifted, but only to cover the costs of training and cultivating their endowments and for putting them to use in a way which improves the position of the less fortunate. We are led to the difference principle if we wish to arrange the basic social structure so that no one gains (or loses) from his luck in the natural lottery of talent and ability, or from his initial place in society, without giving (or receiving) compensating advantages in return. (The parties in the original position are not said to be attracted by this idea and so agree to it; rather, given the symmetries of their situation, and particularly their lack of knowledge, and so on, they will find it to their interest to agree to a principle which can be understood in this way.) And we should note also that when the difference principle is perfectly satisfied, the basic structure is optimal by the efficiency principle. There is no way to make anyone better off without making someone worse off, namely, the least fortunate representative man. Thus the two principles of justice define distributive shares in a way compatible with efficiency, at least as long as we move on this highly abstract level. If we want to say (as we do, although it cannot be argued here) that the demands of justice have an absolute weight with respect to efficiency, this claim may seem less paradoxical when it is kept in mind that perfectly just institutions are also efficient.

Our second question is whether it is possible to arrange the institutions of a constitutional democracy so that the two principles of justice are satisfied, at least approximately. We shall try to show that this can be done provided the government regulates a free economy in a certain way. More fully, if law and government act effectively to keep markets competitive, resources fully employed, property and wealth widely distributed over time, and to maintain the appropriate social minimum, then if there is equality of opportunity underwritten by education for all, the resulting distribution will be just. Of course, all of these arrangements and policies are familiar. The only novelty in the following remarks, if there is any novelty at all, is that this framework of institutions can be made to satisfy the difference principle. To argue this, we must sketch the relations of these institutions and how they work together.

First of all, we assume that the basic social structure is controlled by a just constitution which secures the various liberties of equal citizenship. Thus the legal order is administered in accordance with the principle of legality, and liberty of conscience and freedom of thought are taken for granted. The political process is conducted, so far as possible, as a just procedure for choosing between governments and for enacting just legislation. From the standpoint of distributive justice, it is also essential that there be equality of opportunity in several senses. Thus, we suppose that, in addition to maintaining the usual social overhead capital, government provides for equal educational opportunities for all either by subsidizing private schools or by operating a public school system. It also enforces and underwrites equality of opportunity in commercial ventures and in the free choice of occupation. This result is achieved by policing business behaviour and by preventing the establishment of barriers and restriction to the desirable positions and markets. Lastly, there is a guarantee of a social minimum which the government meets by family allowances and special payments in times of unemployment, or by a negative income tax.

In maintaining this system of institutions the government may be thought of as divided into four branches. Each branch is represented by various agencies (or activities thereof) charged with preserving certain social and economic conditions. These branches do not necessarily overlap with the usual organization of government, but should be understood as purely conceptual. Thus the allocation branch is to keep the economy feasibly competitive, that is, to prevent the formation of unreasonable market power. Markets are competitive in this sense when they cannot be made more so consistent with the requirements of efficiency and the acceptance of the facts of consumer preferences and geography. The allocation branch is also charged with identifying and correcting, say by suitable taxes and subsidies wherever possible, the more obvious departures from efficiency caused by the failure of prices to measure accurately social benefits and costs. The stabilization branch strives to maintain reasonably full employment so that there is no waste through failure to use resources and the free choice of occupation and the deployment of finance is supported by strong effective demand. These two branches together are to preserve the efficiency of the market economy generally.

The social minimum is established through the operations of the transfer branch. Later on we shall consider at what level this minimum should be set, since this is a crucial matter; but for the moment, a few general remarks will suffice. The main idea is that the workings of the transfer branch take into account the precept of need and assign it an appropriate weight with respect to the other common-sense precepts of justice. A market economy ignores the claims of need altogether. Hence there is a division of labour between the parts of the social system as different institutions answer to different common-sense precepts. Competitive markets (properly supplemented by government operations) handle the problem of the efficient allocation of labour and resources and set a weight to the conventional precepts associated with wages and earnings (the precepts of each according to his work and experience, or responsibility and the hazards of the job, and so on), whereas the transfer branch guarantees a certain level of well-being and meets the claims of need. Thus it is obvious that the justice of distributive shares depends upon the whole social system and how it distributes total income, wages plus transfers. There is with reason strong objection to the competitive determination of total income, since this would leave out of account the claims of need and of a decent standard of life. From the standpoint of the original position it is clearly rational to insure oneself against these contingencies. But now, if the appropriate minimum is provided by transfers, it may be perfectly fair that the other part of total income is competitively determined. Moreover, this way of dealing with the claims of need is doubtless more efficient, at least from a theoretical point of view, than trying to regulate prices by minimum wage standards and so on. It is preferable to handle these claims by a separate branch which supports a social minimum. Henceforth, in considering whether the second principle of justice is satisfied, the answer turns on whether the total income of the least advantaged, that is, wages plus transfers, is such as to maximize their long-term expectations consistent with the demands of liberty.

Finally, the distribution branch is to preserve an approximately just distribution of income and wealth over time by affecting the background conditions of the market from period to period. Two aspects of this branch may be distinguished. First of all, it operates a system of inheritance and gift taxes. The aim of these levies is not to raise revenue, but gradually and continually to correct the distribution of wealth and to prevent the concentrations of power to the detriment of liberty and equality of opportunity. It is perfectly true, as some have said,[3] that unequal inheritance of wealth is no more inherently unjust than unequal inheritance of intelligence; as far as possible the inequalities founded on either should satisfy the difference principle. Thus, the inheritance of greater wealth is just as long as it is to the advantage of the worst off and consistent with liberty, including equality of opportunity. Now by the latter we do not mean, of course, the equality of expectations between classes, since differences in life-prospects arising from the basic structure are inevitable, and it is precisely the aim of the second principle to say when these differences are just. Indeed, equality of opportunity is a certain set of institutions which assures equally good education and chances of culture for all and which keeps open the competition for positions on the basis of qualities reasonably related to performance, and so on. It is these institutions which are put in jeopardy when inequalities and concentrations of wealth reach a certain limit; and the taxes imposed by the distribution branch are to prevent this limit from being exceeded. Naturally enough where this limit lies is a matter for political judgment guided by theory, practical experience, and plain hunch; on this question the theory of justice has nothing to say.

The second part of the distribution branch is a scheme of taxation for raising revenue to cover the costs of public goods, to make transfer payments, and the like. This scheme belongs to the distribution branch since the burden of taxation must be justly shared. Although we cannot examine the legal and economic complications involved, there are several points in favour of proportional expenditure taxes as part of an ideally just arrangement. For one thing, they are preferable to income taxes at the level of common-sense precepts of justice, since they impose a levy according to how much a man takes out of the common store of goods and not according to how much he contributes (assuming that income is fairly earned in return for productive efforts). On the other hand, proportional taxes treat everyone in a clearly defined uniform way (again assuming that income is fairly earned) and hence it is preferable to use progressive rates only when they are necessary to preserve the justice of the system as a whole, that is, to prevent large fortunes hazardous to liberty and equality of opportunity, and the like. If proportional expenditure taxes should also prove more efficient, say because they interfere less with incentives, or whatever, this would make the case for them decisive provided a feasible scheme could be worked out.[4] Yet these are questions of political judgment which are not our concern; and, in any case, a proportional expenditure tax is part of an idealized scheme which we are describing. It does not follow that even steeply progressive income taxes, given the injustice of existing systems, do not improve justice and efficiency all things considered. In practice we must usually choose between unjust arrangements and then it is a matter of finding the lesser injustice.

Whatever form the distribution branch assumes, the argument for it is to be based on justice: we must hold that once it is accepted the social system as a whole—the competitive economy surrounded by a just constitutional and legal framework—can be made to satisfy the principles of justice with the smallest loss in efficiency. The long-term expectations of the least advantaged are raised to the highest level consistent with the demands of equal liberty. In discussing the choice of a distribution scheme we have made no reference to the traditional criteria of taxation according to ability to pay or benefits received; nor have we mentioned any of the variants of the sacrifice principle. These standards are subordinate to the two principles of justice; once the problem is seen as that of designing a whole social system, they assume the status of secondary precepts with no more independent force than the precepts of common sense in regard to wages. To suppose otherwise is not to take a sufficiently comprehensive point of view. In setting up a just distribution branch these precepts may or may not have a place depending upon the demands of the two principles of justice when applied to the entire system. . . .

The sketch of the system of institutions satisfying the two principles of justice is now complete. . . .

In order . . . to establish just distributive shares a just total system of institutions must be set up and impartially administered. Given a just constitution and the smooth working of the four branches of government, and so on, there exists a procedure such that the actual distribution of wealth, whatever it turns out to be, is just. It will have come about as a consequence of a just system of institutions satisfying the principles to which everyone would agree and against which no one can complain. The situation is one of pure procedural justice, since there is no independent criterion by which the outcome can be judged. Nor can we say that a particular distribution of wealth is just because it is one which could have resulted from just institutions although it has not, as this would be to allow too much. Clearly there are many distributions which may be reached by just institutions, and this is true whether we count patterns of distributions among social classes or whether we count distributions of particular goods and services among particular individuals. There are indefinitely many outcomes and what makes one of these just is that it has been achieved by actually carrying out a just scheme of co-operation as it is publicly understood. It is the result which has arisen when everyone receives that to which he is entitled given his and others' actions guided by their legitimate expectations and their obligations to one another. We can no more arrive at a just distribution of wealth except by working together within the framework of a just system of institutions than we can win or lose fairly without actually betting.

This account of distributive shares is simply an elaboration of the familiar idea that economic rewards will be just once a perfectly competitive price system is organized as a fair game. But in order to do this we have to begin with the choice of a social system as a whole, for the basic structure of the entire arrangement must be just. The economy must be surrounded with the appropriate framework of institutions, since even a perfectly efficient price system has no tendency to determine just distributive shares when left to itself. Not only must economic activity be regulated by a just constitution and controlled by the four branches of government, but a just saving-function must be adopted to estimate the provision to be made for future generations. . . .

NOTES

1. In this essay I try to work out some of the implications of the two principles of justice discussed in 'Justice as Fairness' which first appeared in the *Philosophical Review,* 1958, and which is reprinted in *Philosophy, Politics and Society,* Series II, pp. 132–57.
2. This question is discussed very briefly in 'Justice as Fairness,' see pp. 138–41. The intuitive idea is as follows. Given the circumstances of the original position, it is rational for a man to choose as if he were designing a society in which his enemy is to assign him his place. Thus, in particular, given the complete lack of knowledge (which makes the choice one under uncertainty), the fact that the decision involves one's life-prospects as a whole and is constrained by obligations to third parties (e.g., one's descendants) and duties to certain values (e.g., to religious truth), it is rational to be conservative and so to choose in accordance with an analogue of the maximin principle. Viewing the situation in this way, the interpretation given to the principles of justice earlier is perhaps natural enough. Moreover, it seems clear how the principle of utility can be interpreted; it is the analogue of the Laplacean principle for choice uncertainty. (For a discussion of these choice criteria, see R. D. Luce and H. Raiffa, *Games and Decisions* (1957), pp. 275–98).
3. Example F. von Hayek, *The Constitution of Liberty* (1960), p. 90.
4. See N. Kaldor, *An Expenditure Tax* (1955).

The Principles of a Liberal Social Order

FRIEDRICH A. HAYEK

1. By 'liberalism' I shall understand here the conception of a desirable political order which in the first instance was developed in England from the time of the Old Whigs in the later part of the seventeenth century to that of Gladstone at the end of the nineteenth. David Hume, Adam Smith,

Published in *Il Politico,* 1966. Reprinted in *Studies in Philosophy, Politics and Economics,* ed. Friedrich A. Hayek, by permission of the University of Chicago Press. Reprinted by permission of the editors of *Il Politico.*

Edmund Burke, T. B. Macaulay and Lord Acton may be regarded as its typical representatives in England. It was this conception of individual liberty under the law which in the first instance inspired the liberal movements on the Continent and which became the basis of the American political tradition. A few of the leading political thinkers in those countries like B. Constant and A. de Tocqueville in France, Immanuel Kant, Friedrich von Schiller and Wilhelm von Humboldt in Germany, and James Madison, John Marshall and Daniel Webster in the United States belong wholly to it.

2. This liberalism must be clearly distinguished from another, originally Continental European tradition, also called 'liberalism' of which what now claims this name in the United States is a direct descendant. This latter view, though beginning with an attempt to imitate the first tradition, interpreted it in the spirit of a constructivist rationalism prevalent in France and thereby made of it something very different, and in the end, instead of advocating limitations on the powers of government, ended up with the ideal of the unlimited powers of the majority. This is the tradition of Voltaire, Rousseau, Condorcet and the French Revolution which became the ancestor of modern socialism. English utilitarianism has taken over much of this Continental tradition and the late-nineteenth-century British liberal party, resulting from a fusion of the liberal Whigs and the utilitarian Radicals, was also a product of this mixture.

3. Liberalism and democracy, although compatible, are not the same. The first is concerned with the extent of governmental power, the second with who holds this power. The difference is best seen if we consider their opposites: the opposite of liberalism is totalitarianism, while the opposite of democracy is authoritarianism. In consequence, it is at least possible in principle that a democratic government may be totalitarian and that an authoritarian government may act on liberal principles. The second kind of 'liberalism' mentioned before has in effect become democratism rather than liberalism and, demanding *unlimited* power of the majority, has become essentially anti-liberal. . . .

6. Liberalism . . . derives from the discovery of a self-generating or spontaneous order in social affairs (the same discovery which led to the recognition that there existed an object for theoretical social sciences), an order which made it possible to utilize the knowledge and skill of all members of society to a much greater extent than would be possible in any order created by central direction, and the consequent desire to make as full use of these powerful spontaneous ordering forces as possible.

7. It was thus in their efforts to make explicit the principles of an order already existing but only in an imperfect form that Adam Smith and his followers developed the basic principles of liberalism in order to demonstrate the desirability of their general application. In doing this they were able to presuppose familiarity with the common law conception of justice and with the ideals of the rule of law and of government under the law which were little understood outside the Anglo-Saxon world; with the result that not only were their ideas not fully understood outside the English-speaking countries, but that they ceased to be fully understood even in England when Bentham and his followers replaced the English legal tradition by a con-

structivist utilitarianism derived more from Continental rationalism than from the evolutionary conception of the English tradition.

8. The central concept of liberalism is that under the enforcement of universal rules of just conduct, protecting a recognizable private domain of individuals, a spontaneous order of human activities of much greater complexity will form itself than could ever be produced by deliberate arrangement, and that in consequence the coercive activities of government should be limited to the enforcement of such rules, whatever other services government may at the same time render by administering those particular resources which have been placed at its disposal for those purposes.

9. The distinction between a *spontaneous order* based on abstract rules which leave individuals free to use their own knowledge for their own purposes, and an *organization or arrangement* based on commands, is of central importance for the understanding of the principles of a free society and must in the following paragraphs be explained in some detail, especially as the spontaneous order of a free society will contain many organizations (including the biggest organization, government), but the two principles of order cannot be mixed in any manner we may wish.

10. The first peculiarity of a spontaneous order is that by using its ordering forces (the regularity of the conduct of its members) we can achieve an order of a much more complex set of facts than we could ever achieve by deliberate arrangement, but that, while availing ourselves of this possibility of inducing an order of much greater extent than we otherwise could, we at the same time limit our power over the details of that order. We shall say that when using the former principle we shall have power only over the abstract character but not over the concrete detail of that order.

11. No less important is the fact that, in contrast to an organization, neither has a spontaneous order a purpose nor need there be agreement on the concrete results it will produce in order to agree on the desirability of such an order, because, being independent of any particular purpose, it can be used for, and will assist in the pursuit of, a great many different, divergent and even conflicting individual purposes. Thus the order of the market, in particular, rests not on common purposes but on reciprocity, that is on the reconciliation of different purposes for the mutual benefit of the participants. . . .

16. The spontaneous order of the market resulting from the interaction of many . . . economies is something so fundamentally different from an economy proper that it must be regarded as a great misfortune that it has ever been called by the same name. I have become convinced that this practice so constantly misleads people that it is necessary to invent a new technical term for it. I propose that we call this spontaneous order of the market a *catallaxy* in analogy to the term 'catallactics', which has often been proposed as a substitute for the term 'economics'. (Both 'catallaxy' and 'catallactics' derive from the ancient Greek verb *katallattein* which, significantly, means not only 'to barter' and 'to exchange' but also 'to admit into the community' and 'to turn from enemy into friend'.)

17. The chief point about the catallaxy is that, as a spontaneous order, its orderliness does *not* rest on its orientation on a single hierarchy of ends,

and that, therefore, it will *not* secure that for it as a whole the more important comes before the less important. This is the chief cause of its condemnation by its opponents, and it could be said that most of the socialist demands amount to nothing less than that the catallaxy should be turned into an economy proper (i.e., the purposeless spontaneous order into a purpose-oriented organization) in order to assure that the more important be never sacrificed to the less important. The defence of the free society must therefore show that it is due to the fact that we do not enforce a unitary scale of concrete ends, nor attempt to secure that some particular view about what is more and what is less important governs the whole of society, that the members of such a free society have as good a chance successfully to use their individual knowledge for the achievement of their individual purposes as they in fact have.

18. The extension of an order of peace beyond the small purpose-oriented organization became thus possible by the extension of purpose-independent ('formal') rules of just conduct to the relations with other men who did not pursue the same concrete ends or hold the same values except those abstract rules—which did not impose obligations for particular actions (which always presuppose a concrete end) but consisted solely in prohibitions from infringing the protected domain of each which these rules enable us to determine. Liberalism is therefore inseparable from the institution of private property which is the name we usually give to the material part of this protected individual domain. . . .

20. Liberalism recognizes that there are certain other services which for various reasons the spontaneous forces of the market may not produce or may not produce adequately, and that for this reason it is desirable to put at the disposal of government a clearly circumscribed body of resources with which it can render such services to the citizens in general. This requires a sharp distinction between the coercive powers of government, in which its actions are strictly limited to the enforcement of rules of just conduct and in the exercise of which all discretion is excluded, and the provision of services by government, for which it can use only the resources put at its disposal for this purpose, has no coercive power or monopoly, but in the use of which resources it enjoys wide discretion. . . .

22. Liberalism has indeed inherited from the theories of the common law and from the older (pre-rationalist) theories of the law of nature, and also presupposes, a conception of justice which allows us to distinguish between such rules of just individual conduct as are implied in the conception of the 'rule of law' and are required for the formation of a spontaneous order on the one hand, and all the particular commands issued by authority for the purpose of organization on the other. This essential distinction has been made explicit in the legal theories of two of the greater philosophers of modern times, David Hume and Immanuel Kant, but has not been adequately restated since and is wholly uncongenial to the governing legal theories of our day.

23. The essential points of this conception of justice are (a) that justice can be meaningfully attributed only to human action and not to any state of affairs as such without reference to the question whether it has been, or

could have been, deliberately brought about by somebody; (b) that the rules of justice have essentially the nature of prohibitions, or, in other words, that injustice is really the primary concept and the aim of rules of just conduct is to prevent unjust action; (c) that the injustice to be prevented is the infringement of the protected domain of one's fellow men, a domain which is to be ascertained by means of these rules of justice; and (d) that these rules of just conduct which are in themselves negative can be developed by consistently applying to whatever such rules a society has inherited the equally negative test of universal applicability—a test which, in the last resort, is nothing else than the self-consistency of the actions which these rules allow if applied to the circumstances of the real world. These four crucial points must be developed further in the following paragraphs.

24. *Ad (a):* Rules of just conduct can require the individual to take into account in his decisions only such consequences of his actions as he himself can foresee. The concrete results of the catallaxy for particular people are, however, essentially unpredictable; and since they are not the effect of anyone's design or intentions, it is meaningless to describe the manner in which the market distributed the good things of this world among particular people as just or unjust. This, however, is what the so-called 'social' or 'distributive' justice aims at in the name of which the liberal order of law is progressively destroyed. We shall later see that no test or criteria have been found or can be found by which such rules of 'social justice' can be assessed, and that, in consequence, and in contrast to the rules of just conduct, they would have to be determined by the arbitrary will of the holders of power.

25. *Ad (b):* No particular human action is fully determined without a concrete purpose it is meant to achieve. Free men who are to be allowed to use their own means and their own knowledge for their own purposes must therefore not be subject to rules which tell them what they must positively do, but only to rules which tell them what they must not do; except for the discharge of obligations an individual has voluntarily incurred, the rules of just conduct thus merely delimit the range of permissible actions but do not determine the particular actions a man must take at a particular moment. (There are certain rare exceptions to this, like actions to save or protect life, prevent catastrophes, and the like, whether either rules of justice actually do require, or would at least generally be accepted as just rules if they required, some positive action. It would lead far to discuss here the position of such rules in the system.) The generally negative character of the rules of just conduct, and the corresponding primacy of the injustice which is prohibited, has often been noticed but scarcely ever been thought through to its logical consequences.

26. *Ad (c):* The injustice which is prohibited by rules of just conduct is any encroachment on the protected domain of other individuals, and they must therefore enable us to ascertain what is the protected sphere of others. Since the time of John Locke it is customary to describe this protected domain as property (which Locke himself had defined as 'the life, liberty, and possessions of a man'). This term suggests, however, a much too narrow and purely material conception of the protected domain which includes not

only material goods but also various claims on others and certain expectations. If the concept of property is, however, (with Locke) interpreted in this wide sense, it is true that law, in the sense of rules of justice, and the institution of property are inseparable.

27. *Ad (d):* It is impossible to decide about the justice of any one particular rule of just conduct except within the framework of a whole system of such rules, most of which must for this purpose be regarded as unquestioned: values can always be tested only in terms of other values. The test of the justice of a rule is usually (since Kant) described as that of its 'universalizability', i.e., of the possibility of willing that the rules should be applied to all instances that correspond to the conditions stated in it (the 'categorical imperative'). What this amounts to is that in applying it to any concrete circumstances it will not conflict with any other accepted rules. The test is thus in the last resort one of the compatibility or non-contradictoriness of the whole system of rules, not merely in a logical sense but in the sense that the system of actions which the rules permit will not lead to conflict.

28. It will be noticed that only purpose-independent ('formal') rules pass this test because, as rules which have originally been developed in small, purpose-connected groups ('organizations') are progressively extended to larger and larger groups and finally universalized to apply to the relations between any members of an Open Society who have no concrete purposes in common and merely submit to the same abstract rules, they will in this process have to shed all references to particular purposes.

29. The growth from the tribal organization, all of whose members served common purposes, to the spontaneous order of the Open Society in which people are allowed to pursue their own purposes in peace, may thus be said to have commenced when for the first time a savage placed some goods at the boundary of his tribe in the hope that some member of another tribe would find them and leave in turn behind some other goods to secure the repetition of the offer. From the first establishment of such a practice which served reciprocal but not common purposes, a process has been going on for millennia which, by making rules of conduct independent of the particular purposes of those concerned, made it possible to extend these rules to ever wider circles of undetermined persons and eventually might make possible a universal peaceful order of the world. . . .

32. The progressive displacement of the rules of conduct of private and criminal law by a conception derived from public law is the process by which existing liberal societies are progressively transformed into totalitarian societies. This tendency has been most explicitly seen and supported by Adolf Hitler's 'crown jurist' Carl Schmitt who consistently advocated the replacement of the 'normative' thinking of liberal law by a conception of law which regards as its purpose the 'concrete order formation' *(konkretes Ordnungsdenken)*. . . .

34. If it was the nature of the constitutional arrangements prevailing in all Western democracies which made this development possible, the driving force which guided it in the particular direction was the growing recognition that the application of uniform or equal rules to the conduct of

individuals who were in fact very different in many respects, inevitably produced very different results for the different individuals; and that in order to bring about by government action a reduction in these unintended but inevitable differences in the material position of different people, it would be necessary to treat them not according to the same but according to different rules. This gave rise to a new and altogether different conception of justice, namely that usually described as 'social' or 'distributive' justice, a conception of justice which did not confine itself to rules of conduct for the individual but aimed at particular results for particular people, and which therefore could be achieved only in a purpose-governed organization but not in a purpose-independent spontaneous order.

35. The concepts of a 'just price', a 'just remuneration' or a 'just distribution of incomes' are of course very old; it deserves notice, however, that in the course of the efforts of two thousand years in which philosophers have speculated about the meaning of these concepts, not a single rule has been discovered which would allow us to determine what is in this sense just in a market order. Indeed the one group of scholars which have most persistently pursued the question, the schoolmen of the later middle ages and early modern times, were finally driven to define the just price or wage as that price or wage which would form itself on a market in the absence of fraud, violence or privilege—thus referring back to the rules of just conduct and accepting as a just result whatever was brought about by the just conduct of all individuals concerned. This negative conclusion of all the speculations about 'social' or 'distributive' justice was, as we shall see, inevitable, because a just remuneration or distribution has meaning only within an organization whose members act under command in the service of a common system of ends, but can have no meaning whatever in a catallaxy or spontaneous order which can have no such common system of ends.

36. A state of affairs as such, as we have seen, cannot be just or unjust as a mere fact. Only in so far as it has been brought about designedly or could be so brought about does it make sense to call just or unjust the actions of those who have created it or permitted it to arise. In the catallaxy, the spontaneous order of the market, nobody can foresee, however, what each participant will get, and the results for particular people are not determined by anyone's intentions; nor is anyone responsible for particular people getting particular things. We might therefore question whether a deliberate choice of the market order as the method for guiding economic activities, with the unpredictable and in a great measure chance incidence of its benefits, is a just decision, but certainly not whether, once we have decided to avail ourselves of the catallaxy for that purpose, the particular results it produces for particular people are just or unjust.

37. That the concept of justice is nevertheless so commonly and readily applied to the distribution of incomes is entirely the effect of an erroneous anthropomorphic interpretation of society as an organization rather than as a spontaneous order. The term 'distribution' is in this sense quite as misleading as the term 'economy', since it also suggests that something is the result of deliberate action which in fact is the result of spontaneous ordering forces. Nobody distributes income in a market order (as would

have to be done in an organization) and to speak, with respect to the former, of a just or unjust distribution is therefore simple nonsense. It would be less misleading to speak in this respect of a 'dispersion' rather than a 'distribution' of incomes.

38. All endeavours to secure a 'just' distribution must thus be directed towards turning the spontaneous order of the market into an organization or, in other words, into a totalitarian order. It was this striving after a new conception of justice which produced the various steps by which rules of organization ('public law'), which were designed to make people aim at particular results, came to supersede the purpose-independent rules of just individual conduct, and which thereby gradually destroyed the foundation on which a spontaneous order must rest.

39. The ideal of using the coercive powers of government to achieve 'positive' (i.e., social or distributive) justice leads, however, not only necessarily to the destruction of individual freedom, which some might not think too high a price, but it also proves on examination a mirage or an illusion which cannot be achieved in any circumstances, because it presupposes an agreement on the relative importance of the different concrete ends which cannot exist in a great society whose members do not know each other or the same particular facts. It is sometimes believed that the fact that most people today desire social justice demonstrates that this ideal has a determinable content. But it is unfortunately only too possible to chase a mirage, and the consequence of this is always that the result of one's striving will be utterly different from what one had intended.

40. There can be no rules which determine how much everybody 'ought' to have unless we make some unitary conception of relative 'merits' or 'needs' of the different individuals, for which there exists no objective measure, the basis of a central allocation of all goods and services—which would make it necessary that each individual, instead of using *his* knowledge for *his* purposes, were made to fulfil a duty imposed upon him by somebody else, and were remunerated according to how well he has, in the opinion of others, performed this duty. This is the method of remuneration appropriate to a closed organization, such as an army, but irreconcilable with the forces which maintain a spontaneous order.

41. It ought to be freely admitted that the market order does not bring about any close correspondence between subjective merit or individual needs and rewards. It operates on the principle of a combined game of skill and chance in which the results for each individual may be as much determined by circumstances wholly beyond his control as by his skill or effort. Each is remunerated according to the value his particular services have to the particular people to whom he renders them, and this value of his services stands in no necessary relation to anything which we could appropriately call his merits and still less to his needs.

42. It deserves special emphasis that, strictly speaking, it is meaningless to speak of a value 'to society' when what is in question is the value of some services to certain people, services which may be of no interest to anybody else. A violin virtuoso presumably renders services to entirely different people from those whom a football star entertains, and the maker

of pipes altogether different people from the maker of perfumes. The whole conception of a 'value to society' is in a free order as illegitimate an anthropomorphic term as its description as 'one economy' in the strict sense, as an entity which 'treats' people justly or unjustly, or 'distributes' among them. The results of the market process for particular individuals are neither the result of anybody's will that they should have so much, nor even foreseeable by those who have decided upon or support the maintenance of this kind of order. . . .

45. The aim of economic policy of a free society can therefore never be to assure particular results to particular people, and its success cannot be measured by any attempt at adding up the value of such particular results. In this respect the aim of what is called 'welfare economics' is fundamentally mistaken, not only because no meaningful sum can be formed of the satisfactions provided for different people, but because its basic idea of a maximum of need-fulfilment (or a maximum social product) is appropriate only to an economy proper which serves a single hierarchy of ends, but not to the spontaneous order of a catallaxy which has no common concrete ends.

46. Though it is widely believed that the conception of an optimal economic policy (or any judgment whether one economic policy is better than another) presupposes such a conception of maximizing aggregate real social income (which is possible only in value terms and therefore implies an illegitimate comparison of the utility to different persons), this is in fact not so. An optimal policy in a catallaxy may aim, and ought to aim, at increasing the chances of any member of society taken at random of having a high income, or, what amounts to the same thing, the chance that, whatever his share in total income may be, the real equivalent of this share will be as large as we know how to make it.

47. This condition will be approached as closely as we can manage, irrespective of the dispersion of incomes, if everything which is produced is being produced by persons or organizations who can produce it more cheaply than (or at least as cheaply as) anybody who does not produce it, and is sold at a price lower than that at which it would be possible to offer it for anybody who does not in fact so offer it. (This allows for persons or organizations to whom the costs of producing one commodity or service are lower than they are for those who actually produce it and who still produce something else instead, because their comparative advantage in that other production is still greater; in this case the total costs of their producing the first commodity would have to include the loss of the one which is not produced.)

48. It will be noticed that this optimum does not presuppose what economic theory calls 'perfect competition' but only that there are no obstacles to the entry into each trade and that the market functions adequately in spreading information about opportunities. It should also be specially observed that this modest and achievable goal has never yet been fully achieved because at all times and everywhere governments have both restricted access to some occupations and tolerated persons and organizations deterring others from entering occupations when this would have been to the advantage of the latter.

49. This optimum position means that as much will be produced of whatever combination of products and services is in fact produced as can be produced by any method that we know, because we can through such a use of the market mechanism bring more of the dispersed knowledge of the members of society into play than by any other. But it will be achieved only if we leave the share in the total, which each member will get, to be determined by the market mechanism and all its accidents, because it is only through the market determination of incomes that each is led to do what this result requires.

50. We owe, in other words, our chances that our unpredictable share in the total product of society represents as large an aggregate of goods and services as it does to the fact that thousands of others constantly submit to the adjustments which the market forces on them; and it is consequently also our duty to accept the same kind of changes in our income and position, even if it means a decline in our accustomed position and is due to circumstances we could not have foreseen and for which we are not responsible. The conception that we have 'earned' (in the sense of morally deserved) the income we had when we were more fortunate, and that we are therefore entitled to it so long as we strive as honestly as before and had no warning to turn elsewhere, is wholly mistaken. Everybody, rich or poor, owes his income to the outcome of a mixed game of skill and chance, the aggregate results of which and the shares in which are as high as they are only because we have agreed to play that game. And once we have agreed to play the game and profited from its results, it is a moral obligation on us to abide by the results even if they turn against us. . . .

61. In conclusion, the basic principles of a liberal society may be summed up by saying that in such a society all coercive functions of government must be guided by the overruling importance of what I like to call THE THREE GREAT NEGATIVES: PEACE, JUSTICE AND LIBERTY. Their achievement requires that in its coercive functions government shall be confined to the enforcement of such prohibitions (stated as abstract rules) as can be equally applied to all, and to exacting under the same uniform rules from all a share of the costs of the other, noncoercive services it may decide to render to the citizens with the material and personal means thereby placed at its disposal.

PART IV

Contemporary Business Issues

Modern business is undergoing dramatic changes. Smaller businesses find it harder to compete as big corporations account for a larger and larger share of the economy. Today the 1,000 largest U.S. firms are responsible for 72 percent of the sales, 86 percent of the employees, and 85 percent of the profits of all U.S. industrial corporations. Today fewer than 200 corporations hold the same share of manufacturing assets as the 1,000 largest corporations in 1941. But size is only one of the ways in which business has changed. Other changes include alterations in corporate organizational structure, the development of consumer movements, and increasing regulation by government. While these changes have been taking place, business has become more aware of itself not only as an economic institution but as an active participant in the surrounding society.

From an ethical standpoint the transformation of business is significant. Changes in the goals and structure of the corporation have caused changes in the expectations of employees and consumers. For example, the shift away from one-man domination of the corporation has prompted greater participation by employees in corporate decisions. Even if they do not own stock in their companies, professional managers now assume they have a right to participate in governing corporate affairs. Also, technological advances have generated a wider array of products and a vastly more efficient means, television, for advertising them.

Society has also changed its views about economic issues. It was once routinely assumed that economic growth should be pursued: greater production, higher incomes, and larger Gross National Products were the obvious goals for society. Now critics complain that clean air, the abundant wildlife, and adequate energy sources will vanish if we persist in our search for greater economic prosperity. Instead, decreasing growth or "no growth" is sometimes proposed as the optimal policy for society. Certainly the advancing technology of many corporations makes greater and greater demands on our natural resources. We must ask whether an ever-increasing standard of living is possible without endangering the ecological systems that support technology and human life. Also, is a high level of economic prosperity possible without sacrificing the human values of freedom and creativity? Such issues are examined in this part by looking at the ways in which modern corporate society has evolved and by discussing the prognosis for business in the future.

EMPLOYEE RIGHTS

One pressing contemporary concern is the relationship between employers and employees, especially the issue of employee rights. Do employees have rights in the workplace despite having voluntarily entered into a formal employee-employer relationship? For example, does a worker have the right to blow the whistle on a dangerous product without reprisal from management? Does he or she have a right to refuse a lie detector or "polygraph" test without being fired? Does he or she have the right to participate, directly or indirectly, in the management of the organizations for which he or she works? These questions are among those falling under the heading of "employee rights," and their discussion has become among the most heated and controversial in the field of business ethics.

When talking about employee rights, some philosophical distinctions about the concept of a right are in order. We take the term "right" for granted, often forgetting that only a few centuries ago, the term was unknown. The first instance of the word in English was during the sixteenth century in the phrase, "the rights of Englishmen." But the "rights of the Englishmen" referred literally to English*men,* not English*women,* and included only those who owned property. History waited for the English philosopher, John Locke, to provide the word "right" with its present, far-reaching significance. In Locke's writings the word came to refer to something which, by definition, is possessed unconditionally by *all* rational adult human beings. The talk of rights in our own Declaration of Independence and Constitution owes much to Locke's early doctrine of rights.

Philosophers disagree about the precise definition of a right. Two of the most popular definitions are (1) a right is a justified claim or entitlement *to* something, held *against* someone else (for example, the right to free speech is a right *to* speak without restraint and is held against other parties, including the government); and (2) a right is a "trump" over a collective goal. The right to worship as one pleases, for example, overrides or "trumps" the collective goal of ideological unity within our society, and thus overrides any claims by a government that certain religions must be suppressed for the sake of the common good.

Rights may be divided into legal rights and moral rights. The former are rights that are either specified formally by law or protected by it. In the U.S., the right to sue, to have a jury trial, to own property, and to have a free public education are legal rights. Not all such rights were included in the founding documents of the U.S. government: the right to free publication, the right of women and blacks to vote, and the right of workers to form unions, were historical additions made in the nineteenth and twentieth centuries. *Moral* rights, on the other hand, are rights that are not necessarily protected and specified by the laws. They are normative claims which every person is justified in making. These would include, for example, the right to be treated with equal respect, and the right not to be systematically deceived. The law might stop short of preventing private clubs, for instance, from excluding Jews and blacks, yet most of us would agree that Jews and blacks have a *moral* right in such situations not to be excluded. One of the most controversial issues in the area of employee rights is whether, given that employees have some moral rights, those rights should remain only moral rights, or also be protected as legal rights.

Two cases at the beginning of this section highlight the concrete problems and controversies that can arise with employee rights. The Manco Case illustrates the issue of whether or not an employee has a right to favorable treatment even when his capacity to contribute to the company's goals is in doubt. The second case, "Copper O," discusses the dilemma of an employee who wonders whether he should "blow the whistle" on his employer. What are his rights in this instance, and what are the balancing claims of the employer?

The rights to due process and to free expression in the workplace are two rights listed in David Ewings' well-known "A Proposed Bill of Rights," reprinted in this section. Ewing, perhaps the best known modern defender of employee rights, postulates a specific list of rights. This list, he believes, specifies rights that should be guaranteed in all modern organizations. His list has sparked a spirited controversy in which his critics attack both the general idea of employee rights and the specific instances he endorses. One of his critics, Max Ways, takes Ewing to task in the article, "The Myth of the 'Oppressive Corporation.' " In the article, "A Theory of Employee Rights," on the other hand, Patricia Werhane argues for still another employee right, namely, the right to due process. Professor Werhane's argument is closer in spirit to the social practices of Western Europe, where, unlike their U.S. counterparts, corporations are unable to fire or lay off employees for arbitrary reasons.

AFFIRMATIVE ACTION

One important right which directly concerns business is the right of everyone to be treated equally in matters of hiring, pay, and promotion. If a person may be said to have such rights, then presumably business managers have a corresponding obligation not to pursue discriminatory policies. For example, business organizations should be obliged to hire on the basis of applicant competence without being swayed by irrelevant factors such as sex, race, or ethnic origin. Most business people today recognize this obligation. A more controversial issue is whether business has an obligation to go beyond the point of merely "not discriminating," and to pursue what is called affirmative action. Affirmative action programs are of at least two sorts:

1. those which pursue a policy of deliberately favoring qualified minorities and women when hiring or promoting; and
2. those which establish quota systems to regulate the percentage of minority members hired or promoted in accordance with an ideal distribution of race, sex, creed, and/or ethnicity.

Perhaps the most common objection to affirmative action programs is that they are unjust and inconsistent, i.e., that they make the same mistakes they hope to remedy. If discrimination means using a morally irrelevant characteristic, such as a person's skin color, as a factor in hiring, then is affirmative action itself perpetuating unjust discrimination? In giving preference to, say, blacks over whites, are such programs using the same morally irrelevant characteristic previously used in discriminatory practices? This and other criticisms of affirmative action programs are offered by Barry Gross in his article, "Is Turn About Fair Play?"

Defenders of affirmative action argue that these programs are, all things considered, fair and consistent with human rights in that they are necessary to compensate past injustices in employment practices—injustices which clearly damaged the well-being and future prospects of many members of society. Compensation, then, must be made to the victims of discrimination. Moreover, it is maintained that affirmative action programs are necessary to guarantee fairness in hiring and promotion for future generations; how will minority applicants ever seriously compete for positions in, say, medical school, unless the educational and economic opportunities for minorities and nonminorities are equalized? And how will educational and economic opportunities be equalized unless minorities are able to attain a fair share of society's highest level of jobs? In articles reprinted in this section, both Richard Wasserstrom and James Nickel defend the legitimacy of claims against society by minorities.

One of the articles in this section, *"Weber* v. *United Steelworkers,"* is a Supreme Court case that illuminates current disputes in the legal system about affirmative action. In the earlier, well-known Bakke case, the Supreme Court ruled that the University of California Medical School at Davis was guilty of discrimination when it held a specific number of positions open for minorities and thus rejected Allen Bakke, a white, despite his higher qualifications. The Court objected specifically to the "quota" system of affirmative action in the Bakke case, while leaving the door open to nonquota plans. The Weber decision, however, surprised many, for although it also involved a quota plan, the court refused to declare that quota system in violation of the law. One thing seems clear; the Supreme Court's view of the acceptability of affirmative action plans turns on matters more complicated than the mere presence or absence of quota systems.

BUSINESS AND THE ENVIRONMENT

Attention has been drawn in recent years to the fact that we live on a planet which, despite its apparent abundance, possesses finite natural resources. Never-ending economic growth involves either a never-ending consumption of these resources or the discovery of suitable substitutes. Is it wise then, to persist in our goals of technological and economic expansion when our stocks of natural resources are continually dwindling? Critics argue that we live, in effect, on a spaceship—the earth—which contains limited supplies. Considering our rapidly expanding population and economic output, we shall soon approach the limits of those supplies, and human needs will outstrip the technological know-how required to develop substitutes. To avoid this disaster such critics propose a "no-growth" economy in which we actively work to replace lost resources.

In sharp contrast to this argument is the view expressed in the selection by Wilfred Beckerman. Beckerman, a noted Oxford economist, argues that economic growth is both necessary and valuable; that it actually enhances human life rather than discourages it; and that the quality of human life, perhaps its very survival, depends on maintaining both economic and technological growth. Only a fraction of the world's population has achieved a decent standard of living, and economic growth, according to Beckerman, remains indispensable for human welfare. One cannot argue that growth is undesirable until the minimal necessities of life are available for everyone. Moreover, Beckerman points out, people have actively interfered with nature for centuries, and although there have been periodic panics over the exhaustion of natural resources, the resources have not been exhausted. Indeed people continue to find more resources and to invent satisfactory substitutes. The problems connected with our use of resources, Beckerman concludes, cannot be solved by turning to a policy of no growth. Instead, he recommends in some of his writings strict government control of the ecological side effects of business. Such a program, he believes, would not limit economic growth—it would merely guide it in a useful direction.

In his article, "Scarcity Society," William Ophuls discusses the dilemma of economic growth from an ethical point of view. In contrast to Beckerman, Ophuls claims that in order for human life to continue, a program of ecological and economic equilibrium must be instituted to produce an economy in which population, resources, and environment are in balance. The solution recommended by both Beckerman and no-growth proponents is to *control* and *regulate* the economy in order to prevent environmental abuses. But this measure leads immediately, Ophuls says, to the loss of important personal human liberties. Given that people operate in accordance with their own personal ends (Ophuls calls this the "tragedy of the commons"), how is humanity to protect both the environment and vital natural resources *without* generating stifling and oppressive systems of social control?

Ophuls' solution to the problem is an ethical one; improve the ethical nature of man, restore the "civic virtue of a corrupt people." People must, acting as individuals, restore human dignity by developing the moral resources of self-restraint and respect for others. We must impose our own laws and controls upon ourselves—individually. Only then, Ophuls claims, will we solve the dilemma of ecological scarcity.

In the last article in the book, "Ethics and Ecology," the philosopher William Blackstone counters the economic optimism of thinkers such as Beckerman by arguing that, whatever the future holds, we must recognize that persons have a *right* to reasonably clean air and water. Rights, Blackstone asserts, flow from the capacities that make us uniquely human, and these capacities require a livable environment for their proper development.

EMPLOYEE RIGHTS

Case Study—The Manco Corporation

J. J. O'CONNELL

The Manco Corporation serves the consumer field with a broad line of high-quality specialty products. Most of the corporation's 6,000 employees work in Saginaw, Michigan, the headquarters and main plant location. Manco, with the other nine leading companies in its field, invests heavily in R.&D. and relies more on product innovation than on the protection of its numerous patents. Manco's $200 million sales volume is made up of about 75 percent domestic sales and 25 percent foreign sales. Growth over the past half-dozen years has averaged somewhat over 5 percent a year, and profit margins have stayed well in excess of 10 percent before tax.

THE MANAGEMENT SYSTEMS DEPARTMENT

The 55 professional people in the management systems department serve all the operating divisions of the corporation as part of the central staff reporting to Elkin Parker, the vice president of Manco's Administrative Division, through Harold Simken, the director of administrative services.

The department is responsible for performing a broad range of internal consulting activities. The management systems department's major efforts are concentrated in the design and maintenance of computer-based information systems. Project work is also conducted in the areas of organization planning, operations, research, general systems design, and standard operating procedures.

All management systems work is conducted on a project request basis. For example, the customer account system mentioned later resulted from a problem first seen by Ned O'Donnell, manager of the physical distribution department, which in turn is a part of the Sales Division of the company. O'Donnell and the vice president for sales had long wanted a method for keeping customer charge accounts more accurately, and a method for pro-

J. J. O'Connell, "The Manco Corporation," reprinted from *The Managerial Mind,* ed. Charles E. Summer and Jeremiah J. O'Connell (Homewood, Ill.: Richard D. Irwin, Inc., 1964; rpt. 1973), pp. 57–69 (exhibits omitted), reprinted with permission.

cessing these with great speed. They had called the management systems department for help.

The systems department thus forms a central service unit for the whole company. The company has a rule that only if a major operating division requests assistance on its own initiative can work actually commence in the systems department. This rule is designed so that the systems analysts will assume the role of consultants to the other divisions of the company, rather than to assume the active role of managing the operating divisions either by initiating their plans, or by controlling and acting as policemen. According to Simkin, "this means that the systems department is somewhat like a small business seeking customers. We are here to perform services for the operating departments. They must feel a need for our service and, in effect, hire us to perform them. They're also in the position of not buying our services if the services don't genuinely contribute to solving their problems."

After another division requests assistance, the project request is jointly reviewed by the management systems department manager and his five unit supervisors so that a priority might be assigned to the project. The considerable project backlog has made it necessary for managers within the department to devote substantial time to identifying the most important projects.

The organization of management systems (Exhibit 1) reflects Harold Simken's and Walter Davis' strong interest in maintaining satisfactory and stable relationships with all company divisions. Three systems units—the international-marketing unit, the financial-manufacturing unit, and the R.&D.-administrative unit—form the core of the department. Each unit performs work for two company divisions on a continuing basis. The operations research and programming research units provide technical support to the three systems units. Operations research and programming research personnel often work on those systems projects which require very specialized skills, and they are frequently involved in nonproject development work.

The mix of project work and personnel within each of the three systems units is determined by the pattern of project requests made by the various Manco divisions. The potential for meaningful systems design work and the receptivity of key managers vary from division to division. These differences create demands for divergent sets of skills in the three systems units. Project requests from the Research and Development Division, for example, involve the computerized retrieval of scientific information on laboratory experiments. On the other hand, systems work for the Administrative Division primarily consists of issuing and revising standard operating procedures. As a result of these project demands the R.&D.-administrative unit has two distinct types of analysts—programmers and standard procedure specialists.

The requests made by the International and Marketing Divisions demand a still wider set of skills in the international-marketing systems unit. This unit has been involved in large-scale simulations of domestic and international distribution networks, organizational studies of the Marketing Division and several international branches, and other complex systems studies. Since these projects usually require skills different from either pro-

EXHIBIT 1
Partial Manco Organization Chart (June 1966)

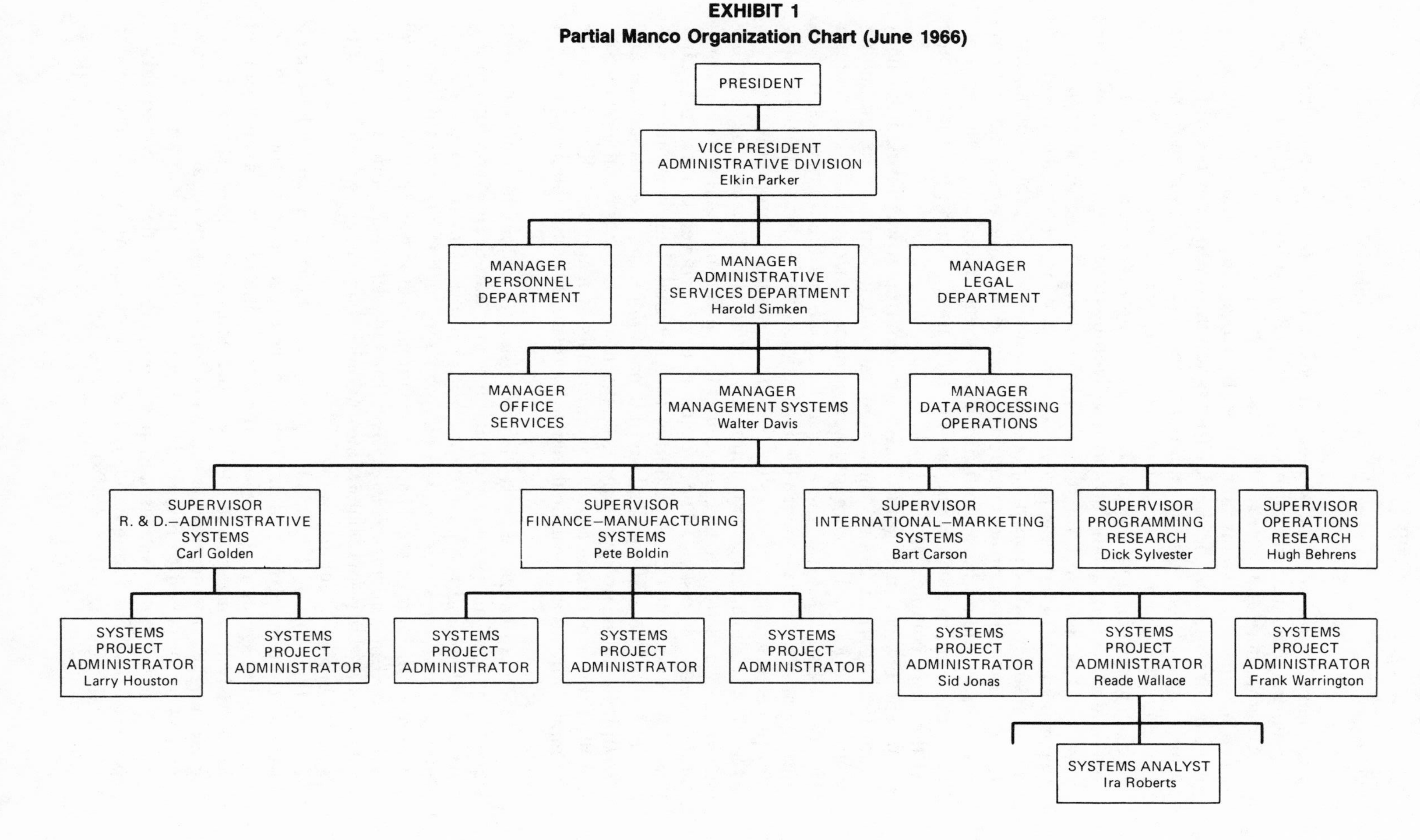
PRESIDENT
VICE PRESIDENT ADMINISTRATIVE DIVISION Elkin Parker
MANAGER PERSONNEL DEPARTMENT
MANAGER ADMINISTRATIVE SERVICES DEPARTMENT Harold Simken
MANAGER LEGAL DEPARTMENT
MANAGER OFFICE SERVICES
MANAGER MANAGEMENT SYSTEMS Walter Davis
MANAGER DATA PROCESSING OPERATIONS
SUPERVISOR R. & D.–ADMINISTRATIVE SYSTEMS Carl Golden
SUPERVISOR FINANCE–MANUFACTURING SYSTEMS Pete Boldin
SUPERVISOR INTERNATIONAL–MARKETING SYSTEMS Bart Carson
SUPERVISOR PROGRAMMING RESEARCH Dick Sylvester
SUPERVISOR OPERATIONS RESEARCH Hugh Behrens
SYSTEMS PROJECT ADMINISTRATOR Larry Houston
SYSTEMS PROJECT ADMINISTRATOR
SYSTEMS PROJECT ADMINISTRATOR
SYSTEMS PROJECT ADMINISTRATOR
SYSTEMS PROJECT ADMINISTRATOR
SYSTEMS PROJECT ADMINISTRATOR Sid Jonas
SYSTEMS PROJECT ADMINISTRATOR Reade Wallace
SYSTEMS PROJECT ADMINISTRATOR Frank Warrington
SYSTEMS ANALYST Ira Roberts

gramming or procedure work, the international-marketing systems unit employs management scientists and organizational planning specialists, as well as programmers and systems analysts.

Within each systems unit, there are two or three systems project administrators, who handle the day-to-day administrative activities of the systems units. Each project administrator is responsible for specific departments in one or two Manco divisions. Thus, in the international-marketing systems unit, one project administrator is responsible for projects in the market research and promotion planning departments, while another supervises project work for the sales, advertising, and general promotion departments. The systems project administrator is, in essence, a working first-line supervisor. From a supervisory standpoint, the project administrators supervise client project requests, plan and schedule work loads, administer salary, and appraise performance of their subordinates. In addition, they spend approximately one third of their time actually performing some of the more complex project work.

The present management systems department was formed during a June 1963 reorganization, which combined all systems and programming activities. Prior to the reorganization, separate systems and programming sections existed. Most of the analysts believed that the reorganization was precipitated by management's dissatisfaction with the divided responsibility for projects, which so often called for both systems and programming work. There had been an increasing number of complaints concerning the inability of the two sections to meet deadlines for converting systems from manual to computer processing. The systems analysts believed that the programmers were at fault for not adhering to schedules. The programmers contended that the systems analysts did not appreciate the magnitude and complexity of the programming task. Because of this lack of understanding, argued the programmers, the systems analysts made unrealistic calendar commitments to the divisional managers responsible for the particular system.

The reorganization was also designed to eliminate the discontent among systems analysts and programmers over advancement opportunities. As a result of the reorganization, the positions of management systems manager and unit supervisor were upgraded to higher salary classifications. The new position of systems project administrator was created one level below the unit supervisor level. Between June 1963 and June 1966, eight former senior systems analysts and senior programmers were elevated to systems project administrators.

In the spirit of the 1963 reorganization, the systems analysts working for each systems project administrator were expected to perform both systems and programming activities. Initially the interests and assignments of most analysts corresponded to their previous specialty—systems or programming. Salary increases and promotions in the new organization, however, were designed to reward the generalist—the man who was able and willing to do both systems and programming and demonstrated this in project work. The hiring and training of new employees were also geared to produce this new breed of systems analyst.

THE INTERNATIONAL-MARKETING SYSTEMS UNIT

The supervisor of the international-marketing systems unit (see Exhibit 1) is Bart Carson. Carson, who had transferred into systems from the Manufacturing Division in 1958, is generally considered by his peers to be the most experienced and talented systems supervisor. Although his (pre-1963) experience had been confined to the systems section, he has been very positive about the new integrated approach of the 1963 reorganization. Carson has made conscious efforts to give his analysts diversified exposure and gradually has begun to develop what is regarded as a well-rounded unit within the context of the new management systems job responsibilities.

One of the three systems project administrators reporting to Carson in the summer of 1966 was Reade Wallace. Carson had given Wallace responsibility for project work in the International Division and the distribution department of the Marketing Division. Wallace, who had joined the company in 1959 after obtaining his MBA degree, had been regarded as a mainstay of the pre-1963 systems section. He had specialized in organization planning, standard operating procedures, and general systems work. Wallace's associates noted that his diplomacy and tact had enabled him to establish excellent rapport with several key managers in the company, in general, and in the International Division, in particular. Harold Simken, manager of administrative services, and Walter Davis, manager of management systems, were keenly interested in generating new international project work, and they both often spoke of how much they valued Wallace's interpersonal skills.

After the 1963 reorganization but before his promotion to systems project administrator, Wallace had made it clear to Bart Carson, systems supervisor, that he had no desire to get involved in EDP or management science projects. He preferred to continue his concentration in organizational planning and general administrative systems and said so publicly. Wallace was, in fact, the only analyst after the 1963 reorganization who overtly resisted Carson's plan for development. Consequently, Wallace's promotion to systems project administrator in October 1964 had been a very controversial move. To many analysts, the promotion represented a flagrant violation of the criteria established for the systems project administrator position. Some analysts attributed the move to pressure exerted on Carson by Simken and/or Davis.

MANAGEMENT SYSTEMS DEPARTMENT EXPANDS

The management systems department experienced rapid growth between June 1963 and June 1965, expanding from a personnel complement of 30 analysts to one of 55 analysts. One source of new people was the company's management training program, a rotational program consisting of several six- to eight-week assignments in various Manco divisions.

Among the trainees in this program was Ira Roberts, a former high school teacher who had taught for four years. As he completed the program in December 1965, Roberts' record showed he had created favorable impressions throughout the company during his rotational assignments. Roberts' first permanent position was as management systems analyst in Bart Carson's international-marketing unit, reporting to Reade Wallace. Roberts had performed poorly on the programming aptitude test administered to all prospective management systems employees. He had received a B- on the exam, lower than anyone currently in the department. The independent psychological consulting firm, which administers the test, placed Roberts in the "Not Recommended" category on the analysis accompanying his test score. Since Roberts' principal work was to be in the general systems area, Carson and Wallace agreed that Roberts' personal strengths offset his relatively weak performance on the aptitude test. Carson and Wallace planned to increase Roberts' exposure to programming at some later date.

Roberts' first assignment was to develop a small-scale system to centralize information on grants to foundations and charities made by various company departments. His second project involved procedural work with various company divisions to insure companywide compliance with new federal legislation affecting the sale of company products. After some training in network scheduling techniques, Roberts performed admirably in developing a PERT chart to plan and schedule the introduction of Manco's first product in the Australian market. Co-workers observed Roberts working yeoman's hours, and the manager of the new Australian Branch was unstinting in his praise of Roberts and his network schedule.

Roberts' performance during his first year in systems was formally appraised by Wallace in January 1967. He noted the following strengths:

1. Quick mind.
2. Ability to shoulder responsibility.
3. Works well with others.
4. Loyal and excellent attitude towards the company.
5. Documents work well and is both cost and profit conscious.

Wallace listed project planning as Roberts' major area for improvement. He rated Roberts satisfactory overall and concluded the appraisal by discussing his potential:

> Roberts handles work very well and has high potential. Could develop into one of our better senior analysts with a bit more programming experience.

At the bottom of the appraisal sheet in the section entitled "Promotability," Wallace checked off "Promotable within two years." The only rating superior to this was "Promotable immediately." The appraisal was reviewed and signed by Carson, in accordance with company policy.

During the early part of 1967, the personnel department notified Roberts that several managers in the company were interested in offering him positions in their departments. These offers of employment in the public relations, distribution, and personnel departments were transmitted through the company's formal system for recruiting internal candidates. Each of these opportunities represented a promotion for Roberts. While these advancement opportunities all appeared attractive, Roberts expressed enthusiasm for his work in systems and was reluctant to leave. When he discussed the situation with Wallace and Carson, they both spoke optimistically about his future progress and their plans for him. Roberts decided to turn down the various internal opportunities and remain in management systems.

On April 1, 1967 Wallace and Carson jointly announced that Roberts had been promoted from management systems analyst to senior management systems analyst.

THE CUSTOMER ACCOUNT COMPUTER SYSTEM (CACS) PROJECT

As part of his plan to increase Roberts' programming experience, Wallace assigned him in April 1967 to a major EDP project, under the direction of another analyst. The basic purpose of this project was to create a computerized information system of all retail and wholesale accounts that distributed a major section of the product line. The system was designed to assist in processing orders during the hectic fall and winter sale periods. A secondary objective was to use the system for recording salesmen's call activities. The system was scheduled to go "on-line" in the fall of 1967.

In May 1967, the project was dealt a serious setback when the senior systems analyst leading the project resigned from the company. Wallace decided to have Roberts direct the project and assigned a new analyst to assist him. Between May and September, Roberts worked feverishly to complete the system. He worked a considerable amount of overtime each week, including six Saturdays during the summer months. Throughout this period, he assured Wallace and Carson and the management of the distribution department that the system would be ready to go into operation by September 1, 1967.

In the midst of Roberts' efforts on the CACS project, corporate organization changes affected the management systems department.

THE CORPORATE REORGANIZATION

In July 1967, a major corporate reorganization was announced. The objectives of the reorganization were the separation of planning activities from operations and the introduction of a strong profit center philosophy.

As a result of the reorganization, some key management changes occurred in the management systems department. Walter Davis, manager of the department, was appointed director, organization and policy planning, on the new corporate staff. Carl Golden, supervisor of the R.&D.-administrative systems unit, joined Davis' staff as manager of organization planning.

Bart Carson replaced Davis as management systems manager (see Exhibit 2). Dick Sylvester, previously supervisor, programming research,

EXHIBIT 2
Partial Manco Organization Chart (August 1967)

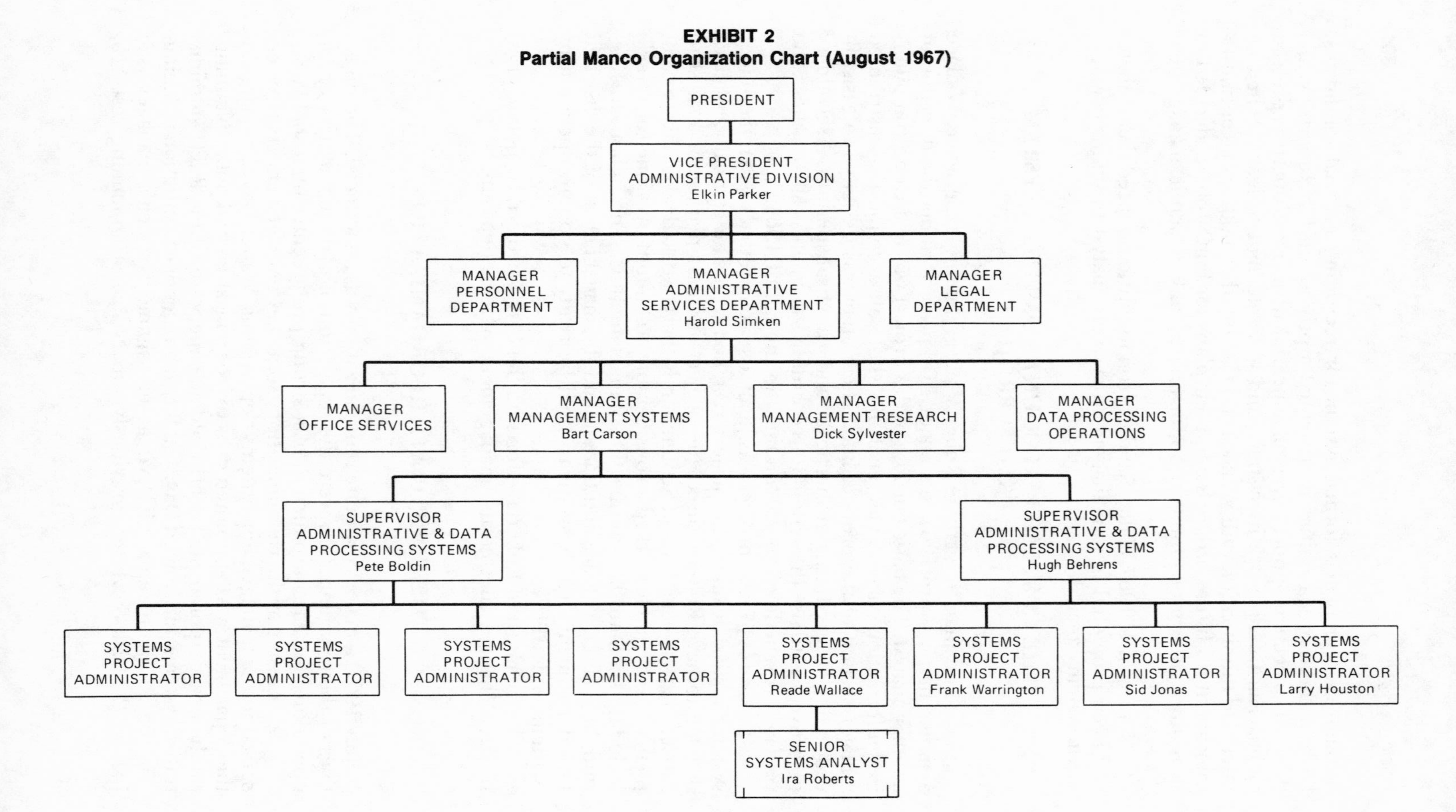

was named to direct a new management research group. The three systems units were merged into new units, reporting to Pete Boldin and Hugh Behrens. Behrens who had previously served as supervisor, operations research, assumed responsibility for Carson's international-marketing systems unit and for all R.&D. systems. The administrative systems would henceforth be designed by the new corporate staff group headed by Walter Davis and Carl Golden. Boldin retained responsibility for all financial and manufacturing systems.

THE JULY 1967–OCTOBER 1967 PERIOD

After the initial excitement generated by the announcement of management appointments, management systems activities continued with no major changes in direction. Carson and his two direct subordinates, Boldin and Behrens, conferred regularly to establish project objectives for 1968, plan the impending conversion to a 360 computer, and develop a new project control system.

Behrens' four systems project administrators (Sid Jonas, Frank Warrington, Larry Houston, and Reade Wallace) found him more conservative and less communicative than Carson, and yet by late summer they felt they had good rapport with him. Behrens started with Manco as a programmer in 1960, and had since served in various capacities in the programming section, systems section, and operations research section. He was credited with conducting the company's most successful operations research effort —a large-scale simulation of the entire Manco distribution network. His several diverse skills had enabled him to establish an excellent reputation throughout the corporation.

Behrens called informal meetings of his four systems project administrators whenever he felt it necessary to review plans or communicate information. These hour-long meetings occurred about every two weeks during the late summer and early fall.

On October 18, Behrens called a 1:30 meeting of his systems project administrators. The only unusual aspect of the scheduling was the short two-hour notice. When the group assembled, they noted that Behrens, who was typically a very calm individual, seemed upset. Warrington, Jonas, and Houston were also surprised to see that Wallace was not present. Behrens began the meeting by announcing:

> I've called you together to tell you that our unit has been reorganized as of this afternoon. Reade Wallace's job has been eliminated and he is leaving the company today. Sid Jonas will pick up Reade's responsibilities for all systems and management science projects in International. Ira Roberts will report to you, and we'll continue to recruit for a replacement for Ira's predecessor on the CACS project. Frank will handle all EDP projects for International. Barbara Mellor and Murray Hankins [Wallace's other analysts] will report to you.

Jonas was the first to speak after a long silence. "Does that mean that Reade was fired due to unsatisfactory performance?" "No," replied Behrens, "Reade was doing a satisfactory job, but we no longer had a position for him in our organization." Jonas reacted sharply to Behrens' answer:

> Now, how can you do a thing like that? We have a very involved system for placing unsatisfactory performers on warning for 30 to 90 days and advising them that they will be canned if they don't shape up. You just subverted the whole system by reorganizing him out of a job. That system's supposed to protect the employee. Now all of the analysts will think that this is a completely arbitrary system and the axe can fall on them any time. We all know that Reade was deficient in certain respects. Why don't you call a spade a spade?

Interrupting, Behrens said:

> Hold on a minute, Sid. Some of your points are valid, but you don't have all the facts. First of all, Wallace did get severance pay amounting to over $5,000. More important, we talked to all the personnel experts, and they said it would be in his best interest to do it this way. The company can give him a good reference without any black marks on his record. And, as an aside, we tried to place him elsewhere in the company. Distribution and International were interested, but because of the budget cutbacks throughout the company, they couldn't afford someone at his salary level. It's been my most traumatic experience since I've been with the company. What more can I say?

Jonas was preparing to resume the verbal battle but thought better of it and added, "I'm sorry, Hugh, but I don't agree. I'm probably unfair arguing with you over this since Reade only worked for you for three months. It's Bart Carson who's responsible, and I plan to tell him that I think the whole situation was handled poorly." With that the meeting was adjourned.

THE CUSTOMER ACCOUNT COMPUTER SYSTEM FAILS

Following the announcement of Wallace's departure, Jonas and Warrington met with their newly assigned analysts to review work loads and project plans. The main topic during the first meeting between Jonas and Roberts on October 20 was the CACS project. Roberts first explained the system to Jonas, pointing out its objectives and major features. He explained that the system began operating in September, although a few "bugs" still had to be ironed out. Roberts expressed confidence that the system would be operating smoothly before too long.

The CACS project seemed to be moving toward final completion when Jonas was called into Behrens office on Thursday, November 9. Behrens informed Jonas that one of the scheduled computer runs for the CACS project had produced incorrect results and Ned O'Donnell, the distribution department manager, had phoned a complaint to Bart Carson. Behrens expressed the fear that there might be some major problem with the entire system. Jonas suggested they speak to Roberts. Behrens phoned Roberts, requesting that he come to his office. Roberts explained that the error in sales totals resulted from 50 duplicate records on the master file. He had scheduled a computer printout of the master file so that the clerks in the distribution department could correct the errors. He assured Jonas and Behrens that he would take care of the problem.

The master file printout was checked by the distribution clerks on Monday, November 13, and Tuesday, November 14. On the 15th, Ned O'Donnell asked Harold Simken, manager of administrative services, to come to his office. When Simken arrived, he saw that O'Donnell had several hundred pages of a computer report on his desk. O'Donnell began to shout at Simken, "Harold, you see this printout? You know how much it's worth? This much!" And with that O'Donnell stuffed the printout in the waste basket. O'Donnell continued, "What's wrong with your damn department? If it's not one kind of mistake, it's another. Now that guy has gone and dropped all of our accounts in Northern California from the file. I can't make any sense out of this."

Simken returned to his office and asked to see Jonas, since Carson and Behrens were both out of the office. Carson was at a week-long management training session, and Hugh Behrens was attending a seminar in operations research. Simken gave Jonas a monotone hello when he entered and asked him what he was doing about the CACS situation. Jonas identified the various problems as best he could and reviewed the instructions he had given Roberts. Simken listened without comment until Jonas was through and then began to speak in a very stern voice. "Sid, I know you weren't involved in this system from the start, and you aren't responsible for these problems. But, it's yours now, and I'm holding you responsible for correcting this mess. Now, get busy on this and keep me informed of your progress."

When Behrens returned to the office the following morning, he was treated to a similar—in his words—"severe harangue," from Simken. Behrens decided to form a task force of himself, Pete Boldin, Jonas, and Roberts to conduct a comprehensive review of the system. After a three-day review, Behrens submitted a report to Carson and Simken, outlining the various technical problems and the proposed remedial action. The review had made it clear to Jonas and Behrens that Roberts did not have the technical EDP expertise to direct a project as complex as CACS. Moreover, some aspects of the system were misrepresented to marketing management in that the system was touted as a panacea for all of distribution's information problems. The cost of the system was vastly underestimated. Original estimates for development costs and annual operating costs were $14,000 to $19,000 and $8,500 to $14,000. Actual development costs exceeded $32,000, while annual operating costs zoomed to $30,000.

When Jonas and Behrens reviewed the report, Behrens began to discuss Roberts' capabilities:

> Sid, we really gave you a personnel problem. That review convinced me that Roberts is not capable of senior analyst performance. There's no question about his technical deficiencies as far as I'm concerned. We knew he wasn't a technical whiz but, if that wasn't bad enough, he did a terrible job of directing the project. There's no evidence of any planning. He missed every deadline, and I'm not sure he properly represented the critical status of the system to marketing or us. He probably didn't know how bad off he really was. You better think about how you're going to use him in the future. Given the type of things we expect from you in the future, I'm not sure where he fits in.

Jonas raised some questions about the apparently poor supervision and direction which Roberts had received from Wallace. Behrens agreed that this was a consideration. Behrens' secretary interrupted to remind him of a meeting, and he abruptly ended the discussion, "Well, give it some thought, Sid, and let's discuss it in a few days."

On Wednesday, November 22, Jonas arranged a session with Carson and Behrens to discuss the Roberts situation. Jonas opened the discussion by summarizing his position for Carson:

> Bart, I've given this issue considerable thought, and I'm very troubled by it. I'm not reluctant to be a so-called "tough-minded manager" and place Roberts on warning for unsatisfactory performance. The problem with this approach is that it's the easy way out because it avoids the real troubling issues. Someone in this organization has to accept responsibility for the things that were said to Roberts six months ago. We told him that his future was very bright in systems and dissuaded him from accepting other jobs in the company. In fact, we promoted him in a relatively short span of time. In retrospect, that was the wrong decision. He's better suited for less technical work, such as personnel or public relations. So far, he hasn't demonstrated that he can perform at a senior level. And, don't forget, one big reason for his poor performance was the lack of proper supervision from Wallace.
>
> If you want me to, I'll try to compensate for our past errors by getting back to basics and developing Roberts the right way. But I can't do this if you're not willing to adjust your expectations of my group. Hugh thinks that Roberts doesn't fit into my operation. So now it seems that if I try to develop one of my less adequate subordinates, I don't meet my technical responsibilities. If I stick to the technical goals, I ship Roberts out the door.

Carson answered:

> Sid, I don't want you to worry about things that were said to Roberts before he started working for you. Perhaps we were premature in promoting him. I'll accept responsibility for all of that. We expect big things of you, and you need the proper blend of skills in your group. It's very easy for Hugh and me to sit here and tell you what to do. But, if we did that, we'd impair your development as a supervisor. All I can say is do what you have to do.

Case Study—The Copper "O" Company

THOMAS F. McMAHON, C.S.V.

The XYZ Company is a multinational electronics corporation. It is listed in *Forbes* as one of the top fifty companies in total assets. XYZ has a plant on Chicago's near northwest side which manufactures printed circuit boards. High concentrations of copper are flushed down the sewer. The Metropoli-

Reprinted by permission of the author.

tan Sanitary District allows 3 milligrams per litre; any amount above 3 milligrams per litre is in violation of the City's Pure Air and Water Ordinance. XYZ has been flushing 5 to 6 milligrams per litre of copper—both particulate and solution—into the city sewerage system. Copper is toxic to water creatures but has little effect on humans (unless it becomes copper sulfate). The sanitary district is much more concerned with cadmium and cyanide than with copper contamination. When the engineers of the sanitary district observe excessive chemical discharge, they generally provide a "reasonable" time (six months) to correct the infringement through systems of filters, settling tanks, or other equipment.

On a number of occasions during the past three years, Bill Jones, plant manager, has confronted his immediate superiors about the existing violation. They keep postponing any definite answer about installing antipollution equipment. During Bill's most recent confrontation six months ago, they told Bill (1) that the present plant has been sold to another company; (2) that XYZ is building a new plant installed with the most advanced antipollution equipment in the suburbs within two years; (3) that no city inspector has ever tested this particular discharge since the inception of the printed circuit boards about four years ago.

Bill frequently wonders about his responsibility to the firm, his superiors, his workers, and his own family as well as his obligation to his profession, local community, and a healthy environmental "quality-of-life." During the last few months, he found out that the XYZ hired a public relations firm to promote the "concerned citizen about the environment" stance which XYZ is taking on its new plant. He wondered whether he should "blow the whistle" on the XYZ company. He also mused over the role of the public relations firm: one black shoe from the sludge in Chicago; one white shoe from the clean environment in the suburbs.

A Proposed Bill of Rights

DAVID EWING

What should a bill of rights for employees look like?

First, it should be presented in the form of clear and practical injunctions, not in the language of desired behavior or ideals.

In 1789, when James Madison and other members of the first U.S. Congress settled down to write the Bill of Rights (the first ten amendments to the Constitution), Madison insisted on using the imperative "shall" instead of the flaccid "ought," which had been used in the declarations of rights by the states, from which the ideas for the federal Bill of Rights were taken. For instance, where Virginia's historic Declaration of Rights of 1776 stated that "excessive bail ought not to be required," and where the amendments proposed in 1788 by Virginia legislators were identically worded, the amendment proposed by Madison (and later accepted) read: "Excessive bail shall not be required. . . ."

The imperative has precisely the same advantage in a bill of rights for members of a corporation, government bureau, university administration, or other organization. An analogy is a traffic light. It does not contain various shades of red but just one shade which means clearly and unequivocally, "Stop." Nor does a stop sign say "Stop If Possible" or "Stop If You Can." It says simply "Stop."

Second, as a general rule, it is wise to phrase a bill of rights in terms of negative injunctions rather than positive ones. A bill of rights does not aim to tell officials what they can do so much as it aims to tell them what they cannot do. It is not like the delegation of powers found in constitutions. Here again it is instructive to recall the writing of the federal Bill of Rights in 1789. Madison insisted that the positive grants of government powers had been well provided for in the main body of the Constitution and did not need to be reiterated in the first ten amendments.

In addition, a "Thou shalt not" type of commandment generally can be more precise than a "Thou shalt" type of commandment; the latter must be worded and interpreted to cover many possibilities of affirmative action. Since it is more precise, a "Thou shalt not" injunction is more predictable —not quite as predictable as a traffic light, but more so than most positive injunctions can be.

Also, since it is more limited, a negative injunction is less of a threat to the future use of executive (and legislative) powers. For instance, the injunction "Congress shall make no law respecting an establishment of religion" (first item in the U.S. Bill of Rights) inhibits Congress less, simply because it is so precise, than a positive command such as "Congress shall respect various establishments of religion" (rejected by the Founding Fathers when proposed in the 1789 discussions), which is more protean and expansible.

Third, an organization's bill of rights should be succinct. It should read more like a recipe in a cookbook than the regulations of the Internal Revenue Service. It is better to start with a limited number of rights that apply to familiar situations and that may have to be extended and amended in a few years than try to write a definitive listing for all time. Rights take time to ingest.

Fourth, a bill of rights should be written for understanding by employees and lay people rather than by lawyers and personnel specialists. It should not read like a letter from a credit company or a Massachusetts auto insurance policy. If an organization desires to make everything clear for experts, it could add a supplement or longer explanation that elaborates in technical terms on the provisions and clarifies questions and angles that might occur to lawyers.

Fifth, a bill of rights should be enforceable. Existence as a creed or statement of ideals is not enough. While creeds indeed may influence behavior in the long run, in the short run they leave too much dependent on good will and hope.

The bill of rights that follows is one person's proposal, a "working paper" for discussion, not a platform worked out in committee. . . . The slight variations in style are purposeful—partly to reduce monotony and partly to suggest different ways of defining employee rights and management prerogatives.

1. *No organization or manager shall discharge, demote, or in other ways discriminate against any employee who criticizes, in speech or press, the ethics, legality, or social responsibility of management actions.*

Comment: This right is intended to extend the U.S. Supreme Court's approach in the *Pickering* case‡ to all employees in business, government, education, and public service organizations.

What this right does not say is as important as what it does say. Protection does not extend to employees who make nuisances of themselves or who balk, argue, or contest managerial decisions on normal operating and planning matters, such as the choice of inventory accounting method, whether to diversify the product line or concentrate it, whether to rotate workers on a certain job or specialize them, and so forth. "Committing the truth," as Ernest Fitzgerald called it, is protected only for speaking out on issues where we consider an average citizen's judgment to be as valid as an expert's—truth in advertising, public safety standards, questions of fair disclosure, ethical practices, and so forth.

Nor does the protection extend to employees who malign the organization. We don't protect individuals who go around ruining other people's reputations, and neither should we protect those who vindictively impugn their employers.

Note, too, that this proposed right does not authorize an employee to disclose to outsiders information that is confidential.

This right puts publications of nonunionized employees on the same basis as union newspapers and journals, which are free to criticize an organization. Can a free press be justified for one group but not for the other? More to the point still, in a country that practices democratic rites, can the necessity of an "underground press" be justified in any socially important organization?

2. *No employee shall be penalized for engaging in outside activities of his or her choice after working hours, whether political, economic, civic, or cultural, nor for buying products and services of his or her choice for personal use, nor for expressing or encouraging views contrary to top management's on political, economic, and social issues.*

Comment: Many companies encourage employees to participate in outside activities, and some states have committed this right to legislation. Freedom of choice of products and services for personal use is also authorized in various state statutes as well as in arbitrators' decisions. The third part of the statement extends the protection of the First Amendment to the employee whose ideas about government, economic policy, religion, and

‡[ed.] In the *Pickering* case, the Supreme Court found in favor of a public employee, a school teacher, who had been fired for criticizing school policies in the local newspaper.

society do not conform with the boss's. It would also protect the schoolteacher who allows the student newspaper to espouse a view on sex education that is rejected by the principal. . ., the staff psychologist who endorses a book on a subject considered taboo in the board room, and other independent spirits.

Note that this provision does not authorize an employee to come to work "beat" in the morning because he or she has been moonlighting. Participation in outside activities should enrich employees' lives, not debilitate them; if on-the-job performance suffers, the usual penalties may have to be paid.

3. *No organization or manager shall penalize an employee for refusing to carry out a directive that violates common norms of morality.*

Comment: The purpose of this right is to . . . afford job security (not just unemployment compensation) to subordinates who cannot perform an action because they consider it unethical or illegal. It is important that the conscientious objector in such a case hold to a view that has some public acceptance. Fad moralities—messages from flying saucers, mores of occult religious sects, and so on—do not justify refusal to carry out an order. Nor in any case is the employee entitled to interfere with the boss's finding another person to do the job requested.

4. *No organization shall allow audio or visual recordings of an employee's conversations or actions to be made without his or her prior knowledge and consent. Nor may an organization require an employee or applicant to take personality tests, polygraph examinations, or other tests that constitute, in his opinion, an invasion of privacy.*

Comment: This right is based on policies that some leading organizations have already put into practice. If an employee doesn't want his working life monitored, that is his privilege so long as he demonstrates (or, if an applicant, is willing to demonstrate) competence to do a job well.

5. *No employee's desk, files, or locker may be examined in his or her absence by anyone but a senior manager who has sound reason to believe that the files contain information needed for a management decision that must be made in the employee's absence.*

Comment: The intent of this right is to grant people a privacy right as employees similar to that which they enjoy as political and social citizens under the "searches and seizures" guarantee of the Bill of Rights (Fourth Amendment to the Constitution). Many leading organizations in business and government have respected the principle of this rule for some time.

6. *No employer organization may collect and keep on file information about an employee that is not relevant and necessary for efficient management. Every employee shall have the right to inspect his or her personnel file and challenge the accuracy, relevance, or necessity of data in it, except for personal evaluations and comments by other employees which could not reasonably be obtained if confidentiality were not promised. Access to an employee's file by outside individuals and organizations shall be limited to inquiries about the essential facts of employment.*

Comment: This right is important if employees are to be masters of their employment track records instead of possible victims of them. It will help to eliminate surprises, secrets, and skeletons in the clerical closet.

7. *No manager may communicate to prospective employers of an employee who is about to be or has been discharged gratuitous opinions that might hamper the individual in obtaining a new position.*

Comment: The intent of this right is to stop blacklisting. The courts have already given some support for it.

8. *An employee who is discharged, demoted, or transferred to a less desirable job is entitled to a written statement from management of its reasons for the penalty.*

Comment: The aim of this provision is to encourage a manager to give the same reasons in a hearing, arbitration, or court trial that he or she gives the employee when the cutdown happens. The written statement need not be given unless requested; often it is so clear to all parties why an action is being taken that no document is necessary.

9. *Every employee who feels that he or she has been penalized for asserting any right described in this bill shall be entitled to a fair hearing before an impartial official, board, or arbitrator. The findings and conclusions of the hearing shall be delivered in writing to the employee and management.*

Comment: This very important right is the organizational equivalent of due process of law as we know it in political and community life. Without due process in a company or agency, the rights in this bill would all have to be enforced by outside courts and tribunals, which is expensive for society as well as time-consuming for the employees who are required to appear as complainants and witnesses. The nature of a "fair hearing" is purposely left undefined here so that different approaches can be tried, expanded, and adapted to changing needs and conditions.

Note that the findings of the investigating official or group are not binding on top management. This would put an unfair burden on an ombudsperson or "expedited arbitrator," if one of them is the investigator. Yet the employee is protected. If management rejects a finding of unfair treatment and then the employee goes to court, the investigator's statement will weigh against management in the trial. As a practical matter, therefore, employers will not want to buck the investigator-referee unless they fervently disagree with the findings.

In Sweden, perhaps the world's leading practitioner of due process in organizations, a law went into effect in January 1977 that goes a little farther than the right proposed here. The new Swedish law states that except in unusual circumstances a worker who disputes a dismissal notice can keep his or her job until the dispute has been decided by a court.

Every sizable organization, whether in business, government, health, or another field, should have a bill of rights for employees. Only small organizations need not have such a statement—personal contact and oral communications meet the need for them. However, companies and agencies need not have identical bills of rights. Industry custom, culture, past history with employee unions and associations, and other considerations can be taken into account in the wording and emphasis given to different provisions.

For instance, Booz, Allen and Hamilton, the well-known consulting company, revised a bill of rights for its employees in 1976 (the list included several of the rights suggested here). One statement obligated the company to "Respect the right of employees to conduct their private lives as they choose, while expecting its employees' public conduct to reflect favorably upon the reputation of the Firm." The latter part of this provision reflects the justifiable concern of a leading consulting firm with outward appearances. However, other organizations—a mining company, let us say, or a testing laboratory—might feel no need to qualify the right of privacy because few of their employees see customers.

In what ways can due process be assured? There are certain procedures that the organization itself can establish, . . . In addition, society can undertake to assure due process for employees. . . .

The Myth of the "Oppressive Corporation"

MAX WAYS

If enough voices declare that the pace of change in the workplace is "too slow," and that this should be blamed on concentrated corporate power, then, obviously, somebody is going to limit the power of the corporate Leviathan.

Proposals along this line are set forth in *Freedom Inside the Organization* by David W. Ewing, an editor of the *Harvard Business Review.* Subtitled *Bringing Civil Liberties to the Workplace,* the book falls into a familiar pattern: generalizations about existing conditions are drawn from atrocity stories and selected opinions of employees. In the dark picture of corporate oppression that results, the author sees an urgent need for drastic legal remedies.

"For nearly two centuries," Ewing begins, "Americans have enjoyed freedom of press, speech, and assembly, due process of law, privacy, freedom of conscience, and other important rights—in their homes, churches, political forums, and social and cultural life. But Americans have not enjoyed these civil liberties in most companies, government agencies, and other organizations where they work. Once a U.S. citizen steps through the plant or office door at 9:00 A.M., he or she is nearly rightless until 5:00 P.M., Monday through Friday."

Ewing has in this opening passage disclosed a fundamental misconception about the nature of our cherished rights. A few pages later, this mistake leads him into a shocking distortion.

"For all practical purposes," he writes, "employees are required to be as obedient to their superiors, regardless of ethical and legal considerations, as are workers in totalitarian countries."

A writer so insensitive that he can equate U.S. corporate practices, even at their worst, with the system that produced the Gulag Archipelago is hardly qualified to lecture businessmen on their lack of concern for human rights.

The historic rights enjoyed by Americans protect them against the abuse of government police power, not against all unpleasant consequences that may follow from their speech or action. Free speech, for instance, means that Americans cannot be fined or imprisoned for what they say; the exceptions are a small and shrinking number. It does not mean that they cannot be sued for slander. It does not mean that what they say may not deprive them of the respect of their children, the affection of their parents or spouses, the company of their friends. If an American's speech is rude enough, or malicious enough, or silly enough he may find that people don't listen to him and he may even be ostracized. Cases where such penalties are "unjust" do occur. But these instances are not violations of our right of free speech.

The human damage that can be done by words is so great and so plain that (most) children learn early to watch what they say. These inhibitions can be psychologically or socially hurtful, but civilized life would be impossible without them and the person-to-person sanctions by which they are maintained.

Most corporations today allow employees great latitude in their personal behavior, including speech. But corporations, like individuals, retain the power to employ all private sanctions that are not illegal in themselves (e.g., assault and battery) to express disapproval of an individual's speech. They can argue, remonstrate, and warn. The most extreme penalty at their disposal is to dissolve their association with the speaker by firing him. This can be, indeed, a serious penalty—but not necessarily more serious than divorce, which is frequently provoked by speech.

Reciting a number of instances where corporations have fired employees for what they said, Ewing deems many, though not all, of these to be "unjust." He points out that some companies invoke penalties only after a scrupulously enforced "due process." He cites an IBM policy that guarantees many freedoms to employees and establishes internal procedures to review penalties imposed by managers. More and more companies have moved in this direction.

Ewing's argument is that if some corporations choose to behave in this way then all corporations should be required by law to do likewise. The legal reasoning is reminiscent of that which produced the Eighteenth Amendment. First, the human damage done by alcohol was exaggerated, then "the power of the liquor interest" was blown up out of all proportion to reality, then attention was called to the fact that many Americans—perhaps half the adult population—hardly ever used alcohol. Ergo, let's have a law requiring everyone to conform to the best practice.

Sure enough, Ewing, too, wants an amendment to the Constitution of the United States. His draft starts, "No public or private organization shall discriminate against an employee for criticizing the ethical, moral, or legal policies and practices of the organization. . . ."

In addition to protecting individual employees, Ewing frankly desires to encourage "whistle blowing" in cases of corporate wrongdoing. That might accomplish some desirable changes in corporate behavior. But this hypothesized advantage has to be weighed against some foreseeable disadvantages. Who is to distinguish between whistle blowing and spiteful accusation? Speech now is protected from government penalty, in most cases, even if the utterance is proved untrue. Would Ewing's amendment continue this broad protection? Or would courts have to sift evidence to discover whether the employee's charge against the corporation was true? In the first case an organization might be required to keep on its payroll an employee who continually lied about it. In the second case, courts, which are not winning much public applause for the way they discharge their present responsibilities, would have to take on a huge new burden of deciding not only whether charges were true or false, but whether ethical norms had or had not been violated by the defendant organization.

The incidence of these cases could become such a nuisance to companies that all employees might wind up having, in effect, life tenure in their jobs, like the Civil Service or the tenured faculty of universities. Neither of these examples is necessarily reassuring.

It's true, of course, that a company's right to fire has long been limited by the National Labor Relations Act, which has worked rather well in forbidding firing for union activity. In this narrow class of cases it is relatively easy to determine whether the forbidden practice has occurred. In a much larger group of cases under equal-opportunity acts, corporations are forbidden to discriminate in respect to race or sex. Enforcement here has been less effective and has caused more confusion. Ewing's amendment is so much broader than the equal-opportunity laws, and its criteria so much vaguer, that the imagination boggles at the legal chaos that might ensue.

Such practical objections Ewing brushes aside with a quote from Judge Learned Hand: "To keep our democracy, there must be one commandment: Thou shalt not ration justice." The distinguished jurist said many wise things, but this was not one of them. In any society justice must always be less than perfect. A free society recognizes that its government should not pretend to dispense total justice. In that sense justice in a democracy must always be "rationed."

Much injustice that occurs among citizens is beyond the reach of courts or of any government instrument. The state in which that limitation is not recognized, the state that believes itself empowered to set all norms of conduct and to deal with every incident of ethical transgression, is the absolute state, Leviathan.

A Theory of Employee Rights

PATRICIA H. WERHANE

In 1981 The Supreme Court of the State of Illinois made what should prove to be a monumental decision. It said that an employee of International Harvester Corporation, Ray Palmateer, was wrongly fired for supplying information to local police about employee theft at International Harvester. The company had tried to justify its firing of Palmateer on the basis of a doctrine called Employment at Will. Under this common law principle in this country, unless specified by law or by contract, an employer has the right to hire, demote, promote or fire "at will" whom and when it wishes. The Palmateer decision is a landmark decision, because it reverses the standing tradition that employer wishes take precedence over employee rights in the workplace. The case indicates a changing view toward employee rights in this country—recognition that employees or workers have certain claims even though they are working for someone else.[1]

It would appear that if one has guarantees to basic human rights and if one is also assured of the rights to equal opportunity and to minimum wages, such guarantees would be enough to assure fair treatment in the workplace. At first glance it is difficult to imagine how any society which guarantees basic rights would not also assure their entitlement in the workplace. Interestingly, however, until recently rights of the majority of employees in this country have not been enforced in the workplace. At least 64 percent of all employees in this country are "at will," employees unprotected by collective bargaining agreements or legislation[2]. These employees can be hired or fired at the discretion of the employer without cause, due process, or prior notice. And the principle of Employment at Will is sometimes used as a weapon to "punish" unruly, disobedient, as well as inefficient employees. In these instances it is not literally the case that the Constitution does not protect employee rights in the workplace. Rather it is that the law does not restrain employers who penalize employees for their exercise of rights. The Palmateer case illustrates a much overlooked issue in the workplace, and the subject of employee rights is a very current and controversial issue.

This paper will present a theoretical argument that employees have rights in employment. Specifically, employees have the right to due process in the workplace. It shall be claimed that the common law doctrine of Employment at Will (hereafter abbreviated EAW) is an unjust principle because it does not recognize equal employer and employee rights. Due process in the workplace, it will be argued, helps alleviate unfair disadvantages in the workplace created by the right to private property and the principle of EAW. Thus due process is an important employee *and* employer right, because it enhances the justice of a private property economic system. In what follows, the terms "employee" and "worker" will be used interchangeably to refer to any person who is in the employ of another. For the sake of abbreviating the argument the term "employer" will represent the person or institution who has the power to hire, demote, promote, or fire an employee. Thus in this context "employer" could refer to an individual, an owner, a corporation, a personnel officer, a manager, a supervisor, or a foreman.

One point should be emphasized at the outset. It is not true that most employers are ogres. Many places of employment are decent places to work, jobs are not unpleasant, and one's superior or employer normally treats its employees with decency and respect. What is troublesome is not that fair treatment never occurs in the workplace. What is at issue is that the *right* to fair treatment has not been firmly established in employment. The determination of this right is important in order that one need not depend merely on the kindness of one's superiors for fair treatment and respect.

Due process is the means by which one can appeal a decision in order to get a disinterested, objective, or fair judgment as to its rightness or wrongness. In the workplace due process is, or should be, the right of employees and employers to grievance, arbitration, or some other appeals procedure in questioning a decision in hiring, firing, promotion, demotion, or other employee treatment. Due process should not be confused with a claim to a right not to be fired. Due process is meant to insure fair procedures in firing, but not to rule out that employer action.

The justification for not according due process in the workplace is stated in the principle of EAW. Since the employer or the corporation owns the means of production as private property, and because every person has the right to freedom, the employer has the right to dispose of its property as it pleases. Because the employee is working on and affecting the property of the employer and is paid for his or her work, the employer has the absolute right, in the absence of any contract, to employ or dismiss whom and when it wishes. The employer need not explain or defend its treatment of employees in this regard, or give a hearing to an employee before he or she is dismissed. According to defenders of EAW, the principle also recognizes equal rights of employees, because the employee, too, is free and may choose or change his or her job at any time.[3]

The right to due process in the workplace simply reiterates what is standardly accepted that every accused person, guilty or innocent, has a right to a fair hearing and an objective evaluation of his or her guilt or innocence. To deny due process in the workplace would appear to argue that this right does not extend to every sector of society, or it might be to claim that the right to dispose freely of the use of one's property may sometimes override an employee's right to due process.

One may argue, however, that while in general, the right to due process is a universal right, the right to private property is also a universal right, and the latter entails the right to dispose of that property freely. According to this view, when an employee is working on the property of another, this labor affects, positively or negatively, that property. Because one has property rights and because this right entails the right to control what happens to one's property, one thus has the right to dispose of the labor of employees whose work changes that property. In dismissing or demoting employees, one is not denying *persons* the political right to due process; rather, the employer is simply excluding that person's *labor* from its property.

This argument makes three questionable judgments. First, it asserts that property rights are absolute rights. Secondly, it purports that one can separate a person from his or her labor in the same fashion that one can separate a person from his or her property. Finally, it fails to recognize that the absence of due process places employees at an unfair disadvantage vis-a-vis other employers, a disadvantage which creates unfair inequalities and thus injustices in the workplace. I shall explain these.

If the right to private property is a legitimate claim, and I shall assume for the sake of the argument in this paper that this is the case, it follows that property owners have other rights connected with that, e.g., the right to use, dispose, and sell their properties as they please. But two conditions for these rights are important. First, one's property rights are not absolute rights. If when disposing of my property I affect the property of another, my right to such disposal is brought into question. For example, when burning on my property causes smoke damage to my neighbor's property, my right to engage in that activity is usually curtailed. And if my property rights infringe on other rights, such as when my burning affects the quality of the atmosphere, my property rights are also restricted. Therefore property rights are limited by the equal property claims of others and by other human rights claims.

Secondly, the relation between a person or an institution to its property is different from the relation of a person to his or her labor. A person is distinct from his or her property, but the same cannot be said of the separation of a person from his or her labor. For example, in buying or selling property one's wealth is changed, but what one is as a human personality is not necessarily affected. If one is denied rightfully acquired property, one's rights are violated, but one's person is not violated. The relationship between a person and her property is not an inalienable one, because a person is not identified with his or her property, and is distinct from it.

On the other hand, labor, unlike material property, is an inseparable part of a person. In "selling one's labor" or taking a job, for example, one is in a sense selling part of oneself, because one cannot detach oneself from the activity of working. Notice that the products of labor, like other properties, are distinct from the laborer or employee. One can, for instance, in principle work at home and send the results of that work to one's employer. But the activity of working itself cannot be "sent in" because that activity is an inalienable part of oneself. In hiring and firing, unlike buying or selling property, one hires and fires persons, even though primarily an employer is interested only in the labor of that person. Thus property and labor are different in this important sense, that a person can be separated from his or her property without damaging his or her person, a separation which allows the creation of fictional persons such as corporations or trusts who can own property. But a person cannot be so distinguished from his or her work. This, incidentally, is why slavery violates more rights than the nationalization of property without compensation. Slavery does not merely deny an employee pay; it uses persons as well. Thus if one denies another person his or her personal rights, e.g., rights to freedom, to equal opportunity, or to fair treatment in the workplace, one is disrespecting that person.

When an employer denies an employee due process in the workplace the employer is presuming that he or she has the absolute right to decide what should be done to his or her property even when exercising that right affects the rights of other persons. This presumption, alone, is highly questionable. Moreover, when an employer arbitrarily fires an employee, the employer is not merely rejecting the labor of the employee; the employer is rejecting that person as well. In treating employees "at will" this treatment is analogous to regarding the employee as if his or her labor were a piece of property owned or at the disposal of the employer. The principle of EAW, then, advocates the treatment of labor of persons as if it were property. It confuses property rights with rights of persons since it advocates the disposal of labor as it if were a material thing. Thus the denial of due process in the workplace, while defended on the basis of property rights, makes the rash assertion that property rights are absolute rights. And in treating labor like property it denies basic respect for persons, since labor, unlike property, cannot be distinguished from the employee.

The argument defending property rights against the right to due process in the workplace fails on a third set of grounds. If I take away someone else's property, I place that person or institution in an unfair disadvantage vis-a-vis other persons or institutions who continue to own property. This is not only because of the obvious disadvantages created by the loss of property. It is also because it is often assumed, rightly or wrongly, that the property owner in question *deserved* this loss. For example, when a business goes bankrupt it is forced to sell its properties. And it is commonly supposed, whether or not there is good reason, that the business deserved to go bankrupt because of mismanagement or some other logically connected reason. Persons connected with the bankrupt business often have difficulties thereafter borrowing money or getting new jobs because it is thought that these persons are bad managers.

Similarly, when one is demoted or fired the reduction or loss of the job is only part of an employee's disadvantage. When one is demoted or fired it is commonly taken for granted that one deserved that treatment, whether or not this is the case. Without a hearing or an objective appraisal of this treatment no employee can appeal if he or she is mistreated, nor has the employee any way to demonstrate that he or she was fired arbitrarily without good reason. Fired or demoted employees, then, have much more difficulty getting new jobs than those who are not fired, even when the employee dismissal was unwarranted. The absence of due process in the workplace places an employee at an unfair disadvantage with fellow workers. The absence of due process denies employees a very basic right—the right to equal opportunity—since those who do not deserve to be fired are treated equally with those who do. Thus the assertion of absolute property rights which include the right to hire and fire at will may conflict and violate the right to equal opportunity, a right commonly held as a most basic human entitlement.

From these arguments it may be concluded that while the principle of EAW claims to espouse equal rights for employees and employers by protecting the right to freedom of both parties, this is not the case. The principle of EAW is to the advantage of the property owner or employer and to the disadvantage of the employee, because the employee's so-called right to change jobs is restricted by whether or not the employee was fired or demoted, while the employer's right to dispose of its property is not similarly constrained. The employee's freedom to dispose of his or her labor, then, is not equal to the employer's freedom to dispose of its property, and the latter creates unfair disadvantages and thus limits the freedom and equal opportunities for those employed.

Defenders of EAW will make the following objection to the right to due process in the workplace. EAW, they claim, balances employee and employer rights because, just as the employer has the right to dispose of its property, so too, the employee has the right to accept or not to accept a job, and he or she has the absolute freedom to quit "at will." Due process creates an imbalance of rights, because it restricts the freedom of the employer without restricting the choices of the employee. What this objection fails to notice is that the right to due process in the workplace distinguishes between property and labor, a distinction blurred by at will employment practices. It argues that property rights are not absolute rights, and therefore the freedom to dispose of property cannot override freedom and equal consideration of persons. However, in making the distinction between property and labor the right to due process merely restricts the employer's right to arbitrary treatment of persons working for the employer, a restriction which propagates rather than disturbs equal rights for employees and employers. But due process does *not* infringe on an employer's right to dispose of its property, a right which balances the right of employees to dispose of their labor as they see fit. Finally, despite employer fears, due process does not preclude firing and demotion in the workplace. Due process does not require that employers never dismiss employees. But due process requires that any employee have a hearing and an objective evaluation before being dismissed.

Some contemporary theorists will complain that the arguments in defense of due process in the workplace are based on an eighteenth century Lockean notion of property and property ownership. The relation of an employer to property is much different from the eighteenth and even from the nineteenth centuries. Today employers are, by and large, corporations. The corporation is owned by stockholders who have little or no say in the management and hence in the employment practices of the corporation, and the corporation is run by managers who hire and fire but who do not own the business. Thus, it will be contended a defense of the right to due process cannot be sustained by criticizing abuses of property rights, but must be argued for on other grounds.[4]

This sort of criticism is correct in pointing out the enormous changes which have occurred in employer-property arrangement. What has not changed, however, is the principle of EAW which, while based on a Lockean theory of property, is still in force as the justification for at will employment practices in modern corporations. The evolution of property from single ownership to the corporate arrangement is not reflected in the principle of EAW. The fact that this evolution has occurred gives further reason for abolishing this outdated obsolete principle.

What is to be concluded is that if employers and other owners of private property have an equal right to dispose of their property, employees too have an equal right to due process to protect their freedom to dispose of their labor. The principle of EAW is an inconsistent doctrine because it violates rights and creates disadvantages for one set of persons, employees, while granting advantages on the basis of the rights to freedom and to property to employers. Due process in the workplace helps to abrogate that inconsistency. Due process helps to adjudicate unfair disadvantages created by property ownership and employer power. It reduces injustices in a private property economic system without changing the basic tenets of that system. Therefore its importance for employees *and* employers cannot be exaggerated.

NOTES

1. *Palmateer v. International Harvester Corportion*, 85 Ill. App. 3d 50 (1981).
2. MaryAnn Glendon and Edward R. Lev, "Changes in the Bonding of the Employment Relationship: An Essay on the New Property," *Boston College Law Review* XX (1979), pp. 457-84.
3. For further discussion of EAW see for example, Lawrence Blades, "Employment at Will versus Individual Freedom: On Limiting the Abusive Exercise of Employer Power," *Columbia Law Review* 67 (1967), pp. 1405–1457; Clyde Summer, "Individual Protection Against Unjust Dismissal. Time for a Statute," *Virginia Law Review* 62, Pt. 1–4 (1976), pp. 481–532.
4. See, for example, George Cabot Lodge, *The New American Ideology* (New York: Alfred Knopf, 1975), especially Chapter 7 reprinted in this volume.

Argues against Employment-at-Will & for due process on the basis of:
(1) non-absolute property rights
(2) integration of person & one's labor vs. distinction bet/ person & one's property
(3) competitive disadvantage getting fired places an employee in

AFFIRMATIVE ACTION

Weber v. Kaiser Aluminum and United Steelworkers

(U.S. SUPREME COURT, 1979)*

Decision: Corporation's voluntary affirmative action plan, granting preference to black employees over more senior white employees in admission to in-plant craft training programs, held not violative of 42 USCS §§ 2000e-2(a), (d). [Title VII]

SUMMARY

A union and a corporation entered into a master collective bargaining agreement covering terms and conditions of employment at several of the corporation's plants. Among other things, the agreement contained an affirmative action plan designed to eliminate conspicuous racial imbalances in the corporation's almost exclusively white craft work force. After setting black craft hiring goals for each plant equal to the percentage of blacks in the respective local labor forces, the plan established on-the-job training programs to teach unskilled production workers the skills necessary to become craft workers. At one particular plant, where the craft work force was less than 2% black even though the local work force was 39% black, the corporation established a training program and selected trainees on the basis of seniority, with the proviso that at least 50% of the new trainees were to be black until the percentage of black skilled craft workers in the plant approximated the percentage of blacks in the local labor force. During the plan's first year of operation, the most junior black trainee selected had less seniority than several white production workers whose bids for admission to the program were rejected. One such white worker instituted a class action in the United States District Court for the Eastern District of Louisiana alleging that the manner of filling craft trainee positions discriminated against him and other similarly situated white employees in violation of §§ 703(a) and 703(d) of Title VII of the Civil Rights Act of 1964 (42 USCS §§ 2000e-2(a), (d)). The District Court held that the plan violated Title VII, entered a judgment in favor of the class of white employees, and granted a permanent injunction prohibiting the corporation and the union from

*443 U.S. 193 (1979)

denying members of the class access to on-the-job training programs on the basis of race.... The United States Court of Appeals for the Fifth Circuit affirmed, holding that all employment preferences based upon race, including those preferences incidental to bona fide affirmative action plans, violated Title VII's prohibition against racial discrimination in employment....

On certiorari, the United States Supreme Court reversed. In an opinion, by BRENNAN, J., joined by STEWART, WHITE, MARSHALL, and BLACKMUN, JJ., it was held that (1) the prohibition in §§ 703(a) and 703(d) of Title VII against racial discrimination does not condemn all private, voluntary, race-conscious affirmative action plans, since any contrary interpretation of §§ 703(a) and 703(d) would bring about an end completely at variance with the purpose of the statute, the inference that Congress did not wish to ban all voluntary, race-conscious affirmative action being further supported by its use only of the word "require," rather than the phrase "require or permit," in § 703(j) of Title VII . . . which provides that nothing in Title VII shall be interpreted to "require" any employer to grant preferential treatment to any group, because of that group's race, on account of a de facto racial imbalance in the employer's work force, and (2) the affirmative action plan under consideration, which was designed to eliminate traditional patterns of conspicuous racial segregation, was permissible under Title VII, especially in light of the fact that it did not require the discharge of white workers and their replacement with new black hirees, did not create an absolute bar to the advancement of white employees, and was a temporary measure not intended to maintain racial balance but simply to eliminate a manifest racial imbalance.

BLACKMUN, J., concurring, expressed the view that while it would have been preferable to uphold the corporation's craft training program as a "reasonable response" to an "arguable violation" of Title VII, the court's reading of Title VII, permitting affirmative action by an employer whenever the job category in question is "traditionally segregated," was an acceptable one.

BURGER, Ch. J., dissenting, expressed the view that the quota embodied in the collective-bargaining agreement discriminated on the basis of race against individual employees seeking admission to on-the-job training programs, such discrimination being an "unlawful employment practice" under the plain language of 42 USCS § 2000e-2(d). [i.e, Title VII]

REHNQUIST, J., joined by BURGER, Ch. J., dissenting, expressed the view that the corporation's racially discriminatory admission quota was flatly prohibited by the plain language of Title VII, and furthermore was sanctioned by neither the Act's legislative history nor its "spirit."

POWELL. and STEVENS, JJ., did not participate.

OPINION OF THE COURT

Mr. Justice ***Brennan*** *delivered the opinion of the Court.*

[1a] Challenged here is the legality of an affirmative action plan—collectively bargained by an employer and a union—that reserves for black

employees 50% of the openings in an in-plant craft training program until the percentage of black craft workers in the plant is commensurate with the percentage of blacks in the local labor force. The question for decision is whether Congress, in Title VII of the Civil Rights Act of 1964 as amended, ... left employers and unions in the private sector free to take such race-conscious steps to eliminate manifest racial imbalances in traditionally segregated job categories. We hold that Title VII does not prohibit such race-conscious affirmative action plans.

In 1974 petitioner United Steel workers of America (USWA) and petitioner Kaiser Aluminum & Chemical Corporation (Kaiser) entered into a master collective-bargaining agreement covering terms and conditions of employment at 15 Kaiser plants. The agreement contained, inter alia, an affirmative action plan designed to eliminate conspicuous racial imbalances in Kaiser's then almost exclusively white craft work forces. Black craft hiring goals were set for each Kaiser plant equal to the percentage of blacks in the respective local labor forces. To enable plants to meet these goals, on-the-job training programs were established to teach unskilled production workers—black and white—the skills necessary to become craft workers. The plan reserved for black employees 50% of the openings in these newly created in-plant training programs.

[2a] This case arose from the operation of the plan at Kaiser's plant in Gramercy, La. Until 1974 Kaiser hired as craft workers for that plant only persons who had had prior craft experience. Because blacks had long been excluded from craft unions, few were able to present such credentials. As a consequence, prior to 1974 only 1.83% (five out of 273) of the skilled craft workers at the Gramercy plant were black, even though the work force in the Gramercy area was approximately 39% black.

Pursuant to the national agreement Kaiser altered its craft hiring practice in the Gramercy plant. Rather than hiring already trained outsiders, Kaiser established a training program to train its production workers to fill craft openings. Selection of craft trainees was made on the basis of seniority, with the proviso that at least 50% of the new trainees were to be black until the percentage of black skilled craft workers in the Gramercy plant approximated the percentage of blacks in the local labor force. . . .

During 1974, the first year of the operation of the Kaiser-USWA affirmative action plan, 13 craft trainees were selected from Gramercy's production work force. Of these, 7 were black and 6 white. The most junior black selected into the program had less seniority than several white production workers whose bids for admission were rejected. Thereafter one of those white production workers, respondent Brian Weber, instituted this class action in the United States District Court for the Eastern District of Louisiana.

The complaint alleged that the filling of craft trainee positions at the Gramercy plant pursuant to the affirmative action program had resulted in junior black employees receiving training in preference to more senior white employees, thus discriminating against respondent and other similarly situated white employees in violation of §§ 703(a) and (d) of Title VII. The

District Court held that the plan violated Title VII, entered a judgment in favor of the plaintiff class, and granted a permanent injunction prohibiting Kaiser and the USWA "from denying plaintiffs, Brian F. Weber and all other members of the class, access to on-the-job training programs on the basis of race." A divided panel of the Court of Appeals for the Fifth Circuit affirmed, holding that all employment preferences based upon race, including those preferences incidental to bona fide affirmative action plans, violated Title VII's prohibition against racial discrimination in employment. . . . We reverse.

We emphasize at the outset the narrowness of our inquiry. Since the Kaiser-USWA plan does not involve state action, this case does not present an alleged violation of the Equal Protection Clause of the Constitution. Further, since the Kaiser-USWA plan was adopted voluntarily, we are not concerned with what Title VII requires or with what a court might order to remedy a past proven violation of the Act. The only question before us is the narrow statutory issue of whether Title VII forbids private employers and unions from voluntarily agreeing upon bona fide affirmative action plans that accord racial preferences in the manner and for the purpose provided in the Kaiser-USWA plan. That question was expressly left open in McDonald v. Santa Fe Trail Trans. Co., . . . (1976) which held, in a case not involving affirmative action, that Title VII protects whites as well as blacks from certain forms of racial discrimination.

Respondent argues that Congress intended in Title VII to prohibit all race-conscious affirmative action plans. Respondent's argument rests upon a literal interpretation of §§ 703(a) and (d) of the Act. Those sections make it unlawful to "discriminate . . . because of . . . race" in hiring and in the selection of apprentices for training programs. Since, the argument runs, McDonald v Santa Fe Trans. Co., . . . settled that Title VII *forbids* discrimination against whites as well as blacks, and since the Kaiser-USWA affirmative action plan operates to discriminate against white employees solely because they are white, it follows that the Kaiser-USWA plan violates Title VII.

[1b, 2] Respondent's argument is not without force. But it overlooks the significance of the fact that the Kaiser-USWA plan is an affirmative action plan voluntarily adopted by private parties to eliminate traditional patterns of racial segregation. In this context respondent's reliance upon a literal construction of §§ 703(a) and (d) and upon McDonald is misplaced. . . . It is a "familiar rule, that a thing may be within the letter of the statute and yet not within the statute, because not within its spirit, nor within the intention of its makers." Holy Trinity Church v. United States, . . . (1892). The prohibition against racial discrimination in §§ 703(a) and (d) of Title VII must therefore be read against the background of the legislative history of Title VII and the historical context from which the Act arose. See Train v Colorado Public Interest Research Group, . . . (1976); Woodworkers v NLRB, . . . (1967); United States v American Trucking Assns. . . . (1940). Examination of those sources makes clear that an interpretation of the sections that forbade all race-conscious affirmative action would "bring

about an end completely at variance with the purpose of the statute" and must be rejected. . . .

Congress' primary concern in enacting the prohibition against racial discrimination in Title VII of the Civil Rights Act of 1964 was with "the plight of the Negro in our economy." 110 Cong Rec 6548 (remarks of Sen. Humphrey). Before 1964, blacks were largely relegated to "unskilled and semi-skilled jobs. . . ." at 6548 (remarks of Sen. Humphrey). Because of automation the number of such jobs was rapidly decreasing. As a consequence "the relative position of the Negro worker [was] steadily worsening. In 1947 the non-white unemployment rate was only 64 percent higher than the white rate; in 1962 it was 124 percent higher." (remarks of Sen. Humphrey). See also id., at 7204 (remarks of Sen. Clark). Congress considered this a serious social problem. As Senator Clark told the Senate:

> The rate of Negro unemployment has gone up consistently as compared with white unemployment for the past 15 years. This is a social malaise and a social situation which we should not tolerate. That is one of the principal reasons why this bill should pass.

Congress feared that the goals of the Civil Rights Act—the integration of blacks into the mainstream of American society—could not be achieved unless this trend were reversed. And Congress recognized that that would not be possible unless blacks were able to secure jobs "which have a future." As Senator Humphrey explained to the Senate:

> What good does it do a Negro to be able to eat in a fine restaurant if he cannot afford to pay the bill? What good does it do him to be accepted in a hotel that is too expensive for his modest income? How can a Negro child be motivated to take full advantage of integrated educational facilities if he has no hope of getting a job where he can use that education?
>
> Without a job, one cannot afford public convenience and accommodations. Income from employment may be necessary to further a man's education, or that of his children. If his children have no hope of getting a good job, what will motivate them to take advantage of educational opportunities?

These remarks echoed President Kennedy's original message to Congress upon the introduction of the Civil Rights Act in 1963.

> There is little value in a Negro's obtaining the right to be admitted to hotels and restaurants if he has no cash in his pocket and no job.

Accordingly, it was clear to Congress that "the crux of the problem [was] to open employment opportunities for Negroes in occupations which have been traditionally closed to them," (remarks of Sen. Humphrey), and it was to this problem that Title VII's prohibition against racial discrimination in employment was primarily addressed.

It plainly appears from the House Report accompanying the Civil Rights Act that Congress did not intend wholly to prohibit private and voluntary affirmative action efforts as one method of solving this problem. The Report provides:

> No bill can or should lay claim to eliminating all of the causes and consequences of racial and other types of discrimination against minorities. There is reason to believe, however, that national leadership provided by the enactment of Federal legislation dealing with the most troublesome problems *will create an atmosphere conducive to voluntary or local resolution of other forms of discrimination.* 88th Cong, 1st Sess (1963), (Emphasis supplied.)

Given this legislative history, we cannot agree with respondent that Congress intended to prohibit the private sector from taking effective steps to accomplish the goal that Congress designed Title VII to achieve. The very statutory words intended as a spur or catalyst to cause "employers and unions to self-examine and to self-evaluate their employment practices and to endeavor to eliminate, so far as possible, the last vestiges of an unfortunate and ignominious page in this country's history," Albemarle v Moody, ... (1975), cannot be interpreted as an absolute prohibition against all private, voluntary, race-conscious affirmative action efforts to hasten the elimination of such vestiges. It would be ironic indeed if a law triggered by a Nation's concern over centuries of racial injustice and intended to improve the lot of those who had "been excluded from the American dream for so long," (remarks of Sen. Humphrey), constituted the first legislative prohibition of all voluntary, private, race-conscious efforts to abolish traditional patterns of racial segregation and hierarchy.

[1c] Our conclusion is further reinforced by examination of the language and legislative history of § 703(j) of Title VII. Opponents of Title VII raised two related arguments against the bill. First, they argued that the Act would be interpreted to *require* employers with racially imbalanced work forces to grant preferential treatment to racial minorities in order to integrate. Second, they argued that employers with racially imbalanced work forces would grant preferential treatment to racial minorities, even if not required to do so by the Act. See 110 Cong Rec (remarks of Sen Sparkman). Had Congress meant to prohibit all race-conscious affirmative action, as respondent urges, it easily could have answered both objections by providing that Title VII would not require or *permit* racially preferential integration efforts. But Congress did not choose such a course. Rather Congress added § 703(j) which addresses only the first objection. The section provides that nothing contained in Title VII "shall be interpreted to *require* any employer ... to grant preferential treatment ... to any group because of the race ... of such ... group on account of" a de facto racial imbalance in the employer's work force. The section does *not* state that "nothing in Title VII shall be interpreted to *permit*" voluntary affirmative efforts to correct racial imbalances. The natural inference is that Congress chose not to forbid all voluntary race-conscious affirmative action.

The reasons for this choice are evident from the legislative record. Title VII could not have been enacted into law without substantial support from legislators in both Houses who traditionally resisted federal regulation of private business. Those legislators demanded as a price for their support that "management prerogatives and union freedoms ... be left undisturbed to the greatest extent possible. ..." Section 703(j) was proposed by Senator

Dirksen to allay any fears that the Act might be interpreted in such a way as to upset this compromise. The section was designed to prevent § 703 of Title VII from being interpreted in such a way as to lead to undue "Federal Government interference with private businesses because of some Federal employee's ideas about racial balance or imbalance." 110 Cong Rec, (remarks of Sen. Miller). . . . Clearly, a prohibition against all voluntary, race-conscious, affirmative action efforts would disserve these ends. Such a prohibition would augment the powers of the Federal Government and diminish traditional management prerogatives while at the same time impeding attainment of the ultimate statutory goals. In view of this legislative history and in view of Congress' desire to avoid undue federal regulation of private businesses, use of the word "require" rather than the phrase "require or permit" in § 703(j) fortifies the conclusion that Congress did not intend to limit traditional business freedom to such a degree as to prohibit all voluntary, race-conscious affirmative action.

[1d] We therefore hold that Title VII's prohibition in §§ 703(a) and (d) against racial discrimination does not condemn all private, voluntary, race-conscious affirmative action plans.

We need not today define in detail the line of demarcation between permissible and impermissible affirmative action plans. If suffices to hold that the challenged Kaiser-USWA affirmative action plan falls on the permissible side of the line. The purposes of the plan mirror those of the statute. Both were designed to break down old patterns of racial segregation and hierarchy. Both were structured to "open employment opportunities for Negroes in occupations which have been traditionally closed to them." 110 Cong Rec (remarks of Sen. Humphrey.)

[1e] At the same time the plan does not unnecessarily trammel the interests of the white employees. The plan does not require the discharge of white workers and their replacement with new black hires. Cf. McDonald v Santa Fe Trail Trans. Co., supra. Nor does the plan create an absolute bar to the advancement of white employees; half of those trained in the program will be white. Moreover, the plan is a temporary measure; it is not intended to maintain racial balance, but simply to eliminate a manifest racial imbalance. Preferential selection of craft trainees at the Gramercy plant will end as soon as the percentage of black skilled craft workers in the Gramercy plant approximates the percentage of blacks in the local labor force. . . .

We conclude, therefore, that the adoption of the Kaiser-USWA plan for the Gramercy plant falls within the area of discretion left by Title VII to the private sector voluntarily to adopt affirmative action plans designed to eliminate conspicuous racial imbalance in traditionally segregated job categories. Accordingly, the judgment of the Court of Appeals for the Fifth Circuit is reversed.

Mr. Justice **Powell** and Mr. Justice **Stevens** took no part in the consideration or decision of this case.

Mr. Justice ***Blackmun****, concurring.*

While I share some of the misgivings expressed in Mr. Justice Rehnquist's dissent, post, concerning the extent to which the legislative history of Title VII clearly supports the result the Court reaches today, I believe that additional considerations, practical and equitable, only partially perceived, if perceived at all, by the 88th Congress, support the conclusion reached by the Court today, and I therefore join its opinion as well as its judgment.

In his dissent from the decision of the United States Court of Appeals for the Fifth Circuit, Judge Wisdom pointed out that this case arises from a practical problem in the administration of Title VII. The broad prohibition against discrimination places the employer and the union on what he accurately described as a "high tightrope without a net beneath them." 563 F2d 216, 230. If Title VII is read literally on the one hand they face liability for past discrimination against blacks, and on the other hand they face liability to whites for any voluntary preferences adopted to mitigate the effects of prior discrimination against blacks.

In this case, Kaiser denies prior discrimination but concedes that its past hiring practices may be subject to question. Although the labor force in the Gramercy area was approximately 39% black, Kaiser's work force was less than 15% black, and its craft work force was less than 2% black. Kaiser had made some effort to recruit black painters, carpenters, insulators and other craftsmen, but it continued to insist that those hired have five years prior industrial experience, a requirement that arguably was not sufficiently job-related to justify under Title VII any discriminatory impact it may have had. . . .

Respondents' reading Title VII, endorsed by the Court of Appeals, places voluntary compliance with Title VII in profound jeopardy. The only way for the employer and the union to keep their footing on the "tightrope" it creates would be to eschew all forms of voluntary affirmative action. Even a whisper of emphasis on minority recruiting would be forbidden. Because Congress intended to encourage private efforts to come into compliance with Title VII, see Alexander v Gardner-Denver Co. . . . (1974), Judge Wisdom concluded that employers and unions who had committed "arguable violations" of Title VII should be free to take reasonable responses without fear of liability to whites . . . Preferential hiring along the lines of the Kaiser program is a reasonable response for the employer, whether or not a court, on these facts, could order the same step as a remedy. The company is able to avoid identifying victims of past discrimination, and so avoids claims for back pay that would inevitably follow a response limited to such victims. . . .

The "arguable violation" theory has a number of advantages. It responds to a practical problem in the administration of Title VII not anticipated by Congress. It draws predictability from the outline of present law, and closely effectuates the purpose of the Act. Both Kaiser and the United States urge its adoption here. Because I agree that it is the soundest way to approach this case, my preference would be to resolve this litigation by applying it and holding that Kaiser's craft training program meets the requirement that voluntary affirmative action be a reasonable response to an "arguable violation" of Title VII.

The Court, however, declines to consider the narrow "arguable violation" approach and adheres instead to an interpretation of Title VII that permits affirmative action by an employer whenever the job category in question is "traditionally segregated. . . ." The sources cited suggest that the Court considers a job category to be "traditionally segregated" when there has been a societal history of purposeful exclusion of blacks from the job category, resulting in a persistent disparity between the proportion of blacks in the labor force and the proportion of blacks among those who hold jobs within the category.

"Traditionally segregated job categories," where they exist, sweep far more broadly than the class of "arguable violations" of Title VII. The Court's expansive approach is somewhat disturbing for me because, as Mr. Justice Rehnquist points out, the Congress that passed Title VII probably thought it was adopting a principle of nondiscrimination that would apply to blacks and whites alike. While setting aside that principle can be justified where necessary to advance statutory policy by encouraging reasonable responses as a form of voluntary compliance that mitigates "arguable violations," discarding the principle of nondiscrimination where no countervailing statutory policy exists appears to be at odds with the bargain struck when Title VII was enacted.

A closer look at the problem, however, reveals that in each of the principal ways in which the Court's "traditionally segregated job categories" approach expands on the "arguable violations" theory, still other considerations point in favor of the broad standard adopted by the Court, and make it possible for me to conclude that the Court's reading of the statute is an acceptable one.

Mr. Chief Justice ***Burger,*** *dissenting.*

The Court reaches a result I would be inclined to vote for were I a Member of Congress considering a proposed amendment of Title VII. I cannot join the Court's judgment, however, because it is contrary to the explicit language of the statute and arrived at by means wholly incompatible with long-established principles of separation of powers. Under the guise of statutory "construction," the Court effectively rewrites Title VII to achieve what it regards as a desirable result. It "amends" the statute to do precisely what both its sponsors and its opponents agreed the statute was not intended to do.

When Congress enacted Title VII after long study and searching debate, it produced a statute of extraordinary clarity, which speaks directly to the issue we consider in this case. In § 703(d) Congress provided:

> It shall be an unlawful employment practice for any employer, labor organization, or joint labor-management committee controlling apprenticeship or other training or retraining, including on-the-job training programs to discriminate against any individual because of his race, color, religion, sex, or national origin in admission to, or employment in, any program established to provide apprenticeship or other training

Often we have difficulty interpreting statutes either because of imprecise drafting or because legislative compromises have produced genuine ambiguities. But here there is no lack of clarity, no ambiguity. The quota embodied in the collective-bargaining agreement between Kaiser and the Steelworkers unquestionably discriminates on the basis of race against individual employees seeking admission to on-the-job training programs. And, under the plain language of § 703(d), that is "an unlawful employment practice."

Oddly, the Court seizes upon the very clarity of the statute almost as a justification for evading the unavoidable impact of its language. The Court blandly tells us that Congress could not really have meant what it said, for a "literal construction" would defeat the "purpose" of the statute—at least the congressional "purpose" as five Justices divine it today. But how are judges supposed to ascertain the purpose of a statute except through the words Congress used and the legislative history of the statute's evolution? One need not even resort to the legislative history to recognize what is apparent from the face of Title VII—that it is specious to suggest that § 703(j) contains a negative pregnant that permits employers to do what §§ 703(a) and (d) unambiguously and unequivocally forbid employers from doing. Moreover, as Mr. Justice Rehnquist's opinion—which I join—conclusively demonstrates, the legislative history makes equally clear that the supporters and opponents of Title VII reached an agreement about the statute's intended effect. That agreement, expressed so clearly in the language of the statute that no one should doubt its meaning, forecloses the reading which the Court gives the statute today.

Arguably, Congress may not have gone far enough in correcting the effects of past discrimination when it enacted Title VII. The gross discrimination against minorities to which the Court adverts—particularly against Negroes in the building trades and craft unions—is one of the dark chapters in the otherwise great history of the American labor movement. And, I do not question the importance of encouraging voluntary compliance with the purposes and policies of Title VII. But that statute was conceived and enacted to make discrimination against *any* individual illegal, and I fail to see how "voluntary compliance" with the nondiscrimination principle that is the heart and soul of Title VII as currently written will be achieved by permitting employers to discriminate against some individuals to give preferential treatment to others.

Until today, I had thought the Court was of the unanimous view that "discriminatory preference for any group, minority or majority, is precisely and only what Congress has proscribed" in Title VII. Griggs v Duke Power Co., . . . (1971). Had Congress intended otherwise, it very easily could have drafted language allowing what the Court permits today. Far from doing so, Congress expressly prohibited in §§ 703(a) and (d) the discrimination against Brian Weber the Court approves now. If "affirmative action" programs such as the one presented in this case are to be permitted, it is for Congress, not this Court, to so direct.

It is often observed that hard cases make bad law. I suspect there is some truth to that adage, for the "hard" cases always tempt judges to exceed the limits of their authority, as the Court does today by totally rewriting a crucial part of Title VII to reach a desirable result. Cardozo no doubt had this type of case in mind when he wrote:

> The judge, even when he is free, is still not wholly free. He is not to innovate at pleasure. He is not a knight-errant, roaming at will in pursuit of his own ideal of beauty or of goodness. He is to draw his inspiration from consecrated principles. He is not to yield to spasmodic sentiment, to vague and unregulated benevolence. He is to exercise a discretion informed by tradition, methodized by analogy, disciplined by system, and subordinated to 'the primordial necessity of order in the social life.' Wide enough in all conscience is the field of discretion that remains. B. Cardozo, *The Nature of the Judicial Process* 141 (1921).

What Cardozo tells us is beware the "good result," achieved by judicially authorized or intellectually dishonest means on the appealing notion that the desirable ends justify the improper judicial means. For there is always the danger that the seeds of precedent sown by good men for the best of motives will yield a rich harvest of unprincipled acts of others also aiming at "good ends."

Mr. Justice ***Rehnquist,*** *with whom The* ***Chief Justice*** *joins, dissenting.*

In a very real sense, the Court's opinion is ahead of its time: it could more appropriately have been handed down five years from now, in 1984, a year coinciding with the title of a book from which the Court's opinion borrows, perhaps subconsciously, at least one idea. Orwell describes in his book a governmental official of Oceania, one of the three great world powers, denouncing the current enemy, Eurasia, to an assembled crowd:

> "It was almost impossible to listen to him without being first convinced and then maddened. . . .
>
> The speech had been proceeding for perhaps twenty minutes when a messenger hurried onto the platform and a scrap of paper was slipped into the speaker's hand. He unrolled and read it without pausing in his speech. Nothing altered in his voice or manner, or in the content of what he was saying, but suddenly the names were different. Without words said, a wave of understanding rippled through the crowd. Oceania was at war with Eastasia! . . . The banners and posters with which the square was decorated were all wrong! . . .
>
> "[T]he speaker had switched from one line to the other actually in mid-sentence, not only without a pause, but without even breaking the syntax." G. Orwell, *Nineteen Eighty-Four,* 182–183 (1949).

Today's decision represents an equally dramatic and equally unremarked switch in this Court's interpretation of Title VII.

The operative sections of Title VII prohibit racial discrimination in employment simpliciter. Taken in its normal meaning, and as understood by all Members of Congress who spoke to the issue during the legislative debates, . . . this language prohibits a covered employer from considering race when making an employment decision, whether the race be black or white. Several years ago, however, a United States District Court held that "the dismissal of white employees charged with misappropriating company property while not dismissing a similarly charged Negro employee does not raise a claim upon which Title VII relief may be granted." McDonald v Santa Fe Trail Transp. Co., . . . (1976). This Court unanimously reversed, concluding from the "uncontradicted legislative history" that "Title VII prohibits racial discrimination against the white petitioners in this case upon the same standards as would be applicable were they Negroes. . . ."

We have never waivered in our understanding that Title VII "prohibits *all* racial discrimination in employment, without exception for any particular employees." . . . In Griggs v Duke Power Co., . . . (1971), our first occasion to interpret Title VII, a unanimous court observed that "[d]iscriminatory preference, for any group, minority or majority, is precisely and only what Congress has proscribed." And in our most recent discussion of the issue, we uttered words seemingly dispositive of this case: "It is clear beyond cavil that the obligation imposed by Title VII is to provide an equal opportunity for *each* applicant regardless of race, without regard to whether members of the applicant's race are already proportionately represented in the work force." Furnco Construction Corp. v Waters, . . . (1978) (emphasis in original).

Today, however, the Court behaves much like the Orwellian speaker earlier described, as if it had been handed a note indicating that Title VII would lead to a result unacceptable to the Court if interpreted here as it was in our prior decisions. Accordingly, without even a break in syntax, the Court rejects "a literal construction of § 703(a)" in favor of newly discovered "legislative history," which leads it to a conclusion directly contrary to that compelled by the "uncontradicted legislative history" unearthed in McDonald and our other prior decisions. Now we are told that the legislative history of Title VII shows that employers are free to discriminate on the basis of race: an employer may, in the Court's words, "trammel the interests of white employees" in favor of black employees in order to eliminate "racial imbalance." . . . Our earlier interpretations of Title VII, like the banners and posters decorating the square in Oceania, were all wrong.

As if this were not enough to make a reasonable observer question this Court's adherence to the oftstated principle that our duty is to construe rather than rewrite legislation, United States v Rutherford, . . . (1979), the Court also seizes upon § 703(j) of Title VII as an independent, or at least partially independent, basis for its holding. Totally ignoring the wording of that section, which is obviously addressed to those charged with the responsibility of interpreting the law rather than those who are subject to its proscriptions, and totally ignoring the months of legislative debates preceding the section's introduction and passage, which demonstrate clearly that it was enacted to prevent precisely what occurred in this case, the Court infers from § 703(j) that "Congress chose not to forbid all voluntary race-conscious affirmative action."

Thus, by a tour de force reminiscent not of jurists such as Hale, Holmes, and Hughes, but of escape artists such as Houdini, the Court eludes clear statutory language, "uncontradicted" legislative history, and uniform precedent in concluding that employers are, after all, permitted to consider race in making employment decisions. It may be that one or more of the principal sponsors of Title VII would have preferred to see a provision allowing preferential treatment of minorities written into the bill. Such a provision, however, would have to have been expressly or impliedly excepted from Title VII's explicit prohibition on all racial discrimination in employment. There is no such exception in the Act. And a reading of the legislative debates concerning Title VII, in which proponents and opponents alike uniformly denounced discrimination in favor of, as well as discrimination against, Negroes, demonstrates clearly that any legislator harboring an unspoken desire for such a provision could not possibly have succeeded in enacting it into law.

Is Turn About Fair Play?

BARRY R. GROSS

. . . The balance of argument weighs against reverse discrimination for four interrelated sets of reasons. First, the procedures designed to isolate the discriminated are flawed. Second, the practice has undesirable and dangerous consequences. Third, it fails to fit any of the models of compensation or reparations. Fourth, it falls unjustly upon both those it favors and those it disfavors. I conclude that if to eliminate discrimination against the members of one group we find ourselves discriminating against another, we have gone too far.

Sociologically, groups are simply not represented in various jobs and at various levels in percentages closely approximating their percentage of the population. When universities in general and medical schools in particular discriminated heavily against them, Jews were represented in the medical profession in far greater percentages than their percentage of the population. At the same time, they were represented in far lower percentages in banking, finance, construction, and engineering than their percentage in the population, especially the population of New York City. A similar analysis by crudely drawn group traits—Jew, Roman Catholic, WASP, Irish, and so forth—of almost any trade, business or profession would yield similar results.

But the argument from population percentages may be meant not as an analysis of what is the case, but as an analysis of what ought to be the case. A proponent might put it this way: It is true that groups are not usually represented in the work force by their percentage in the population at large, but minority C has been systematically excluded from the good places. Therefore, in order to make sure that they get some of them, we should

From *Reverse Discrimination,* ed. Barry R. Gross (Buffalo, N.Y.: Prometheus Books, 1977); reprinted from the *Journal of Critical Analysis,* Vol. 5 (Jan.-Apr. 1975).

systematically include them in the good places, and a clear way of doing it is by their percentage in the population. Or we might conclude instead: therefore, in order to make up for past exclusion, they should be included in the good places as reparation, and an easy way to do it is by their percentage in the population.

If the definition of a minority discriminated against is ipso facto their representation in certain jobs in percentages less than their percentage in the general population, then one has to remark that the reasoning is circular. For we are trying to prove: (1) that minority C is discriminated against.

We use a premise (3) that minority C is underrepresented in good jobs. Since (1) does not follow from (3) (mere underrepresentation not being even prima facie evidence of discrimination), it is necessary to insert (2) that their underrepresentation is due to discrimination. But this completes the circle.

A critic might reply that we know perfectly well what is meant. The groups discriminated against are blacks, Puerto Ricans, Mexican-Americans, American Indians, and women. He is correct, though his answer does not tell us *how to find out* who is discriminated against. This critic, for example, left out Jews and Orientals. If he should reply that Jews and Orientals do well enough, we point out that the question was not "Who fails to do well?" but rather, "Who is discriminated against?" This argument shows that the mechanisms for identifying the victims of discrimination and for remedying it are seriously deficient.

Even if we allow that the percentage of the group in the work force versus its percentage in the population is the criterion of discrimination, who is discriminated against will vary depending upon how we divide the groups. We may discover that Republicans are discriminated against by our literary or intellectual journals—*New York Review, Dissent, Commentary.* We may also discover that wealthy Boston residents are discriminated against by the Los Angeles Dodgers, that women are discriminated against by the Army, and that idiots (we hope) are discriminated against by universities.

What employment or profession a person chooses depends upon a number of variables—background, wealth, parents' employment, schooling, intelligence, drive, ambition, skill, and not least, luck. Moreover, the analysis will differ depending upon what group identification or stratification you choose. None seems to have priority over the others. Every person can be typed according to many of these classifications. It seems, therefore, that the relevant analysis cannot even be made, much less justified.

In addition, some proponents of the population-percentage argument seem to hold: (4) From the contingent fact that members of the group C were discriminated against, it follows necessarily that they are underrepresented in the good positions. They then go on to assert (5) if members of group C were not discriminated against they would not be underrepresented, or (6) if they are underrepresented, then they are discriminated against.

But clearly (4) is itself a contingent, not a necessary truth. Clearly also neither (5) nor (6) follows from it, (5) being the fallacy of denying the antecedent and (6) the fallacy of affirming the consequent. Lastly, neither

(5) nor (6) is necessarily true. The members of a group might simply lack interest in certain jobs (for example, Italians in the public-school system are in short supply). Could one argue that, even though neither (4), (5), nor (6) is *necessarily* true, the mere fact of underrepresentation in certain occupations does provide evidence of discrimination? The answer is no—no more than the fact of "overrepresentation" in certain occupations is evidence of favoritism.

At most, underrepresentation can be used to support the contention of discrimination when there is *other* evidence as well.

FAIR PLAY: OUGHT WE TO DISCRIMINATE IN REVERSE?

There are at least three difficulties with reverse discrimination: first, it is inconsistent; second, it licenses discrimination; third it is unfair.

If we believe the principle that equal opportunity is a right of everyone, then if members of group C are excluded from enjoying certain opportunities merely because they are members of group C, their right is being abrogated. They are entitled to this right, but so is everybody else, even those persons who presently deny it to them. If both are made to enjoy equal opportunity, then both are enjoying their right. To give either oppressors or oppressed more than equal opportunity is equally to deny the rights of one or the other in violation of the principle of equal opportunity.

Proponents of reverse discrimination seem to be caught on the horns of a dilemma: either discrimination is illegitimate or it is not. If it is illegitimate, then it ought not to be practiced against anyone. If it is not, then there exists no reason for *now* favoring blacks, Puerto Ricans, Chicanos, Indians, women, and so forth over whites.

Two strategies present themselves. Either we can analyze one disjunct with a view to showing that distinctions can be made which require compensation or reparations in the form of reverse discrimination to be made to wronged individuals or groups; or we can try to soften one of the disjuncts so as to make a case for exceptions in favor of the wronged. The first appeals both to our reason and our sense of justice. The second appeals to our emotions. I shall argue that neither strategy works.[1]

Now reverse discrimination can take several forms, but I think that what many of its proponents have in mind is a strong form of compensation —a form which requires us to discriminate against non-C members and favor C members even if less qualified. One may well wonder whether there is not a little retribution hidden in this form of compensation.

THE "SOFTENED" GENERAL PRINCIPLE

The argument for construing reverse discrimination as compensation or reparation has a great appeal which can be brought out by contrasting it with another approach. One might agree that as a general rule reverse discrimination is illegitimate but that it need not be seen as universally illegitimate.

In particular, in the case where people have been so heavily discriminated against as to make it impossible for them now to gain a good life, there is no possibility of their having a fair chance, no possibility of their starting out on anything like equal terms, then and only then is it legitimate to discriminate in their favor and hence against anyone else.

Against this "softened" general principle I shall urge two sorts of objections which I call respectively "practical" and "pragmatic." Against the reparations type of argument, I shall urge first that there is some reason to think the conditions for exacting and accepting them are lacking, and second that, owing to the peculiar nature of the reparations to be exacted (reverse discrimination), the very exaction of them is unreasonable and unfair to both parties—exactors and exactees.

I mention briefly two sorts of practical objections to the "softened" general principle. First, it is simply the case that when discrimination is made in favor of someone regardless of his qualifications, there is the greatest possible danger that the person getting the position will not be competent to fill it. Second, when a person is placed in a position because of discrimination in his favor, he may come to feel himself inferior.[2] This may easily lead to the permanent conferral of inferior status on the group, an inferiority which is all the stronger because self-induced. Its psychological effects should not be underestimated.

The pragmatic objection to the "softened" general principle is much stronger. Discrimination in any form is invidious. Once licensed, its licenses rebound upon its perpetrators as well as others. Principles tend to be generalized without consideration of restrictions or the circumstances to which they were intended to apply. Students of the Nazi movement will have noticed that in licensing the discrimination, isolation, persecution, and "final solution" of the Jews, the Nazis (foreign and German) licensed their own. (Hitler's plans for extermination included political groups, for example, the Rohm faction of the SA, as well as other racial groups, for example, Slavs and Balts who fought on the German side.) It is necessary to be quite careful what principles one adopts. In view of the long and bloody history of discrimination, one ought to be very chary of sanctioning it.

COMPENSATIONS, REPARATIONS, AND RESTITUTION

Because it escapes most of these objections, the reparations argument becomes very attractive. What is more obvious than the principle that people ought to be compensated for monetary loss, pain and suffering inflicted by others acting either as agents of government or as individuals? From the negligence suit to reparations for war damage, the principle is comfortable, familiar, and best of all, legal. For victims of broken sidewalks, open wells, ignored stop signs, the conditions under which damages are awarded are quite clear. (1) There is specific injury, specific victim, specific time and place. (2) A specific individual or set of individuals must be found responsible either (a) by actually having done the injury, or (b) by failing to act in such a way (for example, repairing the sidewalk, sealing the well) so as to remove a particular potential source of injury on their property. (3) A reasonable assessment of the monetary value of the claim can be made. In such cases no moral blame is attached to the person forced to pay compensation.

But reparations are somewhat less clear. How much does Germany owe France for causing (losing?) World War I? Can we say that *Germany* caused the war? Germany did pay, at least in part, based upon rough calculations of the cost of the Allied armies, including pensions, the loss of allied GNP, indemnities for death and for the destruction of property. . . .

INAPPLICABILITY OF THESE PARADIGMS

Can reverse discrimination be construed to fit any of these paradigms? Can favoring blacks, Chicanos, Indians, women, and so forth over whites or males be seen as compensation, reparations, or restitution? The answer is no for two general reasons and for several which are specific to the various paradigms. The general reasons are, first, that responsibility for discrimination past and present and for its deleterious consequences is neither clearly assigned nor accepted. Some seem to think that the mere fact of its existence makes all whites (or males in the case of antifeminism) responsible.[3] But I do not know an analysis of responsibility which bears out this claim. Second, there is a great difficulty, if not an impossibility, in assigning a monetary value to the damage done and compensation allegedly owed—that is to say, reverse discrimination.

If we turn to the negligence paradigm, all the conditions seem to fail. *Specific* injury is lacking, *specific* individual responsibility is lacking, and there is no way to assess the monetary value of the "loss." Indeed, in the case of reverse discrimination it is not monetary value which is claimed but preferential treatment. Under the large-scale reparations paradigm two conditions beyond responsibility are lacking. There are no governments or government-like agencies between which the transfer could take place, and there is no *modus agendi* for the transfer to take place.

Where the transfer is to be of preferential treatment, it is unclear how it is even to be begun. So we come to the third paradigm: individual restitution. This is much closer, for it deals with compensating individual victims of persecution. Again, however, it fails to provide a model, first, because reverse discrimination cannot be looked at in monetary terms, and second, even if it could, the restitution is designed to bring a person back to where he was before deprivation. In the case of the minorities in question, there can be no question of restoring them to former positions or property. Precisely, the point of the reparation is to pay them for what they, because of immoral social practices, never had in the first place. . . .

JUSTICE

Finally, if we ignore all that has been said and simply go ahead and discriminate in reverse, calling it reparation, it remains to ask whether it would be either reasonable or just? I think the answer is no. It is possible to hold that in some set of cases, other things being equal, compensation is required and yet to argue either that since other things are not equal compensation is not required, or that even if some compensation is required it ought not to take the form of reverse discrimination. Certainly, from the fact that some form of compensation or reparation must be made it does not follow that any *specific* form of compensation is in order. If X is discriminated against in awarding professorships because he is a member of C group, it scarcely follows that if compensation is in order it *must* take the form of his being discriminated in favor of for another professorship, at least not without adopting the principle of "an eye for an eye" (and only an *eye* for an eye?). Consider X being turned down for an apartment because he is a C member. Must compensation consist just in his being offered another ahead of anybody else? Even if he has one already? To go from the relatively innocuous principle that where *possible* we ought to compensate for damages, to sanction reverse discrimination as the proper or preferred form of redress, requires us to go beyond mere compensation to some principle very much like "let the punishment mirror the crime." But here the person "punished," the person from which the compensation is exacted, is often not the "criminal." Nor will it help to say that the person deprived of a job or advancement by reverse discrimination is not really being punished or deprived, since the job did not belong to him in the first place. Of course it didn't; nor did it belong to the successful candidate. What belonged to both is equal consideration, and that is what one of them is being deprived of.[4]

There is an element of injustice or unfairness in all reparations. The money derived from taxes paid by all citizens is used for reparations regardless of whether they were responsible for, did nothing about, opposed, or actually fought the policies or government in question. Yet we say that this is the only way it can be done, that the element of unfairness is not great, and that on the whole it is better that this relatively painless way of appropriating money from Jones, who is innocent, be used than that the victims of persecution or crime go uncompensated. But the consequences of reverse discrimination are quite different, especially when it is based upon group membership rather than individual desert. It is possible and is sometimes the case that though most C members are discriminated against, Y is a C member who has met with no discrimination at all. Under the principle that all C members should be discriminated in favor of, we would offer "compensation" to Y. But what are we compensating him *for?* By hypothesis he was no victim of discrimination. Do we compensate him for what happened to others? Do we pay Jones for what we buy from Smith? We seem to be compensating him for being a C member, but why? Do we secretly hold C members inferior? Some claim that society as a whole must bear the burden of reparation. But then reverse discrimination will hardly do the trick. It does not exact redress from the government, or even from all white (responsible?) citizens equally, but falls solely against those who apply for admissions, or jobs *for which blacks or other minorities are applying at the same time.* By the same token, it does not compensate or "reparate" all minority persons equally but merely those applying for admission, jobs, promotions, and so forth. Those whose positions are secure would not be paid. A white person who fought for civil rights for blacks may be passed over for promotion or displaced, a victim of reverse discrimination, while a Ku Klux Klan man at the top of the job ladder pays nothing. This would be a laughably flawed system if it were not seriously advocated by responsible people, and partly implemented by the government. Surely, it violates the principles of both compensatory and distributive justice.

NOTES

1. For examples of these strategies, see the article by J. W. Nickel . . . herein.
2. *Contra* this objection see Irving Thalberg, "Justifications of Institutional Racism," *The Philosophical Forum,* Winter 1972.
3. See Thalberg. For an interesting catalogue of "irresponsible use of 'responsibility' " see Robert Stover, "Responsibility for the Cold War—A Case Study in Historical Responsibility," *History and Theory,* 1972. For a clear-cut analysis that more than mere presence on the scene is required to show responsibility, see S. Levinson, "Responsibility for Crimes of War," *Philosophy and Public Affairs,* Spring 1973.
4. See Gertrude Ezorsky, "It's Mine," *Philosophy and Public Affairs,* Spring 1974.

A Defense of Programs of Preferential Treatment

RICHARD WASSERSTROM

Many justifications of programs of preferential treatment depend upon the claim that in one respect or another such programs have good consequences or that they are effective means by which to bring about some desirable end, e.g., an integrated, equalitarian society. I mean by "programs of preferential treatment" to refer to programs such as those at issue in the *Bakke* case—programs which set aside a certain number of places (for example, in a law school) as to which members of minority groups (for example, persons who are non-white or female) who possess certain minimum qualifications (in terms of grades and test scores) may be preferred for admission to those places over some members of the majority group who possess higher qualifications (in terms of grades and test scores).

Many criticisms of programs of preferential treatment claim that such programs, even if effective, are unjustifiable because they are in some important sense unfair or unjust. In this paper I present a limited defense of such programs by showing that two of the chief arguments offered for the unfair-

Richard Wasserstrom, "A Defense of Programs of Preferential Treatment," *Phi Kappa Phi Journal,* LVIII (Winter 1978), based in part on Part III of "Racism, Sexism, and Preferential Treatment: An Approach to the Topics," which appeared in 24 U.C.L.A. Law Review, 581 (1977).

ness or injustice of these programs do not work in the way or to the degree supposed by critics of these programs.

The first argument is this. Opponents of preferential treatment programs sometimes assert that proponents of these programs are guilty of intellectual inconsistency, if not racism or sexism. For, as is now readily acknowledged, at times past employers, universities, and many other social institutions did have racial or sexual quotas (when they did not practice overt racial or sexual exclusion), and many of those who were most concerned to bring about the eradication of those racial quotas are now untroubled by the new programs which reinstitute them. And this, it is claimed, is inconsistent. If it was wrong to take race or sex into account when blacks and women were the objects of racial and sexual policies and practices of exclusion, then it is wrong to take race or sex into account when the objects of the policies have their race or sex reversed. Simple considerations of intellectual consistency—of what it means to give racism or sexism as a reason for condemning these social policies and practices—require that what was a good reason then is still a good reason now.

The problem with this argument is that despite appearances, there is no inconsistency involved in holding both views. Even if contemporary preferential treatment programs which contain quotas are wrong, they are not wrong for the reasons that made quotas against blacks and women pernicious. The reason why is that the social realities do make an enormous difference. The fundamental evil of programs that discriminated against blacks or women was that these programs were a part of a larger social universe which systematically maintained a network of institutions which unjustifiably concentrated power, authority, and goods in the hands of white male individuals, and which systematically consigned blacks and women to subordinate positions in the society.

Whatever may be wrong with today's affirmative action programs and quota systems, it should be clear that the evil, if any, is just not the same. Racial and sexual minorities do not constitute the dominant social group. Nor is the conception of who is a fully developed member of the moral and social community one of an individual who is either female or black. Quotas which prefer women or blacks do not add to an already relatively overabundant supply of resources and opportunities at the disposal of members of these groups in the way in which the quotas of the past did maintain and augment the overabundant supply of resources and opportunities already available to white males.

The same point can be made in a somewhat different way. Sometimes people say that what was wrong, for example, with the system of racial discrimination in the South was that it took an irrelevant characteristic, namely race, and used it systematically to allocate social benefits and burdens of various sorts. The defect was the irrelevance of the characteristic used—race—for that meant that individuals ended up being treated in a manner that was arbitrary and capricious.

I do not think that was the central flaw at all. Take, for instance, the most hideous of the practices, human slavery. The primary thing that was wrong with the institution was not that the particular individuals who were assigned the place of slaves were assigned there arbitrarily because the assignment was made in virtue of an irrelevant characteristic, their race. Rather, it seems to me that the primary thing that was and is wrong with slavery is the practice itself—the fact of some individuals being able to own other individuals and all that goes with that practice. It would not matter by what criterion individuals were assigned; human slavery would still be wrong. And the same can be said for most if not all of the other discrete practices and institutions which comprised the system of racial discrimination even after human slavery was abolished. The practices were unjustifiable—they were oppressive—and they would have been so no matter how the assignment of victims had been made. What made it worse, still, was that the institutions and the supporting ideology all interlocked to create a system of human oppression whose effects on those living under it were as devastating as they were unjustifiable.

Again, if there is anything wrong with the programs of preferential treatment that have begun to flourish within the past ten years, it should be evident that the social realities in respect to the distribution of resources and opportunities make the difference. Apart from everything else, there is simply no way in which all of these programs taken together could plausibly be viewed as capable of relegating white males to the kind of genuinely oppressive status characteristically bestowed upon women and blacks by the dominant social institutions and ideology.

The second objection is that preferential treatment programs are wrong because they take race or sex into account rather than the only thing that does matter—that is, an individual's qualifications. What all such programs have in common and what makes them all objectionable, so this argument goes, is that they ignore the persons who are more qualified by bestowing a preference on those who are less qualified in virtue of their being either black or female.

There are, I think, a number of things wrong with this objection based on qualifications, and not the least of them is that we do not live in a society in which there is even the serious pretense of a qualification requirement for many jobs of substantial power and authority. Would anyone claim, for example, that the persons who comprise the judiciary are there because they are the most qualified lawyers or the most qualified persons to be judges? Would anyone claim that Henry Ford II is the head of the Ford Motor Company because he is the most qualified person for the job? Part of what is wrong with even talking about qualifications and merit is that the argument derives some of its force from the erroneous notion that we would have a meritocracy were it not for programs of preferential treatment. In fact, the higher one goes in terms of prestige, power and the like, the less qualifications seem ever to be decisive. It is only for certain jobs and certain places that qualifications are used to do more than establish the possession of certain minimum competencies.

But difficulties such as these to one side, there are theoretical difficulties as well which cut much more deeply into the argument about qualifications. To begin with, it is important to see that there is a serious inconsistency present if the person who favors "pure qualifications" does so on the ground that the most qualified ought to be selected because this promotes maximum efficiency. Let us suppose that the argument is that if we have the most qualified performing the relevant tasks we will get those tasks done in the most economical and efficient manner. There is nothing wrong in principle with arguments based upon the good consequences that will flow from maintaining a social practice in a certain way. But it is inconsistent for the opponent of preferential treatment to attach much weight to qualifications on this ground, because it was an analogous appeal to the good consequences that the opponent of preferential treatment thought was wrong in the first place. That is to say, if the chief thing to be said in favor of strict qualifications and preferring the most qualified is that it is the most efficient way of getting things done, then we are right back to an assessment of the different consequences that will flow from different programs, and we are far removed from the considerations of justice or fairness that were thought to weigh so heavily against these programs.

It is important to note, too, that qualifications—at least in the educational context—are often not connected at all closely with any plausible conception of social effectiveness. To admit the most qualified students to law school, for example—given the way qualifications are now determined—is primarily to admit those who have the greatest chance of scoring the highest grades at law school. This says little about efficiency except perhaps that these students are the easiest for the faculty to teach. However, since we know so little about what constitutes being a good, or even successful lawyer, and even less about the correlation between being a very good law student and being a very good lawyer, we can hardly claim very confidently that the legal system will operate most effectively if we admit only the most qualified students to law school.

To be at all decisive, the argument for qualifications must be that those who are the most qualified deserve to receive the benefits (the job, the place in law school, etc.) because they are the most qualified. The introduction of the concept of desert now makes it an objection as to justice or fairness of the sort promised by the original criticism of the programs. But now the problem is that there is no reason to think that there is any strong sense of "desert" in which it is correct that the most qualified deserve anything.

Let us consider more closely one case, that of preferential treatment in respect to admission to college or graduate school. There is a logical gap in the inference from the claim that a person is most qualified to perform a task, e.g., to be a good student, to the conclusion that he or she deserves to be admitted as a student. Of course, those who deserve to be admitted should be admitted. But why do the most qualified deserve anything? There is simply no necessary connection between academic merit (in the sense of being most qualified) and deserving to be a member of a student body. Suppose, for instance, that there is only one tennis court in the community. Is it clear that the two best tennis players ought to be the ones permitted to use it? Why not those who were there first? Or those who will enjoy playing the most? Or those who are the worst and, therefore, need the greatest opportunity to practice? Or those who have the chance to play least frequently?

We might, of course, have a rule that says that the best tennis players get to use the court before the others. Under such a rule the best players would deserve the court more than the poorer ones. But that is just to push the inquiry back on stage. Is there any reason to think that we ought to have a rule giving good tennis players such a preference? Indeed, the arguments that might be given for or against such a rule are many and varied. And few if any of the arguments that might support the rule would depend upon a connection between ability and desert.

Someone might reply, however, that the most able students deserve to be admitted to the university because all of their earlier schooling was a kind of competition, with university admission being the prize awarded to the winners. They deserve to be admitted because that is what the rule of the competition provides. In addition, it might be argued, it would be unfair now to exclude them in favor of others, given the reasonable expectations they developed about the way in which their industry and performance would be rewarded. Minority-admission programs, which inevitably prefer some who are less qualified over some who are more qualified, all possess this flaw.

There are several problems with this argument. The most substantial of them is that it is an empirically implausible picture of our social world. Most of what are regarded as the decisive characteristics for higher education have a great deal to do with things over which the individual has neither control nor responsibility: such things as home environment, socioeconomic class of parents, and, of course, the quality of the primary and secondary schools attended. Since individuals do not deserve having had any of these things vis-à-vis other individuals, they do not, for the most part, deserve their qualifications. And since they do not deserve their abilities they do not in any strong sense deserve to be admitted because of their abilities.

To be sure, if there has been a rule which connects say, performance at high school with admission to college, then there is a weak sense in which those who do well at high school deserve, for that reason alone, to be admitted to college. In addition, if persons have built up or relied upon their reasonable expectations concerning performance and admission, they have a claim to be admitted on this ground as well. But it is certainly not obvious that these claims of desert are any stronger or more compelling than the competing claims based upon the needs of or advantages to women or blacks from programs of preferential treatment. And as I have indicated, all rule-based claims of desert are very weak unless and until the rule which creates the claim is itself shown to be a justified one. Unless one has a strong preference for the status quo, and unless one can defend that preference, the practice within a system of allocating places in a certain way does not go very far at all in showing that that is the right or the just way to allocate those places in the future.

A proponent of programs of preferential treatment is not at all committed to the view that qualifications ought to be wholly irrelevant. He or she can agree that, given the existing structure of any institution, there is probably some minimal set of qualifications without which one cannot participate meaningfully within the institution. In addition, it can be granted that the qualifications of those involved will affect the way the institution works and the way it affects others in the society. And the consequences will vary depending upon the particular institution. But all of this only establishes that qualifications, in this sense, are relevant, not that they are decisive. This is wholly consistent with the claim that race or sex should today also be relevant when it comes to matters such as admission to college or law school. And that is all that any preferential treatment program—even one with the kind of quota used in the *Bakke* case—has ever tried to do.

I have not attempted to establish that programs of preferential treatment are right and desirable. There are empirical issues concerning the consequences of these programs that I have not discussed, and certainly not settled. Nor, for that matter, have I considered the argument that justice may permit, if not require, these programs as a way to provide compensation or reparation for injuries suffered in the recent as well as distant past, or as a way to remove benefits that are undeservedly enjoyed by those of the dominant group. What I have tried to do is show that it is wrong to think that programs of preferential treatment are objectionable in the centrally important sense in which many past and present discriminatory features of our society have been and are racist and sexist. The social realities as to power and opportunity do make a fundamental difference. It is also wrong to think that programs of preferential treatment could, therefore, plausibly rest both on the view that such programs are not unfair to white males (except in the weak, rule-dependent sense described above) and on the view that it is unfair to continue the present set of unjust—often racist and sexist—institutions that comprise the social reality. And the case for these programs could rest as well on the proposition that, given the distribution of power and influence in the United States today, such programs may reasonably be viewed as potentially valuable, effective means by which to achieve admirable and significant social ideals of equality and integration.

Classification by Race in Compensatory Programs

JAMES W. NICKEL

Suppose that a person who favors compensatory programs for American blacks because of America's history of slavery and discrimination is charged with inconsistency in the following way: "When blacks are denied benefits and given heavier burdens because of race you claim that race is irrelevant and hence claim that discrimination is being practiced.[1] But when racial

From *Ethics,* Vol. 84 (1974); © 1974 by the University of Chicago. Reprinted by permission of the author and the publisher, The University of Chicago Press.

classifications are used to give preferential treatment to blacks you claim that race is a relevant consideration and deny that this is reverse discrimination." I want to consider two replies that can be made to this charge of inconsistency. The first reply holds that race, the characteristic which is held to be irrelevant when blacks are mistreated, is not the characteristic which is being held to be relevant when compensatory programs are defended. This reply denies that race is the basis for compensation; it claims that the real basis is the wrongs and losses blacks have suffered and the special needs that they have. Hence the characteristic which is held to be relevant in connection with compensatory programs is not race but a different characteristic, and there is no inconsistency. I will call this the "different-characteristics reply." The second reply allows that race is the characteristic about which differing relevance claims are made, but it denies that there is any inconsistency since claiming that race is irrelevant to whether someone should be mistreated is not incompatible with claiming that race is relevant to whether someone should be helped. Different issues are involved, and what is relevant to one issue can be irrelevant to another. I will call this the "different-issues reply."

This reply claims that there is no inconsistency in condemning racial discrimination while favoring compensatory programs for blacks because race, the characteristic which is held to be irrelevant when blacks are mistreated, is not the characteristic which is the basis for providing compensation to blacks. And since race is not the basis for compensatory programs, it need not be claimed that race is relevant in such contexts. The reason for providing compensatory programs for blacks is not their race but the fact that they have been victimized by slavery and discrimination. Not race, but the wrongs that were done, the losses that were suffered and the special needs resulting from these provide the basis for special treatment now. On this view, race is not held to be relevant in defending compensatory programs, and hence there is no inconsistency with the original claim that race is irrelevant to how people should be treated.[2]

I think this reply is helpful in many cases, but in cases where explicit racial classifications are used by compensatory programs, the person who takes this approach must either claim that such explicit racial classifications are unjustifiable or suggest that they are an unavoidable administrative expediency. To suggest the latter is to suggest that this is a case where the administrative basis for a program (i.e., the characteristic which is used by administrators to decide who is to be served by the program) is different from the justifying basis (i.e., the characteristic which is the reason for having the program). It is not uncommon for these two to differ, although they should overlap substantially. If the justifying basis is a characteristic which occurs in more individuals than the characteristic which is the administrative basis, the latter is underinclusive. And if the justifying basis is a characteristic which occurs in fewer individuals than the characteristic which is the administrative basis, the latter is overinclusive. When resources are limited it is not uncommon to use an underinclusive administrative basis (e.g., when a poverty program only serves those with an income of less than

$2,000 per year), even though this forces the program to ignore deserving cases. And difficulties in identifying those with the characteristic which is the justifying basis may cause the program, for reasons of efficiency, to serve more people than those who have the characteristic which is the justifying basis (e.g., when everyone in a certain county—the administrative basis—is inoculated in order to eliminate a disease—the justifying basis—which 60 percent of the people have but which is difficult to detect except in advanced stages).[3]

The advocate of the "different-characteristics reply" is committed to denying that race is the justifying basis for compensatory programs. But if the justifying basis for such programs is the losses and needs resulting from slavery and discrimination there will be a high correlation between being black and having suffered these losses and having these needs, and because of this the advocate of this reply can allow, without inconsistency, that race can serve as part of the administrative basis for such a program. Efficiency in administering large-scale programs often requires that detailed investigations of individual cases be kept to a minimum, and this means that many allocative decisions will have to be made on the basis of gross but easily discernible characteristics. This may result in a certain degree of unfairness, but it does help to decrease administrative costs so that more resources can be directed to those in need. Programs designed to help victims of discrimination are probably of this sort. Since it is usually quite difficult to determine the extent to which a person has suffered from racial discrimination, it may be necessary simply to take the susceptibility to this discrimination (and perhaps some other gross criterion such as present income) as the basis for allocation. The use of such an administrative basis would result in a certain degree of both over and underinclusiveness, but in most cases this degree would probably not be an intolerable one from the perspective of fairness and efficiency.

This reply to the charge of inconsistency ignores possible differences in the characteristic which is the justifying basis; it presupposes, as does the person making the charge of inconsistency, that race is the justifying basis for compensatory programs. This reply claims that even if race is held to be irrelevant when blacks are being mistreated and relevant when blacks are being helped, there is no inconsistency in this since different issues are involved, and a characteristic which is relevant to one issue is often irrelevant to another. Relevance involves a relation between a characteristic and an issue, *C* is relevant to *I*, and because of this "C_1 is relevant to I_1" is not inconsistent with "C_1 is not relevant to I_2."

But for this reply to work it must be shown that there really are two issues here, that the issue of deciding whether to allocate a penalty or loss is a different issue from deciding whether to allocate a benefit. This seems to be what Mark Green is suggesting in his article, "Reparations for Blacks," when he says, "It is a verbal gimmick to elide past prejudice with preferential treatment. A subsidy is obviously dissimilar to a penalty, a beneficiary different from a victim, although both fit under the discrimination rubric."[4] Green seems to hold that the crucial difference is between subsidies and penalties, between helping and harming, and that it is the fact that racial classifications are used in compensatory programs to do good that makes them permissible. Green's view seems to be that it is one thing to use race as a basis for doing harm but quite another to use it as a basis for providing help.

But is there a sufficient difference between deciding to allocate a subsidy and deciding to allocate a penalty or loss to enable us to say that different issues are being decided and that race can be relevant to the former and irrelevant to the latter? The best reason I have been able to discover for thinking that there is a sufficient difference derives from the fact that the allocation of losses and penalties is a much more dangerous enterprise than the allocation of help and benefits. Deciding to impose a penalty or loss involves making a person worse off, whereas deciding not to provide a benefit usually involves merely leaving a person as he is. Since the former decision involves weightier consequences in most cases, we may be inclined to allow that it is a different decision than the latter and to allow that different considerations can be relevant to the two issues. This will be to claim that because of this difference there are and should be tighter moral and legal restriction on grounds that can serve as a basis for distributing penalties and losses, and that even though it is impermissible to use race as the basis for imposing losses and penalties, it is permissible to use race as the basis for distributing benefits.

One problem with putting so much weight on the distinction between distributing benefits and distributing penalties and losses is that in many cases a single distribution does both. If the item which is being allocated is a scarce and important benefit (like a good job), giving it to one person will often be tantamount to denying it to another person with an equally good claim to it, and denying it to this person will often be a considerable loss to him. Here the allocative decision concerns both providing a benefit and causing a loss, and hence one cannot merely say that race is a permissible basis for the decision because it is a decision about whom to help. If in a situation like this we decide to help Jones because he is black, this may be tantamount to causing Smith to suffer a loss because he is nonblack. Cases like this do exist,[5] and in these cases the "different-issues" approach provides no help.

Leaving this problem aside, there is another difficulty with the "different-issues reply." Even if it is allowed that what is relevant to the distribution of a benefit is sometimes different from what is relevant to the distribution of penalties and losses, it still remains to be shown that race is the justifying basis for programs which provide special help to blacks. If this cannot be shown then one must fall back on the claim that race is only the administrative basis for such programs.

So the question that we must ask is whether race or ancestry as such can serve as a justifying basis for a program which distributes benefits rather than many burdens. And I am inclined to think that it cannot. The mere fact that many people in this country are of African ancestry does not in itself provide any justification for a program of benefits to these people—no more than the mere fact that many people in California are of Oklahoman ancestry provides a justifying basis for a program of benefits to them. One's race or ancestry could serve as a justifying basis for special benefits only if having this race or ancestry was, in itself, a special merit which deserved reward or special lack which required compensation. But unless one is prepared to return to racist and aristocratic principles, one must deny that one's race or ancestry is in itself a matter of special merit or special lack. And hence one must deny that race or ancestry, in itself, can serve as a justifying basis for a program of special benefits.

It might be replied, however, that this overlooks important aspects of the context. In a context where the members of one race have over a long period been subject to discrimination and mistreatment it might be argued that race can be the justifying basis for a program of benefits. I think, however, that as soon as one begins to emphasize the wrongs done to blacks, the losses they have suffered, and the special needs they have now, it becomes clear that these things are the justifying basis for help to blacks and not race per se.

Suppose, however, that the person making this reply continues by asserting that in this period in America so many people think that being black is a special defect or lack that in effect it is a special defect or lack which requires compensation. But again one must insist that it is not race itself that justifies compensation; it is rather the effects of people's misconceptions about race that do this. Race or ancestry in itself constitutes no merit or defect; it is only in combination with people's misconceptions about it that it can aspire to this status. It is the adverse effects of these misconceptions, not race per se, that provide the justifying basis for special help programs. Race simply is not plausible as a justifying basis for a program, even for a program of benefits.

If I am right about this the "different-issues reply" turns out not to be helpful since it presupposes that race is the justifying basis for compensatory programs. Unless some other option emerges, the defender of compensatory programs will have to use the "different-characteristics reply" to the charge of inconsistency. This view allows that race can sometimes serve as the administrative basis for programs but makes its use contingent on considerations of fairness and efficiency. Whether race or ancestry can serve as a reasonable administrative basis (or a part of such a basis) for a program designed to provide special benefits to victims of slavery and discrimination will depend on whether among the possible alternatives it is the classification which is most workable and involves the combination of over- and underinclusiveness which is least unfair.

NOTES

1. There are two senses of "discrimination." One of these is morally neutral and applies to the simple discernment of differences. The other implies moral disapproval and applies to differentiations which involve bias, prejudice, and the use of irrelevant characteristics. My concern here is with "discrimination" in the latter sense.

2. This is the position that I took in my article, "Discrimination and Morally Relevant Characteristics," *Analysis* 32 (1972): 113–14. Also see J. L. Cowan's reply, "Inverse Discrimination," *Analysis* 33 (1972): 10–12.
3. The distinction between over-and underinclusive classifications is derived from Tussman and tenBroek, "The Equal Protection of the Laws," *California Law Review* 37 (1949): 341.
4. "Reparations for Blacks," *Commonweal* 90 (June 1969): 359. In saying that both subsidies and penalties "fit under the discrimination rubric," Green seems to overlook the connection between discrimination and the use of an irrelevant characteristic. He seems, that is, to slip into using the morally neutral sense when it is the other sense of "discrimination" that is in question.
5. See, for example, Bob Kuttner, "White Males and Jews Need Not Apply," *The Village Voice,* August 31, 1972.

ENVIRONMENTAL ISSUES

Case Study—Three Mile Island

It began with a brief but terrible bump in the night and quickly grew into the worst commercial nuclear accident in U.S. history. At the Three Mile Island power plant near Harrisburg, Pa., a balky valve malfunctioned, setting off an intricate chain of mechanical and human failures. In the control room of the plant's Unit II, warning lights flashed and an electronic alarm rang. Craig Faust, 32, and Ed Frederick, 29, working the night shift, studied the alarms and meters as the plant veered toward a state of emergency. They kept their heads, pushed and pulled as many as 50 buttons and levers in fifteen seconds and the reactor shut down. "What we saw we understood and we controlled," Frederick said. But it wasn't enough.

Within minutes, there was a serious leak of radioactive steam—and several more in the days following—spreading over an area up to 20 miles from the plant. Many experts agreed that the radiation posed no immediate threat to health, but others warned of cancer, genetic damage and other long-term effects from the low-level emissions.

'TIME BOMB': Pennsylvania Gov. Richard Thornburgh considered a mass evacuation of parts of four surrounding counties. Instead, he advised people to stay inside their homes, then urged pregnant women and preschool children to move beyond a 5-mile radius of the plant. In Middletown, Goldsboro, Harrisburg and other surrounding towns, few panicked. But schools closed, families packed up and gasoline stations did a brisk business as an estimated 50,000 to 60,000 people headed away, for the weekend at least. "I just get the feeling we're all sitting on a time bomb," said Louise Hardison of Londonderry Township. "It's rotten—the whole thing is rotten."

The episode came precariously close to turning into Everyman's nuclear nightmare—an out-of-control reactor spewing radioactivity into the countryside. At the weekend, there was still a distant possibility that the chain of events could take a nightmarish turn. Unless engineers were able to cool the crippled reactor, said Joseph M. Hendrie, the chairman of the

Nuclear Regulatory Commission, it might still be necessary to evacuate thousands of people living 10 to 20 miles downwind of the plant. "They are way out in an unknown land with a reactor whose instruments and controls were never designed to cope with this situation," said MIT professor Henry Kendall, an outspoken nuclear critic. "They are like children playing in the woods."

There was no danger that the plant would explode like a nuclear bomb, but there were other possibilities nearly as apocalyptic. The problem was to cool the reactor. But damage suffered by its radioactive core in the first moments of the accident interfered with the cooling process, and the high heat spread the damage to up to half the 36,816 nuclear fuel rods. A gas bubble inside the reactor vessel also threatened to block the circulation of water around the rods. To make matters worse, highly flammable hydrogen gas was accumulating inside the huge containment structure that holds the reactor, posing the threat of a conventional explosion that could scatter dangerous radioactive gas and debris widely through the area.

The greatest risk of all was a catastrophic "meltdown" of the sort fictionalized in a . . . film called "The China Syndrome." In theory, the experts said, the core could melt its way through the thick steel walls of the reactor vessel, penetrate the floor of the containment structure, contaminate the soil or hit a water pocket and send up gushers of radioactive steam and contaminants. If that happened, there might be thousands of deaths later on. "There is some risk of meltdown," Dr. Roger Mattson of the NRC told members of a Senate subcommittee on nuclear regulation last week.

Officials of the Metropolitan Edison Co., operators of the plant, consistently down-played the seriousness of the situation, and their accounts often disagreed with those of staff members from the NRC who were rushed to the scene. Radioactive steam apparently vented automatically—and uncontrollably. Government officials were not alerted in advance, raising complaints that the monitoring by Met-Ed and government agencies was so haphazard that the cumulative radiation absorbed by people in the vicinity might never be known. Beyond that, the General Accounting Office reported that Pennsylvania—like most states with nuclear facilities—did not have a federally approved plan for dealing with such on-site emergencies. And the GAO said there was no single Federal Agency that could direct the mass evacuation that might be prompted by a major disaster.

'DECISIONS': Industry officials insisted that the accident, as bad as it was, showed that safety systems did indeed prevent any immediate injuries or deaths. "We didn't injure anybody, we didn't seriously contaminate anybody and we certainly didn't kill anybody," said John Herbein, a Met-Ed vice president. . . .

* * *

Under the circumstances, the public fallout from the accident was bound to have a lengthy half-life of its own. "Every dose of radiation is an overdose," said Nobel Prize-winning biochemist George Wald, professor emeritus at Harvard. Protestors duly went on the march from New England to southern California. . . . And in Washington, the NRC itself came under attack. "Three Mile Island has had a very short operating period but a very long and troubled history," said Richard Pollock, head of Critical Mass, a Ralph Naderite group. "The NRC let this plant go forward despite the red flags which were waving. They look—but they do not see."

CASH: In the beginning, it looked like Three Mile Island would generate nothing more menacing than megawatts. Completed in 1974 on a forested little island in the Susquehanna River, it replaced a small farm and a few cabins used by fishermen. Most local residents welcomed it because Federal economizing had closed nearby Olmstead Air Force Base, punching a hole in the local economy. With their high pay and overtime, men hired at the new plant could earn between $25,000 and $35,000 a year. In sleepy Middletown, workers coming off their shift began to fill Mat's Wining Wench tavern with good company and clinking cash. When people asked the watering hole's owner whether the new plant made him nervous, he said: "What happens, happens."

There appeared to be nothing to be nervous about: the plant seemed a marvel of advanced technology. Unit I and Unit II each had a reactor with a core of 36,816 fuel rods sheathed in zirconium and containing pellets of uranium oxide. The reactor produced heat by nuclear fission. Giant pumps pushed water heated by the reactor to two towering steam generators. Within the generators, the heat from each reactor's pressurized water loop was "exchanged" through tiny tubes to a second independent water loop that produced steam. This steam drove turbines that turned generators that sent 880,000 kilowatts of electricity humming out over high-tension wires to the 346,000 residents of Berks, York and Lebanon counties.

'INCIDENTS': The plant was fitted out with multiple fail-safe protective systems. The core of the reactor was sealed in a 41-foot-high vessel with walls of steel 8 7/16ths inches thick. This awesome tube stood within a containment dome 190 feet high and 140 feet across. The dome, with its massive walls of concrete 4 feet thick over a sheathing of carbonized steel, would hold in the fiercest radiation. In an emergency in the reactor core, the industry's scientific experts predicted, several cooling systems could flood the core, in effect turning the containment into a nuclear hot-water bottle that could be drained slowly and safely if the plant suffered what nuclear engineers often call nuclear "incidents."

No one expected any trouble at Three Mile Island. But when Unit II plugged into the northeastern power grid for full commercial operations on Dec. 30, 1978, it promptly developed a number of worrisome bugs. In mid-January, it had to be shut down for almost two weeks after two safety valves ruptured during a test of the turbine. On Feb. 1, a throttle valve developed a leak. The next day, a heater pump blew a seal. On Feb. 6, a pump on a feedwater line tripped off. All the difficulties were promptly repaired, though the reason the feedwater pump had stuttered remained something of a mystery.

ALARMS: Similar trouble apparently returned to haunt the plant last week. Early Wednesday, at about 4 A.M., Unit II was generating at 97 per cent capacity, with the third shift manning the controls and machinery. "Somebody was screwing around with some of the equipment in the feedwater system," said Edson Case, deputy director of nuclear-reactor regulation for the NRC. "Whatever he was doing resulted in tripping the feedwater pumps off the line." Ordinarily, when the feedwater pumps go off, the turbine shuts down and the reactor cuts back on power. This time the turbine perfomed normally but the reactor did not. Heat and pressure in the reactor's primary water loop began to rise above normal operating levels (582 degrees Fahrenheit and 2,155 pounds per square inch pressure)—and alarms in the control room began to flash and beep.

When the pressure hit 2,350 psi, about 200 pounds above normal, the reactor automatically "scrammed"—its boron control rods dropped down into the core to "poison" and finally shut down the fission process. There was never any danger of a nuclear explosion. "A reactor is not like a bottled-up bomb," says Mark Mills of the Atomic Industrial Forum, an industry group. "It won't explode. It can't run away like a fire."

Officials at Three Mile Island denied that the malfunction could have melted the core enough to produce the China syndrome—so named because the fiercely hot molten core eats its way into the floor of the containment building and straight through the earth below. It may stop about 50 feet down, cool into a glassy blob and emit intense radiation in all directions—or hit the water table and throw back a deadly radioactive geyser.

VALVE: It didn't happen last week, but the Three Mile Island syndrome was unsettling enough in itself. As utility and NRC officials piece things together, the scrammed reactor kept producing residual heat from the decay of fission products in its core. Heat and pressure in the primary water loop then mounted until a relief valve in a pressurizer opened, allowing the excess water to flow safely into a quench tank. But, instead of shutting off again, the valve stuck open. Water surged through the stuck relief valve, filled the quench tank and flooded out onto the floor of the reactor containment building. Water pressure in the primary loop then fell dangerously low. The main cooling pumps were shut off. An emergency cooling system kicked in, injecting still more water into the loop. It, too, flooded through the valve and out of the quench tank.

"Now things get conjectural," Case said. He speculated that while the emergency core-cooling system was on, a technician may have watched the water pressure build up—then turned off the system manually, thinking the crisis had passed. When the system was turned off, the water pressure in the loop fell again. "Whether he was right is not clear; whether he should have turned it back on again later is not clear," Case said. "But in any event, it was turned off for a long enough period of time that the pressure went back down again. At that point—and we're guessing—the water level got low enough that the core became uncovered, at least momentarily."

A hot and uncovered core is the nuclear engineer's nightmare. The best guess last week was that the heat grew severe enough to burst the protective zirconium cladding of some of the fuel rods. Radioactive elements—xenon and krypton gases—could then have contaminated water in the primary loop. This "hot" hot water then flowed out the relief valve through the broken quench tank and into the containment area. In very short order, there were 6 feet of radioactive water on the containment floor, clouds of deadly steam billowing to the roof and a "shine" of gamma radiation passing directly through the walls.

SUMP: Plant operators said that the containment system had functioned properly. "There is no way the water could escape through the walls," said Frederick, because the walls were secure. But escape it did—the only question was how. Ordinarily, safety systems shut off all pipes into the containment building when the emergency core-cooling system is on. NRC investigators speculated last week that when the emergency core-cooling system was turned off, a basement sump pump was activated, pumping thousands of gallons of radioactive water out of the containment building into tanks in an auxiliary building never meant to contain high-intensity radiation. Utility officials conceded that the pump had indeed gone into operation. At least one of the tanks overflowed onto the floor of the auxiliary building—and radioactivity shot through a vent stack. . . .

The results were disturbing. The monitors detected between 20 and 30 millirems of radiation per hour in the atmosphere over the island and 5 to 7 millirems (or about one-eighth of the dose in a chest X-ray) in the air 2 to 3 miles away. Radioactivity traveled 20 miles on winds that shifted from southeast to northwest. Maggie Reilly, chief of the environmental radiation unit of Pennsylvania's DER, said the most radiation anyone in the plant's vicinity had received was 100 millirems at the time of the accident. That added up to half the annual exposure for an average U.S. citizen—in a single flash—but it was still one-tenth of the level the U.S. Environmental Protection Agency considers immediately dangerous. Later, it turned out that four plant employees received mild overdoses of gamma radiation.

Met-Ed officials, trying earnestly to calm the growing crisis, only created more confusion and anxiety. "We aren't at the China syndrome level," plant spokesman William Gross said, but a few hours later, Met-Ed official Don Curry said: "We concede that it's not just a little thing." The same day, Sen. Gary Hart of Colorado, head of the Senate nuclear regulation subcommittee, arrived for an inspection. Hart told reporters that three key questions would need further investigation: Had Met-Ed recognized the emergency quickly enough? Did Unit II have inherent design flaws? Were the plant's systems adequate to handle a large overflow of radioactive water? Gov. Richard Thornburgh was more soothing: "There is no reason to disrupt your daily routine," he told Pennsylvanians late that afternoon, "nor any reason to feel that the public health has been affected by events on Three Mile Island."

But that reassurance faded on the next day, when the reactor failed to cool down as quickly as expected and new puffs of radiation escaped from the hot plant. One meter picked up 1,200 millirems per hour in a steam plume above the plant site; ground levels shot up to 25 millirems within a

3-mile radius. For a moment, Governor Thornburgh considered evacuating parts of four counties around the plant. After consulting the NRC and Met-Ed, he decided instead to advise residents to stay indoors and close their windows. He received a phone call from President Carter. "He was concerned that there be no panic, that there be no going off half-cocked," Thornburgh said. He later urged the evacuation of all pre-school toddlers and pregnant women within 5 miles of the plant. "There is no reason to panic," he said. But the alarm was palpable . . . and a small exodus was soon under way.

'A BIG BALLOON': Back at the plant, the immediate task was to cool down a very hot reactor. Dozens of engineers and more than 50 workers, clad in raincoats over white protective suits and equipped with scuba-like breathing gear or gas masks, desperately tried to shrink the bubble of gas trapped in the top of the reactor vessel. "You have to be very careful about the method you use to bring the reactor to a cold shutdown position," said Harold R. Denton, nuclear-reactor regulation director for the NRC—who arrived at the plant as President Carter's personal man on the scene. Reducing vessel pressure to cool the reactor would also allow the bubble to expand. "It's like a big balloon," said one worried Met-Ed official. If the bubble grew too large, it could block the flow of coolant or drive water levels down far enough to expose the damaged core—raising the risk of a meltdown. None of the available solutions looked very attractive and all took time. "If there were a clear choice, it wouldn't take us this long to decide," said the NRC's Case. The first option was to continue slowly to cool the reactor, venting small amounts of the gas bubble through a pressurizer valve with the cooling water. The risk was that the process was so slow that oxygen and hydrogen might build up and explode. Another idea was to "purge" the reactor vessel with oxygen in the hope that it would combine with the hydrogen in the bubble to form water. But safety experts estimated that tactic could take up to 30 days. A third option was to turn on the emergency core-cooling system and attempt to blow the bubble out through the coolant pipes, but enough water might be lost to raise the risk of a meltdown.

Given the manifest dangers, NRC chairman Joseph M. Hendrie said it was possible that all residents in a wedge-shaped area 10 to 20 miles downwind of the plant might be evacuated before any attempt was made to do something about the bubble. "It may turn out to be a prudent, precautionary measure," said Hendrie. "We wouldn't necessarily at all wait for a demonstrated disaster."

. . . The ripples of the accident also promised to spread a long way. In New England, the Clamshell Alliance organized vigils at the Seabrook, Maine Yankee and Millstone nuclear power plants. The Clamshellers also planned to leaflet California Gov. Jerry Brown when he visited the New Hampshire legislature this week to argue for a balanced Federal budget. The complaint: that Brown has not been hard enough on the Diablo Canyon nuclear plant being constructed in his state. In Austin, Texas, where voters have narrowly approved referendums on the proposed South Texas Nuclear Project five times in the past, a sixth vote next week hung in the balance after the accident at Three Mile Island. "It hurt—it hurt bad," complained John Rogers of the Committee for Economic Energy, a pro-nuclear group.

The accident did nothing to ease the Carter Administration's rough passage through the energy crunch. Energy Secretary James Schlesinger, a nuclear advocate, said sunnily that the accident "underscores how safe nuclear [energy] has been in the past." That reassured no one, and it seemed likely Congress would look doubly hard at Administration plans for funding a revamped breeder-reactor program and for speeding up the regulatory process for licensing a nuclear plant. It can now take up to a dozen years to license and build. Sen. Edward Kennedy, chairman of the House-Senate Joint Economic Committee's subcommittee on energy, shot off a tart letter to Schlesinger attacking the license speed-up. "It's more important to build these plants safely than to build them quickly," he said. Carter himself told a group of editors that the incident "will make all of us reassess our present safety regulations . . . and will probably lead inexorably toward even more stringent safety-design mechanisms and standards."

Whether the shock of the accident would jolt citizens and elected officials into broader action remained to be seen. The Government Accounting Office released the final draft of a report to Congress calling for the expansion of emergency planning zones around nuclear plants to a radius of 10 miles. So far only ten states—Pennsylvania not among them—have federally approved peacetime nuclear-emergency plans. The lapse alarmed critics. Robert D. Pollard, a former staffer of the NRC, charged that problems similar to those that touched off the accident at Three Mile Island had turned up at Rancho Seco in California, Oconee Units I, II and III in South Carolina, Davis-Besse Unit I in Ohio, Crystal River Unit III in Florida and Arkansas Nuclear One-I and One-II. "If anyone had been paying attention, Three Mile Island wouldn't have happened," he said.

Now that it has, the nation is in an exceptionally difficult energy bind. Every form of energy production involves risks. Coal, the chief alternative to nuclear power, has already claimed thousands of lives in mining accidents, and air pollution is a serious health menace. There isn't enough available oil and natural gas to carry the load, and solar energy for electricity is still years away.

Both Schlesinger and Carter were counting on more nuclear plants to reduce America's dependence on imported oil. They will try to keep on that course, undoubtedly coupled with tighter safety regulations. But anti-nuclear forces, backed now by a more worried populace, will be more potent than ever. Meltdowns and millirems are now part of America's vocabulary—and it remains to be seen whether the industry can recover from the nightmare that almost was.

The Case for Economic Growth

WILFRED BECKERMAN

For some years now it has been very unfashionable to be in favor of continued long-run economic growth. Unless one joins in the chorus of scorn for the pursuit of continued economic growth, one is in danger of being treated either as a coarse Philistine, who is prepared to sacrifice all the things that make life really worth living for vulgar materialist goods, or as a short-sighted, complacent, Micawber who is unable to appreciate that the world is living on the edge of a precipice. For it is widely believed that if growth is not now brought to a halt in a deliberate orderly manner, either there will be a catastrophic collapse of output when we suddenly run out of key raw materials, or we shall all be asphyxiated by increased pollution. In other words, growth is either undesirable or impossible, or both. Of course, I suppose this is better than being undesirable and inevitable, but the anti-growth cohorts do not seem to derive much comfort from the fact. . . .

Hence it is not entirely surprising that the antigrowth movement has gathered so much support over the past few years even though it is 99 per cent nonsense. Not 100 per cent nonsense. There does happen to be a one per cent grain of truth in it.

This is that, in the absence of special government policies (policies that governments are unlikely to adopt if not pushed hard by communal action from citizens), pollution will be excessive. This is because—as economists have known for many decades—pollution constitutes what is known in the jargon as an "externality." That is to say, the costs of pollution are not always borne fully—if at all—by the polluter. The owner of a steel mill that belches smoke over the neighborhood, for example, does not usually have to bear the costs of the extra laundry, or of the ill-health that may result. Hence, although he is, in a sense, "using up" some of the environment (the clean air) to produce his steel he is getting this particular factor of production free of charge. Naturally, he has no incentive to economize in its use in the same way as he has for other factors of production that carry a cost, such as labor or capital. In all such cases of "externalities," or "spillover effects" as they are sometimes called, the normal price mechanism does not operate to achieve the socially desirable pattern of output or of exploitation of the environment. This defect of the price mechanism needs to be corrected by governmental action in order to eliminate excessive pollution.

But, it should be noted that the "externality" argument, summarized above, only implies that society should cut out "excessive" pollution; not *all* pollution. Pollution should only be cut to the point where the benefits from reducing it further no longer offset the costs to society (labor or capital costs) of doing so.

Mankind has always polluted his environment, in the same way that he has always used up some of the raw materials that he has found in it. When

Wilfred Beckerman, "The Case for Economic Growth," *Public Utilities Fortnightly,* Sept. 26, 1974, abridged and reprinted by permission of the publisher.

primitive man cooked his meals over open fires, or hunted animals, or fashioned weapons out of rocks and stones, he was exploiting the environment. But to listen to some of the extreme environmentalists, one would imagine that there was something immoral about this (even though God's first injunction to Adam was to subdue the earth and every living thing that exists in it). If all pollution has to be eliminated we would have to spend the whole of our national product in converting every river in the country into beautiful clear-blue swimming pools for fish. Since I live in a town with a 100,000 population but without even a decent swimming pool for the humans, I am not prepared to subscribe to this doctrine.

Anyway, most of the pollution that the environmentalists make such a fuss about, is not the pollution that affects the vast mass of the population. Most people in industrialized countries spend their lives in working conditions where the noise and stench cause them far more loss of welfare than the glamorous fashionable pollutants, such as PCB's or mercury, that the antigrowth lobby make such a fuss about. Furthermore, such progress as has been made over the decades to improve the working conditions of the mass of the population in industrialized countries has been won largely by the action of working-class trade unions, without any help from the middle classes that now parade so ostentatiously their exquisite sensibilities and concern with the "quality of life."

The extreme environmentalists have also got their facts about pollution wrong. In the Western world, the most important forms of pollution are being reduced, or are being increasingly subjected to legislative action that will shortly reduce them. In my recently published book ("*In Defense of Economic Growth*")[1] I give the facts about the dramatic decline of air pollution in British cities over the past decade or more, as well as the improvement in the quality of the rivers. I also survey the widespread introduction of antipollution policies in most of the advanced countries of the world during the past few years, which will enable substantial cuts to be made in pollution. By comparison with the reductions already achieved in some cases, or envisaged in the near future, the maximum pollution reductions built into the computerized calculations of the Club of Rome[2] can be seen to be absurdly pessimistic.

The same applies to the Club of Rome's assumption that adequate pollution abatement would be so expensive that economic growth would have to come to a halt. For example, the dramatic cleaning up of the air in London cost a negligible amount per head of the population of that city. And, taking a much broader look at the estimates, I show in my book that reductions in pollution many times greater than those which the Club of Rome purports to be the upper limits over the next century can, and no doubt will, be achieved over the next decade in the advanced countries of the world at a cost of only about one per cent to 2 per cent of annual national product.

When confronted with the facts about the main pollutants, the antigrowth lobby tends to fall back on the "risk and uncertainty" argument. This takes the form, "Ah yes, but what about all these new pollutants, or what about undiscovered pollutants? Who knows, maybe we shall only learn in a 100 years' time, when it will be too late, that they are deadly." But life is full of risk and uncertainty. Every day I run the risk of being run over by an automobile or hit on the head by a golf ball. But rational conduct requires that I balance the probabilities of this happening against the costs of insuring against it. It would only be logical to avoid even the minutest chance of some catastrophe in the future if it were costless to do so. But the cost of stopping economic growth would be astronomic. This cost does not merely comprise the loss of any hope of improved standards of living for the vast mass of the world's population, it includes also the political and social costs that would need to be incurred. For only a totalitarian regime could persist on the basis of an antigrowth policy that denied people their normal and legitimate aspirations for a better standard of living.

But leaving aside this political issue, another technical issue which has been much in the public eye lately has been the argument that growth will be brought to a sudden, and hence catastrophic, halt soon on account of the impending exhaustion of raw material supplies. This is the "finite resources" argument; i.e., that since the resources of the world are finite, we could not go on using them up indefinitely.

Now resources are either finite or they are not. If they are, then even zero growth will not save us in the longer run. Perhaps keeping Gross National Product at the present level instead of allowing it to rise by, say, 4 per cent per annum, would enable the world's resources to be spread out for 500 years instead of only 200 years. But the day would still come when we would run out of resources. (The Club of Rome's own computer almost gave the game away and it was obliged to cut off the printout at the point where it becomes clear that, even with zero growth, the world eventually begins to run out of resources!) So why aim only at zero growth? Why not cut output? If resources are, indeed, finite, then there must be some optimum rate at which they should be spread out over time which will be related to the relative importance society attaches to the consumption levels of different generations. The "eco-doomsters" fail to explain the criteria that determine the optimum rate and why they happen to churn out the answer that the optimum growth rate is zero.

And if resources are not, after all, finite, then the whole of the "finite resources" argument collapses anyway. And, in reality, resources are not finite in any meaningful sense. In the first place, what is now regarded as a resource may not have been so in the past decades or centuries before the appropriate techniques for its exploitation or utilization had been developed. This applies, for example, to numerous materials now in use but never heard of a century ago, or to the minerals on the sea bed (e.g., "manganese nodules"), or even the sea water itself from which unlimited quantities of certain basic minerals can eventually be extracted.

In the second place, existing known reserves of many raw materials will never appear enough to last more than, say, twenty or fifty years at current rates of consumption, for the simple reason that it is rarely economically worthwhile to prospect for more supplies than seem to be salable, at prospective prices, given the costs of exploitation and so on. This has always been the case in the past, yet despite dramatic increases in consumption, supplies have more or less kept pace with demand. The "finite resource" argument fails to allow for the numerous ways that the economy and society react to changes in relative prices of a product, resulting from changes in the balance between supply and demand.

For example, a major United States study in 1929 concluded that known tin resources were only adequate to last the world ten years. Forty years later, the Club of Rome is worried because there is only enough to last us another fifteen years. At this rate, we shall have to wait another century before we have enough to last us another thirty years. Meanwhile, I suppose we shall just have to go on using up that ten years' supply that we had back in 1929.

And it is no good replying that demand is growing faster now than ever before, or that the whole scale of consumption of raw materials is incomparably greater than before. First, this proposition has also been true at almost any time over the past few thousand years, and yet economic growth continued. Hence, the truth of such propositions tells us nothing about whether the balance between supply and demand is likely to change one way or the other. And it is this that matters. In other words, it may well be that demand is growing much faster than ever before, or that the whole scale of consumption is incomparably higher, but the same applies to supply. For example, copper consumption rose about fortyfold during the nineteenth century and demand for copper was accelerating, around the turn of the century, for an annual average growth rate of about 3.3 per cent per annum (over the whole century) to about 6.4 per cent per annum during the period 1890 to 1910. Annual copper consumption had been only about 16,000 tons at the beginning of the century, and was about 700,000 tons at the end of it; i.e., incomparably greater. But known reserves at the end of the century were greater than at the beginning.

And the same applies to the postwar period. In 1946 world copper reserves amounted to only about 100 million tons. Since then the annual rate of copper consumption has trebled and we have used up 93 million tons. So there should be hardly any left. In fact, we now have about 300 million tons!

Of course, it may well be that we shall run out of some individual materials; and petroleum looks like one of the most likely candidates for exhaustion of supplies around the end of this century—if the price did not rise (or stay up at its recent level). But there are two points to be noted about this. First, insofar as the price does stay up at its recent level (i.e., in the $10 per barrel region) substantial economies in oil use will be made over the next few years, and there will also be a considerable development of substitutes for conventional sources, such as shale oil, oil from tar sands, and new ways of using coal reserves which are, of course, very many times greater than oil reserves (in terms of common energy units).

Secondly, even if the world did gradually run out of some resources it would not be a catastrophe. The point of my apparently well-known story about "Beckermonium" (the product named after my grandfather who failed to discover it in the nineteenth century) is that we manage perfectly well without it. In fact, if one thinks about it, we manage without infinitely more products than we manage with! In other words, it is absurd to imagine that if, say, nickel or petroleum had never been discovered, modern civilization would never have existed, and that the eventual disappearance of these or other products must, therefore, plunge us back into the Dark Ages.

The so-called "oil crisis," incidentally, also demonstrates the moral hypocrisy of the antigrowth lobby. For leaving aside their mistaken interpretation of the technical reasons for the recent sharp rise in the oil price (i.e., it was not because the world suddenly ran out of oil), it is striking that the antigrowth lobby has seized upon the rise in the price of oil as a fresh argument for abandoning economic growth and for rethinking our basic values and so on. After all, over the past two or three years the economies of many of the poorer countries of the world, such as India, have been hit badly by the sharp rise in the price of wheat. Of course, this only means a greater threat of starvation for a few more million people in backward countries a long way away. That does not, apparently, provoke the men of spiritual and moral sensibility to righteous indignation about the values of the growth-oriented society as much as does a rise in the price of gasoline for our automobiles!

The same muddled thinking is behind the view that mankind has some moral duty to preserve the world's environment or supplies of materials. For this view contrasts strangely with the antigrowth lobby's attack on materialism. After all, copper, oil, and so on are just material objects, and it is difficult to see what moral duty we have to preserve indefinitely the copper species from extinction.

Nor do I believe that we have any overriding moral duty to preserve any particular animal species from extinction. After all, thousands of animal species have become extinct over the ages, without any intervention by mankind. Nobody really loses any sleep over the fact that one cannot now see a live dinosaur. How many of the people who make a fuss about the danger that the tiger species may disappear even bother to go to a zoo to look at one? And what about the web-footed Beckermanipus, which has been extinct for about a million years. . . .

In fact, I am not even sure that the extinction of the human race would matter. The bulk of humanity lead lives full of suffering, sorrow, cruelty, poverty, frustration, and loneliness. One should not assume that because nearly everybody has a natural animal instinct to cling to life they can be said, in any meaningful sense, to be better off alive than if they had never been born. Religious motivations apart, it is arguable that since, by and large (and present company excepted, of course), the human race stinks, the sooner it is extinct the better. . . .

Whilst economic growth alone may never provide a simple means of solving any of these problems, and it may well be that, by its very nature, human society will always create insoluble problems of one kind or another, the absence of economic growth will only make our present problems a lot worse.

NOTES

1. Jonathan Cape, London. The U.S.A. edition, under the title *"Two cheers for the Affluent Society,"* was published by the St. Martins Press in the fall of 1974.
2. The Club of Rome is an informal international organization of educators, scientists, economists, and others which investigates what it conceives to be the overriding problems of mankind. Its study, "The Limits to Growth," has become the bible of no-growth advocates (Potomac Associates, 1707 L Street, N.W., Washington, D.C., $2.75). The study assembled data on known reserves of resources and asked a computer what would happen if demand continued to grow exponentially. Of course, the computer replied everything would break down. The theory of "Beckermonium" lampoons this. Since the author's grandfather failed to discover "Beckermonium" by the mid-1800's, the world has had no supplies of it at all. Consequently, if the club's equations are followed, the world should have come to a halt many years ago. "Beckermonium's" foundation is that the things man has not yet discovered are far more numerous and of greater importance than what has been discovered. (Editor's of *Public Utilities Fortnightly* Note.)

The Scarcity Society

WILLIAM OPHULS

. . . For the past three centuries, we have been living in an age of abnormal abundance. The bonanza of the New World and other founts of virgin resources, the dazzling achievements of science and technology, the availability of "free" ecological resources such as air and water to absorb the waste products of industrial activities, and other lesser factors allowed our ancestors to dream of endless material growth. Infinite abundance, men reasoned, would result in the elevation of the common man to economic nobility. And with poverty abolished, inequality, injustice, and fear—all those flowers of evil alleged to have their roots in scarcity—would wither away. Apart from William Blake and a few other disgruntled romantics, or the occasional pessimist like Thomas Malthus, the Enlightenment ideology of progress was shared by all the West. The works of John Locke and Adam Smith, the two men who gave bourgeois political economy its fundamental direction, are shot through with the assumption that there is always going to be more—more land in the colonies, more wealth to be dug from the ground, and so on. Virtually all the philosophies, values, and institutions typical of modern capitalist society—the legitimacy of self-interest, the primacy of the individual and his inalienable rights, economic laissez-faire, and democracy as we know it—are the luxuriant fruit of an era of apparently endless abundance. They cannot continue to exist in their current form once we return to the more normal condition of scarcity.

Worse, the historic responses to scarcity have been conflict—wars fought to control resources, and oppression—great inequality of wealth and the political measures needed to maintain it. The link between scarcity and oppression is well understood by spokesmen for underprivileged groups and nations, who react violently to any suggested restraint in growth of output.

Our awakening from the pleasant dream of infinite progress and the abolition of scarcity will be extremely painful. Institutionally, scarcity demands that we sooner or later achieve a full-fledged "steady-state" or "spaceman" economy. Thereafter, we shall have to live off the annual income the earth receives from the sun, and this means a forced end to our kind of abnormal affluence and an abrupt return to frugality. This will require the strictest sort of economic and technological husbandry, as well as the strictest sort of political control.

The necessity for political control should be obvious from the use of the spaceship metaphor: political ships embarked on dangerous voyages need philosopher-king captains. However, another metaphor—the tragedy of the commons—comes even closer to depicting the essence of the ecopolitical dilemma. The tragedy of the commons has to do with the uncontrolled self-seeking in a limited environment that eventually results in competitive overexploitation of a common resource, whether it is a commonly owned field on which any villager may graze his sheep, or the earth's atmosphere into which producers dump their effluents.

Francis Carney's powerful analysis of the Los Angeles smog problem indicates how deeply all our daily acts enmesh us in the tragic logic of the commons:

> Every person who lives in this basin knows that for twenty-five years he has been living through a disaster. We have all watched it happen, have participated in it with full knowledge. . . . The smog is the result of ten million individual pursuits of private gratification. But there is absolutely nothing that any individual can do to stop its spread. . . . An individual act of renunciation is now nearly impossible, and, in any case, would be meaningless unless everyone else did the same thing. But he has no way of getting everyone else to do it.

If this inexorable process is not controlled by prudent and, above all, timely political restraints on the behavior that causes it, then we must resign ourselves to ecological self-destruction. And the new political structures that seem required to cope with the tragedy of the commons (as well as the imperatives of technology) are going to violate our most cherished ideals, for they will be neither democratic nor libertarian. At worst, the new era could be an anti-Utopia in which we are conditioned to behave according to the exigencies of ecological scarcity.

Ecological scarcity is a new concept, embracing more than the shortage of any particular resource. It has to do primarily with pollution limits, complex trade-offs between present and future needs, and a variety of other physical constraints, rather than with a simple Malthusian over-population. The case for the coming of ecological scarcity was most forcefully argued in the Club of Rome study *The Limits to Growth.* That study says, in essence, that man lives on a finite planet containing limited resources and that we appear to be approaching some of these major limits with great speed. To use ecological jargon, we are about to overtax the "carrying capacity" of the planet.

Critical reaction to this Jeremiad was predictably reassuring. Those wise in the ways of computers were largely content to assert that the Club of Rome people had fed the machines false or slanted information. "Garbage in, garbage out," they soothed. Other critics sought solace in less empirical directions, but everyone who recoiled from the book's apocalyptic vision took his stand on grounds of social or technological optimism. Justified or not, the optimism is worth examining to see where it leads us politically.

The social optimists, to put their case briefly, believe that various "negative feedback mechanisms" allegedly built into society will (if left alone) automatically check the trends toward ever more population, consumption, and pollution, and that this feedback will function smoothly and gradually so as to bring us up against the limits to growth, if any, with scarcely a bump. The market-price system is the feedback mechanism usually relied upon. Shortages of one resource—oil, for example—simply make it economical to substitute another abundant supply (coal or shale oil). A few of these critics of the limits-to-growth thesis believe that this process can go on indefinitely.

Technological optimism is founded on the belief that it makes little difference whether exponential growth is pushing us up against limits, for technology is simultaneously expanding the limits. To use the metaphor popularized during the debate, ecologists see us as fish in a pond where all life is rapidly being suffocated by a water lily that doubles in size every day (covering the whole pond in thirty days). The technological optimists do not deny that the lily grows very quickly, but they believe that the pond itself can be made to grow even faster. Technology made a liar out of Malthus, say the optimists, and the same fate awaits the neo-Malthusians. In sum, the optimists assert that we can never run out of resources, for economics and technology, like modern genii, will always keep finding new ones for us to exploit or will enable us to use the present supply with ever-greater efficiency.

The point most overlooked in this debate, however, is that politically it matters little who is right: the neo-Malthusians *or* either type of optimist. If the "doomsdayers" are right, then of course we crash into the ceiling of physical limits and relapse into a Hobbesian universe of the war of all against all, followed, as anarchy always has been, by dictatorship of one form or another. If, on the other hand, the optimists are right in supposing that we can adjust to ecological scarcity with economics and technology, this effort will have, as we say, "side effects." For the collision with physical limits can be forestalled only by moving toward some kind of steady-state economy—characterized by the most scrupulous husbanding of resources, by extreme vigilance against the ever-present possibility of disaster should breakdown occur, and, therefore, by right controls on human behavior. However we get there, "Spaceship Earth" will be an all-powerful Leviathan—perhaps benign, perhaps not.

The scarcity problem thus poses a classic dilemma. It may be possible to avoid crashing into the physical limits, but only by adopting radical and unpalatable measures that, paradoxically, are little different in their ultimate political and social implications from the future predicted by the doomsdayers.

Why this is so becomes clear enough when one realizes that the optimistic critics of the doomsdayers, whom I have artificially grouped into "social" and "technological" tendencies, finally have to rest their different cases on a theory of politics, that is, on assumptions about the adaptability of leaders, their constituencies, and the institutions that hold them together. Looked at closely, these assumptions also appear unrealistic.

Even on a technical level, for example, the market-price mechanism does not coexist easily with environmental imperatives. In a market system a bird in the hand is always worth two in the bush.* This means that resources critically needed in the future will be discounted—that is, assessed at a fraction of their future value—by today's economic decision-makers. Thus decisions that are economically "rational," like mine-the-soil farming and forestry, may be ecologically catastrophic. Moreover, charging industries—and, therefore, consumers—for pollution and other environmental harms that are caused by mining and manufacturing (the technical solution favored by most economists to bring market prices into line with ecological realities) is not politically palatable. It clearly requires political decisions that do not accord with current values or the present distribution of political power; and the same goes for other obvious and necessary measures, like energy conservation. No consumer wants to pay more for the same product simply because it is produced in a cleaner way; no developer wants to be confronted with an environmental impact statement that lets the world know his gain is the community's loss; no trucker is likely to agree with any energy-conservation program that cuts his income.

We all have a vested interest in continuing to abuse the environment as we have in the past. And even if we should find the political will to take these kinds of steps before we collide with the physical limits, then we will have adopted the essential features of a spaceman economy on a piecemeal basis—and will have simply exchanged one horn of the dilemma for the other.

Technological solutions are more roundabout, but the outcome—greater social control in a planned society—is equally certain. Even assuming that necessity always proves to be the mother of invention, the management burden thrown on our leaders and institutions by continued technological expansion of that famous fishpond will be enormous. Prevailing rates of growth require us to double our capital stock, our capacity to control pollution, our agricultural productivity, and so forth every fifteen to thirty years. Since we already start from a very high absolute level, the increment of required new construction and new invention will be stagger-

*Of course, noneconomic factors may temporarily override market forces, as the current Arab oil boycott illustrates.

ing. For example, to accommodate world population growth, we must, in roughly the next thirty years, build houses, hospitals, ports, factories, bridges, and every other kind of facility in numbers that almost equal all the construction work done by the human race up to now.

The task in every area of our lives is essentially similar, so that the management problem extends across the board, item by item. Moreover, the complexity of the overall problem grows faster than any of the sectors that comprise it, requiring the work of innovation, construction, and environmental management to be orchestrated into a reasonably integrated, harmonious whole. Since delays, planning failures, and general incapacity to deal effectively with even our current level of problems are all too obvious today, the technological response further assumes that our ability to cope with large-scale complexity will improve substantially in the next few decades. Technology, in short, cannot be implemented in a political and social vacuum. The factor in least supply governs, and technological solutions cannot run ahead of our ability to plan, construct, fund, and man them.

Planning will be especially difficult. For one thing, time may be our scarcest resource. Problems now develop so rapidly that they must be foreseen well in advance. Otherwise, our "solutions" will be too little and too late. The automobile is a critical example. By the time we recognized the dangers, it was too late for anything but a mishmash of stopgap measures that may have provoked worse symptoms than they alleviated and that will not even enable us to meet health standards without painful additional measures like rationing. But at this point we are almost helpless to do better, for we have ignored the problem until it is too big to handle by any means that are politically, economically, and technically feasible. The energy crisis offers another example of the time factor. Even with an immediate laboratory demonstration of feasibility, nuclear fusion cannot possibly provide any substantial amount of power until well into the next century.

Another planning difficulty: the growing vulnerability of a highly technological society to accident and error. The main cause for concern is, of course, some of the especially dangerous technologies we have begun to employ. One accident involving a breeder reactor would be one too many: the most minuscule dose of plutonium is deadly, and any we release now will be around to poison us for a quarter of a million years. Thus, while we know that counting on perfection in any human enterprise is folly, we seem headed for a society in which nothing less than perfect planning and control will do.

At the very least, it should be clear that ecological scarcity makes "muddling through" in a basically laissez-faire socioeconomic system no longer tolerable or even possible. In a crowded world where only the most exquisite care will prevent the collapse of the technological society on which we all depend, the grip of planning and social control will of necessity become more and more complete. Accidents, much less the random behavior of individuals, cannot be permitted; the expert pilots will run the ship in accordance with technological imperatives. Industrial man's Faustian bargain with technology therefore appears to lead inexorably to total domination by technique in a setting of clockwork institutions. C. S. Lewis once said that "what we call Man's power over Nature turns out to be a power exercised by some men over other men with Nature as its instrument," and it appears that the greater our technological power over nature, the more absolute the political power that must be yielded up to some men by others.

These developments will be especially painful for Americans because, from the beginning, we adopted the doctrines of Locke and Smith in their most libertarian form. Given the cornucopia of the frontier, an unpolluted environment, and a rapidly developing technology, American politics could afford to be a more or less amicable squabble over the division of the spoils, with the government stepping in only when the free-for-all pursuit of wealth got out of hand. In the new era of scarcity, laissez-faire and the inalienable right of the individual to get as much as he can are prescriptions for disaster. It follows that the political system inherited from our forefathers is moribund. We have come to the final act of the tragedy of the commons.

The answer to the tragedy is political. Historically, the use of the commons was closely regulated to prevent overgrazing, and we need similar controls—"mutual coercion, mutually agreed upon by the majority of the people affected," in the words of the biologist Garrett Hardin—to prevent the individual acts that are destroying the commons today. Ecological scarcity imposes certain political measures on us if we wish to survive. Whatever these measures may turn out to be—if we act soon, we may have a significant range of responses—it is evident that our political future will inevitably be much less libertarian and much more authoritarian, much less individualistic and much more communalistic than our present. The likely result of the reemergence of scarcity appears to be the resurrection in modern form of the preindustrial polity, in which the few govern the many and in which government is no longer of or by the people. Such forms of government may or may not be benevolent. At worst, they will be totalitarian, in every evil sense of that word we know now, and some ways undreamed of. At best, government seems likely to rest on engineered consent, as we are manipulated by Platonic guardians in one or another version of Brave New World. The alternative will be the destruction, perhaps consciously, of "Spaceship Earth."

There is, however, a way out of this depressing scenario. To use the language of ancient philosophers, it is the restoration of the civic virtue of a corrupt people. By their standards, by the standards of many of the men who founded our nation (and whose moral capital we have just about squandered), we are indeed a corrupt people. We understand liberty as a license for self-indulgence, so that we exploit our rights to the full while scanting our duties. We understand democracy as a political means of gratifying our desires rather than as a system of government that gives us the precious freedom to impose laws on ourselves—instead of having some remote sovereign impose them on us without our participation or consent. Moreover, the desires we express through our political system are primarily for material gain; the pursuit of happiness has been degraded into a mass quest for what wise men have always said would injure our souls. We have yet to learn the truth of Burke's political syllogism, which expresses the essential wisdom of political philosophy: man is a passionate being, and there must therefore be checks on will and appetite; if these checks are not self-imposed, they must be applied externally as fetters by a sovereign power. The way out of our difficulties, then, is through the abandonment of our political corruption.

The crisis of ecological scarcity poses basic value questions about man's place in nature and the meaning of human life. It is possible that we may learn from this challenge what Lao-tzu taught two-and-a-half millennia ago:

> Nature sustains itself through three precious principles, which one does well to embrace and follow.
>
> These are gentleness, frugality, and humility.

A very good life—in fact, an affluent life by historic standards—can be lived without the profligate use of resources that characterizes our civilization. A sophisticated and ecologically sound technology, using solar power and other renewable resources, could bring us a life of simple sufficiency that would yet allow the full expression of the human potential. Having chosen such a life, rather than having had it forced on us, we might find it had its own richness.

Such a choice may be impossible, however. The root of our problem lies deep. The real shortage with which we are afflicted is that of moral resources. Assuming that we wish to survive in dignity and not as ciphers in some ant-heap society, we are obliged to reassume our full moral responsibility. The earth is not just a banquet at which we are free to gorge. The ideal in Buddhism of compassion for all sentient beings, the concern for the harmony of man and nature so evident among American Indians, and the almost forgotten ideal of stewardship in Christianity point us in the direction of a true ethics of human survival—and it is toward such an ideal that the best among the young are groping. We must realize that there is no real scarcity in nature. It is our numbers and, above all, our wants that have outrun nature's bounty. We become rich precisely in proportion to the degree in which we eliminate violence, greed, and pride from our lives. As several thousands of years of history show, this is not something easily learned by humanity, and we seem no readier to choose the simple, virtuous life now than we have been in the past. Nevertheless, if we wish to avoid either a crash into the ecological ceiling or a tyrannical Leviathan, we must choose it. There is no other way to defeat the gathering forces of scarcity.

Ethics and Ecology

WILLIAM BLACKSTONE

THE RIGHT TO A LIVABLE ENVIRONMENT AS A HUMAN RIGHT

. . . Let us first ask whether the right to a livable environment can properly be considered to be a human right. For the purposes of this paper, however, I want to avoid raising the more general question of whether there are any human rights at all. Some philosophers do deny that any human rights exist.[1] In two recent papers I have argued that human rights do exist (even though such rights may properly be overridden on occasion by other morally relevant reasons) and that they are universal and inalienable (although the actual exercise of such rights on a given occasion is alienable).[2] My argument for the existence of universal human rights rests, in the final analysis, on a theory of what it means to be human, which specifies the capacities for rationality and freedom as essential, and on the fact that there are no relevant grounds for excluding any human from the opportunity to develop and fulfill his capacities (rationality and freedom) as a human. This is not to deny that there are criteria which justify according human rights in quite different ways or with quite different modes of treatment for different persons, depending upon the nature and degree of such capacities and the existing historical and environmental circumstances.

If the right to a livable environment were seen as a basic and inalienable human right, this could be a valuable tool (both inside and outside of legalistic frameworks) for solving some of our environmental problems, both on a national and on an international basis. Are there any philosophical and conceptual difficulties in treating this right as an inalienable human right? Traditionally we have not looked upon the right to a decent environment as a human right or as an inalienable right. Rather, inalienable human or natural rights have been conceived in somewhat different terms; equality, liberty, happiness, life, and property. However, might it not be possible to view the right to a livable environment as being entailed by, or as constitutive of, these basic human or natural rights recognized in our political tradition? If human rights, in other words, are those rights which each human possesses in virtue of the fact that he is human and in virtue of the fact that those rights are essential in permitting him to live a human life (that is, in permitting him to fulfill his capacities as a rational and free being), then might not the right to a decent environment be properly categorized as such a human right? Might it not be conceived as a right which has emerged as a result of changing environmental conditions and the impact of those conditions on the very possibility of the realization of other rights such as liberty and equality?[3] Let us explore how this might be the case.

Given man's great and increasing ability to manipulate the environment, and the devastating effect this is having, it is plain that new social institutions and new regulative agencies and procedures must be initiated on both national and international levels to make sure that the manipulation is in the public interest. It will be necessary, in other words, to restrict or stop some practices and the freedom to engage in those practices. Some look upon such additional state planning, whether national or international, as unnecessary further intrusion on man's freedom. Freedom is, of course, one of our basic values, and few would deny that excessive state control of human action is to be avoided. But such restrictions on individual freedom now appear to be necessary in the interest of overall human welfare and the rights and freedoms of *all* men. Even John Locke with his stress on freedom as an inalienable right recognized that this right must be construed so that it is consistent with the equal right to freedom of others. The whole point of the state is to restrict unlicensed freedom and to provide the conditions for equality of rights for all. Thus it seems to be perfectly consistent with Locke's view and, in general, with the views of the founding fathers of this country to restrict certain rights or freedoms when it can be shown that such restriction is necessary to insure the equal rights of others. If this is so, it has very important implications for the rights to freedom and to property. These rights, perhaps properly seen as inalienable (though this is a controversial philosophical question), are not properly seen as unlimited or unrestricted. When values which we hold dear conflict (for example, individual or group freedom and the freedom of all, individual or group rights and the rights of all, and individual or group welfare and the welfare of the general public) something has to give; some priority must be established. In the case of the abuse and waste of environmental resources, less individual freedom and fewer individual rights for the sake of greater public welfare and equality of rights seem justified. What in the past had been properly regarded as freedoms and rights (given what seemed to be unlimited natural resources and no serious pollution problems) can no longer be so construed, at least not without additional restrictions. We must recognize both the need for such restrictions and the fact that none of our rights can be realized without a livable environment. Both public welfare and equality of rights now require that natural resources not be used simply according to the whim and caprice of individuals or simply for personal profit. This is not to say that all property rights must be denied and that the state must own all productive property, as the Marxist argues. It is to insist that those rights be qualified or restricted in the light of new ecological data and in the interest of the freedom, rights, and welfare of all.

The answer then to the question, Is the right to a livable environment a human right? is yes. Each person has this right qua being human and because a livable environment is essential for one to fulfill his human capacities. And given the danger to our environment today and hence the danger to the very possibility of human existence, access to a livable environment must be conceived as a right which imposes upon everyone a correlative moral obligation to respect.[4] . . .

ECOLOGY AND ECONOMIC RIGHTS

We suggested above that it is necessary to qualify or restrict economic or property rights in the light of new ecological data and in the interest of the freedom, rights, and welfare of all. In part, this suggested restriction is predicated on the assumption that we cannot expect private business to provide solutions to the multiple pollution problems for which they themselves are responsible. Some companies have taken measures to limit the polluting effect of their operations, and this is an important move. But we are deluding ourselves if we think that private business can function as its own pollution police. This is so for several reasons: the primary objective of private business is economic profit. Stockholders do not ask of a company, "Have you polluted the environment and lowered the quality of the environment for the general public and for future generations?" Rather they ask, "How high is the annual dividend and how much higher is it than the year before?" One can hardly expect organizations whose basic norm is economic profit to be concerned in any great depth with the long-range effects of their operations upon society and future generations or concerned with the hidden cost of their operations in terms of environmental quality to society as a whole. Second, within a free enterprise system companies compete to produce what the public wants at the lowest possible cost. Such competition would preclude the spending of adequate funds to prevent environmental pollution, since this would add tremendously to the cost of the product—unless all other companies would also conform to such antipollution policies. But in a free enterprise economy such policies are not likely to be self-imposed by businessmen. Third, the basic response of the free enterprise system to our economic problems is that we must have greater economic growth or an increase in gross national product. But such growth many ecologists look upon with great alarm, for it can have devastating long-range effects upon our environment. Many of the products of uncontrolled growth are based on artificial needs and actually detract from, rather than contribute to, the quality of our lives. A stationary economy, some economists and ecologists suggest, may well be best for the quality of man's environment and of his life in the long run. Higher GNP does not automatically result in an increase in social well-being, and it should not be used as a measuring rod for assessing economic welfare. This becomes clear when one realizes that the GNP

> aggregates the dollar value of all goods and services produced—the cigarettes as well as the medical treatment of lung cancer, the petroleum from offshore wells as well as the detergents required to clean up after oil spills, the electrical energy produced and the medical and cleaning bills resulting from the air-pollution fuel used for generating the electricity. The GNP allows no deduction for negative production, such as lives lost from unsafe cars or environmental destruction perpetrated by telephone, electric and gas utilities, lumber companies, and speculative builders.[5]

To many persons, of course, this kind of talk is not only blasphemy but subversive. This is especially true when it is extended in the direction of additional controls over corporate capitalism. (Some ecologists and economists go further and challenge whether corporate capitalism can accommodate a stationary state and still retain its major features.)[6] The fact of the matter is that the ecological attitude forces one to reconsider a host of values which have been held dear in the past, and it forces one to reconsider the appropriateness of the social and economic systems which embodied and implemented those values. Given the crisis of our environment, there must be certain fundamental changes in attitudes toward nature, man's use of nature, and man himself. Such changes in attitudes undoubtedly will have far-reaching implications for the institutions of private property and private enterprise and the values embodied in these institutions. Given that crisis we can no longer look upon water and air as free commodities to be exploited at will. Nor can the private ownership of land be seen as a lease to use that land in any way which conforms merely to the personal desires of the owner. In other words, the environmental crisis is forcing us to challenge what had in the past been taken to be certain basic rights of man or at least to restrict those rights. And it is forcing us to challenge institutions which embodied those rights.

Much has been said . . . about the conflict between these kinds of rights, and the possible conflict between them is itself a topic for an extensive paper. Depending upon how property rights are formulated, the substantive content of those rights, it seems plain to me, can directly conflict with what we characterize as human rights. In fact our moral and legal history demonstrate exactly that kind of conflict. There was a time in the recent past when property rights embodied the right to hold human beings in slavery. This has now been rejected, almost universally. Under nearly any interpretation of the substantive content of human rights, slavery is incompatible with those rights.

The analogous question about rights which is now being raised by the data uncovered by the ecologist and by the gradual advancement of the ecological attitude is whether the notion of property rights should be even further restricted to preclude the destruction and pollution of our environmental resources upon which the welfare and the very lives of all of us and of future generations depend. Should our social and legal system embrace property rights or other rights which permit the kind of environmental exploitation which operates to the detriment of the majority of mankind? I do not think so. The fact that a certain right exists in a social or legal system does not mean that it ought to exist. I would not go so far as to suggest that all rights are merely rule-utilitarian devices to be adopted or discarded whenever it can be shown that the best consequences thereby follow.[7] But if a right or set of rights systematically violates the public welfare, this is prima facie evidence that it ought not to exist. And this certainly seems to be the case with the exercise of certain property rights today.

In response to this problem, there is today at least talk of "a new economy of resources," one in which new considerations and values play an important role along with property rights and the interplay of market forces. Economist Nathaniel Wollman argues that "the economic past of 'optimizing' resource use consists of bringing into an appropriate relationship the ordering of preferences for various experiences and the costs of acquiring those experiences. Preferences reflect physiological-psychological responses to experience or anticipated experience, individually or collectively revealed, and are accepted as data by the economist. A broad range of noneconomic investigations is called for to supply the necessary information."[8]

Note that Wollman says that noneconomic investigations are called for. In other words the price system does not adequately account for a number of value factors which should be included in an assessment. "It does not account for benefits or costs that are enjoyed or suffered by people who were not parties to the transaction."[9] In a system which emphasizes simply the interplay of market forces as a criterion, these factors (such as sights, smells and other aesthetic factors, justice, and human rights—factors which are important to the well-being of humans) are not even considered. Since they have no direct monetary value, the market places no value whatsoever on them. Can we assume, then, that purely economic or market evaluations provide us with data which will permit us to maximize welfare, if the very process of evaluation and the normative criteria employed exclude a host of values and considerations upon which human welfare depend? The answer to this question is plain. We cannot make this assumption. We cannot rely merely upon the interplay of market forces or upon the sovereignty of the consumer. The concept of human welfare and consequently the notion of maximizing that welfare requires a much broader perspective than the norms offered by the traditional economic perspective. A great many things have value and use which have no economic value and use. Consequently we must broaden our evaluational perspective to include the entire range of values which are essential not only to the welfare of man but also to the welfare of other living things and to the environment which sustains all of life. And this must include a reassessment of rights.

ETHICS AND TECHNOLOGY

I have been discussing the relationship of ecology to ethics and to a theory of rights. Up to this point I have not specifically discussed the relation of technology to ethics, although it is plain that technology and its development is responsible for most of our pollution problems. This topic deserves separate treatment, but I do want to briefly relate it to the thesis of this work.

It is well known that new technology sometimes complicates our ethical lives and our ethical decisions. Whether the invention is the wheel or a contraceptive pill, new technology always opens up new possibilities for human relationships and for society, for good and ill. The pill, for example, is revolutionizing sexual morality, for its use can preclude many of the bad consequences normally attendant upon premarital intercourse. *Some* of the strongest arguments against premarital sex have been shot down by this bit of technology (though certainly not all of them). The fact that the use of the pill can prevent unwanted pregnancy does not make premarital sexual intercourse morally right, nor does it make it wrong. The pill is morally neutral, but its existence does change in part the moral base of the decision to engage in premarital sex. In the same way, technology at least in principle can be neutral—neither necessarily good nor bad in its impact on other aspects of the environment. Unfortunately, much of it is bad—very bad. But technology can be meshed with an ecological attitude to the benefit of man and his environment.

I am not suggesting that the answer to technology which has bad environmental effects is necessarily more technology. We tend too readily to assume that new technological developments will always solve man's problems. But this is simply not the case. One technological innovation often seems to breed a half-dozen additional ones which themselves create more environmental problems. We certainly do not solve pollution problems, for example, by changing from power plants fueled by coal to power plants fueled by nuclear energy, if radioactive waste from the latter is worse than pollution from the former. Perhaps part of the answer to pollution problems is less technology. There is surely no real hope of returning to nature (whatever that means) or of stopping *all* technological and scientific development, as some advocate. Even if it could be done, this would be too extreme a move. The answer is not to stop technology, but to guide it toward proper ends, and to set up standards of antipollution to which all technological devices must conform. Technology has been and can be used to destroy and pollute an environment, but it can also be used to save and beautify it. What is called for is purposeful environmental engineering, and this engineering calls for a mass of information about our environment, about the needs of persons, and about basic norms and values which are acceptable to civilized men. It also calls for priorities on goals and for compromise where there are competing and conflicting values and objectives. Human rights and their fulfillment should constitute at least some of those basic norms, and technology can be used to implement those rights and the public welfare.

NOTES

1. See Kai Nielsen's "Scepticism and Human Rights," *Monist,* 52, no. 4 (1968): 571–94.
2. See my "Equality and Human Rights," *Monist,* 52, no. 4 (1968): 616–39 and my "Human Rights and Human Dignity," in Laszlo and Gotesky, eds., *Human Dignity.*
3. Almost forty years ago, Aldo Leopold stated that "there is as yet no ethic dealing with man's relationship to land and to the non-human animals and plants which grow upon it. Land, like Odysseus' slave girls, is still property. The land relation is still strictly economic entailing privileges but not obligations." (See Leopold's "The Conservation Ethic," *Journal of Forestry,* 32, no. 6 (October 1933): 634–43. Although some important changes have occurred since he wrote this, no systematic ethic or legal structure has been developed to socialize or institutionalize the obligations to use land properly.
4. The right to a livable environment might itself entail other rights, for example, the right to population control. Population control is obviously essential for

quality human existence. This issue is complex and deserves a separate essay, but I believe that the moral framework explicated above provides the grounds for treating population control both as beneficial and as moral.

5. See Melville J. Ulmer, "More Than Marxist," *New Republic,* 26 December 1970, p. 14.
6. See Murdock and Connell, "All about Ecology," *Center Magazine,* 3, no. 1 (January-February 1970), p. 63.
7. Some rights, I would argue, are inalienable, and are not based merely on a contract (implicit or explicit) or merely upon the norm of maximizing good consequences. (See David Braybrooke's *Three Tests for Democracy: Personal Rights, Human Welfare, Collective Preference* (New York: Random House, 1968), which holds such a rule-utilitarian theory of rights, and my "Human Rights and Human Dignity," for a rebuttal.)
8. Nathaniel Wollman, "The New Economics of Resources," *Daedalus* 96, pt. 2, (Fall 1967): 1100.
9. Ibid.

ETHICS AND THE ECONOMIC FUTURE

Law and the Culture of the Corporation

CHRISTOPHER D. STONE

In Where The Law Ends I demonstrate why our present legal system is less than adequate when it comes to dealing with business corporations. And I outline some new measures the society shall have to prescribe. At the heart of my proposals is the idea that the law cannot continue to influence the corporation's inner world only indirectly by threats to the company's bank accounts. Nor are tougher measures aimed at key executives an adequate solution (although I generally support them). Increasingly, we shall have to augment these traditional approaches by new ones in which the larger society itself locates the specific organizational variables that are critical to corporate direction (its information nets, its management structure, etc.)

* * *

To be realistic, with the American business corporation the dominant orientation of the institution is going to remain toward profit, expansion, and prestige. Those who labor in it are going to remain concerned about providing for their wives and kids, for the approval of their peers, for "moving up" in the organization. What ideas can we gather up in our entire society that are powerful enough to set in competition with these, with "self-interest" as so many centuries of the culture have defined it?

To recognize these basic constraints is not to say we are powerless, however. We live with the fact that human beings are dominated by certain ego-centered goals/drives (sexual gratification, power, self-preservation). But through various acculturating mechanisms we have been able, not to do away with these forces, but at least to put constraints on them. On a parity of reasoning, even if we accept profit *orientation* as a basic and inalterable fact of American corporate life, we don't have to accept, or expect, sheer corporate hedonism. What I am asking of our chemical companies, for example, is not that they abandon profits. Producing fertilizers and chemi-

Christopher D. Stone, "Law and the Culture of the Corporation," *Business and Society Review,* 15 (Fall, 1975), pp. 5–17, reprinted by permission of the author and publisher.

cals that will get the world fed would be, and should be, a profitable activity. But what we want, too, is that the companies will manifest enough concern about the effects their products are having on the health of the field workers who use them; that they will accept the internal structures we deem appropriate; that in cooperation with the imposed systems they will perform some amount of follow-up; that, if suspicious circumstances are apparent, they will undertake appropriate studies and notify health authorities; that they will make data available to interested parties—rather than cover up the apparent risks and deny their very possibility.

* * *

Someone may ask, "why isn't the corporation more responsible than it is?" The answers are not all obvious; they are, moreover, important because any program to change corporate attitudes has to begin by identifying the particular social attitudes that we are up against.

The first point to remember is that while the corporation is *potentially* immune from a single-minded profit orientation, in any particular company that potentiality is able to become reality only after some satisfactory level of profits has been achieved. A corporation that is operating "on the margin" is going to cut as many corners as it can get away with on worker safety, product quality, and everything else.

Then, too, it would be a mistake to believe that the desire to turn profits is the only attitude that causes us problems. We know, for example, that many companies—especially the major dominant companies—go through periods in which they are well enough off that they could put a little something extra into, say, environmental protection, and not have to face (what is a real rarity) a shareholder coup d'état. The true range of attitudes we have to confront is much deeper and more complex than "profits"—but not necessarily any the less intractable.

One range of attitudes we might call "profit-connected." Even when the company is achieving enough profits that the managers can protect their own tenure, they may continue to pursue much the same course of conduct, but now as a reflection of other motives. Prestige in the business world comes of being connected with a firm listed on the New York Stock Exchange, one whose sales are rising, or which appears in the *Fortune* 500. The problem here is a lack of most other measures of success, other guarantors of prestige, than those which can be read off the company's ledgers.

Some other of the attitudes we are up against are even further removed from profits. Consider corporate insensitivity to their workers. The received wisdom on "blue-collar blues" is a purely economic one: that the worker is crushed in the corporation's never-ending push for profits. In part, this is true. But any bureaucracy, and not only the modern corporation, evolves toward depersonalized relationships. Its very "success" depends upon the mobilization of personalities into roles—the better for the synchronization of behavior. Thus, if corporations appear insensitive (to the world as well as to their workers) they may be insensitive for many of the same reasons that many nonprofit bureaucracies are insensitive (a hospital is the first example that comes to my mind). I am not saying that we therefore give up on attempts to sensitize them. I am just suggesting that if we are going to confront such problems, we have to be prepared to deal with subtler and more pervasive features than "capitalist greed."

* * *

Why is it that different corporations, and different industries, exhibit these differences in attitude? Can we identify the variables that make some more responsible than others, and put this knowledge to work by directly manipulating those variables? We simply do not know the answer to these and many similar questions. But even in the absence of this knowledge we do have some good clues as to how attitudinal changes can be brought about —clues that suggest two broad approaches suited to two distinguishable situations.

The key characteristic of the first situation is that the attitudes we want to inculcate can be connected with, and find support in, norms and/or subgroups that preexist in the organization. An example of this is provided in the aftermath of the electrical equipment conspiracy cases.

* * *

Price-fixing in the industry—certainly in the heavy-equipment section of the industry—had become so widespread as to constitute something of a behavioral norm. To change this corporate culture that had grown up within it, Westinghouse appointed an outside advisory panel.

The advisory panel insisted not merely on the company's instructing its employees that price-fixing was illegal. Despite all the industry protests about the "vagueness" of the antitrust laws, none of those involved in the secret meetings had any doubts about the illegality of price-fixing. And that knowledge, of itself, obviously had not pulled enough freight. Instead, the panel decided to aim for an affirmative demonstration "that competition, properly pursued, can produce far more consistent profits than . . . conspiracy."

In-house programs were established—management courses, workshops, conferences—all adopting the positive approach that the company's business success in the future, over the long haul, depended "to a considerable degree on the adoption . . . of policies of vigorous (and even aggressive) flexible, competitive initiative."

The presentation, in other words, was not that the company had to "submit" to a stronger, outside force—that is, the government. Rather, the price-fixing was depicted as itself a foreign element, inimical to the more fundamental corporate ideal of increasing one's share of the market through better salesmanship, superior design, and the like: the norm of competition. In fact, I am authoritatively informed that at discussions among employees, a sentiment emerged that the price-fixing had been "the sales force's thing: a way to avoid the hard work of really going after sales." The same source reports that the design engineers actually resented what had been going on. Their self-esteem had been based on their ability to build better mousetraps; suddenly they discovered that their share of the market for heavy equipment had been fixed at a ratio that had no real bearing on their own contribution.

This brings me to the second point. Securing conformity to the compliance norm was not based solely on demonstrating its link to a preexistent, supposedly dominant, corporate *ideal.* In addition, there already existed within the organization certain *groups* potentially more supportive of the desired attitude than the corporation as a whole. Part of the trick of changing the attitude manifested by the corporation as a whole is to locate the critical support group and strengthen its hand.

* * *

True, the Westinghouse situation is a special case in that no one there doubted that unless certain attitudes were changed the money damages to the corporation could be enormous. The directors, too, although saved from liability this time on the theory that they had "no reason to suspect" the wrongdoing, had now become an additional support group. They simply had to make some gesture of concern to "cover" themselves in case of a repeat performance.

Still, there are any number of roughly comparable situations where the same sort of approach should and could be invoked to alter unwanted attitudes.

* * *

In a second class of situation, however, the problem of dealing with the corporate culture is stickier. I am thinking now of the cases where the attitudes the society wants to inculcate are at odds with all the dominant norms of the corporation and can find no alliance with any of the attitudinal groups I mentioned (the work group, industry, business community).

For example, where worker-safety problems are concerned, we can at least consider mobilizing some internal alliance with the unions; for product quality and safety, with the engineers; for resource conservation (as through recycling energy), with the investors. But consider, by contrast, the problem of getting "insiders" to give notice of the company's pollution; to halt industrial espionage and campaign law violations; to keep clear of political adventures in foreign countries; to exercise concern for land-use aesthetics. In these cases, the attitudes desired by the "outside" world have barely a toehold on the "inside."

REWARDS FOR EXCELLENCE

At present, just about the only positive reward corporations achieve is in the form of profits (or sales, or other measures of financial growth). Essentially, all other social feedback is negative—public criticisms or legal punishments for doing things badly. This need not be the case. During World War II, for example, "E" awards were bestowed on defense companies that had exceeded their allotted production. The presentation of the "E" to a qualifying corporation was the occasion of a high ceremony, at which government representatives, executives, and workers joined. The company would get a flag, and each of the workers an "E" pin. Why should not the Environmental Protection Agency, for example, be authorized to give out its own Environmental Protection "E"s to companies that accelerate beyond their "cleanup" timetables, or come up with ingenious new environment-protecting methods?

SOCIAL AUDIT

A great deal has been written recently about devising a "social audit" for corporations to supplement their traditional financial audits. Their aim would be to represent on paper the total social costs and benefits of a corporation's activities, over and above those that are now reflected in its financial statements.

The problem with the traditional statements is that they developed to reflect the interests of the financial community. Investors—and potential investors—have no particular need for a breakdown of figures displaying, for example, how much the company has put into quality-control systems or how much it has done to increase minority worker mobility. A paper company's statement will reflect the cost of the lumber it consumes; but if it uses the local river as a sewer to carry away waste, and does not have to pay for the damages this causes downstream, those social costs will nowhere appear on the company's books. They don't affect earnings.

A reporting system that measured these hidden costs and benefits would be—if we had it—quite interesting. But at present, the details of how to implement it are wanting. Much of the value of a true audit, for example, is that it has a set prescribed structure, designed to display the answers to a series of questions which are the same for all companies. This the social auditors are nowhere near achieving. And it may well be beyond their grasp. . . .

INTERCHANGES

There is no more primitive way to alter intergroup attitudes (hopefully, for the better) than to bring the groups together. On an intracorporate scale, there have been a number of experiments in "sensitivity" confrontations among executives and, to a lesser extent I believe, among management and workers.

But insofar as the boundary between the corporation and the outside world is concerned, the exchanges could barely be worse. The government, for its part, relies largely on lawsuits and the threat of suits—certainly a less than ideal way to communicate values. The public at large—or, at least, the activist groups that purport to speak for it—maintain a shrill criticism that is just overstated enough that managers (even otherwise sympathetic managers) can find grounds to dismiss it in their own minds. The corporate response to the public is either a cynical PR bluff, or a defensiveness no less shrill and hysterical than the criticisms it receives. In a recent interview, Union Oil Company's president dismissed the environmental movement as "a question of people being irrational." Then, thinking a little further he added darkly, "It's more than that, actually. I don't know who's behind the Sierra Club, but it obviously isn't people of good will."

What is called for, obviously, is some improved mode of communication and understanding—in both directions. Public criticism of corporate behavior certainly should be maintained. But it should be informed enough, and even sympathetic enough, that it does not induce so extreme and inflexible a defensiveness.

One approach to a better understanding is simply to plead for it (which I hereby do). But, we should also try to set various stages for bringing the groups together. This has been done, in a limited way and after its own fashion, by the Executive Interchange Program. The program, established by President Johnson, sends middle-to upper-level government employees for a brief swing in business posts, and brings private-sector managers to Washington. . . .

PUBLIC EDUCATION

Part of the problem corporate reformers face in changing the corporate culture has been mentioned: that the shriller their criticisms, the more the corporate community inclines to discount them as "one-sided" and ill-informed. The reform movement has some particularly sensitive problems, too, in taking its case to the public. How the issues are handled is important, not only because of the obvious implications for garnering legislative support, but because the reactions of the outside world are themselves one of the more significant determinants of the corporation's internal culture. . . .

The point is, altering corporate behavior may involve reexamining the views that prevail in the outside world. And in this regard, one has to be struck by the fact that while the public may be periodically exercised over corporations, corporate wrongdoing simply doesn't command the same dread and fascination as crimes committed by tangible human beings. To an extent, this difference in public reaction toward corporate as opposed to human wrongs probably owes to the different nature of the offenses that are typically involved, rather than to a difference in who the actor is. That is, the Boston Strangler commands headlines because strangulation (and rape) are embedded in the human psyche as particularly fearful acts, whereas price-fixing, stock frauds, and the range of most offenses associated with corporations seem more "technical."

On the other hand, I think we have to consider another factor that is at work, too—one that involves the nature of the corporation, as much as what the corporation is doing. I strongly suspect—although I cannot prove—that where a corporation rather than an identifiable person is the wrongdoer, the hostility that is aroused is less even where the offense is more or less the same. For example, if we are subjected to the noise of a motorcyclist driving up and down our street at night, I think a deeper and more complex level of anger is tapped in us than if we are subjected to the same disturbance (decibelically measured) from an airline's operations overhead. It is not just that the one seems "uncalled for" while the other seems incidental to commerce and progress. It is also that where a tangible person is involved, we can picture him (even if that means only to fantasize him); whereas when the nuisances we are subjected to are corporate, there is no tangible target to fix our anger upon. And it all seems so hopeless anyway. The consequence, if I am right, is that while various small groups are turning increased publicity onto corporate wrongdoings, they are still a long way from bringing about effective changes in corporate laws and corporate performance. A reform movement, to be effective, needs both widespread indignation and widespread hope to sustain itself. Neither by itself will do. So long as the public continues to perceive the wrongs corporations do as impersonal, market-dictated, and somehow inevitable, the reformers will have as little success forcing a change in corporate consciousness as they will in marshaling a public opposition that can seriously challenge the corporation's legislative clout. In all events, those of us who aim to change things have a job to sort out and deal with the various reasons why corporate reform movements have not been more successful after so many decades of agitation. One principal reason, I am sure, is that the public little cares to be reminded, over and over, that it is being victimized by impersonal forces, without being told what it can do about it. . . .

Resolving Income and Wealth Differences in a Market Economy: A Dialogue

JAMES M. GUSTAFSON AND ELMER W. JOHNSON[1]

JMG:

Let me begin this discussion by recounting a few facts concerning the distribution of wealth and income in the United States. According to Arthur Okun, the top 1 percent of American families have about as much after-tax income as nearly all families in the bottom 20 percent and the top fifth of families have about as much after-tax income as the bottom three-fifths. The distribution of wealth is even more skewed. The richest 1 percent of American families have about one-third of all wealth, and the bottom half of all families hold only 5 percent of total wealth. Even worse, I understand, is the concentration of investment assets, since homes account for most of the wealth of the bulk of the population. It has been estimated that the top half

James M. Gustafson and Elmer W. Johnson, "Income and Wealth Differences in a Market Economy," presented at Loyola University of Chicago November 18, 1980, under the auspices of the Mellon Foundation. Reprinted by permission of the authors.

percent of the adult population owns 49 percent of all privately owned corporate stock.[2]

According to Lester Thurow, the distribution of family income has remained essentially the same over the last thirty years, but only by reason of the rapid rise in income transfer payments ($224 billion in 1978) and labor force participation rates for women. Without these two factors the income differences might have been substantially greater. In short, welfare-state capitalism under our present tax system has made almost no dent in the distribution patterns of thirty years ago.[3]

Given these circumstances can capitalism be defended as a just system? Does it facilitate or impede the realization and develop a just distribution of the economic benefits that it produces?

There are two dominant ways of stating the formal principle of justice in the Western tradition: "To each his or her due," and "equals shall be treated equally." To apply these principles three questions must be kept in mind. *To whom* is X due? (Who are the equals to be treated equally?) *What* kinds of things are due to whom? (What is to be duly distributed?) And, on *what principle* is the distribution to be made? The third is obviously the most critical question.

There is a spectrum of possible principles of distribution. (1) To each the same things. This is the most radical egalitarian principle. (2) To each according to needs. (3) To each according to ascribed social status, that is to "rank" determined by, for example, social tradition. (4) To each according to merit. Merit, like needs, begs for refinement. Merit can refer to contributions to social well-being, to culture, to productivity, etc.; what holds merit criteria together is the assumption that a person is causally accountable for achievements, and thus deserves reward.

In one sense a capitalist social order is radically egalitarian, at least in principle, namely that respect is due to all persons as free agents. The liberty of each is to be respected; the capacities that each has to be self-determining are to be respected. Respect is due each person; respect for persons ought to be evenly distributed to all.

The humane forms of capitalism today attempt to see that the fundamental human needs of persons in the society are met; at least this tends to be the case for "the deserving poor," for those who desire to work and who accept a considerable measure of accountability for the conduct of their lives. On what basis should the "undeserving poor" be treated? The "free-riders?" Those who do not seek work, or in other ways conduct their lives "irresponsibly"?

We do not have a social structure based on the ascription of status such as the designation of various "estates," but the powers that accrue to families of large inherited wealth are not totally dissimilar. Many of the benefits of power and authority, income and education, that families have in our society are certainly not attributable to the merits and achievements of their individual members. Present inheritance tax policies would seem to sustain a kind of "ascribed" social status.

Merit, it would seem, is the dominant, operative principle in the "justice" of present income distribution. And the most determinative kind of merit or achievement in the corporate and professional worlds is that of contributions to the economic well-being of particular organizations. The merit principle is clearly an incentive to achievement; it maximizes the degree to which persons are accountable for what they receive, and it motivates the acceptance of high performance standards. It appeals to self-interest, and sustains aggressive and competitive drives. In principle it operates not only within organizations, but among them. Units that deserve to flourish presumably do, and their flourishing is the result of the collective merits of the leadership and policies that make them successful.

EWJ:

I cannot begin to consider the justice questions you have raised without making some preliminary observations about the case for capitalism. The more thoughtful advocates of capitalism, to my knowledge, have never rested their case on whether it results in a just distribution of the economic output among the members of the society.

Rather they argue on grounds of efficiency and freedom and contend that excessive efforts to approximate economic equality will ultimately undermine liberty and severely contract output. The idea that the material welfare of the masses should depend on society's toleration of substantial wealth and income differences is not easily grasped, but this is the key to achieving adequate long-term capital formation, rewarding managerial training and responsibility, and providing the entrepreneurial incentives for innovation and risk-taking. Our current problems of declining productivity and inadequate capital formation, these advocates argue, are attributable not to capitalism but rather to such factors as (1) a tax system that has favored consumption over saving and investing and (2) a program of social legislation and over-regulation that has sapped the vigor of our market system.

Hayek, Lindblom and others have all paid tribute to the marvelous coordinating function performed by market systems, a function that must otherwise be carried out by government planners. To date, no government has demonstrated the competence to perform this function very well.

We should also remind ourselves that capitalism has raised the material well-being of the masses of citizens in the advanced societies of the world to levels that were never dreamed possible, and this despite the population growth of the last two hundred years. The deliverance of the masses of people in democratic capitalist societies from grinding poverty, they argue, has been accomplished not by pursuing economic justice but by harnessing the energy of private, self-interest. In addition, the capitalist would remind us that our strivings for justice are subject to important constraints. Among these constraints is the need for a strong military defense capability, which in a democratic society requires a great deal of efficiency and dynamism in the economy.

The advocates of market capitalism would point out another important limiting condition: the corrupting nature of power. Capitalism works as well as it does in part because it decentralizes power and responsibility. All utopian forms of economic organization, dedicated to achieving greater economic equality, require an even greater centralization of power than obtains in the case of managerial capitalism. In the process, the managers of the centrally ordered economy tend to be corrupted by the exercise of power, and the system tends to break down. This danger might be less where there has been a long tradition of high ethical standards of conduct in the central government, continually maintained by institutions for the moral nurture and education of central managers, as obtained periodically in ancient China when Confucian ethicists played an important role. But it is doubtful whether the forces for moral nurture in our society today are sufficiently strong that we can be optimistic along these lines. We have enough trouble trying to cope with the corruptibility of corporate managers under capitalism.

Another limiting condition is the obligation to maintain and pass on from generation to generation the torch of high civilization. Surely, the capitalist argues, the preservation and enhancement of our cultural and intellectual heritage require a substantial degree of economic inequality. Tocqueville is good authority on this point.

Having summarized the very powerful utilitarian case for capitalism, I am ready to address your justice concerns. But I think it is important that these concerns be addressed in light of the possible downside risks: the subordination of national defense and international peace-keeping concerns; the spread of mediocrity and the loss of intellectual and cultural richness; declining productivity as self-interest incentives are removed and as government bureaucracy is augmented to handle redistributive schemes; the resulting increase in free-riders throughout the society; the erosion of the capital formation system as incentives to save are removed; the disappearance of what Schumpeter calls the "gales of creative destruction" that make for innovation and progress over the long term; the threat to civil liberties as government comes to pervade every area of our lives; and so forth. With this understanding, the question remains: Can the distributional principles operative in capitalism be defended as Just?

I would generally agree with your very brief summary of the mix of distributive principles that are presently operative in our particular system. Does this mix satisfy my normative concerns? By no means. First, it seems unfair that persons should be rewarded so heavily on the basis of their genetic endowments. Second, I am bothered that many persons are rewarded on the basis of how well they pander to the basest of consumer desires, desires intensified by a powerful advertising engine. Third, it is not fair that some people inherit vast non-human capital assets for whose employment they are richly rewarded without having to develop and apply their own human skills. Fourth, it is unfair that the child who is born into a home where the educational and moral nurture is of the highest order, should therefore be able to earn many times more than the unlucky child born into a home at the opposite end of the spectrum.

The trick, I suppose, is to address these normative concerns without losing sight of the various downside risks that I mentioned earlier. Is it possible to articulate a workable concept of justice, one that takes these kinds of considerations into account? I remember John Rawls qualifying his theory of justice by saying that there are other institutional values besides justice that need to be taken into account, such as stability and efficiency, but that justice is primary. Yet, by the time he has worked out his difference principle (which in effect justifies the unequal distribution of wealth, income and the powers and prerogatives of authority to the extent that such inequality maximizes the well-being of the least advantaged), it seems to me he has incorporated into his concept of justice a great deal of what I would call efficiency values. I just wonder if justice doesn't include efficiency as a component value. Also, Rawls specifically makes the preservation of equal liberty prior to the fair distribution of the other social primary goods, thus taking into account my concerns about freedom and world peace.

JMG:

Let me remark on some of the points of your response.

First you raise an issue that probably gets us into an eddy. The question is, what are the causes of the increase in material well-being of persons in many societies over the past two centuries. You attribute the cause to capitalism. I would attribute it more to the rise of modern technology, which can be supported by various systems of economic organization. The point to be raised is whether modern technology arose only under the incentives of capitalism. But that gets us into a historical argument.

Second, you gradually move toward normative concerns by stating some things that bother you about present arrangements. Three of the four things you list I would put under the heading of luck in the lottery of birth. You do not think people should be especially rewarded for being lucky in their genetic endowments, in being born into wealthy families, and being born into families that provide commendable moral and educational advantages. Underlying this seems to me to be a principle that can be stated in this way: Persons should be rewarded according to their desserts, and their desserts are to be judged according to their individual efforts. Persons should not be rewarded for their luck in the lottery of birth. I take it that one can also say that persons should not be penalized for their unluck in the lottery of birth. We could pursue this point. Should persons be compensated for their unluck in the lottery? How should this be done? What compensation at the expense of the lucky would be fair to the unlucky because they are unlucky? Maybe the lucky, and the lucky who achieve, should be taxed so that the unlucky, and especially the unlucky who achieve to the best of their circumstances, can be compensated. I do not think this line of inquiry gets us into an eddy; it is one route into how different benefits of the economy might, or should be distributed. My impression is that if this route is taken, we are not distributing according to need, or certainly not need alone. We are distributing according to desserts for achievements, with non-penalization (or compensation) of those who have less advantages due to no responsibility of their own.

Next, you indicate the "downside" risks for the health of the economy of a generally more egalitarian distribution system. What might be risks for the economy might also make possible benefits for persons in the relevant community—they would not need to be anxious about the things Jesus had confidence that God would provide, but if God does not, the state should —like adequate nutrition, and so forth. So the downside risks for the economy might be upside benefits for persons and families. And we are coming to the trade-off problem. To the risks for the economy you add the threat to civil liberties. On that I have an empirical query. Are civil liberties put at risk in economies more "mixed" than ours such as the British and the Scandinavian ones? What civil liberties are put at risk?

Finally, you ask whether justice includes efficiency as a competent value. Efficiency is a relational term that needs to be specified according to the ends of activity. Something that is economically efficient—producing a marketable product at very low cost—might be an inefficient procedure for some other human ends.

I think we need now to turn to further specification of what sorts of distribution of benefits from the economy we would deem to be more or less just, and defend them on some moral or religious grounds. Second, we need to ask what we would be willing to "trade off" either of the benefits and their distribution, or of the economic costs that are involved in the downside risk.

Let me propose. I would argue on religious and moral grounds that distribution according to needs is proper. Then I should have to differentiate between real needs and superficial desires, and formulate some gradation of needs so that those deemed basic were sure to be met, and that distribution with reference to others would be graded according to resources available and willingness to make certain trade-offs in the process of meeting them. Meeting "health" needs would be a case in point; while certain forms of medical care ought to be available regardless of capacity to pay for them by the patient, high cost, high technology interventions under certain conditions cannot be provided to all. But to put my point as an assertion, I believe that our society and its government have an obligation of justice to meet a range of human needs that could be defended as basic to all persons. We do not respect persons without providing the necessary conditions for them to survive, and to develop some of their capacities.

My second proposal is that a merit principle of distribution should operate on the second floor of this social structure. This is not simply a concession to "sin," in terms of the observation that persons will not work hard, achieve many things, etc., without some recognition and reward. It is also that having persons accept accountability (within the range of their capacities, obviously) for their own actions is itself a matter of moral worth, and that some reward system (it might be honor and respect as well as money) is fitting recognition. If you agree, we can begin to work these things out in more detail.

There will be no perfect system. Those who are ahead by the lottery of birth might always be ahead (though many of them will squander their gifts), but we cannot penalize persons simply for being lucky. I believe compensatory measures ought to be made available to the unlucky so that they can make the most of their unluck. I believe that we will always have free-riders, and the number that can be tolerated, and the extent to which their costs can be tolerated, has to be looked at in particular classes of cases.

EWJ:

Your suggestion, that a just organization of economic life would meet the basic needs of every member of society without reference to notions of merit and would permit the excess output of the society to be distributed in accordance with some principle of merit, is really what our country has been groping after for several decades, particularly with the social legislation of the last ten or fifteen years. Even Milton Friedman has proposed a negative income tax as a means of further ensuring that each family will be able to satisfy its basic needs, regardless of merit.

Your two-tier concept has an immediate appeal to me. I start with the view that this world is an arena for our moral and rational development, in community. Our economic arrangements provide a limited but indispensable portion of the conditions for this development.

Having agreed with the substance of your two very general proposals, let me now raise some problems that call for clearer definition. As to the first principle, you have already mentioned one of the serious definitional problems: i.e., that of distinguishing between basic needs and all other needs and desires for goods and services. A second, related problem is how should the needs principle be carried out: by means of a negative income tax or through an extensive array of governmental programs for the distribution of basic goods and services in kind, or by some combination of both mechanisms? In other words, how paternalistic should we be if our aim is to produce free and responsible human beings? A third problem is whether the society is obliged by considerations of justice to meet even the basic needs of the able-bodied poor who refuse to work when work is available? If it is not, then perhaps the government should have comprehensive work programs available for the reserve army of the unemployed.

As to your second proposal for some kind of merit principle, what do you think of our present free market idea as a principle of distribution, subject to the heavy qualification it receives in our society by virtue of government regulation and taxation? Or did you have some quite different principle in mind? As I stated earlier, the market principle is basically an efficiency criterion, and it appeals to me for this reason. I mentioned some aspects of this principle that I don't like. Your proposal for a floor eliminates some of my concerns. Appropriate tax reforms would eliminate other concerns of mine. I would then still be left with one more, perhaps insoluble, defect of the market: that it leaves people free, and many people almost certain, to make a mess of their lives, as Schumpeter puts it.

JMG:

I am happy that you consent to the view that respect for persons requires more than respect for their liberty. That, I take it, is a critical difference between us and the radical libertarians. Second, I am pleased that you note the intergenerational responsibilities. I suspect you would not argue against the view that maintenance and improvement of the capital base of our civilization comprehends natural and cultural conservation and preservation as well.

First, the distinction between basic and other needs and desires. There are efforts to draw the distinction more precisely than I have thus far. Basic needs would include food, clothing, and shelter; protection from crime and from rash invasions of privacy, and so forth. But I think no sharp lines, valid through time and across cultures, can be drawn with precision. The minimal conditions for well-being vary. Some opportunities to nurture the human spirit are necessary; that which nurtures differs between cultures. In American cities it can be argued that a telephone is a necessary instrument to meet many needs; in Calcutta it is not. In certain conditions modern transportation is not needed (though it is convenient), and in others it is. One thing I think we can agree upon; a percentage figure of those at the bottom of the income scale ought not to determine "the needy" in a more basic sense. Swedish social services, for example, are so broadly distributed that to call a fixed percentage of the lower-income levels "needy" does not make sense.

Across cultures and national economies the issue of meeting basic needs must be kept in mind, though we cannot get into international economic arrangements here. Not only the luck of the birth lottery, but the fact that some human populations must survive in adverse climatic and geographical circumstances is important to remember.

So, on the point of basic needs, I cannot "define" them in a satisfactory way to meet all circumstances. Historical, technological, and cultural conditions will always make the distinction a moving, rather than fixed, one.

To sum up, I believe that "voluntary consent" and exercise of capacities of self-determination provide a basic line of concern, but I do not believe the community needs to provide the resources that will be used wantonly for the sake of maximizing liberty. The basic point on which I think we agree is that (to polarize) any maximally libertarian way of meeting the needs principle, or any maximally paternalistic way, will have its deleterious as well as approvable consequences. Policy must be based on which risks seem to be worth taking.

There is one term we have not developed much that I think needs some reflection, and that is "power." Just distribution pertains to the distribution of power as well as economic benefits. How the actual distribution of power occurs in the society will be affected by other choices along the way. I take it that distribution according to the need "floor" requires concentration of power in government, for that is the institution that has responsibility for attending to the welfare of all of the citizenry (and by welfare I do not mean doles, but even the preservation of liberties). One of the functions of government is to attend to the interests of those whose interests are not met by other institutional arrangements. The state has an interest in the neglected child not only because the child does not have capacities and power to defend his or her own interests, but also because the common good is threatened in some way. There are legitimate interests of persons that are overlooked without the power of the state attending to them. The civil rights movement in recent history has made that point. Part of what has occurred is the development of new power groups with legitimation by law and court decisions, and with new power groups come different distributions of aspects of the capitalistic social organization's benefits. It is not only power that tends to corrupt, but also the absence of power.

Another term is common good. What is the relation between distributive justice and the common good of the society? That asks the question abstractly. But it can be asked with reference to particular policies for just distribution. And when we get down to particular policies we have to ask about various elements in the common good. Your argument might be that a free system of economic life serves the common good by providing capital accumulation, by setting conditions for the emergence of good leaders in competitive situations, and by providing conditions that serve the common good by maximizing individual responsibility. From another side, one can ask whether the common good in other respects is not served by more egalitarian distribution of more things under the auspices of the state, which is the institution that in principle is concerned for the common good of the nation. I only raise the question here.

EWJ:

Let me summarize our ethical concerns and considerations and then propose to you some very general policy guidelines that I believe are responsive to these concerns.

Much oversimplified, here are the fundamental principles and assumptions on which our policies will be based:

1. Our society is not merely an aggregation of individuals, as the nineteenth century liberals and their philosophic successors suppose. That is, our ideal of the person is not comprehended by such phrases as "free to choose" or "free and responsible." Because the individual can flourish only in community, government is much more than a night watchman and a market referee. Government exists not only to ensure individual freedom, a negative value, but also to provide positively for the common good. Gewirth, Maritain and Rawls have spoken eloquently to this point.
2. All members of our society are entitled to equal respect simply because they are human beings. Through our government institutions we accord this respect not only by guaranteeing individual freedom but also (at our advanced stage of cultural and economic development) by (a) meeting the minimum needs for food, clothing, shelter, education and health of those who are unable to work and thereby meet these needs on their own and (b) by providing work opportunities for the unemployed who are able to work. We cannot be at all precise in defining "minimum needs" in kind or amount for all times and places. We cannot even be very precise in our respect to our particular time and our particular community.
3. Above the "needs" floor, this equal respect can be roughly accorded by means of a market principle of economic organization, which (despite its many imperfections) tends to operate as a merit principle and hold us accountable to each other and to ourselves for successfully developing our talents and making the most productive use of those talents. The effectiveness of the market depends heavily on broad government guarantees to all members of society of positive rights to equality of opportunity and to open access to positions of power and responsibility, based on merit. This is especially important in a highly hierarchical society such as ours in which most persons earn their livings as employees of large organizations. These considerations would seem to call for a tax system designed to prevent undue concentrations of economic wealth from being passed on from generation to generation.
4. In providing for basic needs, questions as to whether and to what extent goods and services should be delivered in kind will be resolved not by reference to abstract principles of freedom vs. paternalism but by considering how these needs can be met in ways that are least costly to the community, least demeaning to the recipient, and most likely to encourage self-help and self-respect.

I think this fairly summarizes our joint conclusions thus far in our discussion. What are the implications of these ethical notions for the organization of our economic life? First, we are not calling for any basic alteration from capitalism to socialism. That is, we are not only content with, but our merit notion calls for, a market principle of economic organization, one of the two chief defining terms of capitalism.

The other defining term, private ownership of the means of production, is also an aspect of capitalism that is entirely consistent with our ethical notions. I really believe the critics of capitalism who think that this second principle is a great evil are quite misguided. That is, there are two basic ways by which the government can see to it that productive resources are deployed so as to promote the common good. One way is to permit individuals and non-governmental associations to "own" and deploy these assets subject to the regulatory and taxing powers of the state. This way reflects a policy that says in effect: "We want as much of the best of both worlds as possible: the much superior efficiency and adaptability afforded by the market accountability of competitive capitalism; and the governmental tools of regulation and taxation for seeing to the common good and eliminating excessive differences in wealth and income. The second way is for government directly to own these capital assets and for everyone in society to work for government. In theory our merit principle could work just as well if the salary and bonus schemes were artfully designed and fairly applied, but with government being the dominant employer and having to rely on the command system of the legislature or agencies to establish appropriate incentive systems, the prospects for our merit principle would be quite dim. Certainly my observations of other societies as well as of our post office confirm this conclusion.

Second, we *are* calling for the kinds of reforms that will (a) help carry out our generation's obligations to maintain and improve the capital base for succeeding generations, and (b) moderate income and wealth differences in light of our "needs" and "merit" principles. Edmund Burke is my authority for the proposition that government is among other things a partnership among generations. A chief function of the state is to ensure that we who are living fulfill our intergenerational responsibilities, particularly in a time such as ours when the institution of the family cannot be relied upon to play the major role in inculcating this aspect of stewardship.

Specifically, I would tend to favor tax reforms (i) replacing the present income tax system with a consumption tax on the lines proposed by Professor William Andrews at Harvard Law School,[4] (ii) removing the tax discrimination against equity capital of corporations, and (iii) imposing a more severe inheritance tax system that is yet consistent with the need for entrepreneural incentives. Professor Cooper has spoken eloquently to this last point.[5] I would favor such tax reforms because (a) we need to encourage saving for investment and discourage consumption; (b) we must prevent long-term, undue concentrations of wealth if we are to have a vigorous merit system, (c) we need to create more fluid markets for the allocation of capital resources, and (d) we should afford to the children of all economic levels, even the wealthy, the opportunity to blossom forth to their full potential under a meritocracy.

My conclusion is that our two principles of "needs" and "merit," far from being mutually incompatible or requiring tragic trade-offs, are mutually supportive. Persons with freedom, but whose basic needs are unmet, never reach the stage of being able to develop under a merit system. Persons with excess wealth likewise often inherit positions of economic power for which they are not fit. Finally, I believe that the downside risks that I referred to much earlier in this dialogue have been adequately taken into account.

JMG:

I am not sufficiently informed about the more technical matters implied in your proposals to say that I am either in firm agreement with all of them, or in firm disagreement with any of them. I think they are very important ways to bring greater justice into the system, and are really quite strong without being revolutionary.

I will make one comment, and then state vigorously one dissent.

I believe that the *most general* principles we agree on can probably be worked out in a democratic quasi-socialist system as well as in the democratic quasi-capitalist system your proposals lead to. The policy proposals you make protect the interests of developing capitalism, and serve the common good in that way. Someone who might favor quasi-socialism would be dissatisfied with your proposals. The difference is that your proposals are readier to limit some justice considerations, and the efficiency considerations require a larger range of freedom of economic choice and a wider spread in income and wealth. Your proposals do, however, lay the groundwork for the need-tier of this justice principle. The debate between you and someone to your left would be primarily about what economically, legally and socially conditions are necessary, and how to establish them, so as to bring about a more equitable distribution. You probably worry more than such a person would about maximizing accountability for one's self as a moral value to be preserved. I, a "liberal" but not a socialist, can live with these proposals comfortably, and support them heartily.

My leaning toward the center continues to be from the left side; yours is from the right side. That is a good thing; if it were not so we would have a monologue.

NOTES

1. James M. Gustafson is University Professor of Theological Ethics at the University of Chicago. Elmer Johnson is a senior partner of the Kirkland and Ellis Law Firm in Chicago.
2. George Cooper, "Taking Wealth Taxation Seriously," *Record of the Association of the Bar of the City of New York* 34 (1979).
3. Lester Thurow, *The Zero Sum Society* (New York: Basic Books, 1980).
4. William D. Andrews, "A Consumption-Type or Cash Flow Personal Income Tax," *Harvard Law Review* 87, p. 1113. A consumption or expenditures tax is one which taxes only that portion of income or wealth that is devoted to spending for consumption purposes as opposed to savings and investment.
5. Cooper, p. 34.